Radical Churchman

Reproduced by kind permission of the Vicar and PCC of St Thomas, Skirbeck Quarter

Radical Churchman

Edward Lee Hicks and the New Liberalism

GRAHAM NEVILLE

CLARENDON PRESS · OXFORD
1998

Oxford University Press, Great Clarendon Street, Oxford OX2 6DP

Oxford New York

Athens Auckland Bangkok Bogotá Buenos Aires Calcutta
Cape Town Chennai Dar es Salaam Delhi Florence Hong Kong Istanbul
Karachi Kuala Lumpur Madrid Melbourne Mexico City Mumbai
Nairobi Paris São Paulo Singapore Taipei Tokyo Toronto Warsaw

and associated companies in
Berlin Ibadan

Oxford is a registered trade mark of Oxford University Press

Published in the United States
by Oxford University Press Inc., New York

British Library Cataloguing in Publication Data
Data available

Library of Congress Cataloging in Publication Data
Radical churchman : Edward Lee Hicks and the
new liberalism / Graham Neville.
Includes bibliographical references and index.
1. Hicks, Edward Lee, 1843–1919. 2. Liberalism—Great Britain—
History. 3. Church and social problems—Great Britain—History.
4. Church of England—England—Lincoln—Bishops—Biography.
5. Bishops—England—Lincoln—Biography. I. Title.
BX5199.H54   1998   283'.092—dc21   98–26750
ISBN 0–19–826977–3

1 3 5 7 9 10 8 6 4 2

Typeset by Graphicraft Limited
Printed in Great Britain on acid-free paper by
Bookcraft (Bath) Ltd., Midsomer Norton

To Margaret

Preface and Acknowledgements

My interest in Edward Lee Hicks first arose in connection with my work for the History of Lincolnshire Committee in contributing to *Twentieth Century Lincolnshire* (Lincoln 1989), the concluding volume of their twelve-volume series. There was a striking difference between Hicks and his predecessor in the see of Lincoln, Edward King; that is, between two kinds of character and two kinds of churchmanship. Then the editing of Hicks's diaries for the Lincoln Record Society revealed his warm and lively personality, even in his declining years. The question arose, how had he become the person and the churchman his diaries revealed. The list of sources at the end of this book indicates something of the route my enquiries then took, from Oxford to Warwickshire, from Manchester to Lincoln. An unexpected reward has been the friendship of members of his family.

Full acknowledgement of my indebtedness to those who have helped me in my research might easily develop into an extensive essay. I hope that they will accept this brief statement of my thanks, with my assurance that it is no less genuine for being brief. First I thank the members of the family of Edward Hicks, and especially Mr Timothy Hicks for making available his collection of family papers. They have enabled me to feel a personal interest in writing this book. The Revd Jonathan Inkpin also helpfully drew my attention to some relevant family letters. My thanks are due to Dr Lionel North of Hull University for his interest and for pointing me to material specially relevant to Hicks as an epigraphist. Local knowledge has been kindly made available by Mr W. H. Stubbings, who gave me advice and help about Fenny Compton and its school; by Mr G. Lewis of the South Holland Family and Local History Group, who transcribed a long article from the *Spalding Free Press*; and by Mr Peter Chapman of the *Grimsby Evening Telegraph*, who searched out information about the case of James Brightmore, the conscientious objector.

I have been given willing help by archivists, official and unofficial, of various institutions with which Hicks was associated. Especially I thank Mr Alastair Macpherson, Honorary Archivist of Haileybury and Imperial Service College, Dr J. Briscoe of Manchester Grammar School, and Mrs P. Hatfield, Eton College Archivist, for detailed responses to my enquiries about their respective schools; and Mr Derek Winterbottom of Clifton College for information about Dean Fry and Mr J. H. Fowler. I am very grateful for the help of the College Archivist of Brasenose College, Mrs Elizabeth Boardman, and the Assistant Archivist of Corpus Christi College Oxford, Mrs C. Butler; and Melanie Barber, Deputy Librarian at Lambeth Palace.

The career of Edward Hicks in Manchester and Salford has been illuminated for me by Dr Michael Poole and two of the clergy who had personal experience of St Philip's, the Revd Canon Gwilym Owen Morgan, and the Revd Michael Price, who made available his thesis on Peter Green, from which I learnt much about the tradition Edward Hicks established. I also thank Mr John Rowlands for information about his grandfather, Captain Rowlands of the Church Army; and Captain John Smith for searching out Church Army records.

I am grateful to Lady Nevile, for kind hospitality and allowing me access to the diaries of Herbert F. Torr; and Lady Morrison and the Honorary Archivist, Dorothy Williams, for access to archives at Madresfield Court.

I also express my gratitude for much assistance in researching library records, from staff of the John Rylands University Library, Manchester, and particularly Mrs J. C. Sen, Deputy Head of Reader Services; the Bodleian Library; the Honnold/Mudd Library, Claremont, California; the Local Studies Unit, Manchester Central Library; Pusey House Library; the Fawcett Library; the Queen's College Library, Birmingham; and the record offices of Oxfordshire, Warwickshire, and Lincolnshire.

The substance of Chapter 4, 'Rural Problems: Fenny Compton 1873–1886', has already been published by the Warwickshire Local History Society, and my thanks are due to Dr Robert Bearman for seeing it through the press.

Finally, I am personally grateful to the Right Revd Robert Hardy, for making available the episcopal diaries of Edward Hicks, to Dr

Dorothy Owen for help in the preparation of an edition of those diaries, to Dr Nicholas Bennett for access to material in Lincoln Cathedral Library; and not least, for encouragement and advice from Professor John Kent and the Revd Dr John Nurser.

G.N.

Worcester 1997

Contents

Abbreviations

CETS   Church of England Temperance Society
CSU   Christian Social Union
Diary   Graham Neville (ed.), *The Diaries of Edward Lee Hicks, Bishop of Lincoln 1910–1919*, Lincoln Record Society, lxxxii (1993)
Fowler J. H. Fowler (ed.), *The Life and Letters of Edward Lee Hicks (Bishop of Lincoln 1910–1919)* (1922)
LDM   *Lincoln Diocesan Magazine*
MG   *Manchester Guardian*
UKA   United Kingdom Alliance

I

Introduction

If we read Ruskin's diatribes against the commercialism he saw all about him, we must often be struck with the curious way in which they match some current criticisms of the worst aspects of society in our own age. It is as though a century has passed and the cycle of history has taken a complete revolution. There is a shift in the level of poverty and deprivation, a change in the degree of pollution, a variation in the rhetoric of self-righteousness which proceeds from the defenders of the *status quo*. But take almost any of Ruskin's writings from about 1860 onwards expressing as they do his miserable unhappiness whenever he considers the condition of the British people and you may find yourself applying his words to the present time:

I have listened to many ingenious persons, who say we are better off now than ever we were before. I do not know how well off we were before; but I know positively that many very deserving persons of my acquaintance have great difficulty in living under these improved circumstances: also, that my desk is full of begging letters, eloquently written by distressed or dishonest people; and that we cannot be called, as a nation, well off, while so many of us are either living in honest or in villainous beggary. For my own part, I will put up with this state of things, passively, not an hour longer.[1]

That may stand as a text for this study. Although it concentrates on the story of a particular churchman who was deeply influenced by Ruskin, it offers a fresh slant on a process which has been described from other angles, the stirring of consciences in the fifty years from 1870 onwards which changed the face of Liberalism in Britain.

Edward Lee Hicks was born in 1843 in Ship Street, Oxford. His story is one of a scholar who abjured scholarship for the sake

---

[1] John Ruskin, *Fors Clavigera: Letters to the Workmen and Labourers of Great Britain*, i, Letter 1 (1891 edn.).

of something he saw as a more vital Christian concern, and of a churchman who believed the institutional church was less important than the total community within which it fulfilled its ministry. In brief outline, his adult career included a fellowship at Oxford (1866–73), the living of Fenny Compton, Warwickshire (1873–86), the wardenship of Hulme Hall, Manchester (1886–92), a residentiary canonry of Manchester Cathedral with the rectory of St Philip's, Salford (1892–1910), and the bishopric of Lincoln (1910–19). There was a turning-point or watershed somewhere between 1886 and 1892. Up to that time it looked as if his life might have been devoted increasingly to scholarship. Afterwards it was clear that his over-riding concern was with the condition of society and the church's responsibility for it. This division curiously echoes the division in the life of John Ruskin, whom he so much admired. Ruskin had turned from art criticism to social reform in the period 1850–60. Both of them were in their forties when they set their lives in a fresh direction.

Hicks has been little remembered, or quite misremembered. Even in Lincoln there lingers a memory of a 'black Protestant', which is the worst possible description of him. His name scarcely appears in any of the standard works dealing with the Church of England during the period of his life. But he was one of a small number of leading churchmen who caught the mood and shared the hopes of the 'New Liberalism' which developed after 1886. His political position, by the time he went to Lincoln, was closely similar to that of C. P. Scott, the editor of the *Manchester Guardian*, who was already looking for a radical coalition of left-wing Liberals and the Labour Party under the leadership of Lloyd George. It did not come into existence, because of the division and then the virtual disappearance of the Liberal Party. Yet one later commentator, writing in the 1970s, could say: 'Ironically it is more or less what we have ended up with. Socialism is forgotten. We have a Whig chancellor of the exchequer, a Liberal home secretary, and a prime minister who has Lloyd George's ingenuity without his inspiration.'[2] The sacramental socialism of 'Gore's men' captured neither the church nor the nation, but some at least of Hicks's hopes were realized after his death. That is a matter of history; but there are deeper

[2] A. J. P. Taylor, 'Saving Lloyd George's Soul', in Chris Wrigley (ed.), *From the Boer War to the Cold War: Essays on Twentieth-Century Europe* (1995), 266; first published June 1970. The references are to Roy Jenkins, James Callaghan, and Harold Wilson.

questions implicit in the study of his life and opinions, mostly related
to the meaning of the ambiguous word 'liberal'.

There are as many kinds of liberalism as there are liberals. When
their liberalism is combined with denominational allegiance a further variant enters the mix. It is, therefore, a truism to say that
Edward Hicks was unique. He developed his own particular variety of liberal churchmanship in a period when the religious excitements of earlier decades had to some extent subsided. He was never
identified with any of the various organized parties within the
Church of England, and he exercised his ministry chiefly outside
the areas which have tended to command most attention—London
and Oxford. His liberalism was also explicitly political. He moved
from the left wing of the Liberal Party to support of Labour, and
was in many ways the most radical of the bishops on the bench
when he died in 1919. His story may, therefore, act as a corrective
to other descriptions of religious developments in the Victorian
and Edwardian periods which stress the importance of partisan
religious groups, underestimate the significance of events in the
provinces, and interpret the political involvement of the Church
of England mainly in terms of a tension between Conservatism
and Christian Socialism.

Those who knew him personally saw much more in him than
the image of the temperance reformer which was inclined to oblit-
erate his real character. One of his Lincoln clergy, in his reminiscences, described him as 'a great man in every sense of the word'.
A later clerical gossiper, who had possibly never met Hicks, wrote
of the succession of bishops of Lincoln, 'It is said that Bishop King
was a saint, Bishop Lee Hicks a scholar, and Bishop Swayne a statesman.'[3] All three verdicts are open to question. Bishop King was
the particular kind of saint moulded by the Oxford Movement in
its early stage, and therefore almost entirely unconcerned about
questions of social justice. Bishop Swayne's statesmanship does not
particularly emerge from a reading of his memoirs.[4] As for Bishop
Edward Hicks, it is true that he had to the end of his life many of
the traits his early scholarship had developed, and instances of his
precision in the use of language were still remembered thirty years

[3] F. W. Hutchinson, *Reminiscences of a Lincolnshire Parson* (Ely n.d.), 53; Humphrey
P. W. Burton, *Weavers of Webs* (1954), 107.
[4] Graham Neville, 'Bishop King: Right Heart, Wrong Head', *Modern Churchman* 28/3
(1986); W. S. Swayne, *Parson's Pleasure* (Edinburgh and London 1934).

after his death.[5] But he progressively turned his back on a scholar's career. In Salford he had been regarded as one of the leading church-men in the north-west and one of the few who had established good relations with nonconformists. In personal relationships he had shown devotion to pastoral duty. He had occupied a number of positions with distinction. It is only part of the truth to describe him as a scholar. He was pastor and administrator as well; and his preferred description of himself was that of social reformer.

Another verdict was that of Hensley Henson, who received Hicks's steady support during the controversy over his consecration in 1917 and 1918. In spite of that, Henson wrote him off ungener-ously as 'a feminist, a total abstainer, and three parts a pacifist'.[6] That at least recognizes a cluster of concerns, all equally abhor-rent to Henson. In Bell's *Randall Davidson* he appears only as one of three bishops dissenting from a motion in Convocation calling for strenuous opposition to the disestablishment of the church in Wales—the other two being Charles Gore (Oxford) and John Percival (Hereford).[7] This is an interesting coalition and hints at both similarities and differences, though Bell makes no comment on them. Gore and Percival were contrasted in character, the one a liberal catholic, the other a Low-Church political Liberal. Hicks was different from them both, most obviously in lacking the author-itarianism of the other two—aristocratic in Gore and headmasterly in Percival.

For all his evident merits, there were those in high places in the church who mistrusted him. The papers at Lambeth Palace show how he was regarded by Randall Davidson and others. In November 1909 the archbishop was in correspondence with the Prime Minister, H. H. Asquith, about the vacant see of Norwich, to which Asquith eventually nominated the evangelical Dr B. Pollock, the candidate preferred by the king. Davidson says he is

[5] *Lincoln Diocesan Magazine* (1950), 122–3 (subsequently cited as '*LDM*'); *Diary* for 26 Aug. 1914; J. H. Fowler (ed.), *The Life and Letters of Edward Lee Hicks (Bishop of Lincoln 1910–1919)* (1922), 188. It was certainly a scholar's relaxation to turn the Te Deum into hexameters.

[6] H. H. Henson, *Retrospect of an Unimportant Life*, i (1942), 259, quoted in Owen Chadwick, *Hensley Henson: A Study in the Friction between Church and State* (1983), 145. The index of Chadwick's book witnesses to his obscurity by confusing him with the other Bishop Hicks of Lincoln, Nugent Hicks, author of *The Fulness of Sacrifice*, whose episcopate at Lincoln was from 1933 to 1942.

[7] G. K. A. Bell, *Randall Davidson, Archbishop of Canterbury*, 2 vols. (Oxford 1935), i. 643.

'indisposed to such an appointment' and runs down a list of five other names. 'Hicks of Manchester' is the third on the list, and Davidson's assessment is 'a fine scholar, good speaker, strong Liberal in politics, great temperance advocate: but (I am told) rather faddist, and (from my point of view) slightly too High Church'. Six days later he elaborates this opinion, when it seems that Asquith is inclined to favour Hicks. 'I cannot think that you would feel happy or satisfied in nominating Canon Hicks of Manchester. He is a fine enthusiastic fellow, who throws himself eagerly, not to say fanatically, into any cause which he espouses. But he has always seemed to me to lack (very *markedly*) the Scriptural requirement of σεμνότης—and his Churchmanship is, I believe, of a very advanced type. I say this without I hope derogating at all from his high merits and his fine character.'[8] These are shallow judgements from the archbishop, based on hearsay. He is transparently attempting to play on the Prime Minister's prejudices.

The most significant word is 'faddist'. It was a vogue-word of the Edwardian period and it points to an important aspect of political life at the time. The prolific journalist and author G. W. E. Russell found the topic so intriguing that he devoted an entire article to 'The Faddist', noting that the term is always connected with some projected reform, and always applied to reforms the speaker does not support. In another article he had written:

One may be a very good reformer oneself and yet dislike other people's reforms. In that case we call them 'fads' and stigmatise their authors as 'Faddists'. The plain man . . . has a holy horror of a Fad. When the Head Mastership of Eton was last vacant we were assured by those who ought to know that no Faddist need apply.[9]

The use of the term was rife in two areas of public life, the religious and the political, but it crept into some unusual contexts. In the record of a Bishops' Meeting at Lambeth in 1911, during a discussion of the administration of Holy Communion and possible infection from the chalice, there is a reference to 'bacteriological faddists'.[10] The archbishop had long mistrusted those who made particular causes the focus of their energies and interests. Back in

---

[8] Davidson papers, 10: Appointments 1903–15, fos. 59–60.
[9] G. W. E. Russell, *Social Silhouettes* (1906), 18, 95–101.
[10] Lambeth papers, Bishops' Committees 23 May 1911.

1882, while still chaplain to Archbishop Tait, he had addressed the Church Congress on 'Unity of Belief in relation to Diversities of Thought' and had made fun of the journals which presented minority fads: 'Every sort of human craze and crochet, good, bad, and indifferent, has its own organ. Anti-vaccination reformers, women's suffrage reformers, and every separate grade and sort of temperance reformers; each of these and twenty more have a newspaper peculiarly their own.' He went on to make a joke about *The Mineral Waters Advocate* and *The Haberdashers' Chronicle*, among the two thousand different newspapers every week in the United Kingdom. It was intended as a humorous section of his speech, leading into a more serious argument that the things which united believers were more significant than the things which divided them. But taken at face value it shows a failure to discriminate between the good, the bad, and the indifferent among minority causes. They were, and are, an important feature of democratic life.[11]

In an illuminating discussion of Faddism, D. A. Hamer has drawn attention to its political significance. The various pressure-groups which earned the epithet set out to be non-party movements operating outside parliament, but were inevitably drawn into party politics because the reforms they desired could only be achieved by parliamentary action.[12] The democratization of the parliamentary process had encouraged the development of organizations intent upon bringing about social change, and it followed that those members of the churches who took up hopes of reform became organized as pressure-groups in a way which had been unthinkable before the widening of the suffrage. Faddists were assumed to believe that a particular reform would act as a panacea of social ills. But that was certainly not always the case. To take a single instance, Sir Wilfrid Lawson has been remembered, if at all, as the parliamentary leader of the temperance movement for over forty years. Yet his interests were far wider than that particular issue, so that it does not even come first in a list of the causes he espoused given by G. W. E. Russell in an article in 1900, in which he says that Lawson 'is chiefly known as a pro-Boer and anti-everything else; a little Englander, a Peace-at-any-Price Man, a would-be destroyer of the Established Church, the House of Lords, the Liquor-Traffic,

---

[11] Church Congress Report (1882), 44–7.
[12] D. A. Hamer, *The Politics of Electoral Pressure* (1977), 1–6.

and several other institutions scarcely less robust'. Temperance reform was only one of a number of reforms he wanted to promote.[13] 'Single-issue reformer' was a loaded description deliberately minimizing the significance of both the issue and the reformer.

But if there was one cause more than any other which attracted the description of Faddism it was the temperance cause, and Edward Hicks undoubtedly became a temperance advocate. That may have been uppermost in the archbishop's mind. But his own words show that his knowledge of Hicks was at best second-hand, and closer acquaintance would have revealed a deeper unifying motivation underlying his concern for temperance and other reforming causes. Some temperance advocates may have wanted to put a stop to working-class drunkenness without changing much else in the state of society, but that was not the case with Hicks. In one of his articles in the *Manchester Guardian* he unconsciously sketched a self-portrait in saying that the church too often regarded as faddists and cranks those who were concerned about the conditions of labour, the overthrow of the betting mania, the lessening of the drink bill, the abatement of militarism, the growth of better international and interracial morality and the spread of the doctrine of government by consent.[14]

He was fully aware of the currency of the term and its application to himself. He hit back by criticizing what he saw as its opposite. In the second of a series of Lent addresses given in Manchester in 1900 he attacked the spirit of compromise which he saw lurking behind common-sense phrases, and argued for openness and honesty in the church. 'The spirit of immoral compromise can always be detected in the cant phrases it affects, such as "It's of no use trying to alter it"; "They all do it"; "It is the custom of the trade"; "One must live"; "Don't be a faddist"; "The idea is Utopian".'[15] He was himself no compromiser. That was recognized by one of the archbishop's closest advisers, Bishop E. S. Talbot. He had known Hicks personally since his time as Warden of Keble College and had in fact preached at Hicks's ordination to the priesthood in 1870, and later stayed with him in Manchester. He had been offered, and declined, the see of Lincoln only a few weeks before it was offered to Hicks, and was later translated from

[13] G. W. E. Russell (ed.), *Sir Wilfrid Lawson: A Memoir* (1909).
[14] *Manchester Guardian* (18 May 1905) (subsequently cited as '*MG*').
[15] *Addresses on the Temptation* (1903).

Southwark to Winchester. He wrote to Davidson in April 1910: 'I had just written to Hicks. Very able—with scholarship given to *res sacrae*. A churchman of good tradition. A man of most fearless & virile morals: keen for things of liberty—&, of course, temperance. Then, his honourable refusal of the "conditioned" Deanery offer.'[16] The details of that offer will be noticed later. Put briefly, Hicks had turned down an appointment he would have liked to accept on grounds of principle. It was a recurrent feature of his career to make decisions on principle even to his own disadvantage and not to mind what company it threw him into, whether 'pro-Boers' or teetotal nonconformists or pacifists or Modernists. An archbishop might well think such a man in a bishopric would endanger the stability of the church. People like that were good to have in the church, but preferably not on the bench of bishops.

Archbishop Davidson also thought Hicks lacked the scriptural requirement of σεμνότης. Whatever the precise significance of that word in the New Testament, it is reasonable to assume that the archbishop interpreted it as meaning 'dignity' or 'gravity'—a certain presence or weightiness of outward deportment appropriate for public occasions. In consultations between Prime Ministers and archbishops and their sovereigns it was often mentioned.[17] Curiously enough, Edward Hicks is very likely to have agreed with the archbishop's verdict on him at this point. His diaries include occasional self-criticisms, particularly on the anniversaries of his consecration as bishop. He finds fault with himself over a number of things including the failure to control his temper, his tongue, his passions. But he also writes: 'I must be dignified, without pride or self-consciousness: for some men need keeping in place: all this is not easy for me' (24 June 1911). Perhaps fortunately, he did not succeed. He much more enjoyed relaxing with congenial company. When he stayed the night with the very same clergyman who later described him as 'a great man in every sense of the word', his own comment in his diary is, 'A happy little supper at the Hutchinsons, where I was *too* hilarious and happy, I fear.' He seemed acutely aware of the mismatch between the image of a bishop he was required to display, or needed to project for his inevitable disciplinary duties, and his inner unruly disposition to see the funny side of things.

---

[16] Davidson papers, 164: Official letters 1910, fo. 213.

[17] See Bernard Palmer, *High and Mitred: A Study of Prime Ministers as Bishop-makers 1837–1977* (1992), 77, 82, 101, 210, 290.

His work for the temperance movement must have involved the same kind of tension between the outward persona and the inner man. There could be no one less like the stereotyped image of the teetotaller as killjoy. It must have tried his sense of humour sometimes to hear, let alone to sing, some of the more trite or crude verses composed for temperance gatherings. His daughter Christina noted his strenuous attempts to keep his composure on temperance platforms. No doubt, too, he startled quite a few members of the diocesan conference in 1910 when he said, 'I regard dancing, under proper safeguards, as one of the most healthy amusements young people can enjoy for their physical development. Don't be afraid of it. I could tell you so many experiences of mine in connection with that in the slums of Manchester.'[18] It was not usual for a bishop to advocate dancing, even with 'safeguards'. In his own family he enjoyed dancing and amateur dramatics, and it is no great surprise to learn that Christina was at one time friendly with the young Ivor Novello. She subsequently married E. V. Knox, who as 'Evoe' of *Punch* no doubt kept laughter alive in the family.[19] Hicks himself evidently enjoyed the theatre and was happy, as bishop, to take out a clergyman and his wife to a show, to thank them for their hospitality. This was a far cry from the penalization of Stewart Headlam, the Anglo-Catholic socialist priest, for forming the Church and Stage Guild. The anti-puritanism of many Anglo-catholics, on the other hand, in opposition to the rigidities of evangelicalism, as they saw them, seldom left them room to embrace the temperance cause. Edward Hicks and Peter Green were among those who did.

Alongside this evidence of the lighter side of Hicks's character should be set the testimony of a witness to its sterling quality. In 1946 the former secretary of the United Kingdom Alliance, G. B. Wilson, recorded some of his memories of work with Edward Hicks, who had held the post of Honorary Secretary. He wrote:

He was a remarkable man. His judgments of men were wise and kind. He looked out for the best and found what he sought; but while he

---

[18] Report of Proceedings of Lincoln Diocesan Conference (1910), 159. Another advocate was Bishop Winnington Ingram, who approved dancing as a 'healthy and graceful amusement' (*Guardian*, 27 October 1911).

[19] Penelope Fitzgerald, *The Knox Brothers* (1977), 114. Ivor Novello stayed at the Old Palace, Lincoln, in 1911 and signed himself with his original name, 'Ivor Novello Davies'.

always preferred peace, he was not afraid of war where questions of principle were at stake . . . His eyes would blaze and his jaw would set sternly with indignation against wrong. He hated injustice. Courtly, with the politeness of the 'old school', there was no patronage in his manner . . . His joyous nature and culture came as a great surprise to those members of his Diocese who had always associated Total Abstinence with gloom.[20]

That was the judgement of someone who worked closely with Hicks for more than ten years, and who knew him as Randall Davidson never did.

A great part of the interest in sketching his life consists in trying to trace the steps by which he came to be a significant liberal churchman. He did not fall conveniently into any of the categories which come to hand when placing church leaders. He did not adopt the stance of a typical partisan of the evangelical or catholic wing of the church and therefore could not call on the backing of any organized ecclesiastical group. And although he was overtly a political bishop he was not entirely at home in the mildly left-wing company of the Christian Social Union, which indeed he regarded as not political enough. His life is conveniently marked out into stages by his movement from one context to the next. In retrospect they seem to trace a coherent progression, in which each stage carries forward into the next something of vital importance, which then forms part of a more mature and complex personality. He becomes scholar, pastor, trainer of clergy, reformer, social critic, prophet. Every stage of development relates to, and throws light on, some wider movement in the church or in society.

The study of Hicks's life provides additional insights into the religious development of the time in two ways. First, that period is not usually seen as an entity, because it spans late Victorian and Edwardian times and the early years of the reign of King George V. From the religious point of view the period under consideration can be seen as the last phase in the contribution of political Liberalism to national life and therefore the last phase in the relation of the churches to the Liberal Party in opposition and in power. It is the period of the 'New Liberalism'. For a number of churchmen who aimed at social reform, including Edward Hicks, this determined the nature of their witness. It was also the heyday of

[20] G. B. Wilson, *Looking Back* (UKA 1946).

extra-parliamentary pressure-groups campaigning on single issues, and Hicks's life shows that the understanding of the complexities of English Christianity at the time must take account of organizations which were not denominational or even religious in basis, as well as the church parties which have been made the object of study in ways which bias some accounts of the religious life of the period. In the preceding period political Liberalism had worn a different aspect; and after the end of the First World War there were so many changes in English society that the participation of leading churchmen in national life inevitably took a different form. But Hicks himself, in moving towards the Labour Party, foreshadows the shift of interest among those Anglicans who aimed at social and political reform.

The second consideration which supports the validity of this study is that the geographical focus of Hicks's ministry at this period was away from London and Oxford. His work was principally in Salford, Manchester, and Lincolnshire, and reveals characteristics of church life rather different from those which tend to bulk large in general studies of English religion. For example, the influence of ritualism and the problems which it created for church discipline were less noticeable in the areas of Hicks's ministry as parish priest, residentiary canon, and bishop than in London and some southern dioceses. The two dioceses of Manchester and Lincoln, though very different from each other, escaped some of the disruptive effects of partisanship; but for different reasons. The church life of Manchester was predominantly Low Church. That characteristic was specially noticeable after 1903 during the episcopate of E. A. Knox, but it was not created by the arrival of such a leading evangelical in the see. In Lincoln, on the other hand, the prosecution of Bishop King for ritual offences in 1888 exposed the vindictiveness of extreme Protestant elements and won a more sympathetic tolerance for Anglo-catholic tendencies favoured by a bishop universally regarded as saintly and humane. The personal character of Bishop King muted criticism of his churchmanship, even among nonconformists; critical comment on him only survived as a whisper among those who deplored his Toryism.

But the story also illustrates the interaction of factors which enabled him to become what he was during the climax of his ministry in Salford and Manchester. The broad context was the attempted adjustment of the Church of England to an increasingly secularized society in which it could no longer assume an authoritarian role, pretend that it was successfully ministering to 'the unchurched masses', ignore the worst effects of competitive capitalism, or turn its back upon scholarly disciplines affecting religion which had established their right to autonomy. A description of the early stages of his development also provides a gloss on the characterization of the Anglican clergy as becoming increasingly professionalized in the aftermath of the Oxford Movement. Along with other leading churchmen of his generation, he escaped the influence of the new theological colleges, and consequently drew upon largely lay sources of inspiration in the formation of his general outlook.

It was perhaps the last phase of a dying tradition among English clergy going back to the Reformation. That was when the mystique of the priesthood largely evaporated. The intellectual culture of the clergy became indistinguishable from that of their lay contemporaries, which was itself closely involved with the Christian tradition. But the traditional participation of the clergy in the general culture of their age was put under strain by the development in the nineteenth century of autonomous scholarly disciplines —of historical study, of analytical literary criticism, of inductive scientific study—and a division arose between those of the clergy who welcomed these secularizing developments and tried to work out their implications for Christian belief and practice and those who turned back to earlier Christian traditions in the hope of resisting the damage which they saw such developments as inflicting on church and nation. This division correlated roughly with a political division between Liberals and Conservatives. Hicks can be seen to represent the tradition of clerical participation in lay contemporary culture.

The study of Hicks's life also throws some light on the apparent division of the Church of England in the nineteenth century into distinct parties. Certain critical events in the earlier part of that century have cast long shadows over the interpretation of church history in the rest of the century and beyond. Each has called forth an extensive literature; and the volume of discussion has inevitably given a bias to our understanding of what was going on in English religion at the time. The most obvious of these is the Tractarian episode beginning in 1833. In retrospect it is interpreted as having transformed the Church of England, and indeed the whole English religious scene.[21] Another is the episode of Christian Socialism prompted by the fiasco of the Chartist demonstration in 1848. That is seen as having sown a seed which germinated in the later Christian social movement, with effects continuing at least to the Second World War. Less dramatic, though brought into prominence by high points of public debate, is the controversy over science and the scriptures, of which the publication of *Essays and Reviews* in 1860 is a potent symbol. This movement of ideas is seen as culminating in the English version of Modernism, which (unlike Modernism in the continental Roman Catholic Church) was not forced out of the mainstream churches and has contributed a generally tolerant element to English religion.[22]

Each of these important movements, however, contained within itself distinguishable elements. The Oxford Movement upheld ideals of spiritual authority inherent in the priesthood; but it also incorporated a concern for reverent liturgical worship which others shared.[23] The Christian social movement claimed Christian justification for political reorganization, but it also asserted more generally the spiritual significance of secular life. The Modernist movement tended to represent the past traditions of Christian doctrine as obscurantist, but it also asserted more broadly the need for criticism of religious texts by historical criteria and of religious doctrines in the light of scientific principles. Each movement had a hard core, and a softer periphery. The enthusiasts in each of these movements, if they were members of the Church of England, could easily find themselves moving towards its perimeter, and perhaps beyond. But in historical retrospect it is clear that most members of the Church of England were never committed to the entirety of any one of these schemes propounded by the enthusiasts. It was possible to welcome greater reverence in worship without conceding

---

[21] e.g. S. L. Ollard in additional chapter to H. O. Wakeman, *An Introduction to the History of the Church of England* (8th edn. 1914), 485. 'The story of the English Church since 1896 has been the record of a gradual development in Church life along the lines of the Oxford movement.'

[22] *Doctrine in the Church of England*, The Report of the Commission on Christian Doctrine appointed by the Archbishops of Canterbury and York in 1922 (1938), 2–3: 'the utmost liberty of thought compatible with maintenance of spiritual fellowship should be secured'.

[23] Cf. P. B. Nockles, *The Oxford Movement in its Context: Anglican High Churchmanship 1760–1857* (Cambridge 1994), 213: 'few criticisms of the Tractarians focused on ceremonial'.

divine authority to the priesthood.[24] It was possible to take the realm
of the secular as the appointed scene of discipleship and even to
feel sympathy with socialistic ideas without maintaining that there
was a divinely authorized eucharistic pattern for society. It was
possible to welcome light on Christian origins and doctrines from
historical and scientific advances without supposing that they in-
validated all the insights of religion from a pre-scientific age.

The average English Christian (which is to say, the average lay
person) seems always to have taken an eclectic approach in matters of belief. Perhaps that is due to the historical experience of the
English people in the turmoils of the Reformation period. Today
most church-going members of the Church of England are luke-
warm about apostolic succession, but look for reverence in worship. They reject the notion of an ideal collectivist society, but believe
that their life in the secular world is the proper place to work out
their discipleship. They accept the need for open-mindedness in
interpreting and even criticizing the scriptures and formularies of
religion, but continue to reverence the Bible and to accept the
historic creeds, whatever private reservations they may feel about
a faith once delivered to the saints and hence immutable.

Such eclecticism was to be found in the pew and even the pulpit in previous generations. Certainly more people took theology
seriously in the Victorian age than now. But seriousness does not
necessarily lead to total acceptance of someone else's orthodoxy;
indeed it may have the very opposite effect. If this case needs an
exemplar, we may consider one of the greatest of laymen in the
Victorian age: William Ewart Gladstone. He was fully conscious
of the wide range of religious attitudes in the Church of England,
and noted in the midst of the controversy over Tractarianism that
for over three hundred years the English church had comprised
almost every shade of opinion from absolute Romanism to 'the naked
scheme of Geneva'.[25] He was accounted a High-Churchman, but
had reached that position independently of the Oxford Movement. He continued to hold the essentials of his earlier evangelical

[24] Cf. C. C. J. Webb, *Religious Thought in the Oxford Movement* (1928), 9: 'While its
doctrinal teaching probably affected the religion of the nation as a whole less than is often
supposed, it unquestionably created a new ideal of the Church's ministry and a new type
of clergyman.'
[25] B. L. Add. Ms. 44733 fo. 150 (12 November 1845), quoted in Perry Butler, *Gladstone: Church, State and Tractarianism* (1982), 199; and see ibid., 51, 53, 64.

religion along with a profound reverence for the sacraments. He was anxious not to unchurch dissenters, though he thought some of their doctrine erroneous. He remained a close friend of Lord Acton and others whose religious opinions were not his own. As J. L. Hammond has written: 'Gladstone's friendships are significant. He was as zealous for his religion as Shaftesbury, but nobody can imagine Shaftesbury intimate with the Catholic Acton or the agnostic Morley.'[26] It was part and parcel of the life of a politician to find a *modus vivendi* with those whose religious opinions he thought mistaken. The more totalitarian schemes of Christian doctrine which denied ultimate salvation to those who were labelled heretics fell into the background or lost coherence in the minds of men and women who dedicated themselves to secular objectives, whether in politics, in social reform or even in scholarship.

Hicks was not formed by the Oxford Movement, though he spoke with appreciation of its legacy to the church. He was not a Christian Socialist, though he regarded Maurice as a great prophet. He was not a Modernist, though he accepted without hesitation the need to subject scriptures and doctrines to critical examination. The fundamental reason for his eclecticism was that his Christian commitment became focused outside the realm of the sacred, narrowly defined. For him, as for Acton, politics transcended religion. The long shadows of the Oxford Movement, of Christian Socialism, of biblical controversy, did not finally distract him from the other great process at work during the decades of his maturity: the process of democratization. Here his early acceptance of a critical approach to the scriptures and the development of Christian doctrine was crucial, because it freed him from the temptation to look for immutable patterns of social organization in the Bible or the Fathers, as evangelicals and sacramental socialists were tempted to do.[27] And he was fortunate in coming from a commonplace family background. That ensured that he was free from the authoritarian attitudes of the well-to-do, which we can see in such otherwise dissimilar characters as Charles Gore, Ralph Inge, and even Conrad Noel and Hewlett Johnson. His entry into polite society was through his proficiency in classical scholarship; but in

---

[26] J. L. Hammond, 'Gladstone and the League of Nations Mind', in *Essays in Honour of Gilbert Murray* (1936), 111 n.

[27] See for a later example L. S. Thornton, 'The Necessity of Catholic Dogma' in A Group of Churchmen, *The Return of Christendom* (1922), 63–86.

this, too, he was fortunate in the chance that pointed his studies away from literary or philosophical subjects, which tempt students to postulate 'values' transferable from one age to another, and towards the everyday practicalities revealed by classical epigraphy and the language of the market-place. That resulted from contact with the first of four formative influences: Sir Charles Newton. The others were John Ruskin, Sir Wilfrid Lawson, and the great editor, C. P. Scott. The deepest and most abiding influence, however, may have been that of his home. For it was there that he learnt to take politics seriously, as the only road to the amelioration of society. The politics of amelioration was the politics of the Liberal Party. Hicks's father was a small businessman who neglected his business to work for the return to parliament of good Liberal members. Even his mother, who led a quiet private life, had firm political opinions. In a letter to Hicks's wife Agnes she declared roundly, 'I am sure Liberalism and not Toryism is most in agreement with the religion of the Christ of the New Testament.'[28] This lesson, learnt at home, was more potent even than the influence of his friends.

During his university career Hicks came into contact with other views about the relation of religion to politics, even among those he considered his friends. Ruskin, in particular, declared himself a Tory. He was, however, of an older generation, and Hicks was more a discerning admirer than a disciple, choosing what to accept and what to reject among Ruskin's manifold prophetic denunciations. Of his own age, a particular friend was John Wordsworth, later Bishop of Salisbury, with whom he was elected to a Craven scholarship in 1867. They both won fellowships at Oxford colleges. They remained friends until Wordsworth's death in 1911. They corresponded about all kinds of things, from recommended country walks to inscriptions in the Middle East. When Wordsworth died, Hicks made a little Latin note in his diary, recalling his friend's great learning, the closeness of their friendship, the loss he felt.[29] Remarkably their friendship continued in spite of the radical divergence of their views on politics. John Wordsworth was a Conservative. He quite possibly agreed with the unequivocal statement made by his father, Bishop Christopher Wordsworth:

[28] Private letter to Hicks's wife Agnes (1893).
[29] *Vir doctissimus, amicissimus, valde deflendus.*

What, gentlemen, is Conservatism? It is the application of Christianity to civil government. And what is English Conservatism? It is the adoption of the principles of the Church of England as the groundwork of legislation. Gentlemen, I say it with reverence, the most Conservative book in the world is the Bible, and the next most Conservative book in the world is the Book of Common Prayer.[30]

If it seems strange that devout believers within the same communion could diverge to that extent in political opinions which they claimed to derive from the gospel, we can add to the strangeness a third opinion: 'Christianity is the religion of which socialism is the practice.'[31] It is improbable that Hicks heard anything like that dictum at Oxford, but the most significant period of his ministry in Salford and Manchester, between 1886 and 1910, was a time of the multiplication of Christian groups attracted by socialist theories of various kinds, and Hicks was in touch with many of the active members of these groups. But he was unwilling to adopt any theory of the ideal basis of social organization; least of all when it pretended to find authorization in theology.

The reasons for this refusal were of two kinds. First, his scholarship revealed to him both the continuities and the changes in the historical process which had created the contemporary world, with new patterns of society emerging to which the foundation documents of the Christian faith had not been addressed. Secondly, his way into active political involvement had been through concern with the kind of practical problems which required for their solution the co-operative efforts of all who could be persuaded to act together, irrespective of their beliefs and attitudes in other matters. The most obvious of these were the related problems of drink and poverty. But his temperance activities were the beginning, not the end, of his social concerns. Unfortunately temperance is one of those topics on which it was, and is, almost impossible for people to take an unimpassioned view. The humane learning, the broad culture, the enjoyment of literature and art and the natural world, the capacity for friendship, which characterized Edward Hicks often counted for little with those who condemned all talk of total abstinence from alcohol as an absurd prejudice. Sometimes his critics

---

[30] Reported in the *Guardian* (1865), 96, and quoted in Owen Chadwick, *The Secularization of the European Mind in the Nineteenth Century* (Cambridge 1975), 108.

[31] Lewis Donaldson, quoted by Maurice B. Reckitt in *Maurice to Temple: A Century of the Social Movement in the Church of England* (1947), 148.

could see that there were other facets of his concern for social reform, but few seemed able to penetrate to the unifying convictions at the heart of them all.

The starting-point of this study, in Part I, is the making of a Radical churchman in the period after the controversies of the 1830s and the 1850s. It begins in Oxford. It shows initially a multiplicity of influences on a young scholar, influences both secular and religious. But it leads, in Part II, to the witness of a Radical churchman chiefly in the very different situation provided by Salford and Manchester, at a time when the Liberal Party was renewing its strength, for the last time, and Liberal churchmen were, for the last time, trying to work together to change social conditions through their influence with the party. It ends, in Part III, with an assessment of the nature of liberalism in religion more generally. Hicks's biography, edited by J. H. Fowler, and published in 1922, remains an indispensable source of information.[32] But although Fowler was a long-standing friend of the family, his interests were not chiefly political or ecclesiastical. He had a distinguished career as a teacher, and was a founding member of the English Association. He shared some of Hicks's political attitudes during the time of their friendship in Manchester, where Fowler was on the staff of the Grammar School, but they were not closely in touch with each other during the most effective period of Hicks's ministry, and it is noticeable that only a small part of the *Life and Letters* is devoted to his political and social activities. It is possible that Hicks's wife Agnes preferred the emphasis to fall elsewhere. His episcopal diary mentions, among a very small number of observations about Agnes's opinions, an occasion when she was worried about his outspokenness on political matters in a University Sermon at Cambridge. A different picture would have been presented by someone who had worked closely with him in the causes which he championed. A letter from one of them, Samuel Proudfoot, to the *Modern Churchman* after Fowler's book had been reviewed, included this testimony to Hicks's character:

In his advocacy of Reform he was advanced, clear and definite, and never showed any fear of democracy. His constancy to progressive politics was unswerving, because it was a passion. The horrors of the slums, the uncertainties of employment, the inadequate wages, the jerry-built cottages,

---

[32] Fowler, *Life and Letters* (subsequently cited as 'Fowler').

the complete absence of 'sweetness and light' from whole tracts of his Salford Parish, these things stirred him to the very depths, and made him feel ashamed of the more complacent members of the Christian Church, believing this to be so dishonouring to God. It is idle to deny that he distrusted Conservative politicians. In them he saw nothing but danger. He was almost a fanatical Radical; and would have voted for an advanced Socialist rather than a Tory. His nature and temperament were sweetness and graciousness itself, being thoroughly Christian, and under perfect control, and this frequently gave the impression that he was more 'moderate' than the above suggests, but only to the superficial observer.[33]

By these standards Fowler's portrait, with its contributions from Hicks's successor in Salford, Canon Peter Green, and his chaplain at Lincoln, Canon Boulter, is too domestic and too uncontroversial.

Unfortunately few of his own letters have survived, and much of the material used by Fowler is no longer available. But a collection of family papers has been treasured and provides information about Hicks's life, particularly at Oxford and Fenny Compton.[34] The bulk of evidence about his attitudes and ideas is to be found in a great quantity of occasional writings, which adequately document, together with material included in Fowler's biography, his activities and ideas during the double culmination of his life's work at Salford and at Lincoln. In Salford he was a regular contributor to the *Manchester Guardian*, first as a frequent letter writer, with over seventy letters published between 1892 and 1910, and then for six years as one of two official religious correspondents, contributing on an almost weekly basis a commentary on religious and national affairs. He also contributed to a number of journals, notably the *Optimist*, which took its origin from a reunion of former students of the short-lived Manchester theological college, Scholae Episcopi, in 1905. It changed its title to the *Church Socialist Quarterly* in 1909, but reverted to its original title two years later. The CSU journal, the *Commonwealth*, from 1896 until almost the end of Hicks's life, is important for filling in some of the background to his activities. He made a few contributions to its columns, and

---

[33] *Modern Churchman* 12/12 (March 1923): Letter from S. Proudfoot, Pendleton Vicarage. Manchester, Proudfoot had been assistant curate to Hewlett Johnson in Altrincham, and later served under Hicks in Lincoln diocese.

[34] These include a bound volume of letters written by his mother between 1871 and her death in 1897.

there are more frequent references to meetings he attended or addressed in Manchester and further afield, but its value lies in providing much background material relating to that amorphous group of religious people who were attracted by radical social ideas and hovered over the borderline between Liberalism and socialism.

Hicks's episcopate is more fully documented than his earlier ministry. There are, as in the case of every diocesan, the official and unofficial records of the bishops in Convocation, in Bishops' Meetings, and in correspondence with the archbishop. But, more importantly, it was the last period at Lincoln during which the proceedings of the diocesan conference were reported verbatim; and although much of the record is tedious, it does catch informal comments by the bishop which are sometimes as revealing as his prepared speeches and sermons. His Primary Visitation Charge, delivered in June 1912, was printed in full, though the restrictions of wartime prevented publication of his later Charge, delivered in May and June 1918. The *Lincoln Diocesan Magazine* all through his episcopate chronicled events in the diocese at a length unimaginable today, as well as carrying serious articles relating to the diocese and verbatim reports of addresses by the bishop and other clergy. Then there are the two massive volumes of his manuscript diary, covering the entire period of his episcopate. The printed edition is readily accessible.[35] This contains only about one-third of the whole manuscript, but what has been omitted consists mainly of material of a factual nature which throws little light on the bishop's character. What has been printed offers a wealth of detail relating to an age which is rapidly passing beyond the memory of the living.[36] Yet that kind of picture of the intersection of recorded history and an individual's life, intriguing though it may be, is not the chief merit of the diaries. That lies in showing us what kind of man, and what kind of churchman, had been created by seventy years of experience in Oxford, in a Warwickshire parish, in a civic university, in a parish and a cathedral in Salford and Manchester, and in a largely rural diocese with over 580 benefices, suddenly filled with camps and hospitals during four years of total war.

[35] Graham Neville (ed.), *The Diaries of Edward Lee Hicks, Bishop of Lincoln 1910–1919*, Lincoln Record Society, lxxxii (1993) (subsequently cited as 'Diary').

[36] For a short account of the characteristics of the diaries, see *Diary*, Introduction, pp. vii–xiii.

With this material it is possible to provide the fuller view of Hicks which his friend Samuel Proudfoot had vainly hoped would be provided by Fowler, and which goes far to release him from the stereotypes of Anglican churchmen sometimes imposed upon figures from the past. But the major concern of this study is to enlarge, however little, our understanding of the complex story of English religion under stress from the interplay of social forces, the variety of partisan groups and societies, the remaking of relations between church and state, and perhaps above all the assertive autonomy claimed by secular studies from the constraints of religious orthodoxy. Hicks lived and thought in several borderlands or points of transition: old universities were changing, and the place of the church within them was being transformed; the legacy of the Oxford Movement was being wrested by its inheritors in fresh directions as they faced the experience of life in industrial centres; Christian apologetic was reacting, positively or negatively, to new understandings of history and science; social change was challenging traditional Christian ideas about the family and women's place in society. The story of a particular man in such a time is part of the story of the church's response to change.

PART I

The Making of a Radical Churchman

2

Oxford in Transition

Hicks began his life in Oxford as a townsman. He can hardly have been aware of what was going on in the university until after he became a scholar of Brasenose in 1862. He left Oxford to take up a college living in 1873, but evidently remained in touch with university affairs for many years after that. During that period, from 1862 to the 1880s, there were important issues which were being debated and fought over and restated—issues both for the university and for the church. Church parties were being redefined. The perceived functions of the university in national life and its relation to its Christian heritage were changing. At a deeper level, methods of scholarship were falling into line with the new scientific and historical spirit of the age. Hicks was inevitably affected by these changes, but it is only with hindsight that we can recognize their influence from the beginning in his experience. There are clues we can pick up as we trace the stages of his life. But it was another question which was brought earliest to the young Edward Hicks's attention: the political implications of Christian belief.

Picture Gloucester Green at Oxford some time in the 1840s, full of a great crowd which had come together for a feast of anti-Corn-Law oratory by Cobden and Bright. Among them is 'a man of middle height, fair and somewhat sandy in complexion' with a little boy two or three years old on his shoulders, brought along, not to understand the arguments of the orators speaking from a wagon, but just so that he could in after years say he had heard them. The little boy was Edward Lee Hicks, on the shoulders of his father. Nearly seventy years later he was to write a review of G. M. Trevelyan's *Life of John Bright*. That is, of course, far from proving a continuity of influence and interest. But Hicks claimed to remember how, as a little boy, he had sat on his father's knee 'spelling out Peel's speeches', and that he had enough curiosity to look through his father's papers and find some anti-Corn-Law League pamphlets. His childhood home in Oxford, first in Ship

Street and later in the High, was alive with political interests. His father was active in a number of parliamentary elections, to the detriment of his business.

He was a good Liberal, and worked hard for Edward Cardwell (afterwards Viscount Cardwell, and Minister of War), and for Sir William Harcourt, successively members for Oxford. He took a vigorous part in the famous election when W. M. Thackeray put up as a Radical against the 'Peelite' Cardwell, who at the time was absent abroad.[1]

Cardwell was one of a group of close associates of Gladstone which also included Roundell Palmer, who was appointed Lord Chancellor in Gladstone's first ministry. Roundell Palmer's youngest brother, Edwin, became Corpus Professor of Latin, and was a close friend of Hicks when he was a young fellow of that college. In the course of time Hicks married Edwin's niece, Agnes. So the web of politics and university life began to be woven round the Hicks household, and it was natural for him to see political agitation as a proper part of life. He was neither insulated from politics by indifference or subservience in the home, nor discouraged from political thought by an atmosphere of contentment with the *status quo*. His father took it for granted that things ought to be changed, and could be changed by the pressure of popular opinion. That certainly was an assumption of the radical churchman Hicks grew up to be. The influence of his mother, Catherine Hicks, was also important. She had more decided religious views than her husband; but she was also equally firm in her political opinions.

The Christian faith was much in evidence in the home; but it was not a clerical household, such as was so often the setting in which church leaders were nourished. Of the bishops with whom Hicks eventually sat on the bench more than half had grown up in parsonages. Probably they were more familiar with so-called party allegiances in the church than with parliamentary parties and their subdivisions. The lay religion of the Hicks household took little account of the nuances of Christian belief. The father, Edward Hicks, had forebears who had held office as churchwardens of Wolvercote, a few miles from Oxford. There they had resented the intrusion of Methodists into the parish, but in Oxford he joined his wife in attending Methodist worship for some time. When the

[1] These and other details included in Fowler, 2 ff., are taken from a manuscript memoir written by Hicks and bound up with his mother's letters (see notes on sources).

Wesleyans were embroiled in the 'Fly-sheets' controversy of 1844–9, Hicks's father took the side of the reformers, who stood up for the rights of the laity and aimed at greater local independence within the connexion. That controversy also generated bitter personal rivalries, and the family welcomed the opportunity to turn to the Church of England under the sympathetic ministry of a local parish priest.

Hicks remembered as an important lesson he had learnt from his father the readiness to accept truth wherever it might be found. His mother was remembered as having sat under preachers of all varieties in Oxford, and enjoyed all kinds of clerical biography, whether of E. B. Pusey or of Dean Stanley. It is a salutary reminder that there is a lay spirituality which can draw nourishment from many different sources, picking out what seems right and seems relevant, and ignoring differences over things believed to be indifferent or even wrong. Again, it would be too much to claim continuity from childhood to maturity, but it was true of the mature bishop who had been born into that household that he was praised by an evangelical bishop for having written one of the best of evangelical biographies and mistrusted by an archbishop for being too High Church. He neither looked for, nor was offered, the support of an ecclesiastical party.

There is one other factor in Edward Hicks's early experience of family life which resonates in his thoughts as a mature man. His father was 'in trade'. He appears in local directories as a 'dyer'—not a trade of much repute. Not only so, but he was an unsuccessful tradesman who got into debt. Hicks grew up determined to clear those debts and provide his father with a peaceful retirement in old age. Somehow or other he succeeded. But he remained sensitive all his life to the way so-called gentlemen, and not least clerical gentlemen, regarded 'trade'. An extreme instance is seen in the sentiments expressed by the future Archbishop of Canterbury, Edward White Benson, while an undergraduate at Cambridge in the 1840s. His mother, a widow in straitened circumstances, owned her late husband's patent for the manufacture of cobalt, and she had the sensible idea of starting a business to exploit it. Benson was horrified. 'I do hope and trust you will keep out of it. It will do me so much harm here, and my sisters so much harm for ever! I trust that the scheme may be abandoned once and for all.'[2] Another

---

[2] E. F. Benson, *As We Were* (1930), 55.

clerical snob, Charles Kingsley, believed that 'the shopkeeping class' were unable to bear fatigue, danger, or pain 'which would be considered as sport by an average public schoolboy'.[3] An attitude of superiority persisted when its overt expression was muted, and Hicks remained sensitive about it to the end of his life. He told against himself the story of his acute embarrassment as an undergraduate when carrying his uncle's 'hideous red-patterned carpet-bag' for him to the station in term-time.

Even late in life that sensitivity comes out noticeably in diary entries which refer to the Bishops' Meetings at Lambeth. He notes that he always feels 'out of it'. On one occasion (21 October 1914) he writes: 'I was miserable. I feel always out of my element here at Lambeth: an "outsider": I hear the same men say the same things, & the Archbp. turning ever to Winton, or Oxford. I fear I am thought a bore, or a bear, or a bounder.' Perhaps he felt so acutely isolated on that occasion because the discussion had been about alcohol in wartime, and he knew that he stood out as an advocate of total abstinence. Teetotalism itself had class overtones; there were far more gentlemanly ways of advocating temperance. Most of the bishops who did not come from clerical families had professional backgrounds, in law or medicine. Several had connections with the nobility, including E. S. Talbot, whose grandfathers were Earl Talbot and Lord Wharncliffe, and Charles Gore, whose grandfathers were the Earl of Arran and the Earl of Bessborough. No doubt Archbishop Davidson relied heavily on them because they were intelligent and experienced men, but Hicks suspected that it was also because they were from a particular class. In fact, Davidson's own father was a wood merchant in Leith, having chosen that way of life in preference to the bar, but one of his grandmothers was sister to a Scottish Law Lord. So there is a lifetime's sensitivity in the thought Hicks confided to his diary, at the age of seventy-four: 'I have been what the world calls "successful": but that is a poor thing after all—yet being a poor lad, & without any influence to push me, I just did what I could, & here I am. *Deo gratias*.'[4]

The 'thanks be to God' was not for having his origins as a 'poor lad', but in having become something quite different. Hicks may

---

[3] Susan Chitty, *The Beast and the Monk: A Life of Charles Kingsley* (1974), 159.
[4] *Diary*, 18 Dec. 1917.

have resented the superiority of those who looked down on 'trade', never having needed to earn a living by 'the disgusting vice of shopkeeping'.[5] But he never looked back with nostalgia to a tradesman's life. Christian leaders from upper-class backgrounds who became social reformers tended to favour socialism rather than Liberalism. Hicks lacked that kind of background, and was less strongly attracted to socialistic theories.

Two men who influenced him, Gladstone and Ruskin, were themselves to some degree refugees from the commercial classes. One commentator has said of Gladstone that 'in the presence of noble blood, he felt something akin to awe', because of his mercantile background.[6] As for Ruskin, it is noticeable that in some early memories of him by G. W. Kitchin, a former Dean of Durham, he is described as feeling the challenge which Oxford life presented in his undergraduate days as posing the question, 'In the midst of a very aristocratic group of lads, how could he, with his relations in trade, large or small, with his baker cousins and all the rest of it, hold his own, and take his proper part in the life of Christ Church?'[7] Ruskin's father, however, traded in wine, and the status of a successful wine merchant was 'that of a responsible adviser to the aristocracy and gentry in one of its most important and critical departments of gentlemanly conduct'.[8] Perhaps the church in its higher echelons was slower to respond to social change than some other sectors of national life. Even after 1910, when Hicks was made a bishop, the episcopate had some of the marks of a gentleman's club.

It would have been impossible to look at the young Edward Lee Hicks as he went to Magdalen College School, Oxford, in the 1850s and predict which childhood influences would prove significant. From a later vantage point it is easy to see that three factors present in his childhood contributed to the formation of the man he became: reforming politics, comprehensive Christian faith, class consciousness. Each element was appropriated in a distinctive way. Each was effective in his mature life; but for the time being they were all overlaid by other influences, as he was absorbed into the life of the university and made new friends.

---

[5] G. M. Young, *Victorian England: Portrait of an Age* (1953), 7.
[6] Perry Butler, *Gladstone: Church, State and Tractarianism* (Oxford 1982), 18.
[7] G. M. Kitchin, *Ruskin in Oxford and Other Studies* (1904), 8.
[8] J. A. Hobson, *John Ruskin, Social Reformer* (1898), 2.

The future religious commitment of anyone who spent eleven years in the University of Oxford at this period cannot be understood except in relation to the changes that were taking place. During Hicks's childhood and adolescence the excitements of the Oxford Movement had been succeeded by a period of reaction when, it has been said, dons turned from speculation in theology to speculation in railway shares. But the influence of the High Church party, led by Pusey and Liddon, remained strong and there was a continuing conflict between it and the theological liberalism represented by Benjamin Jowett at Balliol and by Arthur Stanley, the disciple of Dr Arnold, who was an important figure in Oxford until he left the university in 1864 to become Dean of Westminster. There were, in fact, identifiable religious parties still, though divisions did not run as deep as in the time of the Tractarian controversy. We need not assume that they were quite sharply defined and that it was always possible to put individual members into the categories of High Church, evangelical and Broad Church. At moments of crisis individual churchmen did, no doubt, allow themselves to be identified by those labels. It does not follow that they shared all the beliefs and attitudes of the party leaders.

Nor was religious life in the colleges and the university merely a matter of partisan polemics. Dons and undergraduates were individuals, and were free in their private thoughts to choose how much of any scheme of belief each one adopted. It had been possible even in the 1830s for the young John Ruskin, who was not at all lacking in Christian belief, to spend his years at Christ Church knowing little about the controversial Dr Pusey;[9] and it was even more possible for an undergraduate with other interests to ignore Puseyism in the 1860s and 1870s. The religious tests which were so much disputed did not exclude superficial conformists; and even the serious-minded might have a religious background in which denominational allegiance played little part. It would be a mistake to give too much emphasis at this period to the figures of controversialists who stood out as important on the national scene. Of equal or greater importance for the formation of Hicks's character and opinions were his day-to-day experiences within the

---

[9] Ruskin, *Praeterita* (1978 edn), vol. i, ch. 11, 190: 'Even Dr Pusey (who also never spoke to me) was not in the least a picturesque or tremendous figure, but only a sickly and rather ill put together English clerical gentleman, who never looked one in the face, or appeared aware of the state of the weather.'

confined community life of small colleges which were only just beginning to feel the winds of change.

From Magdalen College School Hicks had won an open classical scholarship to Brasenose. This was a fair achievement, seeing that a few years earlier his mother had had difficulty in persuading the headmaster to accept him as a pupil on account of his lack of Latin and Greek. He was admitted and went into residence in January 1862. He had been well advised to choose Brasenose as his college. It was described a few years later, by John Wordsworth who took up a fellowship there in 1867, as 'a place for poor men to work in'. There are few remaining evidences of Hicks's undergraduate life. Some details are given in Fowler's biography and there are scanty records in the college archives. What they contain bears witness to a circumscribed existence. His battels—small items of personal expenditure recorded in the college accounts—are regularly lower than those of any other undergraduate, a mere 2s. 2d. a week. Even his friend Henry Bazely, who was no sybarite, always spent a least twice as much as Hicks. For a short time he shared a room in college with another man, the son of a 'gentleman farmer'. There were no other tradesmen's sons in the college. There is no entry for Hicks in the Room Book after the end of 1862, and evidently he economized by living at home, only a few hundred yards away in High Street, on the site of the present Examination Schools. His studies were effective enough, however, and he and Bazely were the only two to be given First Classes in the Brasenose 'Collections' at the beginning of their undergraduate courses. He maintained this high level of achievement, and was awarded First Classes in Classical Moderations and in the Final School of Literae Humaniores.

Alongside his classical studies, Hicks was forming his basic beliefs. His own recollections, recorded much later, were of two distinct religious influences in his early years: his debt to Methodism, and his debt to the Anglo-catholic movement. The latter was not due to the preaching of leading High-Churchmen, but to the pastoral care of the Vicar of St Peter-in-the-East, the Revd E. Hobhouse, when his father was gravely ill. His regard for the Tractarian tradition had more to do with pastoral faithfulness and the reverence of public worship than with theology. There is something symbolic in the fact that Professor J. M. Wilson, a leading university reformer, gave Hicks a portrait of Newman, which he had been given by one of Newman's friends, and Hicks in due course gave it to his mother. Newman, so to speak, passed him by, as he passed by J. M. Wilson. Perhaps it was the effect of his religious, but non-partisan, upbringing that he never felt the attraction of the Roman Catholic Church. Much of Newman's Anglican writing assumed a problem which was posed precisely by that church's existence. For many another political Liberal like Wilson and Hicks the problem was not its existence but its illiberal autocracy, seemingly perpetuated by the 1864 *Syllabus Errorum*. If, then, Anglocatholicism as a theory did not appeal to Hicks, neither did he commit himself to the doctrinal alternatives of the liberal theologians who either had 'nothing definite to teach',[10] or alternatively grounded their religion on mysticism or some other experiential basis. In fact, although he became highly critical of evangelicalism, his closest friend at Brasenose was an extreme evangelical.

It is a misleading fact that Hicks's longest published writing, apart from his technical work in Greek epigraphy, is his memoir: *Henry Bazely, the Oxford Evangelist*.[11] He expressed his individuality and his convictions much more in his occasional writings, in journalism, in lectures and articles, and during his episcopate in visitation addresses and presidential addresses at diocesan conferences. The memoir of Henry Bazely was not written till many years after he had left Oxford, but its relevance in understanding his development relates to the Oxford period. It is a memorial of friendship and not a statement of personal faith. The bond of sympathy between the two men is shown by the fact that even after leaving Corpus Hicks kept in touch with Bazely on his frequent visits to Oxford from Fenny Compton, and their friendship continued until Bazely's death. Hicks was throughout his life, as many people testified, ready to give a fair hearing to opinions he did not share. In his memoir he presented his friend's beliefs with scrupulous fidelity and without comment, except for a note in the Introduction to the effect that his own theological position was very different from that of Bazely, and that he 'was surprised at his decided objections

---

[10] See Jowett's notebook quoted in W. S. Peterson, *Victorian Heretic: Mrs Humphry Ward's Robert Elsmere* (Leicester 1976), 75.

[11] The genesis of this book is uncertain. The Rector of St Aldates, the Revd Alfred Christopher, wrote to Hicks in 1884 inviting him to contribute to a proposed memorial volume to Bazely to be edited by 'a Scotch clergyman'. This did not appear, and the entire task fell to Hicks (Timothy Hicks papers).

to Episcopacy, his strong Calvinism, his extreme scruples about purity of worship'.

But there was an interesting cross-over in their responses to their religious backgrounds. Bazely did not suffer from the straitened family circumstances which cramped Hicks's social life. His father was Rector of Poplar when his son went up to Brasenose. Hicks described him as belonging to the old High-Church school. There was, however, more to his incumbency at Poplar than the mere acceptance of a college living. The college was at that time the patron of most of the important benefices formed out of the old parish of Stepney. Hicks saw that as the expression of a 'fine ideal, the concentration of the influence and action of one Oxford college upon the spiritual needs of the East End'—an ideal later expressed through the Oxford settlements.[12] That might have led the rector's son in the direction of a social gospel, or towards the kind of colourful religion which the neighbouring Anglo-catholic clergy believed was capable of meeting the religious needs of the deprived. Hicks's background, with the Methodist element to which he often referred favourably in later life, might have led him to devote himself to outgoing, evangelistic efforts to spread the gospel. Neither consequence followed. Bazely became a footloose evangelist, preaching a Calvinistic gospel, replete with the fear of everlasting punishment. Hicks in due course spent eighteen years in a largely slum parish trying in some measure to fulfil the ideal which he thought the Brasenose college livings in the East End were intended to express.

Perhaps the difference between them had something to do with the different kinds of academic work which they undertook. Bazely won a Hulme Exhibition which obliged him to study theology for two years after taking his BA (though in fact he took a BCL to avoid having to sign the Thirty-nine Articles), and went on to take further theological scholarships and to undertake some theological teaching. The result, in his case, was eventually to narrow his interests to purely theological questions, and even those were unrelated to contemporary society. His theology was an attempt to use the Bible as the basis on which to construct not only a gospel message but also an ideal pattern of church life. Having done that to his own satisfaction he looked around for a church which most

[12] *Henry Bazely*, 8.

nearly matched the ideal he had constructed. He thought he had found it in the Presbyterian order of the Church of Scotland, in spite of being alienated by the whisky-drinking and smoking habits of the men studying for the ministry in Scotland.

But the ideal church was nowhere to be found, and he vacillated between the English and Scottish churches. His life's work was to go out to fairs and races, and there to preach, whether men would hear or whether they would forbear. 'If you want to find Bazely,' it was said, 'you must look for him in a crowd.' He was sufficiently well known to attract the supercilious comment of Taine, in his *Notes on England*. He witnessed the outdoor preaching of 'two gentlemen and a member of the middle-class' at the Martyrs' Memorial in Oxford, and commented:

I heartily approve of these proceedings. In the first place they provide a vent for consuming passion, for an intense conviction which for lack of an outlet would degenerate into madness, melancholy and sedition. In the second, they are moralizing and may do good to many consciences. In the third, they keep alive among the public the belief that there are noble ideals, genuine convictions, perfectly zealous souls; for man is only too ready to fancy that indifference and amusement are the end of life.[13]

Hicks confirms that this was a picture of Bazely. He does not reveal whether he himself was then, or ever, a companion in this outdoor preaching, but he certainly practised it personally in his Warwickshire parish, in the slums of Salford, and on Lincolnshire beaches. There was much, he thought, to admire in Bazely. He did not run away from the evil in human life; rather he sought it out. He had once, in 1863, deliberately attended a public execution in Oxford, and had condemned it as brutalizing and disgusting. The only remedy was the preaching of the gospel. He had no interest in changing society, but only in changing individuals. He saw the gospel as a plain, straightforward message describing the way to salvation. To him, Hicks wrote, 'the mystical in religion and the sensual in art were equally abhorrent'.

That remark of Hicks about Bazely also reveals something about himself. His interests were too wide to be accommodated within purely biblical studies. Though it is difficult to discover what theological reading Hicks did at this stage of his life, he knew enough to be accepted for ordination by Bishop Mackarness. But he was

---

[13] H. Taine, *Notes on England* (1872), 236.

first and foremost a classicist, and his working life as a fellow and tutor and eventually Dean of Corpus demanded that he should give priority to classical studies. The chief influences upon him in the formative period of his life at Corpus were not theological, though he was not untouched by theological controversy. When he came to describe his college experience in the 1860s, he wrote:

Among the more intellectual students it was almost a point of honour to be in revolt against clerical restrictions. The wildest theories were agitated; and the system of religious repression only encouraged scepticism. The theological world was then still disturbed by the *Essays and Reviews*, and was further discussing the riots at St George's-in-the-East, and the 'ritualism' of Mr Bryan King—a near neighbour . . . of Mr Bazely at Poplar, and a brother ex-fellow of Brasenose. All these controversies found their echo among the undergraduates.[14]

Perhaps Bazely's deep interest in theological questions and his experience of his father's East-End parish opened a door to controversy which others in other colleges did not peer through. But the subjectivity of all such impressions is demonstrable.

It happens that a different picture, more particularly referring to Corpus, where Hicks in due time became a fellow, is contained in a memoir recorded some fifty years later by Edmund Arbuthnott Knox, who was to have a number of connections with Hicks in after life, but in the late 1860s had been tutored by him. This is his description of religion at Corpus as he remembered it:

Even of Churchmanship we had no great varieties. St Barnabas did not exist; St Thomas was said to use vestments, but I never met an undergraduate who went there. St Philip and St James, for practical purposes, was the high-water mark of churchmanship, and I doubt if it had even risen to coloured stoles. Surpliced choirs and the surplice in the pulpit satisfied Ritualistic aspirations. In the opposite direction we had three Churches with Evangelical Incumbents, but their influence on University life was small. The College Chapel with its monthly Communion, and without choir, indeed without music, and without sermons—and the University sermon, were for most of us the spiritual provision . . . The Oxford Movement had left little trace on University religious life. Broad Churchmanship of the Kingsley type there was none. The negative type thereof had a strong following among the Fellows, and of course of the undergraduates not a few were indifferent. Conformity to the

---

[14] *Henry Bazely*, 23–4.

Church of England of an old-fashioned type was its characteristic. Varieties were few; dissent practically unknown.[15]

That tells us primarily what Knox remembered, not all that he might have noticed. But it helps us to get something of the flavour of the community within which Hicks began the period of his life when he was free to make choices. Its religion sounds dull. But Knox did not think so. In another passage from the memoir he writes:

As we received the bread and drank the wine from vessels that had been used for communicating Jewel, Hooker, Reynolds, Keble, Arnold, and their successors, we entered very really into the Communion of Saints and were profoundly conscious of the presence of our common Lord. Those communions in the Chapel of C. C. C. have never been surpassed by any subsequent spiritual experience in the course of a long life, not even by those of my ordination or consecration. The President had no small share in making them what they were to me.[16]

Such was the reality of Oxford life for the evangelical Knox, as he remembered it. It corresponds only in part with another picture of Corpus, this time in a contemporary letter written by C. P. Scott to his father, after he went into residence there in 1865. 'You might not improbably be told that Corpus was a low-church college, and so indeed it is, so far as an evangelical President and a chapel service entirely without music can make it; but the dons are Jowettites and free-thinkers, while the undergraduates are of decidedly high-church tendencies.' Scott himself, for all his nonconformist background, took an active part in chapel worship, and helped to introduce music into the services.[17] There was real spirituality in the chapel at Corpus, for those who were open to it, as Knox testified, but there was also religious controversy among the undergraduates, which he denied.

In any case, it was as a member of the senior common room that Hicks experienced the intellectual temper of Corpus. In 1866 he had gained a fellowship there. He was in fact the first lay fellow elected by examination under new statutes which derived from the work of the 1850 Royal Commission of inquiry into the University of Oxford. He remained a fellow of Corpus from 1866

---

[15] *Pelican Record* 20, 89–90.   [16] Ibid., 107.

[17] J. L. Hammond, *C. P. Scott of the Manchester Guardian* (1934), 16; *C. P. Scott 1846–1932, The Making of the 'Manchester Guardian'* (1946), 32.

to 1873. He was proceeding along a well-trodden path in classical studies. It was hardly a matter of choice; rather, of acceptance. And since he felt the goad of poverty and the need to support his parents as soon as he could, he was unlikely to turn aside from that path. The character of the man could only appear when choice did not threaten what he saw as his primary goal, the support of his family. The choices before him were not many. He had neither the interest nor the resources required for the profession of the law. The revised statutes did not require him to be ordained in order to retain his fellowship. The obvious course was to remain a don at Oxford. What that would mean was not entirely clear at the end of the 1860s. Reform was not only in the air; it was in actual process. He became aware of the issues which were exercising its senior members, and his liberalism began to take shape. The most obvious of these issues was the relationship of the church to the university, at a time when the role of the Church of England in national life was subject to continuous debate. In spite of all the campaigns and arguments, it continued to be the established church of the English nation throughout Hicks's life-time. It was said, however, by Dr Woodford, Bishop of Ely, in 1881 that disestablishment had been proceeding for fifty years. He was looking back to the repeal of the Test Acts in 1828. G. W. E. Russell, reporting that saying, continued:

Since then have followed in natural sequence the Emancipation of the Roman Catholics; the legalization of marriages in Dissenting chapels; the withdrawal of matrimonial and testamentary jurisdiction from the Ecclesiastical Courts; the admission of Jews to Parliament; the abolition of Church rates; the abolition of University Tests; the admission of Nonconformist funerals to the National churchyards.[18]

Dr Woodford considered that it was by a most gracious Providence that the process had been so gradual, giving the church time to learn how to stand alone.

An important element in this gradual disestablishment (if the term be permitted) was the change brought about by university reform, which initially expressed the convictions of a powerful pressure-group of reformers but then worked its way into the ideas and assumptions of many of the leading personages in national life. That reform was itself a gradual process which began with the

[18] G. W. E. Russell, *Collections and Recollections*, Series 2 (1909), 375–6.

appointment of the Royal Commission in 1850. Perhaps its importance was hardly realized by those who lived through it,[19] and it
is unlikely that the young Edward Hicks in his undergraduate days
at Brasenose took the measure of the change which was proceeding
in Oxford. But when he became a don at Corpus, he entered a
society in which leading men were prominent reformers.[20] Then
his family background made him sympathetic to the proposed
changes. The Royal Commission had been set up precisely to bring
about change, and the University Reform Act of 1854 had begun
a process that was to continue for decades. But the issue was far
from simple. Several battles were being fought simultaneously. There
was the battle over the church dominance of the university; there
was the battle to establish the professional status of college fellows;
and there was the battle over the essential role of the university.
Each aspect of the complex controversy had some relevance to
Hicks's future.

First, there was the struggle to maintain or destroy the dominance of the church in the university. Here it was important that
Hicks had not grown up in a clerical household. He had never lived
in that way at the centre of a parochial organization, though his
father had become churchwarden at St Peter-in-the-East. School
and college had provided the context within which he experienced
the practice of religion. He was unlikely to share the defensive attitude about the privileged place of the church in the university,
common among the clerical members of Congregation sympathetic
to Tractarianism.[21] Knox's memoir hints that the senior members
of the college were more open to radical thought than their juniors.
Doubts about Christian belief encouraged questions about the relation of the church to the university. If the church was no longer
what it had been; if the church was in danger of splitting into fac-
tions; if it could not organize its own life effectively: then the connection of church and university, taken for granted for decades,
seemed problematical. At Corpus Hicks was soon brought into
the arena of argument about the role of the church in the colleges.

[19] Cf. Owen Chadwick, *The Victorian Church* (2nd edn. 1972), pt. II, p. 446.

[20] W. R. Ward, *Victorian Oxford* (1965), 254.

[21] A. J. Engel, *From Clergyman to Don: The Rise of the Academic Profession in Nineteenth
Century Oxford* (Oxford 1983), 114. Engel notes the increase of resident MAs not engaged
in official academic work from 1858 to 1874 as from 15 per cent of Congregation to 25
per cent.

While he was still a Probationer Fellow it was proposed at a College Meeting (27 February 1868) that no declaration should be required of any fellow or candidate for a fellowship as to his intention of taking Holy Orders, and that no fellow should be deprived of his fellowship for not taking Holy Orders. It was also proposed that a layman should be eligible for the headship of the college. A petition was drawn up, to be presented to the Visitor. It was signed by all the fellows, including Hicks. He was still a layman, and would hesitate to argue that others should not be as he was. Having joined in the declaration of laymen's rights, he then characteristically exercised his freedom to make his own choice. He was ordained deacon by Bishop Mackarness in 1870, and priest in 1871. The colleges, with permission from parliament, might declare their independence from ecclesiastical control. Their freedom, however, must not constrain the freedom of their members.

Hicks's vote at the College Meeting put him alongside others who were academically liberal and opposed to the retention of university tests and clerical fellowships. The element of conservatism in the college was represented by the elderly President, Dr Norris. He must have been a man of some devotion, to have impressed the young E. A. Knox as he did. But he did not welcome change. Indeed Hicks's election to his fellowship was (so tradition relates) nearly jeopardized by Dr Norris's wish to offer it to a candidate within the college membership, which had to be overcome by a 'knock-for-knock' argument that Corpus must welcome merit from outside if it wanted to ensure equal opportunities for its own men elsewhere. When the petition to the Visitor about lay fellowships was agreed among the fellows, the President declared that he could not conscientiously support it. And when he welcomed Ruskin to membership of the corporate body, he was relieved to hear him declare himself a Tory, and said, 'You will, I am afraid, find the Tutors great Radicals.'[22] Hicks, then, was on the side of university reform in the matter of clerical fellowships and headships. Generally speaking, that went with what Knox called 'negative' Broad-Churchmanship; but Hicks did not align himself with churchmanship of that type.

Meanwhile another battle was agitating university life in addition to the battle over the church's place in the colleges and the

[22] Bernard Richards, 'Ruskin at Corpus', *Pelican Record* 38/4 (Jan. 1971).

university. It had two aspects, though they were closely related. The first was concerned with the professional status of tutors. In the movement for reform there were, apart from the 'church party', three groups whose understanding of the purpose of fellowships diverged widely.[23] A small group embraced those who wanted to promote the research function of the university as contrasted with its teaching function. A second group included those who held 'prize fellowships', which carried no teaching duties and were limited in tenure only by the requirement of celibacy and by a ceiling of income from other sources above which the emoluments of the fellowship would not be tenable. They argued that such prize fellowships were valuable as providing a temporary base upon which men could launch into the professions, notably into law. Unfortunately many of them did no such thing, but lived on a small but reliable income for life.

The main group organized themselves in a Tutors Association and kept in touch with Gladstone while he was MP for the university. Many of them lacked independent means and were determined to take the opportunity, presented by the reform movement, to consolidate their professional status. They aimed to be released from what Mandell Creighton called the drudgery of tutorial work, that is, the unspecialized teaching which was necessitated by the attempt to restrict each undergraduate's lectures to his own college. Tutors in groups of colleges were already reaching informal agreements to produce joint programmes of lectures, and this made possible some degree of specialization and improved the chances of establishing a reputation within a particular field. The removal of the need to take Holy Orders within a specified period of time, the reduction of clerical fellowships, the new freedom of colleges to permit at least some of their fellows to marry, the allocation of some fellowships to professorial chairs, and the opening of headships to laymen, all contributed to creating a professional class of tutors who saw university teaching as a lifelong commitment with at least some prospects of promotion. In the period between the two parliamentary Acts reforming the university (1850 to 1876) these groups attacked each other vigorously. The outcome of their strife was still uncertain when Hicks took up his fellowship at Corpus, but the possibility of establishing a lifelong career in an

---

[23] See Engel, *Clergyman to Don*, 55.

Oxford Common Room, and as a married man, was becoming more feasible.

The other aspect of the reform debate concerned nothing less than the true nature and function of the university. Was it a mainstay of the church, or a finishing school for gentlemen, or a training ground for public office, or a place of higher research? The first of these options was becoming impossible, and the last was very much a minority view. Merely to raise up a new generation of gentlemen was not enough to satisfy the developed conscience of thinking people in the last quarter of the nineteenth century. By the end of that century, therefore, senior members of the colleges of both Oxford and Cambridge universities had come to accept a role in training men for public office. 'By creating men who would influence the direction of social change, they hoped to affirm their own importance and authority.'[24]

This 'revolution of the dons' had hardly begun when Hicks made the first major decision about his future career. He might have decided differently, if that revolution had already been effected, but it is unlikely. It is clear that he wanted to give his energies to the Christian mission, but in a very different way from his friend Bazely. A lifelong career as a classical scholar, even in changed circumstances, would not satisfy that sense of mission. Nor would he have thought himself fit, at that stage of his life, to prepare others for public life, of which he had no experience. There were deeper influences at work which prepared him, in the long term, to find a role in the movement for social reform. Those influences derived from his contacts at Oxford with Sir Charles Newton and John Ruskin. The struggles mentioned so far belonged to the old Liberalism, with its campaigns against privilege and effete old institutions. The influences to be considered next laid the basis for elements in the new Liberalism which was to modify, if not replace, the old.

[24] Sheldon Rothblatt, *The Revolution of the Dons: Cambridge Society in Victorian England* (1968), 247.

3
Critical Scholarship and Social Concern

While vigorous, and even embittered, debate was going on at Oxford about the two issues of the church's place in the university and the university's role in society, there were two other issues of great moment for English religion, which were beginning to take a salient place in intellectual life during Hicks's time at the university: the development of methods of historical study, with all that they implied for the understanding of Christian origins, and the developing social conscience among the middle and upper classes. The second will become explicit when we come to describe Hicks's friendship with Ruskin. The first is indicated by his work with Charles Newton, but remains implicit rather than explicit at that stage.

The scientific spirit of the age had expressed itself within historical studies in a fresh examination of known facts and documents, and archaeology had begun to reveal fresh evidence bearing on the history and religion of cultures which had contributed to western civilization. That development inevitably affected biblical and theological studies. As Mandell Creighton said later, in 1884: 'The traditions of theological learning have been thoroughly leavened by the historical spirit . . . Theology has become historical, and does not demand that history should become theological.'[1] The way in which this development first impinged upon Hicks's ideas had nothing directly to do with theology. It came about fortuitously when he was approached by Charles Newton for assistance in the deciphering and publication of epigraphical material.

Newton was of an older generation than Hicks, having been born, the son of a clergyman, in 1816. In his undergraduate days his dominant interest was in the scientific study of archaeology. This was by no means a favoured form of scholarship at the time.

[1] Mandell Creighton, *Historical Lectures and Addresses*, 2, quoted in L. E. Elliott-Binns, *The Development of English Theology in the Later Nineteenth Century* (1952), 59.

Hicks himself was later to quote the dismissive verdict of Benjamin Jowett that archaeology could only add a few, and (by implication) a few unimportant, facts to the literary study of classical civilization.[2] That view was widely held in Oxford. The Board of Studies of Literae Humaniores went on rejecting a place for archaeology as late as 1900.[3] It was without any encouragement from his family or his college that Newton, on taking his MA in 1840, decided to enter the British Museum and work in the department of antiquities. This proved, however, to be the beginning of a remarkable career, in the course of which he held consular appointments in the Middle East, carried out significant excavations, and brought back to England a large collection of inscriptions. So when, in 1862, he was appointed Keeper of Greek and Roman antiquities at the British Museum, not only was it a new position created specifically for him, but many of the antiquities would not have been there to keep if he had not personally acquired them. In due course he looked for a young Oxford scholar to assist in deciphering inscriptions.

It is not clear how he came to choose Hicks, though it is possible that the point of contact was John Ruskin. Newton and Ruskin were friends of long standing. They had first met each other as undergraduates at Christ Church, where Newton, the senior of the two, helped Ruskin in his study of architecture. They remained friends, disagreeing about Alpine scenery and the virtue of filling the British Museum with ancient sculptures, but enjoying their disagreements.[4] Ruskin knew Hicks well when he was a young fellow of Corpus, and may have brought his name to the attention of Newton. However that may be, it was a momentous event in Hicks's life, and Newton was not disappointed in his young assistant. The scholar and educationalist, Sir Samuel Dill, later wrote of him:

When I first knew him he was busy on his first volume of Greek inscriptions. And I had daily evidence of the wide range of learning and immense industry which he brought to the task of deciphering and

---

[2] *A Manual of Greek Historical Inscriptions* (Oxford 1882), p. xi.

[3] Engel, *Clergyman to Don*, 215; but Greek Numismatics was accepted as a subject in the Final Schools in 1882, see Sir Charles Oman, *Memories of Victorian Oxford and Some Early Years* (1941), 94. Oman used Hicks's *Greek Inscriptions* as a textbook.

[4] Ruskin, *Praeterita*, 352–3.

historical interpretation. I should say that, perhaps with the exception of [Ingram] Bywater, no young Oxford man of that time had anything like his erudition in Greek; and in finished scholarship Hicks was far superior to Bywater. In fact, it was the combination of the delicate old Oxford scholarship with learning that distinguished Hicks.[5]

The line of study which opened out for Hicks had something of the character of an adventure into new territory. Many years later, when he was speaking about one of his predecessors in the see of Lincoln, Bishop Christopher Wordsworth,[6] he called him 'the last of the old era of English scholarship, and the harbinger of the new' and went on to explain that Wordsworth's work on the New Testament and the Fathers might not always stand the light of newer scholarship. Hicks evidently had in mind, amongst other developments, the new evidence provided by archaeology. Wordsworth was 'one of the pioneers of archaeological travel and study in Greece', but his work came too early to take advantage of its evidence. Hicks did not work in the field of biblical archaeology, but he found himself in Greek historical studies at a turning-point.

Looking back from the beginning of the new century, the pioneering classical scholar Jane Harrison thought of herself and her contemporaries in Hellenic studies as 'a people who sat in darkness' but had seen the two great lights—archaeology and anthropology.[7] The old humane assumption of traditionally educated people in Britain, that there was an affinity between their own standards and those of classical Greece, had been challenged by fresh thought and fresh evidence. The crudity of many myths had been tacitly overlooked in the idealization of fifth- and fourth-century life in the Greek city states. The study of comparative mythology, pioneered in England by Max Müller in the 1850s, opened the eyes of those who were willing to look and made them reconsider their assumptions. The work of Charles Newton provided a further basis for that reconsideration. He showed that archaeology was another contributor to the process of re-examining accepted views of Greek social life, and argued that a very different picture would emerge as the recovered artefacts were studied. Some scholars feared the dissolution of their accepted picture of Greek civilization; others were able to fit the new data into a developmental frame. That

---

[5] Fowler, 28.   [6] *LDM* (July 1912), 100.
[7] Duncan Wilson, *Gilbert Murray O.M. 1866–1957* (Oxford 1987), 118.

commended itself to minds attuned, as many were in mid-century, to evolutionary categories in other fields of thought.

Hicks became absorbed in epigraphic studies at the British Museum, with all the dedication of an explorer of new worlds. It would, however, be wrong to suggest that he wanted to take part in a radical reconstruction of classical studies. He had written a prize Latin essay on myth in 1868, and in it he refrained from taking sides in the current arguments.[8] The title of the essay was 'Quaenam sit mythologicae quam vocant scientiae utilitas?' Fowler translates this neutrally as 'What is the value of the study of mythology?' But there are nuances in the Latin to which Hicks was surely sensitive. He might have read it as 'What is the *use* of the *so-called* science of mythology?' If he took the wording of the essay title as slightly hostile to the new development of comparative mythology, it was wise to be as objective as possible. So he acknowledges the division of opinion among interpreters, and lists the names of some German writers in the field, before going on to make the general point that, however interpreted, myth must be acknowledged as having its origins much further back than the literature of Greece or Rome. The value he sees in the study of myth is its evidence for the study of religion and morality. There is, he says, no surer indication of a people's moral standards or its inherent character than the kind of gods it worships. Here it is easy to criticize in others what is false, difficult to find for oneself what is true. And he cannot resist a final word in favour of his own chief interest. Let scientists use observation, and let historians use monuments and documents. He likes the hard actuality of things. So, many years later, in the Introduction to his *Manual of Greek Historical Inscriptions* he wrote: 'It is impossible to linger, for example, over those awkward-looking numeral letters in the financial inscriptions of the Periklean time, without a peculiar sense of satisfaction. We are here face to face with state documents which Perikles may have issued, and Thukydides may have read.' Then he reproves himself for letting his imagination run away with him, and continues: 'Such reflections, however, it may be said, belong merely to the sentiment of the dilettante. What is the real value

---

[8] 'Quaenam sit mythologicae quam vocant scientiae utilitas?', 29: 'Ut enim deos cuncti venerantur, ita bonos non omnes habent; neque certior ulla nota cuiusque populi morum ingeniique reperiri potest, quam in deorum quos colunt natura . . . Utinam inventio veri tam facilis esset quam erroris animadversio!'

of Greek inscriptions to the serious student of history?' The answer
is that archaeology and literature combine to call to life again the
features of classical civilization.

The *Manual of Greek Historical Inscriptions*, completed while
Hicks was at Fenny Compton, was dedicated to Charles Newton,
'Magistro Discipulus Amicus Amico'. That simple (but carefully
chiasmic) dedication bore witness to one of the major influences
in his life. He continued right to the end to be at heart a classical
scholar, continuing his epigraphic work, encouraging archaeological investigation in Manchester, reviewing scholarly works, chair-
ing the Classical Association, and even as a busy bishop keeping
his eye open for points of epigraphic interest. In what he himself
called the last lap of his life his interest could still be aroused by
the kind of thing he had loved to do as a young man. His diary
for 22 November 1917 contains the entry: '10.30 Prayers in H of
L. Then to BM to see Hill about the Guthlac Inscription: it doubt-
less belongs to the middle 10th Century: note how the *Roman*
letters are just beginning to become "Lombardic".' He became an
internationally recognized authority on Greek epigraphy, with the
dignity implied by being a Corresponding Member of the Imperial Archaeological Society of Berlin, but the course of his life, partly
by chance and partly by choice, turned in other directions.

His classical studies and his work under the guidance of Charles
Newton inducted him into the new tradition of historical scholarship before he turned to any serious theological study. At a later
date he expressed the hope that it would lead to greater object-
ivity in the understanding of Christian origins, and would serve
an ecumenical purpose. That was a hope which took time to mature, but its seed was sown in his Oxford days. In an article in the
Manchester Guardian on 1 July 1909 he declared that Christianity
was faced with industrial and social problems which made the
badge of creed and church seem irrelevant. Historical science might
even prove a healer of schism. He evidently had in mind J. B.
Lightfoot's work on the beginnings of episcopacy, which could be
interpreted as relativizing all claims of divine sanction for particular theories of church government. That, too, had been an issue
in his Oxford days, focused on his disagreement with his friend
Henry Bazely about the true basis of church order to be found
in the New Testament.

The fact that the main focus of his life's work was elsewhere was mostly due to another man's influence at Corpus. That was Ruskin, who alerted him to the ugliness and injustice of contemporary commercialism. Again we see signs of the transition from old to new Liberalism, without which an end to the alienation of High-Churchmen from reform in general and the Liberal Party in particular would hardly have been conceivable. The Tractarians hated Liberalism. They had been provoked by political changes under a Whig administration ('National Apostasy' as Keble called it) to vindicate the independent authority of the church. That was, in effect, to reassert an ancient privilege: just the kind of thing which Whiggism most disliked. Some of those they influenced in the second generation of Anglo-catholicism went out into urban parishes, but they went with a message which carried little or no political content. They were not chiefly concerned to remedy the apostasy of the nation but to recapture the church which was itself in danger of apostasy. There was a strong moral element in their message, but it was directed at individual holiness within the sacramental life of the church. It was only as they became oppressed by the degradation of their parishioners through the operation of the industrial system that they were forced to examine its evils and to look for a remedy. Out of that critical examination, and in line with their corporatist theology, some of them moved towards varieties of socialist idealism. So at last society, rather than the nation, came to feature on the Anglo-catholic agenda.

The theological basis for constructive social ideas was hardly to be found in the teaching of the early Tractarian leaders. Ultimately it had to be supplied by the separate stream of Christian teaching which welled up within the Christian Socialist movement of the 1840s and 1850s. This development took time, and there was something lacking in social thought within the High Church tradition. The influence of F. D. Maurice and his sympathizers was minimal in Oxford during Hicks's years as an undergraduate and fellow of a college. Those senior and junior members of the university who were sensitive to the social problems created by competitive commercialism found their stimulus to thought and action elsewhere. It has been argued that the moral imperatives of evangelicalism were redirected, in those who had moved away from its theology, to social causes. But moral earnestness was not confined to the evangelicals. Men reared in other traditions caught the contagion of conscientiousness, and began to listen to prophetic voices declaiming against current philosophies which presented the existing state of things as unalterable, according to the laws of political economy.

Prominent among the prophetic voices in Oxford at this period was John Ruskin. The most outspoken attacks on competitive commercialism came from someone who had felt, as an undergraduate at Christ Church, that he might be suspect to his upper-class companions through his connection with trade. But it was that very connection which had awakened his conscience. His father's partner in the sherry trade moved in 'the best French circles', and members of his family came once or twice to the Ruskins' house in Denmark Hill. John Ruskin described how these men of sense and honour and women of gentle and amiable disposition 'spoke of their Spanish labourers and French tenantry, with no idea whatever respecting them but that, except as producers by their labour of money to be spent in Paris, they were cumberers of the ground'.[9] That gave him, he said, the first clue to the real sources of wrong in the social laws of modern Europe and led him necessarily into the political field. That change of direction had already taken place when he was invited back to Oxford as Slade Professor.

Hicks had been a fellow of Corpus for three years when they met. Through the interest of members of the Senior Common Room, notably J. W. Oddie ('the heartiest Ruskinite among us', according to Hicks), Ruskin joined the Common Room and became Hicks's near neighbour. Years later, at the request of C. P. Scott, who had been an undergraduate at Corpus, Hicks wrote for the *Manchester Guardian* some reminiscences of those days. They appeared anonymously in the issues of 15 June and 2 July 1903. This is his account of the beginning of Ruskin's connection with Corpus:

John Ruskin was elected Slade Professor of Art at Oxford in August, 1869, being the first occupant of the Chair. Early in the next year he visited the University, with his mind full of plans of teaching and lectures. In company with one of the Fellows, himself a devoted student of art, the new Professor visited Corpus, and was delighted with its old-world peacefulness, its quaint garden abutting the old city wall, and especially

---

[9] Ruskin, *Praeterita*, 378.

the library, with its wealth of early printed books and illuminated manu-
scripts. As he was leaving he let fall the wish that he could have rooms
in Corpus, 'between the two noble towers of Christ Church and Merton.'
Soon after this the President and Fellows sent Ruskin a formal invitation to accept an Honorary Fellowship at the College, and to occupy a
set of rooms in the Fellows' Buildings during his sojourns in Oxford.
The invitation was at once accepted.

Ruskin's influence was, of course, dominant in the arts; but he
also had a notable impact on social thought, particularly on young
men at Oxford. It sometimes took eccentric forms, as when he
emphasized the importance of the 'gospel of labour' and persuaded
some undergraduates to build a road at Hinksey, later described
as the worst road in the kingdom. Amongst the men Ruskin influenced by his social concern were Arnold Toynbee, who founded
the settlement in London later named after him. He rose to the
rank of 'foreman' on the Hinksey road, and was invited to take
breakfast with Ruskin.[10] Another was A. F. Winnington Ingram,
later Bishop of London. A lively description of Ruskin's influence
at a later period, and after Hicks had left Oxford, is given in Henry
Scott Holland's picture of Winnington Ingram as an undergraduate.

He used to be brought up by his Keble Dons to an odd little gathering
which we called Pesec, because it was a tiny, political, ethical, social,
economic sort of club, made up of a few dons and some favoured Under-
grads, who met at Arthur Lyttelton's, in his rooms over a chemist's shop
in St Giles (known therefore as 'the Pill-Box') to talk about cities and
the Poor, and Social Problems, and all that we have heard so much of
since. We thought ourselves rather in 'the forward movement' in those
far-away days. We were burning with Ruskin and Carlyle: we read
together 'Unto this Last': we discussed: we railed at the dry bones of
the older Political Economy: we clamoured for a Breath to come from
the four winds and blow upon these dry bones till they might live.[11]

Other young men who later acknowledged the influence of
Ruskin were Percy Dearmer, best known for his campaign to recall
catholic-minded clergy of the Church of England to traditional

---

[10] E. T. Cook, *The Life of John Ruskin*, ii. 190, quoted in G. Kitson Clark, *Churchmen
and the Condition of England 1832–1885* (1973), 280.
[11] From 'Arthur of London', quoted in S. C. Carpenter, *Winnington-Ingram: The Biography of Arthur Foley Winnington-Ingram, Bishop of London 1901–1939* (1949), 115.

English liturgical practices, and H. D. Rawnsley, the countryside campaigner and joint founder of the National Trust.[12] Henry Scott Holland was overwhelmed by Ruskin's 'most gorgeous eloquence', but at first found his ideas 'almost spitefully revolutionary'. Later, he declared that the Christian Social Union existed 'in memory of Ruskin'. 'How can it be imagined that we have forgotten the grey blue child-like eyes, above the tawny whiskers and the blue-spotted tie? Of course, we owe it to him as much as to any, that CSU exists.'[13]

The history of Christian social thought in the nineteenth century has sometimes been presented as having a lacuna between the first short-lived period of Christian Socialism led by F. D. Maurice and his associates (1848–54) and the period during which the Christian Social Union and other socialist groups of Christians were active in the last quarter of the century. Maurice Reckitt, for example, in his *Faith and Society*, comments that the original Christian Socialist Movement did not live long in its first form, and continues: 'when a later generation returned, after the heyday of Victorian prosperity, to the quarrel with capitalism under a new banner, those who took their stand upon the Faith were first in the field'.[14] That was, no doubt, a deliberate simplification. In fact, during the intervening period prophetic voices continued to be heard, even in the 'heyday of Victorian prosperity'. Indeed it was the prosperity which prompted them. One was that of Carlyle. His *Sartor Resartus*, with its quirky and deliberately mystifying form and its broadly theistic message, had been first published in *Fraser's Magazine* as early as 1833, but he remained influential. Mrs Humphry Ward testified to his influence on her father, Tom Arnold, in the 1850s. He was, with J. M. W. Turner, one of Ruskin's two 'masters'. Acton thought him 'detestable' as a historian, and Mandell Creighton distrusted him and all other 'prophets'. But

<hr />

[12] Nan Dearmer, *The Life of Percy Dearmer* (1941), and Graham Murray, *Founders of the National Trust* (1987).

[13] S. Paget (ed.), *Henry Scott Holland: Memoir and Letters* (1921), 46; *Commonwealth* (Dec. 1902), 371.

[14] Maurice B. Reckitt, *Faith and Society: A Study of the Structure, Outlook and Opportunity of the Christian Social Movement in Great Britain and the United States of America* (1932), 83. This interpretation is adopted in C. E. Hudson and M. B. Reckitt, *The Church and the World, Being Materials for the Historical Study of Christian Sociology*, iii: *Church and Society in England from 1800* (1940), and repeated by John Sleeman, 'The Church and Economic Policy', in G. Moyser (ed.), *Church and Politics Today* (1985), 257 ff.

after his death he became a cult figure for young men like G. M. Trevelyan, who as an undergraduate described *Sartor Resartus* as 'the greatest book in the world'.[15]

Amongst prophetic voices, however, it was that of Ruskin which had most influence on Edward Hicks, on account of their personal friendship in the Corpus Common Room. That personal relationship reinforced the influence widely exercised through his many writings and frequent lectures. These became more eccentric after Hicks left Oxford, and the notorious lawsuit over his criticism of Whistler in 1878 has left on many minds an image of oddity and egotism. Against other unsympathetic portraits we can set the description of Ruskin in Hicks's *Manchester Guardian* article.

Profound as was the impression made upon our minds by the ethical fervour of Ruskin's lectures—wherein his interchange of tenderness and invective and his daring felicity of illustration reminded one of nothing less than the New Testament,—what most struck us, in living and conversing with him day by day, was the astonishing genius of the man. He seemed to have read all literature and to be at home with every author. Whatever he had read he remembered, and he remembered in no mere mechanical way, but critically and with a power of analysis wherein reason and recollection went hand in hand. He seemed to have seen almost all beautiful places, and so often as to know them by heart; he knew all galleries and pictures; he had entered into every kind of innocent pleasure, and could analyse its peculiar sources and conditions of delight. He had studied, for the joy of them, all forms and colours and variations of cloud and sky, of sunshine and storm, of woodland and greensward and ploughing. He knew the sea and the river, the cathedral and the cottage, each kind and colour of cliff and rock, and every form and tint of precious stone or of flower and leaf. His observation was immense in its range, and he entered into everything with the keenest relish . . . You might complain that his method lacked coherence, that he professed to lecture on art and wandered into the tangles of economic or ethical problems; you might be stung by his sarcasm or moved by his pathos; but one thing you had to confess—that he was the most wonderful and unselfish and tender-souled Prophet of his age.

[15] Mrs H. Ward, *A Writer's Recollections* (1918), 19; Hobson, *John Ruskin*, 25; *Letters of Lord Acton to Mary, Daughter of the Right Hon. W. E. Gladstone*, edited with an introductory Memoir by Herbert Paul (1904), 70; Louise Creighton, *Life and Letters of Mandell Creighton 1803–1901 by his wife* (1904), i. 325; David Cannadine, *G. M. Trevelyan: A Life in History* (1992), 29.

Ruskin had already shifted the main focus of his writing from art criticism to social and economic issues. The turning-point for him as an author was the publication in 1860 of the essays which were later put together in book form as *Unto this Last*, although he had begun to give his attention to the evils of competitive commercialism as early as 1855 when he delivered in Manchester the lectures which formed the basis of *A Joy for Ever*. In a manner characteristic of a prophet, he did not develop his views systematically. In fact he set himself a twofold task. On the one hand he wanted to expose the degradation of workmen and the very nature of work itself which had been brought about by the development of the industrial system. On the other hand, he wanted to controvert the current teachings of political economy. At the heart of these two intertwined arguments was, in his view, a total misunderstanding of the nature of wealth. Both the practice of the industrialists and the theory of the political economists equated wealth with money. Ruskin's watchword was, 'There is no wealth but life.' True wealth had nothing to do with 'making money'. The industrial system had degraded working people by depriving them of their best reward, the enjoyment of the work of creation. There was no such thing as 'economic man'—a mere unit of labour. In all economic systems it was necessary to take into account what he called 'social affections'. Good work was the result of good will. Government and co-operation were the laws of life; anarchy and competition were the laws of death.

All these ideas Ruskin believed to be based upon his religious faith. He shared with Carlyle a deep suspicion of 'Hebrew old clothes'—the forms and formalities with which religion habitually encumbers itself. But he did not, like Carlyle, write off the exponents of formal religion as unworthy of his steel. Hicks noted how, at Corpus, he played a sympathetic, yet critical, part in the religious life of the college. 'He was constant in daily attendance at College Chapel at 8 a.m., and equally regular on Sunday, when he received the sacrament with us all. Nothing could exceed his manifest devotion and reverence.' But he was critical of religion and religious language, calling the synonymous doublets of the Prayer Book mere 'Cockney English'. That criticism deals only with the surface of religion; but Ruskin had given thought to its deeper levels, too. Hicks's memories of him included two occasions of close and personal contact. The first showed a kind of fatherly care.

There lies before me a copy of *Fors Clavigera* for March, 1872, on which he wrote my name 'With John Ruskin's sincere regards,' and I know he gave it me because I had recently taken Orders, and because on page 5 he had defined for me the economic place of the clergy in the social organism: 'The first root of distinction between clergyman and peasant is the greater intelligence, which instinctively desires both to learn and teach, and is content to accept the smallest maintenance if it may remain so occupied . . . the word "clergy" properly signifying persons chosen by lot, or in a manner elect, for the practice and exhibition of good behaviour; the visionary or passionate anchorite being content to beg his bread, so only that he may have leave by undisturbed prayer or meditation to bring himself into closer union with the spiritual world; and the peasant being always content to feed him, on condition of his becoming venerable in that higher estate, and, as a peculiarly blessed person, a communicator of blessing.' Nor am I ashamed to confess that this piece of irony has haunted me through life.

That final comment was written when Hicks had behind him the experience of over thirty years' work in the sacred ministry. He was fully aware of the contrast between Ruskin's sketch of clerical poverty and the comparative elevation of the nineteenth-century clergyman, in social and economic terms, above the 'peasant' or industrial worker.

The second occasion of personal contact which Hicks recalled led him on to a general verdict on Ruskin's influence.

He never forgot the significance of the name of our College, which witnessed to our Founder's devotion to the Blessed Sacrament . . . I spent a happy hour with him one day in endeavouring to devise a Latin inscription for a set of his works which he was presenting to the College Library. We know how he loved symbolic language, and he wanted to express in Latin the thought (as he said) that 'he was giving these books to the Fellows and Tutors who were here ministering to the Body of Christ.' I forget whether we found a phrase to satisfy us. But the idea found perfect expression in his own life. If ever there was a man who lived to praise God by showing forth the glory of His handiwork and to please Him by ministering to His children, that man was John Ruskin.

Men like Hicks, who were not antagonized by Ruskin's prophetic vein, could find in his simple and penetrating questions and criticisms of contemporary religion a stimulus to self-examination. During Ruskin's period as Slade Professor he responded to an invitation from the Furness Clerical Society to write a series of

letters for them to discuss at their meetings.[16] These letters began
with questions about the definition of the clergy as a body, and
went on to ask about putting the gospel of Christ in plain words
and short terms. For example, Ruskin asked what would be the
result 'were it more the effort of zealous parish priests, instead of
getting wicked *poor* people to *come* to church, to get wicked rich
ones to stay out of it'. Again he threw down the challenge of
saying that 'all true Christianity is known—as its Master was—in
breaking of bread, and all false Christianity in stealing it'.

These letters date from a time after Hicks had left Corpus, but
similar thoughts and questions were in his mind earlier; and indeed
the marked passage in *Fors Clavigera* points in the same direction.
Hicks continued to refer to Ruskin and his ideas throughout his
life. It was evidently natural for him to recall some of Ruskin's
aphorisms. 'Life without industry is guilt; industry without art is
brutality' (in a Visitation Charge). 'A cat may look at a king. Yes,
but she cannot *see* a king' (in a lecture on 'The Religious Point
of View'). Preaching at the unveiling of a bust of Tennyson in
Somersby church, he could think of no better way to praise the
poet than by comparing him with Ruskin. In the presence of natural phenomena, he said, we feel the presence of something divine:

I always felt so in the company of John Ruskin. His knowledge, his
memory, his sense of the beautiful, his familiarity with all things lovely
in literature, in nature, or in art, were amazing. And withal, he was so
tender, so gentle in the employment of his marvellous powers, that we
felt him to be like one inspired.[17]

All that was equally true, Hicks thought, of Tennyson, with whom
he contrasted the 'breezy optimism' and 'subtle dialectic' of Browning. This was more a public eulogy than a considered piece of literary criticism, but if it tells us little about Tennyson, it tells us
more about the lasting influence of Ruskin.

Some care is needed, however, in assessing the particular ways
in which that influence was operative. The primary element was
evidently one of admiration for a complex and gifted personality.
It must have been a corrective to Hicks's friendship with Bazely, in

---

[16] These were privately printed at the expense of Canon H. D. Rawnsley, and later
published in book form as *The Lord's Prayer and the Church: Letters to the Clergy* (1879).

[17] *LDM* (Sept. 1911), 133; report of sermon preached 6 August.

whom considerable gifts became narrowly focused on a Calvinistic creed. Hicks had as yet little, if any, experience of the world outside Oxford. His own account of his early life shows no more than childhood holidays with relatives. To enjoy a friendship with someone who seemed familiar with the whole range of Western culture must have been like the opening of magic casements. And although Hicks committed himself, first to ordination, and very soon afterwards to the parochial tasks of a country clergyman, he had begun to develop a view of life in which his overriding interest was in human society, rather than the institutional church. The church was an agent, a servant, for God's work in the world, not a substitute for secular society. Hicks could ignore Ruskin's proclaimed Toryism, his militarism, his strange admiration for the squirearchy, as others would do. It is said that at the first meeting of the parliamentary Labour Party the members were asked what had been the determining influence on their lives, and almost all answered 'the works of Ruskin'.[18] That influence within the Labour movement is borne out at a more local level by the report of a special ruri-decanal conference held in Scunthorpe in 1916 on 'Labour and Organised Christianity', with speakers from trade unions and the Independent Labour Party as well as from the churches. Hicks had taken the chair, as Bishop of Lincoln, and in his summing-up remarked that Ruskin had been freely quoted, and referred to his own memories of him at Corpus.[19]

Ruskin's writings were so voluminous, and so miscellaneous, that it was easy to be selective in appealing to his authority. In fact, although Ruskin occupied a particular place in Hicks's hierarchy of prophets, there were others whose writings (though not their friendships) may have been equally influential. In a sermon preached on behalf of the Christian Social Union in Manchester in 1906 Hicks listed the names in his gallery of prophets: Carlyle, Maurice, Kingsley, Browning, Tennyson, 'and Ruskin the greatest of them'. It is noticeable that only one in this list was primarily a theologian. Hicks consistently looked for ways of commending the gospel in untechnical terms. In an Oxford Long Vacation Lecture

[18] Kenneth Clark, *Ruskin Today* (1964), p. xii. It has been doubted whether the early Labour Party men had actually read *Unto This Last*; e.g. Peter Fuller, *Images of God, The Consolations of Lost Illusions* (1985), 280, quoting Quentin Bell. Hicks's experience, however, supports the claim.

[19] *LDM* (Oct. 1916), 156.

to clergy delivered in 1893 he had already argued that one of the greatest needs of the church was that its teachers should learn how to enunciate the gospel in the phrase and ideas of modern life. 'For the industrial classes it certainly has not been done, save very partially, and chiefly outside the Church.' He believed it would best be done by men of learning and thought, whose culture ought to give them an imaginative insight into conditions not their own.[20] He specifically commended Browning's 'Death in the Desert' and 'Easter Day'. But his description of those best fitted to undertake the task fits Ruskin perfectly. His debt to Ruskin was due as much to the example he set in trying to restate the gospel in terms which were meaningful to working people as it was to his criticisms of the dominant ideas of the political economists or the forthright challenges he threw down to the accredited exponents of Christianity.

There were other formative influences at work upon Hicks's mind. His time at Oxford was a watershed in the development of the general philosophical bias of undergraduates and younger dons. A significant moment was the resignation of Hicks's older friend John Matthias Wilson from the White's Professorship of Moral Philosophy in 1874. This was just after Hicks left Corpus, where Wilson had held a fellowship since 1841 and had been elected President in 1872. The vacancy caused by his resignation seemed to open the way for T. H. Green to succeed him. But he was passed over in favour of John Eaton largely because of the electors' dislike of the German metaphysics which Green had introduced to undergraduate audiences through his lectures. Eaton soon resigned and Green obtained the professorship in 1877.[21] But if that was a recognizable turning-point after which Green's brand of philosophic Idealism achieved established status in the intellectual life of Oxford, his influence went back to the early days of Hicks's fellowship.

Corpus, however, was a different world from Green's (and Jowett's) Balliol, and there is no evidence that Hicks was ever attracted by Idealism. His own description of the change, in his *Manchester Guardian* recollections of 1903, is critical, if not dismissive, of the new school of thought.

---

[20] 'St Paul and Hellenism', in *Studia Biblica et Ecclesiastica: Essays Chiefly in Biblical and Patristic Criticism by Members of the University of Oxford*, iv (1896), 13.
[21] Melvin Richter, *The Politics of Conscience* (1964), 149–50.

J. M. Wilson was the last of the Oxford Utilitarians. For a generation young Oxford had been reared on Bentham and the Mills, and the philosophic Radicalism that breathes from the pages of Grote had possessed many a young politician who afterwards left his mark upon the laws and history of England. But with Wilson that tradition died out. When he resigned he very cheerfully handed over his chair of moral philosophy to Thomas Hill Green, of Balliol. Thus Bentham gave way to Kant and Mill to Hegel, and a change came over Oxford which has been among the reactionary influences—religious, speculative and political—of the last thirty years. Mark Pattison in his caustic *Memoirs* puts his finger on this momentous transition (page 165):

> What is curious is that this new *a priori* metaphysic, whoever gave it shape in Germany, was imported into Oxford by a staunch Liberal, the late Professor Green. This anomaly can only be accounted for by a certain puzzle-headedness on the part of the Professor, who was removed from the scene before he had time to see how eagerly the Tories began to carry off his honey to their hive.[22]

Hicks clearly interpreted these remarks of Pattison's as criticizing the social and political implications of a philosophy which could be interpreted as sanctifying the *status quo*, since it proclaimed that the self-realization of God was progressively taking place in the development of human society. No radical reformation could be justified on that basis. Pattison's point is not entirely clear, but the use of the word 'Tories' demands a political meaning.[23] A reactionary interpretation of Green's teaching, in spite of his Liberal politics and his interest in social reform, was implied in the work of his follower, F. H. Bradley, with his emphasis on the individual's station and duties as the place of self-realization. 'There is nothing better than my station and its duties, nor anything higher, nor more truly beautiful.' Even Scott Holland, who came under Green's influence, was sometimes inclined to speak in quietist terms, and then correct himself. 'I do not feel the slightest tinge of desire or expectation that things should be otherwise than they are—and

---

[22] Fowler, 41.

[23] V. F. Storr in *The Development of English Theology in the Nineteenth Century 1800–1860* (1913), 403, quoted the same passage from Pattison's *Memoirs* but gave it an entirely theological reference, suggesting that it referred either to Hegelianism providing a defence of some Christian dogmas or even to the Hegelian doctrine of immanence providing a support for the dogma of the Real Presence. For once Storr's judgement has failed him. Albert Mansbridge also misses the point, and refers to 'churchmen' as the predators (*Edward Stuart Talbot and Charles Gore* (1935), 73).

yet I see that faith in a good God may be defined as "faith in things being otherwise somewhere".'

Life, he said, never struck him as out of order, 'except in gross cases which do not affect me, as it happens'.[24] That was in 1872, when he still enjoyed the life of an Oxford college. He was already beginning to think that experience of slum life might 'do him good', and after his move to St Paul's as residentiary canon contentment with things as they were became impossible, and the reforming element in Green's teaching came to the fore. He did not carry off the honey to a Tory hive.

That stealing of honey by the Tories did not take place till after Hicks had left Oxford. Fowler's summary of the situation in Hicks's most formative years is that Mill and Comte were still the dominant influences, 'or, if Mill's star was waning, it was Herbert Spencer's rather than T. H. Green's as yet, which was in the ascendant'.[25] Hicks did indeed preach a sermon in Manchester which included favourable comment on Spencer. Perhaps he saw good in someone who saw the importance of temperance reform and the improvement of working-class housing. It is, no doubt, a mere coincidence that Edward Hicks's wife Agnes was the niece of Selina Pritchard, who had been a friend of Herbert Spencer; but it indicates that there were relationships within Oxford circles which may have established presuppositions not easily overturned by the new fashion in philosophy.

Agnes Mary Trevelyan Smith was someone capable of watching the tides of intelligent opinion in Oxford with critical interest. Hicks met her when she was living in the household of the Revd Edwin Palmer. He had been a tutor at Balliol with Jowett, moved to Corpus with a fellowship as Professor of Latin in 1870, and later to Christ Church as Archdeacon of Oxford. Agnes was related to Mrs Palmer by marriage, but that does not altogether explain her presence in the house. She may have been attracted by the stimulus of life on the fringe of the university. It not only gave her the benefit of daily contact with a liberal-minded scholar but also brought her into the milieu in which women were beginning to play a new and important role in university life, as the requirement of celibacy for fellows of colleges was progressively relaxed and the movement for the higher education of women

---

[24] Paget, *Henry Scott Holland*, 36.   [25] Fowler, 31.

gathered momentum. Agnes does not appear to have been one of the coterie of intellectual women gathered round Mary Arnold and Louise von Glehn, the future wives of Humphry Ward and Mandell Creighton, but it would have been difficult for a lively-minded young woman to be unaffected by the turmoil of ideas about 'religious, speculative and political' issues which were in the air at the time.

As for Hicks himself, there is no obvious indication that he paid any particular attention to Idealist philosophy, in spite of Green's outspoken Liberalism and his promotion of temperance, among other issues of social reform. In later life, as has been noted, he referred to what he regarded as the political misuse to which Green's philosophy might be put. Bishop King, whom Hicks succeeded at Lincoln, evidently came more under Green's influence. His tenure of the chair of Pastoral Theology at Oxford coincided with the last and most influential period of Green's activity before his death in 1882. He believed that Green had solved the basic philosophical problems and given Christians back the reality of human personality.[26] It was characteristic of Hicks, however, both in his early Oxford days and later in life, to take a more pragmatic view of schemes of philosophy and theology. He always seemed to mistrust claims to exclusive possession of the truth, such as were implied in Green's *a priori* approach to philosophy and ethics. The abiding legacy of Utilitarianism was a habit of mind which gave priority to observable practice. Equity and charity in social life were primary concerns. It was possible to champion them without adopting a particular philosophical or theological theory. One could keep an open mind about competing theories. Commitment to the improvement of social life was what mattered.

Hicks, then, was ready to see value in unexpected quarters. The succession of prophets which he listed later would have been acknowledged by many a liberal churchman of the time. It is less expected that he spoke of Comte with respect on a number of occasions. Notwithstanding the oddities of Comte's fanciful new religion, there was something valuable that he had to say. Hicks saw a connection with the ethical concerns of Ruskin. This was an opinion shared with, or possibly prompted by, J. M. Wilson. Hicks later recalled an occasion when he was walking home with

[26] Edward King, *Pastoral Lectures*, ed. E. Graham (1932), 50.

Wilson after attending one of Ruskin's lectures in 1872: 'We had been listening, as usual, to an exquisite harangue containing quite as much of ethics as of art. Wilson suddenly turned to me and said: "I wonder if he has ever read Comte? The ethics of his lecture are identical with the *Politique Positive*".' Hicks went on to comment that Frederic Harrison, 'the most brilliant exponent and critic of Ruskin's life and work', had noted the general agreement of Ruskin's ethics and Comte's religion of humanity.[27] They both managed to combine an ideal conception of humankind with a deep distrust of the capacity of the people for self-government, and this led both of them to postulate the need for a governing aristocracy.

These attitudes were mirrored in a modified form in many Liberals. They believed in the possibility of realizing an ideal of society by reform, while fearing the power of large groups of working people which led them to use the weapon of strikes. Some controlling force was necessary, and so different exponents of reform postulated different agencies of control, usually of an utopian kind. Ruskin's 'squirearchy' was a figment of his imagination; so was Frederic Harrison's benevolent body of employers who could be relied upon to reach equitable relations with their employees through freedom of contract. Hicks's personal background restrained any temptation to look to an aristocracy for the proper government of society, and he had as yet little experience of the relations between employers and employed. The predominantly liberal atmosphere of the Corpus Common Room protected him from dogmatic attitudes, and he took away from Oxford two treasures, of which Bazely and Ruskin may count as icons: a personal faith in the Christian gospel and an awakened concern for social justice.

These treasures were not held in the earthen vessels of church parties. Hicks did not draw his inspiration or his values from the acknowledged leaders of the Anglo-catholics or the liberals. He did not sit at the feet of Liddon or Jowett, and the evangelicals had no comparable leaders in university life. Evangelicalism was a force in parochial life in Oxford, but by 1871 was close to 'the verge of intellectual bankruptcy'.[28] If anyone upheld the banner of evangelicalism in the university it was probably Professor C. A. Heurtley, who held his chair along with a canonry of Christ Church

[27] *MG* (June 1903), quoted in Fowler, 40.
[28] J. S. Reynolds, *The Evangelicals at Oxford 1735–1871* (1953), 119–20.

for over forty years until his death in 1895, and in whose presence Pusey reverted to the north end position at the Communion even after he had adopted the eastward position as his usual practice.[29] Hicks did indeed attend his lectures, respected him, and succeeded him in the living of Fenny Compton. But Heurtley was in no sense the focus of an evangelical party in Oxford. It was easily possible for a scholar like Hicks to devote himself to the ministry of the historic Church of England with little interest in its partisan divisions and with sympathetic awareness of the faith and devotion exhibited in men within divergent traditions. He set off with his luggage of critical scholarship and social concern to the countryside of Warwickshire and the diocese of Worcester.

[29] Ibid., 149.

4
Rural Problems: Fenny Compton
(1873–1886)

Neither scholarship nor Christian mission existed in an economic vacuum. Neither Oxford University nor the rural incumbency of Fenny Compton to which Hicks proceeded in 1873 could escape the effects of fluctuating conditions of trade. At Oxford, college incomes, largely derived from farms, declined markedly between 1873 and 1896,[1] and this threw into doubt the reformers' hopes of funding an increase in the number of professorial fellowships. The shape of the university was affected by the level of farm prices; and the income of any particular college even depended on whether its agricultural holdings were in wheat-growing areas or in districts where livestock were the chief commodity. In rural parishes the connection between agricultural prosperity or depression and the conditions of the church's ministry was more obvious. Inevitably the relationship between the parson and the farming community came under strain during times of depression. The farmers resented the payment of tithes; the farm workers listened unwillingly to the representatives of a church which could not rescue them from oppression.

In such a situation those members of the clergy who had particularly felt the increasing sensitivity of social conscience noticeable in the universities looked for possible remedies. They were often attracted to various schemes of allotment holding and consumers' co-operatives for the farm workers. Some went so far as to advocate land nationalization, though that inevitably brought them into conflict with the farming interest. These concerns did not feature to any great extent in the early development of the Anglo-Catholic movement, because of its initial concentration on urban parishes. That was partly a result of the wish to minister to

---

[1] Engel, *Clergyman to Don*, 97.

the unchurched masses of the slums; but country parishes were in any case less attractive to Anglo-catholic clergy because of the influence of patrons and landowners who might regard them with great suspicion. It was more likely that patron and incumbent would agree in abominating Puseyism than in wanting to foster the catholic tradition.[2] Only at a later stage did men such as Conrad Noel and P. E. T. Widdrington use country parishes as a base for wider propagation of catholic ideals.[3] When Hicks went to Fenny Compton there were troubles about ritualism in the small nearby town of Southam, but apparently none in his Rural Deanery. The examples in the district of clerical initiative to alleviate the misery of farm labourers come from rural parishes where the churchmanship was liberal or broadly evangelical.

The details of Hicks's activities in a Warwickshire parish may add little to the general picture of clerical life in the Victorian period,[4] but they provide further examples of social concern in the countryside at a time of agricultural depression. They show the particular way in which a man might begin to move from the position of a scholarly clergyman of evangelical sympathies to that of a leading churchman with a deep concern for social reform. All the elements of his Oxford experience contributed to that development; yet there is no sign that he deliberately set out upon a chosen road. He left no account of the reasons which led him to accept the Corpus living of Fenny Compton in 1873. Fowler mentions the appeal of more definitely evangelistic work and the attraction of a home of his own after living in college rooms. He certainly remained all his life an advocate and exponent of 'missionary work', whether at home or abroad. It was a time when the challenge of irreligion in England had been displayed by the 1851 Census, and the challenge of alternative faiths had been brought home by imperial expansion abroad. The attraction of a home of his own must have appealed to a young man looking forward to marriage but lacking the resources to set up house in Oxford. Yet his memories of Oxford written in later years for the *Manchester Guardian* show his delight in the company he enjoyed there. Fowler's quotation

[2] See e.g. Owen Chadwick, *Victorian Miniature* (1960), 15.

[3] Both Noel and Widdrington were nominated by the socialist Lady Warwick, Noel to Thaxted in 1910 and Widdrington to Great Easton in 1918.

[4] For a fuller version of this chapter see 'Edward Lee Hicks: A Liberal Rector of Fenny Compton', Robert Bearman (ed.), *Warwickshire History* 9/4 (Winter 1994/5), 126–46.

from Horace—*O noctes cenaeque deum*—set at the head of his chapter on the years at Corpus hits the mark. The boy from the impoverished dyer's family had entered a new world of culture and companionship, which he would be sorry to leave. But he had learnt his ideals from Charles Newton and John Ruskin, and though each of them held up a different ideal for life, yet both could be realized in some degree in the life of a country clergyman.

Hicks was already looking to the future in 1871 when he took charge of the parish of Byfield in Northamptonshire for Professor Wilson for a short time, while he was reading for priest's orders. His decision to take a country living was unremarkable. Too much has been made of Mandell Creighton's dictum that anyone who decided to take Holy Orders, in the period of liberal reaction after the Tractarian episode, was assumed to be either a fool or a knave. The list of Hicks's own pupils at Corpus shows that there were enough men who were on the Christian side and intellectually able. They included future bishops of Manchester and Liverpool (E. A. Knox and F. J. Chavasse), Walter Lock (Warden of Keble 1897–1920), and J. R. Illingworth, the modest and influential theological writer. The clerical monopoly of fellowships had been broken, but the long-standing tradition of ordination 'on the title of a fellowship' with subsequent presentation to a college living continued. There were still college livings to fill.

Nor was it unusual for men to take up residence in country parishes in order to pursue scholarly interests. Since 1840 the benefice of Fenny Compton had been held by another fellow of Corpus, already mentioned, Charles Abel Heurtley. He held it concurrently with the Margaret Professorship of Divinity,[5] but resigned it to return to Oxford in 1872 and approved Hicks's appointment as his successor. When Hicks left Fenny Compton for Manchester in 1886, he was himself succeeded by the chaplain of Corpus, Charles Bigg, who had that year published his major work on the Christian Platonists of Alexandria. There were some obvious advantages at Fenny Compton. For one thing, it gave easy access by rail to both Oxford and London. The rector need not be an exile from intellectual circles.

---

[5] Another scholarly clergyman who held a professorship simultaneously with a country living was John Stevens Henslow, Charles Darwin's mentor and chairman of the notorious debate at the British Association meeting in Oxford in 1860. See Jean Russell-Gebbett, *Henslow of Hitcham: Botanist, Educationalist and Clergyman* (Lavenham 1977).

The parish was, moreover, of sufficient size to be taken seriously, by the standards of the nineteenth century, as a sphere of pastoral responsibility. The population in 1878 is given as 660. The parsonage house was in reasonable repair. The church, it is true, needed attention. It had been extended in Heurtley's time by the addition of a south aisle, but it still had high-backed pews and an ugly west gallery. Its accommodation was only 300 or so, and fewer than 200 places were free. But an incoming rector could well view shortcomings in the church building as an opportunity for improvement. Another attraction was that the benefice income, though it fluctuated to some extent, was normally in the region of £600 per annum net. Without any private income Hicks needed financial security in his first parish. The income also marked out the parish as a leading place in the rural deanery. Of the ten benefices which it included (in 1878) only two others were of value above £350, and five were under £200, Wormleighton being worth a miserable £90.[6] The comparatively high level of income at Fenny Compton was vital to Hicks. It made him a potential family man, and permitted hopes of travelling more widely than his limited income had so far allowed. The early days of his fellowship at Corpus had been a struggle financially. For the first two years (1866–7) he had received, as a Probationer Fellow, only £100. No doubt there were other sources of income, such as tutorial fees. But the inadequacy of this payment, especially in the case of a poor man like Hicks, was recognized when it was resolved, at a College Meeting held in February 1868, to raise the income of Probationer Fellows from £100 to £200, and to make this increase retrospective in his particular case. He then proceeded to the normal level of Foundation Payments, which were at maximum £300, with tutorial work in addition. Even this hardly allowed any luxuries for someone who was attempting to clear his father's debts. There were, therefore, strong financial reasons for accepting the second offer of a college living—for he had declined one offer already—when it opened a way out of financial difficulty.

There were now three or four strands in his personal life: his home life, his scholarly interests, and his pastoral responsibility, which itself developed in two ways, as responsibility for both the

---

[6] The incumbent of Wormleighton probably had a private income. His patron was Earl Spencer, and he himself had been, among other things, an assistant chaplain at Genoa and a minor canon of Westminster.

spiritual and the material welfare of his parishioners. He set up home in the rectory with his sister Kate as his housekeeper. She was a young woman of considerable gifts. In Oxford she had taken advantage of Ruskin's instruction in drawing, and she shared with her brother musical gifts and an interest in botany. Later in life she qualified as a nurse, and became matron of Wrexham Infirmary. Within a short time, however, Hicks's thoughts turned to marriage. It has already been noticed that in Oxford he was a close friend of Edwin Palmer and through that friendship had met his future wife, Agnes, who was living with the Palmers while her parents continued to live in Frome. Palmer had resigned his professorship to become Archdeacon of Oxford before Hicks's marriage. It was from his house in Norham Gardens that the wedding took place, in St Giles' Church, on 19 September 1876, when Hicks was thirty-three years old. Their first son, born in 1880, died in infancy. Four other children were born at Fenny Compton, and the youngest in 1892 after they had moved to Manchester. Parishioners, particularly in country parishes, have a warm feeling about children at the rectory, and Hicks was happy to conform to the expected role of the family man. In later years he thought it a handicap for the parson in a country parish to be unmarried. A single man could do good work with lads and youths; but could do less with girls.[7] There was no likelihood, however, of a lack of feminine influence in Hicks's parish. At one time his household included his wife, his sister, and his mother, not to mention an infant daughter and three female servants.[8] But his move to a country living involved far more than a change of his domestic circumstances. It was an induction into a different style of living. The urban, intellectual, egalitarian, and largely celibate milieu of his Oxford Common Room was replaced by a rural milieu in which education was a luxury, classes were clearly demarcated, and family life was regarded as the norm. In the parish there were few, if any, intellectual equals, and no possibility of the stimulating exchange of ideas to which he had been accustomed as part of his daily life. He was fortunate in having as one of his churchwardens throughout his thirteen years of incumbency a gentleman farmer with clerical forebears, E. P. R. Knott, whose two daughters became graduates of Somerville Hall. Hicks remained

---

[7] *Diary*, 27 Nov. 1916.   [8] Census return 11 April 1881.

a friend of the family all his life. Apart from the one or two in his own parish, the locality afforded only the clergy of the parishes in the Rural Deanery for intellectual companionship.

Fenny Compton largely escaped the attention of the local press during Hicks's incumbency, but occasional news items reveal something of his new life-style. When, for example, the Dassett Magna Horticultural Society held its show in 1876, the 'large and fashionable gathering' included Miss Hicks and the Revd E. L. Hicks, and he took various prizes for flowers and vegetables. He did not compare, however, with the Archdeacon of Coventry, the Ven. Charles William Holbech, who carried off no fewer than twenty-three. Holbech was described by White's *Warwickshire* in 1874 as one of the principal landowners. He was also Lord of the Manor, his family having obtained the lordship in the seventeenth century, and the patron of his own living. The *Banbury Guardian* reported that at one of the regular stock sales at Fenny Compton market he sold four fine fat beasts and realized over £140, or roughly the entire annual income of each of the four poorest livings in the Rural Deanery, and a great deal more than the yearly earn-ings of any of the farm workers who constituted the majority of its parishioners. So by his own exertions Hicks had risen to be dean of his Oxford college; now he was established, by the mere act of institution to the living, as one of the acknowledged mem-bers of the dominant class in a still feudalistic society.[9]

He did not, however, have to depend on local resources for intellectual stimulus. For one thing, he had his books. Fowler men-tions poetry, history, biography, travels, philosophy, and economics as amongst his interests, and this is to some extent borne out at a much later date by the evidence of his diary. Philosophy rather faded out, but all the other subjects feature in the reading of his Lincoln period. Fowler also says that he read a good deal of prac-tical theology in his early years at Fenny Compton, and mentions the influence on his preaching of a variety of authors. Although the list includes E. B. Pusey, it is more notable for three names which would have been suspect to Anglicans on the more ortho-dox wing of the church: a Lutheran pastor, the ultra-liberal Robertson of Brighton, and the ex-Wesleyan Robert Aitken. He had, in his early years, inherited the practice of looking for truth

<hr>

[9] *Banbury Guardian*, 24 Aug. 1876, 8 May 1873.

in every quarter, and he held to it after ordination. Just as he was willing to learn from Ruskin, for all his Toryism, and from Bazely, for all his Calvinism, so he was willing to learn about preaching from effective preachers, whatever their brand of Christianity.

His main intellectual interests, however, lay elsewhere, in the field of classical epigraphy. He had already done much of the work which bore fruit in the publication of his first contribution to epigraphical studies, and he continued to prepare material for publication until 1890. The dates of his writings suggest that the intensity of his work on classical studies fell off during his first years at Fenny Compton but picked up again in the 1880s. The immediate demands of his parish pushed academic studies into the background for a time. His achievement was nevertheless impressive. Testimonials from abroad, when he was a candidate for the headmastership of Haileybury College, show his standing in the international academic community. The French scholar, M. Waddington, writes with appreciation of his critical judgement, his profound knowledge, and his ability to relate Greek epigraphy to history, philology, and mythology. Dr A. Michaelis, Professor of Archaeology in Strasbourg University, mentions the honour bestowed by the German Archaeological Institute in making Hicks a Corresponding Member.[10] To which we may add the compliment paid much later, in 1906, by Dr J. H. Moulton in inviting him to collaborate in the preparation of a New Testament Lexicon of Hellenistic Greek. When Hicks declined, Moulton regretted 'the loss of expert knowledge which no one in England can rival'.[11]

There is a temptation to dismiss as amateurs the clerical scholars of the Victorian age in their country rectories. Of course, the amount of study which could be accomplished in the midst of parochial cares was limited; but not its quality. There is an engaging picture of the alternation of intellectual and pastoral work given by Agnes Hicks:

I have often seen my husband bring out his 'little fragments', often so small, of impressions which had been taken at the British Museum and sent down for him to decipher. He would leave them, and go off to take a prayer-meeting in a humble cottage room in the one far-off corner of the parish, or in the school near by—just as it happened. All was done with the greatest cheerfulness and quiet devotion.[12]

---

[10] Fowler, 71–2.   [11] Ibid., 129.   [12] Ibid., 70.

This domestic picture must not leave the impression of a life circumscribed by the parish boundaries. Intellectual interests which
took Hicks to Oxford and London helped him to maintain social
contacts as well. In London he visited the home of his mentor in
epigraphical studies, Charles Newton, and that contributed to his
cultural development as well as to his classical studies. Newton had
held consular appointments and was the son-in-law of Keats's friend,
the painter, Joseph Severn.[13] Hicks also began to travel. When a
notorious murder took place in Fenny Compton, the *Banbury Guardian* reported, in passing, that the Vicar (Rector) was in Italy.

For Hicks classical epigraphy was not a refuge from the ordinary affairs of life. Whatever Jowett said about it, archaeology was
not a trivial pursuit. Hicks made clear his own estimation of its
value in the introduction to his *Manual of Greek Historical Inscriptions*. Archaeology and literature combined to call to life again the
features of classical civilization.[14] He was, in fact, becoming a serious student of society—of a past civilization through his epigraphical
studies, and of the contemporary civilization through his pastoral
activities. The influence of Charles Newton was all-important, for
he was among the pioneers in Britain of the view of Hellenism,
not as a static set of values to be preserved with care, but as a
developmental process leading from the barbaric to the humane.[15]
What the archaeologist revealed about Greek life might threaten
the high estimation of Hellenic values which Victorian education
inculcated. But the point was that it revealed a process of development. Classical studies were acquitted, therefore, of the charge
of being backward-looking. In showing a process of change, they
encouraged a hope for the future, not the admiration of the past.

That may not yet have been a prominent thought in Hicks's
intellectual outlook, but he was to work out ideas on these lines
during his time at Manchester. Then he suggested that it was possible to apply to the history of Christianity the methods he had
learnt from Newton, so that Christianity, too, was seen as a process

---

[13] Fowler's statement (p. 70) that visits to Newton's house in Gower Street brought
Hicks into contact with Mrs Newton and the Severns needs qualification. Mrs Mary Newton
had died in 1866. Her father, Joseph Severn, lived in Rome after 1860. But her brother,
Arthur Severn, was no doubt welcome in the Newton household. He became intimate
with Newton's friend Ruskin, when he married his niece and ward, Joan Agnew. See
James S. Dearden (ed.), *The Professor: Arthur Severn's Memoir of John Ruskin* (1967).

[14] *Greek Inscriptions*, Introduction, p. xi.

[15] See Frank M. Turner, *The Greek Heritage in Victorian Britain* (Yale 1981), 63 ff.

rather than a once-for-all set of values. This was an alternative use
of the legacy of the classics to that made of it by people like Matthew
Arnold. For him Hellenism represented an unchanging standard
by which to judge the philistinism of modern life. Hicks's involvement in epigraphic studies aligned him with the school of thought
which came to characterize Cambridge classical scholarship more
than that of Oxford. An exception to that generalization was Gilbert
Murray, with whom Hicks later developed an acquaintance, and
who shared much the same brand of Liberalism.

While he maintained his scholarly interests, the new set of relationships which he had to make as a parish priest involved both
spiritual and secular responsibilities. Like every newly inducted
incumbent, he had to set before him certain spiritual objectives.
Inevitably he had to make decisions about the worship of his parish church, including decisions about the church building, as well
as the details of regular services. His predecessor, Dr Heurtley, was
a moderate evangelical, whose relationship with his parishioners
seems to have been entirely friendly and peaceful, though his tenure
of the Margaret Professorship at Oxford from 1853, with a Canonry
at Christ Church, meant that he was resident in Fenny Compton
only for part of each year.[16] Beneath his modest exterior there was
a firm adherence to religious principle, which caused him to be
involved in several theological disputes at Oxford. That did not
spill over into parochial controversies. In regard to the church building, Heurtley's intention had been to make more room for parishioners to come and take part in the services, which continued
in the old tradition. Hicks did not aim to provide any further accommodation; in fact the seating was slightly reduced as a consequence
of the changes he promoted. He wanted to make the services more
congregational for those who already came to worship. His plan
involved the rearrangement of the chancel and the provision of a
more dignified altar, with lighted candles in time of service. That
innovation gave rise to the episode, well remembered in the parish,
of Hicks's conciliation of the offended parishioner who declared
she would not come to Communion while the candles were on
the altar. He promised that if she would tell him in advance when
she intended to communicate, he would put them on the floor.[17]

[16] *DNB*, xxii, 'Heurtley, Charles Abel, 1806–1895'.
[17] Fowler, 53. For this anecdote, and much else concerning Hicks's time in Fenny Compton, we are indebted to Mrs Westacott, one of the graduate daughters of the churchwarden
Mr Knott, who compiled some historical notes about Fenny Compton (in Warwickshire
Record Office).

It is impossible to judge whether this better illustrates Hicks's conciliatory nature or his sense of humour—both prominent features of his character. But clearly he was moving the worship of the parish gently along the path beaten out by the catholic revival in the church, even while his mind was occupied with the evangelical career of his friend Henry Bazely.[18]

Hicks's lifelong concern with the outreach of the church was first put to practical effect in Fenny Compton. Correspondence with his mother reveals that he travelled to Birmingham to witness the work of three American revivalists. His enthusiasm made him dissatisfied with the size of his congregation—normally about forty—and she offered him as consolation for himself, though not for her, the information that at Blewbury, near Reading, where she was living, the usual attendance was four, plus some children. He was also trying to find ways of rooting Christian experience and belief in the life of the parish outside the church. He held simple services at 'The Tunnel', or Tunnel Houses, a hamlet some two miles from the church which derived its name from the 'tunnelling' of the canal at that point, and also for the navvies working on the railway in the parish. During the summer of 1884 evening services were suspended for special efforts to evangelize outside the church.[19] More unusually, he tried to create a network of small prayer groups, and drew up careful rules for their conduct, from which Fowler quotes the following:

Let men meet with men, women with women: it is better for brothers not to meet with brothers, nor sisters with sisters.

Let each meeting last exactly an hour, and never longer: as soon as the hour is over, let the three friends separate, and not stay longer together for any purpose.

Let no other person be present: let the whole time be taken up with (1) Prayer; (2) Reading of Scripture and conversation upon it; (3) Singing or reading of Hymns; (4) Concluding Prayer.

Extempore Prayer is recommended, but is not necessary: let the week's Collect from the Prayer Book be always used, together with the Lord's Prayer.

---

[18] Heurtley, though an evangelical, might not have disapproved of this change. He later declared himself in favour of special clothing for ministers at the Holy Communion, on the undogmatic ground that he would always put on his best clothes for a special occasion. See the prefatory memoir by Professor William Ince in C. A. Heurtley, *Wholesome Words: Sermons on some Important Points of Christian Doctrine* (1896).

[19] See the *Parish Magazine for Kineton, Harbury, Lighthorne, Chesterton, Gaydon, Chadshunt, Fenny Compton and Burton Dassett* 3, in Warwickshire Record Office DR 220/35.

Avoid argument, and aim only at God's glory, and your own advance-
ment in Practical holiness.

These groups illustrate some points in Hicks's general outlook: the
continuing influence of the Methodism in which he had received
his first religious experiences and which he recalled with gratitude
to the end of his life; the trust he placed in lay people within the
church; and his refusal to anchor his ministry to the church building or to concentrate his energies on the existing congregation.

This last point is illustrated in another way by the Ordination
Sermon which he preached in Worcester Cathedral on Trinity
Sunday 1883, taking his text from Matthew 4: 19, 'Follow me and
I will make you fishers of men.' In it he developed a contrast
between this picture of the fisherman and the more usual picture
of a shepherd of a flock. It led him to characterize contemporary
society as a restless sea, threatened with storms, so that it was possible to detect 'sounds of socialism and anarchy, the accompany-
ing echoes of that development of democracy, which, for good
or for evil, is the marked and inevitable movement of our times'.
And as the work of fishermen required the co-operation of all
hands, so the church needed to learn how to employ the laity in
its work.[20] Typically for him the mission of the church was related
to the movement of political life; that is to say, to the general life
of society, changing and developing in history. In the pulpit Hicks
suspended judgement on the effects of democracy, and spoke of
the opposed threats of anarchy and socialism. His later writings
suggest that at this stage he would have criticized socialism as requiring too high a degree of social conscience in ordinary people to
be launched on an unregenerate world.[21]

So we can turn to the other part of his pastoral concern—his
interest in the material welfare of his parishioners. But before looking at the details of his social concern, we may take stock of the
kind of society in which his ministry was set. The idyllic rural
picture conjured up by the accounts in the local papers of the horticultural society's show, with the rector taking prizes for his pinks
and cucumbers, and of a convivial lunch in Mr Reading's barn
after the reopening of the church, represents only the sunshine
side of life in the district. There were shadows as well. The rough-
ness and violence of life can be represented by two pictures of a

[20] Fowler, 56–7.   [21] See e.g. 'Quartus', *MG* 24 Mar. 1910.

very different sort. In 1879 there was a highway robbery between Ladbroke and Fenny Compton station, when some tramps dragged a traveller from Bloxham off his horse and stole his purse; and in Hicks's final year in the parish the local constable, PC Hine, was murdered and his body dragged down to the canal. The murderers were never apprehended.[22] Hicks wrote to the local papers soliciting donations for the support of his widow. Those were episodes which could be matched in any generation. But there were special reasons for tension and violence in the 1870s and 1880s.

Hicks's incumbency in Fenny Compton coincided with a period of agricultural depression. This created tensions between the three groups which constituted the chief elements of rural life: the landowners, the farmers (many being tenants), and the farm workers. Some of the clergy, too, were caught up in the conflict. As the farmers' incomes declined, they tried to recoup their losses by looking in both directions—towards the landowners above them and the workers below. They pleaded for reduction in rents, and they forced down the wages of their men or reduced the number they employed. The clergy, as tithe owners, also came under pressure. Landowners and clergy sometimes responded by forgoing a part of their entitlement. If it caused them some hardship, however, it was as nothing in comparison with the lot of the farm workers. A shilling lost from a weekly wage of twelve shillings might force a family to the brink of destitution, and that just at a time when compulsory education threatened to remove children's earnings. As Joseph Arch declared:

Things were so bad with the men that they were beginning to grow desperate. The trodden worms, which had so long writhed under the iron heel of the oppressor, were turning at last. The smouldering fire of discontent was shooting out tongues of flame here and there. The sore stricken, who had brooded in sullen anger over their wrongs, were rising to strike in their turn.[23]

Just when it seemed that farm workers might improve their lot by united action, unemployment was undermining their hopes. Warwickshire was the homeland of the National Agricultural

---

[22] A previous murder in the parish in 1863 had been the occasion of a sermon by Dr Heurtley on 'Bloodguiltiness'.

[23] Joseph Arch, *From Ploughtail to Parliament: An Autobiography* (Cresset Library reprint 1986), 63.

Labourers' Union, founded 'under the chestnut tree' in Welles-bourne in 1872 after a meeting addressed by Joseph Arch, and soon developing branches in villages in the neighbourhood, including Fenny Compton. Its headquarters were in Leamington, and the local papers kept a wary eye on its meetings and activities. The Union's success was short-lived; it was defeated by the farmers' lock-out.

That generated much ill-will in the district to which Hicks came in 1873. Local evidence of this is provided by the case of the 'Chipping Norton riot', which was provoked by the senten-cing of seven women to short periods of hard labour for trying to prevent two strike-breaking labourers from going to work on a farm at Ascot.[24] Although this was across the county border, it was widely reported in the local, and even the national, press. Out-rage at the inappropriate sentences was increased by the fact that they had been imposed by clerical magistrates. There was trouble within the immediate neighbourhood, too. Arch addressed a meet-ing of the Union at Warmington in August, criticizing farmers at North End (where Hicks's churchwarden, E. P. R. Knott, had some land) for wanting to reduce wages. In October the archdeacon's harvest festival sermon in his parish of Farnborough referred to 'discord and estrangement between employer and employed, and between masters and their labourers' and the 'sad breach of that happy cordiality and good feeling which ought to exist' which had led to the cancellation of the usual united harvest home. The hardships of the farm workers made some of them seek a remedy in emigration. In May 1873 a party of thirty-five, including chil-dren, had left Mollington and Fenny Compton for Liverpool en route for New York.[25] Hicks responded to this situation with a variety of initiatives, designed to improve the condition of life for the working people of his parish. These included the provision of allotments, the encouragement of a co-operative store in the vil-lage, and educational and temperance programmes.

These were typical of the pastoral work of those clergy who felt the injustices of the existing social system and could not rest

---

[24] Arch, *Ploughtail to Parliament*, 139–44. Arch spells the place-name 'Ascot'; modern maps give 'Ascott-under-Wychwood'. The 'riot' was apparently a peaceful demonstration outside Chipping Norton police station by 2,000 labourers. See also Donald O. Wagner, *The Church of England and Social Reform since 1854* (New York 1930), 158–9.

[25] *Banbury Guardian* 22 May 1873; *Leamington Spa Courier* 9 Aug. 1873, 18 Oct. 1873; *Banbury Guardian* 8 May 1873.

content with the kind of oppressive 'charity' which quieted the conscience of many of their brethren but evoked the scathing criticism of men like Joseph Arch and Joseph Ashby of Tysoe. The policy of providing allotments had been adopted by some of the clergy over a period of years. Even before the Oxford Movement had inspired many of them with a new sense of pastoral responsibility, the casual relief of poverty by charitable acts had been supplemented by this method of providing a permanent barrier against penury. For some it had been part of a 'dream which haunted with a curious persistency almost throughout the nineteenth century the minds of all sorts of benevolent people . . . the dream of solving problems of the country by converting a large section of the poor into smallholders living moral and happy lives upon the products of spade husbandry'.[26] There is no evidence that Hicks ever had that dream, but his connection with Ruskin would have familiarized him with similar ideals.[27] It was the very period during which Ruskin was promoting his strange scheme of the Guild of St George, with its vision of a new kind of rural community. A few years later the Ruskinian tradition bore fruit in the nearby village of Gaydon, when Bolton King, a Balliol graduate and heir to property at Lighthorne, conducted between 1886 and 1889 his own co-operative farming experiment, buying land and building cottages with allotments. That product of 'romantic idealism' was condemned in advance by Joseph Ashby, as being on the wrong farm, with the wrong men, and with the wrong system of management. It suffered the same fate as that of the experiments in co-operative production fostered by the early Christian Socialists.[28]

Hicks had more modest aims, and was carrying further the provision of allotments on glebe lands which his predecessor had begun. He was possibly aware that this was a method of relieving poverty for which there were other local precedents. Only a few miles away, at Stockton near Southam, the 'radical parson', W. Tuckwell, former fellow of New College, Oxford, had tried a scheme of dividing some 200 acres of the glebe into smallholdings,

[26] See Kitson Clark, *Churchmen*, 168–75.

[27] e.g. *Fors Clavigera*, i, letter v (May 1871), which includes an idyllic picture of rural life in the Tyrol and Bavaria.

[28] See R. Bolton King, J. D. Browne and E. M. H. Ibbotson, 'Bolton King, Practical Idealist', *Warwickshire Historical Society* Occasional Paper 2 (1978); M. K. Ashby, *Joseph Ashby of Tysoe, 1859–1919* (Cambridge 1961), 95–8.

and had met the problem that he could not bind his successor to continue the scheme, so that the Bishop of Worcester decided he must veto the attempt to establish it in perpetuity, even though the patrons of the living, Tuckwell's Oxford college, had given approval.[29] The bishop's decision was unnecessarily cautious, for the same uncertainty held in the case of larger tenancies of glebe, yet they were not vetoed. It was later decided that the utmost which glebe law allowed was fourteen years for such tenancies. That was not the only difficulty faced by clergy who proposed to provide sizeable allotments. The provision was often bitterly opposed by the farmers, who argued that they would absorb the energies which ought to be devoted to their own land by their employees. That argument was a respectable-sounding cover for their real objection, which was that it gave their workers a small degree of independence which threatened their domineering attitude to labourers and their families. They might have taken note of the fact that both Arch and Ashby were able to be independent in their actions because they had a small independence in their ownership of a house and a plot of land.

Fortunately Hicks had, in the person of his churchwarden, the support of a liberal-minded landowner. So he persuaded a tenant to give up 17 acres of pasture and divided them into allotments, giving them the biblical name of Beulah (that is, no longer desolate or forsaken). Some years later, in 1885, he tried to persuade one of the other major landowners of the parish, the college of Christ Church, Oxford, to follow his example and provide more land for allotments. The college took no action immediately, but eventually in 1894 added another 15 acres to the allotment provision. His letter to Dean Liddell in 1885 tells us how he saw the need and the possibility of meeting it.

There are numbers of labourers, thrifty, sober, intelligent and resolute men, who are the pick of the agricultural class; and they see the land going to ruin. They hear the farmers' endless complaints, and one after another they are sent adrift by the masters, who say, 'I have got plenty of work for you, but no money to pay you with.' These labourers say, Very well: if you can neither pay rent, nor employ labour, and are leaving both landlord and labourer penniless, and the land to ruin, why may we not have a chance of trying?

---

[29] W. Tuckwell, *Reminiscences of a Radical Parson* (1905). Tuckwell was rector of Stockton from 1878 to 1893.

Hicks went on to quote the examples of Lord Tollemache in Cheshire, and Earl Spencer in the neighbouring parish of Wormleighton, as well as referring to his own action ten years before in providing half-acre allotments. The men, he said, had made them pay admirably, and brought their rent very gratefully.

Long after Hicks had left Fenny Compton he remembered the details of his scheme, and felt that it had been a worthwhile initiative. In 1898 he contributed a long article on 'spade allotments' to the *Manchester Guardian*. In it he wrote of the land-hunger of the labourers, and his response to it.[30]

At that time a terrible land-hunger possessed the souls of the labourers. It seemed to every man as if the end of existence would be obtained if he could only get hold of 'a bit of land'. This passion was made the keener by the fact of the land in that district consisting chiefly of large grazing farms; the cultivated land was small, so small that stubble ('haulms' we called it) for thatching a cottage or even a rick was a dear commodity. Moreover, there was a tendency to lay down what agricultural land there was to grass—a tendency which grew apace under the agricultural depression of the seventies, and the increasing anxiety of every occupier to lessen the wage-bill. The situation for me was a difficult one. My living consisted entirely of glebe lands, let out to considerable tenants . . . Though I had little experience of the country and no practical knowledge of farming, I was so impressed with the requirements of the situation that I determined to cut up certain grazing lands into spade allotments. I formally acquainted my farmer-parishioners with my resolve and frankly invited their help in its execution. To their immense credit be it said, that though agrarian jealousies ran high and the step I was taking fell in as little with their inclination as their judgment, they loyally consented to assist me.

He gave further details of his scheme, which was to provide half-acre plots, the land being so heavy that half an acre seemed to him as much as a man could cultivate by hand, and to include tradesmen and employees on the railways and the canal in the village among those to whom he let out plots. He found that, among the allotment holders, men like the waggoner or the shepherd or the blacksmith, who had generally little leisure, gave work on their allotments to some of the unemployed men in the village. Every year with the assistance of several of the principal farmers, he awarded prizes to two or three of the best cultivators. Harvest-time, when

[30] *MG* 13 Apr. 1898.

the corn was threshed, was an exciting time, as the wagons came in with their loads of corn and straw. The harvest festival was a significant event in the village.

In this scheme the emphasis was essentially on self-help, not charity, and Hicks did not hesitate to claim that the allotment-holders were among his most profitable tenants. He was concerned with justice and fair dealing, not with charity. But he was aware that he was doing something to mitigate the tradition of subservience which the farmers, and sometimes the clergy, encouraged. He admitted that he had 'incurred a good deal of criticism, and some odium and derision' through his action. But even if he was helping to modify personal relationships, he was not espousing the creation of a 'peasant proprietary'. Only the provision of smallholdings, not half-acre allotments, could have contributed to that end, by providing a 'lowest rung' on the farming ladder. Tuckwell had realized that his action only provided 'an immediate remedy', and went on to campaign for a programme of land nationalization, when he spoke on Liberal Party platforms. Hicks never embraced the idea of such a sweeping remedy, and his less abrasive approach saved him from the kind of criticism by fellow clergymen which Tuckwell experienced. Twenty-five years later he moved to the county where the election of an 'allotments candidate' in a parliamentary by-election at Spalding in 1887, defeating a strong Conservative candidate, led to the enactment of the Allotments Bill which had dropped off the parliamentary agenda.[31]

The primary purpose of Hicks's scheme was to alleviate distress; but it also had other aims. He gave the allotment scheme an educational value, and also aimed to win over at least some of the farmers and so build up a new relationship between them and their men. It was a time of social change which even affected rural workers. Shortly before Hicks left Fenny Compton the vote was extended to them in the third Reform Bill of 1884 and he had vivid memories of the first election in which they voted.

How well do I recollect the excitement over the county franchise in 1884–5! No one who was not living in the rural midlands at that time can imagine the upheaval that ran through the peasantry, political and agrarian in one. One felt a quiet but irresistible ground-swell of enthu-

---

[31] Fowler, 62–3; Departmental Committee of Inquiry into Allotments: Report to the Minister of Housing and Local Government (October 1969) HMSO Cmnd. 4166.

siasm. I can never forget the sight of labourers marching in by squadrons of 20, 30 or 40 at a time, four abreast, and arriving from distant villages at the polling centres to record their first vote.[32]

The provision of allotments was one instance in which Hicks could take independent action, because he had the glebe land at his disposal. Another instance was the provision of a reading room for men and lads, managed by the members themselves. Here he had a directly educational end in view. Papers were taken, including the *Daily News* and the *Graphic* as well as the *Banbury Guardian* and the *Alliance News*. The inscription painted round the walls was not a quotation from the Bible, but from Francis Bacon: 'Read, not to contradict and confute, nor to believe and take for granted, nor to find talk and discourse, but to weigh and consider.' If it did not convey much to the men and lads, at least it declared Hicks's belief in the value of secular education. The room was used for a night school for the village lads, as well as for formal lectures on a variety of topics, for which Hicks drew on the expertise of friends and family. In April 1876, for instance, he took the chair for his brother Fred ('F. J. Hicks, M.A.'), who lectured on 'Air and Ventilation'[33]—a more educational approach to cottage improvement than that of Charles Kingsley taking an auger round his parish and boring holes in the cottage walls.

As chairman of the National School managers he had to make the best of a headmaster who despised the standards set by his predecessor, was constantly grumbling about the farmers' interference with regular attendance by the pupils, and never won the confidence of the village. That did not mean that Hicks kept aloof from the school. His fatherly attitude towards the children may be gauged from the fact that on the very day of his final departure from the village, he called at the school on his way to the station, to say goodbye.[34] He not only taught regularly in it, but also influenced its general curriculum.

As a Manager of an Elementary School in a village, where I almost daily taught, I perpetually said it would be far more sensible to teach *Botany* than Grammar. No less certain is it that the rustic child—even apart from school—is a far more civilized creature than the gutter-boy of the slums.

[32] *MG* 6 Jul. 1905 in a review of Tuckwell's book.
[33] *Leamington Spa Courier* 15 April 1876.
[34] School Log Book, 16 November 1886.

The peasant lad has his thought and memory full of the facts of natural life—he has conned the book of nature and has learnt to live by employment of nature. Observation, memory, skill of hand, alertness of mind and body,—all these are necessitated by the life of the peasant. I never came across a labourer in the village who could be called 'unskilled'.[35]

This was written only two years after his move to Manchester, and perhaps represents an early reaction to the life of the slums. Then he thought that 'life in great cities is an outrage on the laws of nature'. Fifteen years later he might possibly have modified that judgement.

In matters unrelated to education or the glebe he had to wait till opportunities arose. The co-operative retail movement provided one such opportunity. Hicks did not possess the private fortune which had enabled the Revd J. W. Leigh to set up a co-operative store in 1867 in his Warwickshire parish of Stoneleigh, but he was ready to give his support to local plans.[36] The movement had taken root in the neighbouring village of Harbury, and Hicks encouraged the opening of a shop in Fenny Compton. There were vested interests at stake here, as in the provision of allotments. The local press carried attacks on the principle of co-operation. One leading article had to admit the success of the movement but argued that it should be defeated by the shopkeepers accepting minimum levels of profit and refusing credit.[37] That would have achieved only one of the two objects which Hicks believed co-operation could effect. Good and cheap clothing and provisions were important; but so was the educative value of the participation of the members in the running of the society. He may have been mindful of Ruskin's saying: 'Competition and Anarchy are Laws of Death; Government and Cooperation are Laws of Life'. He further arranged for the co-operative purchase and distribution of coal, though he did not use the scheme himself, to avoid any accusation of profiting from it. It seems that he also helped to promote a housing scheme in the village.[38] There is no evidence that Hicks shared the hopes of Edward Vansittart Neale, for whom self-improvement was essentially corporate self-improvement, and the profits of co-operative retail stores the basis for the development of self-governing workshops, associated housing facilities, and home colonies. That kind

---

[35] Fowler, 95–6. [36] Kitson Clark, *Churchmen*, 183–4.
[37] *Leamington Spa Courier* 25 Jan. 1879.
[38] *LDM* (Sept. 1919), 143: testimony of his son-in-law, the Revd H. D. Lockett.

of idealistic project was alien to Hicks's cast of mind. He had inherited the staunch individualism of Gladstonian Liberalism, and
would have agreed with Liberals who praised co-operation as a
voluntary means of uplifting labour, with the benevolent neutrality of the state. He took practical steps to deal with a practical
problem, and in such a way as to focus attention chiefly on the
more capable and more disciplined labourers and tradesmen in
the parish.[39]

It was also in Fenny Compton that Hicks first became interested in the temperance cause, with which he became closely associated in later life. He always claimed to have been drawn into it
by meeting a group of working-class abstainers in the village.

A number of working-men and labourers of the village were forming a
Temperance Society and taking the pledge, and they began to interest
me in the subject. In the Advent of 1877 (I think) the Rev. R. M. Grier,
Vicar of Rugeley and Prebendary of Lichfield, a family friend of my
wife, came to preach a ten days' Mission at my request at our church.
He was a leading member of the United Kingdom Alliance. Under his
tuition, during those happy ten days, I became a decided abstainer (I was
more than half convinced before) and a Prohibitionist, and joined the
U.K.A., of which I have remained a working member ever since.[40]

There were two influences at work here. One was through the
family friendship with Prebendary Grier, who significantly supported the UKA, rather than the Church of England Temperance
Society. The CETS was a society with many branches in the diocese, under the presidency of the Dean of Worcester, and with the
bishop as patron. That gave it an air of respectability which took
the edge off its campaigning force. The UKA was not only interdenominational, but preponderantly nonconformist, and pressed
the case for total abstinence vigorously, in contrast to the willing-
ness of the CETS to accept various levels of moderation. The second influence was that of working men, which chimed in with
the more down-to-earth appeal of the UKA. Hicks saw the problem of alcohol primarily as affecting wage-earners and their wives
in families with little enough to waste from meagre earnings. But
in the village there was no reason to dissipate the temperance forces,

[39] On this debate within the Co-operative movement, see especially Philip N. Backstrom, *Christian Socialism and Co-operation in Victorian England: Edward Vansittart Neale and
the Co-operative Movement* (1974).
[40] Fowler, 193.

and so he tried to bring them together in one society. In 1879 he convened a meeting in the reading room which was, according to the local press, largely attended by working men and women, as well as the local Wesleyan minister. It inaugurated a local Temperance Society, with abstainers as members, and non-abstainers (including his churchwarden E. P. R. Knott) as associates.

He also met at first hand the bias of the Church of England towards political conservatism, with clergy openly active in support of the Conservative Party. Although he incurred some odium for his establishment of allotments and was known as a Radical voter, he tried to avoid the appearance of political partisanship and to keep the peace in his village. He did not have to face the difficulties which Tuckwell met, 'the social ostracism, the cutting of his wife and daughters at dances and parties, the emptying of his church, the drying up of subscriptions which might be necessary for the continuance of his work and the welfare of his people' which resulted from his declaration of Radical principles.[41] Each village had its own political character, largely determined by the attitude of its leading landowners, farmers, and gentry, whatever the private opinions of the farm workers might be. They had no role in the political process until shortly before Hicks left Fenny Compton. His own experience was quite different from that of Tuckwell. In the parish magazine of July 1886, with reference to the coming election, he urged Tories and Radicals to respect each other, and wrote: 'May a liberal, who lives in a parish where most are liberals, express his devout hope that the battle may be fought with perfect good humour and mutual toleration?'[42]

Already for Hicks Liberalism meant Radicalism, and his initiatives in social amelioration were linked to his choice of party politics. His close co-operation and lasting friendship with E. P. R. Knott suggests that they also had political sympathies.[43] Whatever may have been the potential for conflict between incumbent and parishioners elsewhere over political opinions, Fenny Compton seems to have given Hicks an easy ride. It was not for political reasons that he decided to leave his country parish. It had given him new

---

[41] Tuckwell, *Reminiscences*.   [42] *Parish Magazine* for Kineton, etc. July 1886.

[43] Hicks's friendship with Knott may also have been strengthened by the fact that Knott had clerical connections. His daughter Mrs E. C. Westacott mentions that the Revd Isaac Knott was curate of the parish in the early nineteenth century, and that the Revd James Monkhouse Knott was incumbent of Wormleighton in 1825.

experiences in human relationships and a new responsibility for social action, though his contact with the Agricultural Labourers' Union was not quite the turning-point in life which Charles Gore claimed to have reached during a tour of Oxfordshire villages in the company of Joseph Arch.[44] His time as a country parson introduced him to the UKA, which was an important outlet for his energies later in life. Above all, his Liberalism not only survived but matured. There was to be, however, no straight line of development for him. His next move was in some sense a detour. He may have thought that he was returning to the educational world, but in fact he was moving to the borders of a previously unknown world of commerce and industry, and into a political world which was itself in ferment as Liberalism put on a new face.

[44] M. B. Reckitt (ed.), *Prospect for Christendom* (1945), 250–1, quoted in James Carpenter, *Gore: A Study in Liberal Catholic Thought* (1960), 244 n. 5.

5
Hulme Hall and Manchester University (1886–1892)

The never-ending, and not yet ended, story of the Church of England's negotiations with successive governments about its role as the nation's educator is often seen as relating principally to schools and school-age children. Its contribution in that field has declined from a position of dominance to a relatively small but significant presence in partnership with local authorities. At Fenny Compton the old order had scarcely changed when Hicks was there. The village school was an important part of the rector's responsibility and he was expected to have ready access to all the village children. The next period of his ministry focused his attention on another, and equally important, aspect of the church's concern with education: its response to the foundation of new universities.

Generalizations about this are sometimes misleading. It has been asserted that the new universities were opposed to religious education; or that there was no concern about residential accommodation; or that their clientele was entirely local. The role of the Student Christian Movement has also been given great prominence.[1] There is some truth in these observations, depending on locality. But Hicks's experience supplies a corrective for Manchester. There Owens College was founded by men of religious conviction and made provision for religious education, residential hostels were set up quite early, and some students came from a distance, perhaps largely for the sake of its medical training. His log book at Hulme Hall mentions no religious society among the students.

His years as Warden can be seen as a critical moment in the church's process of adjustment to changes in the university scene. He had left Oxford when its ancient role as a clerically dominated university was rapidly changing, and he had not been averse to its

[1] e.g. G. Stephen Spinks, E. L. Allen, and James Parkes, 'The Stirring in the Universities', in *Religion in Britain since 1900* (1952).

secularization. He was, after all, a liberal and a Liberal. Many church-men, particularly of an Anglo-catholic persuasion, put up strenuous resistance; but the tide had been flowing against them for decades. When the 'godless' University of London (later renamed University College) had opened in 1828 eminent churchmen had hastened to set up King's College as a rival institution. Its sponsors still supposed that university education required a religious, and indeed an Anglican, basis. King's was eventually forced into partnership with its rival; and meanwhile university colleges were being set up in Manchester and other great cities. There was no question of their control by church interests, and churchmen were made to consider their response.

In the Church of England, however, there was no central policy; indeed in this critical period, from the 1850s to the 1880s, there was no central church body capable of developing such a policy. Consequently there was only haphazard action of the kind taken in Manchester by the Hulme Trustees. It amounted to the surrender of any claim to organize university education (such as the Roman Catholic Church continued to nourish in Ireland) together with a feeling of some responsibility for the pastoral care of students. In Manchester other organizations were later set up specifically concerned with the training of ordinands: Egerton Hall and St Anselm. The latter eventually came under the general superintendence of the Central Board of Finance (incorporated in 1914), largely through the special interest of its secretary, Canon Partridge.[2] That did not lead to the development of a general policy in relation to the civic universities. The last phases of the church's activity in the area of university education were the support of the Student Christian Movement and then the sponsoring of denominational and ecumenical chaplaincies.

It was at an early stage in this process that, in October 1886, Hicks left Fenny Compton for Manchester, exchanging a small agricultural community under clear skies for a smoky industrial city, but also exchanging a social environment still impregnated with feudal notions of rank and class for a city of vigorous political life and controversy. His period of thirteen years at Fenny Compton had been a good stint. There is no evidence that he

---

[2] On St Anselm, see T. E. Lawrenson, *Hall of Residence; Saint Anselm Hall in the University of Manchester, 1907–1957* (Manchester n.d.—*c*.1957).

was disappointed that no preferment had been offered to him, though that was not true of some of his family. He noted wryly that his mother was jealous of anyone who, in her view, had been more favoured or fortunate in life's career than her children. His Oxford friend, John Wordsworth, had been appointed Bishop of Salisbury before Hicks left Fenny Compton, and F. J. Jayne, who had been ordained with him, was already in the great urban benefice of Leeds, commonly regarded as a stepping-stone to the episcopate. Neither of them had moved from their Oxford fellowships to college livings, and perhaps Hicks had begun to wonder whether he had made the right decision in taking a country parish. It was not until he was appointed to Lincoln that he was able to say, in a private letter to C. P. Scott: 'My Fenny Compton experiences, which I had often half thought a loss of time in my career, prove now to be of golden preciousness.'[3]

Since no appointment was offered to him which he felt inclined to accept, he had to establish his own criteria for choosing suitable posts. There is something rather sanctimonious about the attitude of exceptional and usually well-connected men who decide to wait for 'God's will' to be expressed through offers made to them. That was not Hicks's position. He wanted a post which would enable him to combine pastoral responsibility with academic, or at least educational, work. But he had been out of the Oxford tutorial scene for a number of years, and in any case his choice of a specialism in classical studies did not open many opportunities for academic work. Oxford, as we have seen, was slow to recognize the claims of classical epigraphy. He had a growing family to support, for whom few college appointments would have seemed adequate, and the agricultural depression was affecting his benefice income. It was time to look for other work.

His first recorded attempt to find a way forward was his application for the mastership of Haileybury College in 1883. He had little experience of schoolmastering, apart from teaching in the village school. As a young BA he had taken the place of an absent master at his old school for a short time. He had examined at public schools, and had even had the oversight of the rather cosmopolitan Liverpool College as a sort of 'locum' in 1877 when its Principal,

---

George Butler, accompanied his wife Josephine to Switzerland for the great Congress of the International Federation for the Abolition of Government Regulation of Prostitution.[4] But in those days headmasters were not required to have much, or indeed any, relevant experience. Hicks made a considerable impression on the Council of Haileybury College. He was called for interview, with one other candidate, the Revd James Robertson, who proved successful. Robertson had been an assistant master at Rugby and Harrow, and presented testimonials running to eighty pages, printed in booklet form.[5] Hicks's application included testimonials from the Headmaster of Eton, the President of Corpus Christi College, Oxford, the High Master of St Paul's School, the Dean of Christ Church, Mark Pattison, Benjamin Jowett, the Provost of Oriel, Professor Nettleship, Professor Jebb, and the Warden of Keble. The electors' choice was not entirely happy, for Robertson resigned after six years over his involvement in a lawsuit following the expulsion of a boy for stealing.[6]

We can only speculate how Hicks would have fared at a public school with a tradition of 'imperial service' as it became known that he was, amongst other things, an opponent of imperialism. A later headmaster of Haileybury, Canon Lyttelton, earned some notoriety by refusing the boys a holiday on the occasion of the relief of Ladysmith, and the implication was drawn that he was a 'pro-Boer'. Lyttelton probably was no such thing, but Hicks undoubtedly was. For Hicks the attractions of the post, as advertised, included a salary of £2,250 a year, with a house and garden rent and tax free, and the possibility of arranging the education of his sons without the expense of boarding. He may also have known that the first headmaster, after the reorganization of Haileybury on the site of the former Imperial Service College, was an old Rugbeian, Arthur Gray Butler, who had brought Arnoldian ideals with him and had established Haileybury's reputation among the public schools. With hindsight we may judge that his failure at Haileybury was a blessing in disguise. For it is clear that his future development as a liberal churchman was encouraged by his move

---

[4] *Pelican Record* 14 (1919), 122–3; private letter from Josephine Butler to Agnes Hicks in T. Hicks papers.

[5] Details of the Haileybury interview kindly supplied by the college archivist, Alistair Macpherson.

[6] The case was reputedly the inspiration for Terence Rattigan's play, *The Winslow Boy*.

to Manchester to an extent which would have been very unlikely if he had been appointed Master of Haileybury.

Hicks continued in his parish duties for another three years; but he was on the look-out for other work, and in 1886 was appointed Principal (or Warden) of Hulme Hall at Manchester University, a post which he held for six years. Looking back many years later, he described his appointment in these words:

I had kept up my reading and was beginning to desire some work in which I might once again serve both education and the Church. This feeling was sensibly quickened by the recent fall in agricultural values, which threatened to reduce my income below a standard wage. In this mood I chanced to see on the first page of the Spectator (which I perused on a Sunday afternoon, like all good country parsons of that day) an advertisement which just fitted my case. A Churchman was wanted in Manchester as Principal of a Hall of Residence for Students of Owens College. The Hall was to be under Church of England management, but to receive students of all creeds under a conscience clause.[7]

Here was a new beginning. He was to spend twenty-four years altogether in Manchester and Salford, and this was the most significant period of his ministry, during which his powers were at their height, and his intellectual environment most congenial. The decision to apply for the post at Hulme Hall is not surprising in someone who had formed many of his opinions at Oxford in the 1860s. He may have noticed, and been attracted by the coincidence, that the Hulme Trustees had been responsible for the Hulme Exhibition at Brasenose which had been held by his friend Henry Bazely. But it was also relevant that the liberal and reforming forces in the university during the period of his fellowship had begun to take an interest in extending the reach of university education. This interest developed in several ways. One was the advocacy of easier access to the university itself, through abolition of religious tests and the provision of cheaper accommodation on a non-collegiate basis. Another was the development of the Oxford Extension Movement, which organized extramural work in towns like Reading, Cheltenham, and Malvern. In the same vein were proposals to divert funds to the establishment of academic institutions in major centres of population in the provinces. This coincided with plans developed locally in those centres by industrialists and others.

[7] 'The Early Days of Hulme Hall', *Hulme Hall Magazine* (1912).

In Manchester, Owens College had been opened in 1851 under the terms of the will of a local merchant, John Owens, and had become an important centre of academic study. In 1866 its staff was joined by A. W. Ward as professor of history and English language and literature, and he greatly enhanced the academic reputation of the college and worked for its achievement of university status. Ward was a staunch Liberal, descended from Dr Arnold's sister, a collaborator and continuator of Lord Acton in the editing of the Cambridge Modern History, and later Master of Peterhouse and Vice-Chancellor of Cambridge University. In 1880 the Victoria University had been granted a Royal Charter, with Owens College as a constituent college and other constituent colleges at Liverpool and Leeds. Liberal academics at Oxford would have looked on these developments with favour; and indeed T. H. Green himself had once considered going to Owens College. He was attracted by the 'practical openings' which Manchester offered, seeing them as an outlet for his social concerns; but balanced them against the frustration of his proper line as a teacher, believing that 'Manchester clerks would want some shorter cut than my Hegelian philosophy'.[8]

Although Hulme Hall was not, strictly speaking, an Anglican foundation, it was part of the response of church people to the development of university education outside the church's sphere of control. The church's acceptance of a secular foundation in Manchester was signalled by the approval of the bishop, James Fraser, who in 1880 founded a scholarship in classical literature at Owens College, partly funded with a presentation made to him by lay people in the diocese on the occasion of his marriage—at the age of sixty-one. It would, indeed, be wrong to call Owens College a secular foundation without qualification. Owens and his original trustees were all religious men. They had recommended that religious instruction should be given to all students who desired it, by the Principal or one of the other professors, and they defined the scope of religious instruction, in a rather old-fashioned way, as embracing the evidences of Christianity and the foundation of natural and revealed religion.[9] There were, however, to be no religious tests for either teachers or students, and attendance at religious

---

[8] Letter to Bryce, in Bryce papers, quoted in Richter, *Politics of Conscience*, 85.
[9] See H. B. Charlton, *Portrait of a University 1851–1951* (Manchester 1951).

instruction was to be entirely voluntary. Owens College might have been called secular, but never secularist. In due course it was included in the development of the federal university. Later still Manchester University gained independent status and was freed from the prohibition of religious studies imposed through its association with the Liverpool college. Then it instituted a Faculty of Theology, and Hicks became one of its lecturers. But in the mean time the church's attention had been turned to the pastoral care of young students, often away from home for the first time in their lives.

Hulme Hall had had an unpropitious beginning. Following the example of a Quaker foundation, it had been set up in 1870 as a students' hostel which, without imposing any religious tests, would offer them a communal life under the influence of the church. The interest of Oxford people is indicated by the fact that Hicks's friend John Wordsworth had been offered the headship of the Hall but had declined it. The venture failed to attract sufficient students to make it pay and it was closed in 1876 and stood empty for ten years. After the establishment of the federal university the Hulme Trustees obtained the approval of the Charity Commissioners for a new scheme and the Hall was eventually reopened in the same house in Plymouth Grove. It was able to offer twenty scholarships of £25 each and this proved the key to its success in attracting students. Hicks was appointed Principal, from a field of twenty-four applicants, and moved in with his family at the end of 1886.

For the first term there were only two students, but their numbers grew rapidly, to the maximum of thirty-two, with one or two resident tutors. The intentions of the Trustees and Hicks's broad sympathies with members of other denominations gave to Hulme Hall a different tone from that of the later Anglican hall, St Anselm, founded in 1907, whose chief begetter, T. B. Allworthy, had announced in that year the opening of a hostel 'for free training and preparation with maintenance, of candidates for Holy Orders'. And although St Anselm later developed into something more comprehensive, it was explicitly an Anglican institution, unlike Hulme Hall.

Hicks's main responsibility was pastoral. It is fortunately possible to watch him working out this relationship, because the archives of the Hall have preserved the Log Book which he began to keep from the very beginning. It is a record which covers day-to-day

events, and his thoughts about them, for the next five and a half
years. It was evidently intended for his own uses and not for communication to the governors; but it looks as if he sometimes cleared
his own mind by working out in it what he would like to say to
them.

Three topics recur: worship, industriousness, and general behaviour. Worship in chapel is strictly on Prayer Book lines (for
example, Ash Wednesday—7.50 Litany and Commination) and
sometimes full-scale, with chanted canticles, hymns, and a sermon
on Ascension Day, even when the service had been postponed to
9 p.m., to allow students to go to 'Cricket Theatricals at Owens'.
A few students exercised their right, as nonconformists, to stay
away from chapel, but the Anglicans were expected to be in their
places. A small number were prepared for confirmation by Hicks,
but most of the church members had already been confirmed. He
also gave regular religious instruction, based on the New Testament. Hicks was never sectarian in his religion. His background
in Oxford colleges, dating from a period when the heats of Tractarian controversy had dissipated, had given him an uncontentious
love of Anglican ways. To him, they were just an orderly form of
the Christian faith; and it seemed unaggressively natural for family worship in the Hall to take an Anglican form.

The other two recurrent items are more contentious: industriousness and general behaviour. He often has to 'speak to' some
students to try to get them to stick at their studies. Some do not
respond, and are eventually sent down. In his later reminiscences
these failures loom rather large. That may be a common feeling
among wardens of residential halls; but there were particular
difficulties in the early stages of Hulme Hall, which Hicks set out
in a draft report to the governors in 1889. They arose from two
factors embodied in the formal constitution of the Hall. One was
the very thing which had got it going again after its initial failure: the existence of scholarships. 'These were too small in amount
to offer much attraction, and so numerous that it was difficult to
avoid awarding them to commonplace ability.' The other problem
was that the Hall needed to accept all applicants who had places
at Owens College, and some of them could not be made to work.
This, of course, affected the third recurrent topic: general behaviour. If men came, as most of them did, with 'feeble intellectual
interests', and if there were no effective sanctions which could be

enforced, short of expulsion, it was not surprising that they indulged in 'bear-fighting and horse-play' which made life difficult
for those who wanted to work. It was little use appealing to the
parents of the students, because 'the unsatisfactory lad has generally unwise parents'. Hicks yearned for the old staircase system of
most Oxford colleges. 'Corridors make a man defenceless against
the idler'—as at Keble. Outside the Hall the chief difficulty was the
attraction of the theatre and pantomime. Hicks laid down a rule
that students should not go to the theatre more than once in three
weeks. It is not recorded whether the rule was observed. There
were other aspects of the students' behaviour which Hicks found
unacceptable. One of his few exasperated comments in the Log
Book relates to an invitation to patronize a 'Past and Present Dinner'.
It sounded harmless, but Hicks knew that it was to be an occasion
to invite back some students who had left the Hall under a cloud.
He refused, and confided to his Log Book that he thought it 'silly
and contemptible', an attempt to trap him into a false situation.

It would be misleading, however, to over-emphasize these problems, or to leave the impression that he was censorious. Almost
the next item in the Log Book, after the affair of the Past and Present Dinner, is a record of the going-down dance in the Hall—'a
very pretty party'. He threw himself into theatricals and entertain-
ments, enjoyed the students' sporting successes, and even rearranged
services so that the students could go out and enjoy themselves.
And in his reminiscences he balanced his sense of failure by list-
ing many successes:

All sorts of faculties and courses were represented among us—Classics,
Mathematics, Law and Medicine, Chemistry and Engineering—and of
most of our men I have reason to be proud. Indeed, I could make a
goodly list of men who have passed through our hands between 1886 and
1892 and are at this time doing good work in many parts of the world.

There follows a short list of men distinguished in such spheres as
manufacturing, chemistry, engineering, business, and medicine. Nor
should it be supposed that the previous education of his students
was always of poor quality. In 1888 he mentions that there are students from Harrow, Winchester, Repton, Manchester Grammar
School, and other schools of repute. This makes T. H. Green's
image of 'Manchester clerks' look rather ignorant.

The other side of his responsibility was tutorial, and this revealed another side of his character. At Oxford he had initially been the most unassuming of tutors. E. A. Knox, who became his bishop in Manchester, said in some memories recorded long after Hicks's death, 'The Hicks I knew as scholar of CCC was to me no more than a kind, capable, shy tutor.' He had 'a singular beauty of character'. He was 'painfully shy and modest; he never made a correction without asking leave to put "a faint line, just a very faint line" under the faulty words.'[10] Another future bishop who also came under Hicks's tutorial guidance at Corpus, F. J. Chavasse, had written in his diary in 1866: '11 December.—Hicks went through the Cicero paper with me, and cheered me up.'[11] Perhaps that was a general characteristic of his influence on others. There is a pleasant little entry in his episcopal diary for 18 February 1915: 'Bolam came to be cheered up. He was.' Those earlier recollections relate to the first year or two of Hicks's tutorial work at Corpus, and there had been much further experience to develop a firmer side of his character since then. As college dean he can hardly have been so shy and unassuming, and the challenges and responsibilities of parish life must have made a difference. Reminiscences of former students at Hulme Hall, recorded in Fowler's biography, confirm the impression that the academic level of the students, and their social behaviour, left much to be desired. Hicks's intellectual brilliance and his unfailing courtesy may have set him apart from many of them, but the most responsive among them found in him a formative influence, as one of them testified.[12]

Pastoral care in a kind of extended family would have been a circumscribed existence for someone with Hicks's wide range of interests and abounding energy if he had not had other things to do. The post involved a certain amount of teaching of classics, though mostly at an elementary level. Occasionally he had the opportunity to help more able students. One of them, who was working at a postgraduate level in history, and was intending to proceed to Manchester College, Oxford, to train for the Unitarian ministry, has left a brief record of his methods:

[10] *Pelican Record* 20, 112–13.
[11] J. B. Lancelot, *Francis James Chavasse, Bishop of Liverpool* (Oxford 1929), 37–8.
[12] The Revd H. Stones, in Fowler, 83.

I remember well reading the Greek New Testament with him. When he came to passages around which theological controversy had raged, he made no effort to bias my judgment, or to prejudice me in favour of the views or renderings which he himself accepted. Instead of this he would say to me, 'Dr Martineau or Dr Drummond would read this in this way: Westcott and other commentators would take it thus.' This splendid and scholarly impartiality and breadth of view impressed me deeply at the time, and gave me a great love and regard for Canon Hicks himself and an understanding of the attitude of the true scholar and gentleman. His desire was always that we should seek the truth—not that we should be forced to accept certain opinions, and this was an attitude for which I have always felt deeply grateful to him, and honoured him.

That is a testimony, not only to Hicks's sympathetic attitude to religious beliefs which he did not share, but also to the seriousness of his own studies of the New Testament. His learning was soon to be put at the service of ministerial training. But at Hulme Hall the first call on his scholarship was in secular studies.

The duties of the Hall were not all that he had to think about. There was, of course, his family. It is difficult to see how the move had solved any financial problems, in spite of the account which he himself gave of his reasons for the move. He must have had a margin of income over expenditure in Fenny Compton, or else he could not have managed to contribute £200 to church repairs in 1884. He was never careless about money. Even as a bishop he looked carefully at his bank account, and was in the habit of greeting a favourable balance with a *Laus Deo*. It was not, therefore, out of character for him to attribute his desire to leave Fenny Compton in part to the fall in agricultural values, though precisely what he meant by 'a standard wage' is something of a mystery. But his financial position at Hulme Hall was not very comfortable. His Log Book occasionally has details of the annual balance sheet of the Hall, and from it we learn that the Principal's salary was £283. 6s. 8d. in 1887 and £300 in 1890. To that must be added his residential perquisites, which are reckoned as worth £200 in 1891. The total of £500 does not come up to the benefice income of Fenny Compton, even after the fall in its value. Of course, the Principal's salary was guaranteed in a way in which the benefice income was not. But if that were all that is to be said, the post would hardly have been a financial magnet. Hicks refers in his reminiscences to the practicality of the governors.

I was greatly impressed by the men who formed the Governing Body. They struck me as extraordinarily practical, direct and earnest about the business, and yet so wonderfully considerate in word and act. My experience of men had chiefly lain among college dons and country squires and parsons; but here was a new type of Churchman and educationist, evolved amid the mills and markets of Lancashire. For this type of Christian public men I conceived at once an admiration which larger experience has only deepened. I found Lancashire full of such men, both in the Church and out of it; and to their friendship I owe more than I can ever repay. I was fortunate in my first samples of Manchester people. The Chairman of the Governors at my first interview was the late Lord Egerton (not yet made an earl), and his wonderful refinement and charm will not soon pass out of mind. Equal in munificence, and his successor in the chair, was Mr. W. H. Houldsworth, M.P., afterwards made a baronet. I can never forget the practical shrewdness, and withal the perfect delicacy, with which he discussed and settled with me (on behalf of his colleagues) the financial details of my appointment.

The explanation of Hicks's assurance that he was, to say the least, not going to be worse off, must lie in opportunities for earnings over and above the salary and perquisites of the principalship.

The Log Book shows that he undertook other work in addition to his fairly light duties in the Hall. He mentions his appointment as an examiner in the Oxford Theology Honours School, his lecturing at the Grammar School, courses of lectures to the Women's Department of Owens College, examining in classics and divinity at St Paul's School in London and popular lectures given at Owens College. Fowler also says that he gave regular Sunday assistance to Archdeacon Anson at the church of Birch-in-Rusholme. Certainly not all of these engagements were unpaid, and perhaps the likelihood of extra sources of income, together with the availability of good education for his sons as day boys at Manchester Grammar School, tipped the balance in favour of the move to Manchester. What is more important, in our present context, is that other activities enlarged the circles in which he moved. He was brought into contact with new kinds of men and women, and began to get widely known in Manchester and elsewhere. He had regular meetings with the heads of Halls, and became a member of the professors' Common Room at Owens College. It was a time of personal enrichment.

During these years his work on classical epigraphy continued, and led in 1890 to the publication of his edition of the Ephesian inscriptions in the British Museum. In the following year there appeared *The Inscriptions of Cos*, in which he had assisted the dilettante scholar W. R. Paton.[13] Some at least of the students in the Hall were aware of the Warden's enthusiasm and skill. One of them, who was later ordained, wrote in his reminiscences:

While at Hulme Hall I was reading for the Honours Course in Classics, and I was lucky in having Canon Hicks as tutor. He was busy at the time preparing his book on Inscriptions, and our lessons were often interrupted by the arrival of a parcel of pressings from inscriptions. I can see him yet, eagerly opening these parcels, and, forgetting all about my shocking prose translation, he would invite me to join him in deciphering and in supplying the missing portions where they occurred. His eager excitement over the task was like that of a schoolboy.[14]

He was able in July 1887 to travel to Germany, to improve his German and attend lectures in Berlin. In 1889 he was appointed Lecturer in Classical Archaeology in the University—without a museum and with very few students. In his inaugural lecture he emphasized both the demands and the rewards of this aspect of classical studies:

As an epigraphist I know what it is to spend whole days in deciphering a line or two; or to return again and again to the stone, and look at it in every possible light and shadow, in order to recover one word or even a letter. How many hours such a one may spend in piecing together the fragments of marble that once contained perhaps a decree of Alexander or a rescript of Antoninus—fragments which remind one most of all of a torn-up letter, only that some of the bits are lost.[15]

It began to look as if an academic career might be opening up for him. He had his contacts with the Imperial Archaeological Society of Berlin, and enjoyed an Honorary Fellowship of Corpus Christi College, Oxford. But in the event his classical scholarship, though it remained a source of interest and enjoyment throughout his life, became a sideline. He was turning his attention to the relevance of classical studies to Christian thought.

When the Faculty of Theology was set up in 1904, under the direction of A. S. Peake as dean, Hicks was one of the members of the Faculty who delivered inaugural lectures 'to popular audiences'.

[13] Fowler, 91.   [14] The Revd C. Richardson, in Fowler, 86.
[15] Fowler, 89.

This was after he had left Hulme Hall and had relinquished his tutorial duties in classics there. His lecture had the title 'Christian Art in relation to Christian History'. In it he called the attention of theologians to the neglected evidence of Christian art for the history of Christian thought and the attention of archaeologists to the value of Christian antiquities. In the study of Christianity, he said, it was usual to begin with texts and ignore monuments—the opposite of the method he had learnt in the study of Greek religion. On the other hand archaeologists, such as his mentor Sir Charles Newton, in his work on Asia Minor, had neglected 'merely Christian' artefacts.[16] Hicks believed that documents and artefacts needed to be studied together.

The main part of his lecture consisted of a review of successive periods of Christian art. The published version, written up from brief notes, loses interest from the absence of the illustrations Hicks used. It does, however, contain a passage on the Oxford Movement which indicates something of his attitude to the catholic tradition in the Church of England, of which he was regarded as a moderate exponent. After speaking of its 'romantic sentiment, its religious zeal, its passionate appeal to an idealised past', he went on:

It has revolutionised the Church, and has given a new and mighty impetus to English piety. But its influence upon ecclesiastical art has not been wholly good. It has flooded the land with imitative Gothic, which is not better than imitative classicism . . . We are still painfully afraid of anything unconventional . . . But while English art witnesses to the lack of originality and creativeness in the Church revival of the last century, it witnesses no less to the strong hold of religion—albeit of undogmatic and humanitarian religion—upon the heart of the nation.[17]

We can detect here the particular strain of liberal Christianity which he had begun to espouse: a religion of deep personal piety, sustained by the Anglican liturgical tradition, but looking favourably on what has come to be called 'folk religion'—undogmatic and humanitarian.

His increasing commitment to the work of the church and his involvement with the Faculty of Theology was moving him away

---

[16] Arthur Evans said that Newton regarded archaeology as ending with the Christian era. See Geoffrey Faber, *Jowett: A Portrait with a Background* (1957), 387–8. That passage also tends to modify the picture of Jowett as despising archaeology.

[17] A. S. Peake (ed.), *Inaugural Lectures Delivered by Members of the Faculty of Theology* (Manchester 1905), 233–4.

from purely classical studies. When, in 1893, he delivered one of the Oxford Long Vacation Lectures for the clergy on 'St Paul and Hellenism' he was clearly more interested in St Paul than in Hellenism. He argued, as has already been noticed, that one of the greatest needs of the church was that its teachers should learn the method of St Paul; should learn how to enunciate the gospel in the phrase and ideas of modern life.[18] Behind this plea lies the scholar's realization, particularly in the light of developing epigraphical and papyrological discoveries, that the language of the New Testament was neither classical nor scholarly but popular, the lingua franca of the Hellenistic world. The grammar of the Greek in the New Testament and the grammar of the common Greek of the papyri were seen to be the same. The New Testament was not written in a literary language. So the message of the gospel ought to be expressed in the language of everyday. The task of interpretation, he thought, devolved upon those whose culture ought to give imaginative insight into conditions not their own. When he delivered this lecture he was already trying to do so in Salford.

This new focus, however, did not involve the loss of his personal interest in classics or archaeology. He took an active part in the establishment and activities of the Manchester and District branch of the Classical Association of England and Wales, and served as its President. He encouraged and collaborated with local archaeologists such as Charles Roeder, who was investigating the evidence of Roman occupation of the site of Manchester. One of his own specific contributions to local archaeology was a paper on some sculptured stones then in the Peel Park Museum, which he argued were Mithraic, supporting his argument with illustrations of all but one of the Mithraic sculptures in Britain.[19]

In 1906 he was invited to collaborate with another Manchester scholar, Dr J. H. Moulton of Didsbury College, in the preparation of a Lexicon of Hellenistic Greek. When he refused this invitation, Dr Moulton wrote regretfully:

I must not press you: I feel too strong a sympathy for the kind of work in the interests of which you have made a sacrifice only a fellow-student

---

[18] *Studia Biblica et Ecclesiastica: Essays chiefly in Biblical and Patristic Criticism, by Members of the University of Oxford,* iv (1896), 13.

[19] Charles Roeder, 'Roman Manchester reconsidered', *Transactions of the Lancashire and Cheshire Antiquarian Society* 17 (1900); R. S. Conway (ed.), *Melandra Castle* (1906); F. A. Bruton (ed.), *The Roman Fort at Manchester* (1909).

can understand. But while my Temperance, Citizen and Christian sympathies wholly agree with you, the student part of me insists on rebel-
ling against the loss of expert knowledge which no one in England can
rival. Meanwhile I must try to find some other helper, though he cannot be the epigraphist whom I wanted or the neighbour and friend I
wanted more.[20]

Their friendship was none the less close for the difference between
the two men in religious tradition: Hicks the Anglican from Oxford,
and Moulton the Methodist from Cambridge. They were associated in scholarship, but also in Christian evangelism, in opposition
to the brewing interest in Manchester and Salford, and in passionate
advocacy of the cause of international peace.[21]

The university with its associated colleges provided the intellectual stimulus which had not been so readily available to Hicks
in the countryside. Its first Vice-Chancellor, the former Principal
of Owens College, was Sir Alfred Hopkinson, an Oxford-trained
lawyer, a former Liberal MP, 'above all else a Christian gentleman
to whom religion was a thing which he recorded [?regarded] as
vital not only in his own life but also in that of the nation'.[22] Oxford
training, Liberal politics, Christian conviction—those three elements in Hicks's own character—were equally present in the Vice-
Chancellor. But the university was no mere follower of an Oxford
ideal. In two important ways it marked out its own course. One
was the equal place and honour which it gave to science alongside the humanities. As early as 1876 Mark Pattison, in an address
to the Social Science Congress, had spoken of Owens College,
still 'struggling upwards to the ideal of a university', as having a
remarkable scientific eminence with small capital resources.[23] That
eminence had been sustained in the new university. The other distinctive feature, as compared with Oxford, was its close relationship with the region it primarily served and the civic community
within which it was set. Hicks does not seem to have developed
more than a very general interest in the sciences. He spoke of them
with appreciation, and certainly did not see them as enemies of

---

[20] Fowler, 129; J. L. North, ' "I Sought a Colleague": James Hope Moulton, Papyrologist, and Edward Lee Hicks, Epigraphist, 1903–1906', *Rylands Library Bulletin* (Spring
1997), 195–206.

[21] See *James Hope Moulton* by his brother, W. F. Moulton (1919), esp. 99–102.

[22] *DNB*, article by Alfred T. Davies.

[23] H. B. Charlton, *Portrait of a University 1851–1951* (Manchester 1951), 76.

faith. But it was undoubtedly important to him that all academic study should be related to the day-to-day experience of community life. Whether it was the study of Greek epigraphy or of St Paul's letters, the social context was always in his mind.

He also served on the Board of Governors of the Rylands Library and was friendly with its Librarian, Dr Guppy. He made a number of gifts to the library, notably all his copies of the British Museum Catalogue of Coins. He lectured at the Library on Mithras-worship in the early Christian centuries. When he resigned, on his appointment to Lincoln, the governors of the Library expressed their high esteem, and made him an Honorary Governor.[24] The Classical Association, too, opened the door to intellectual companions and friends, for it brought him in touch, amongst others, with the staff of Manchester Grammar School, where for a short time after his arrival Sir Samuel Dill, a former fellow of Corpus, was High Master, and F. A. Bruton, a particular and life-long friend, an assistant master. Even in his seventies he still enjoyed tramping holidays with Bruton, usually with the stimulus of some archaeological quest. At the Grammar School, too, he met J. H. Fowler, who was in due course to be invited to write his biography. But there were other contacts, as well. Mrs Gaskell had lived only a few doors away from Hulme Hall in Plymouth Grove and made her house a kind of literary salon, so that Lord Houghton, who knew the London salons well, had even suggested Manchester as a possible place for people of literary tastes to live, merely on the strength of Mrs Gaskell's residence there.[25] Her daughters continued to live in Plymouth Grove after Mrs Gaskell's death in 1865, and Hicks and his wife were on visiting terms with them. Hicks also took an interest in the Manchester Art Museum, and gave an address at its Annual Meeting in July 1889 and maintained a correspondence with T. C. Horsfall, one of its staunchest supporters and promoters. Such things enriched his intellectual environment.

But the two most important areas of Hicks's interest, outside the work of the college and university, were his commitment to temperance and the journalism which developed through his friendship with C. P. Scott, who had been an undergraduate at Corpus when Hicks held his fellowship. He was soon drawn into

[24] Minutes of the Governors of the John Rylands Library, 1905–1910.
[25] See *DNB*, 'Mrs Gaskell'.

the intellectual circle, mostly of Oxford men, which was created by Scott to give weight and authority to his editorship of the *Manchester Guardian*. He contributed various letters and articles to the paper, and eventually became one of its two regular religious correspondents. But it was more than a formal relationship through the paper; he became a welcome visitor at Scott's home, The Firs, and kept in touch with him long after leaving Manchester for Lincoln. There was, indeed, a network of relationships of Oxford graduates in Manchester, including W. T. Arnold, the grandson of Dr Arnold and sister of Mrs Humphry Ward. He was a Gladstonian Liberal in politics, and also a scholarly student of Roman history and modern literature, whose home was another meeting place for people who shared his literary and artistic tastes. The Hickses counted his family among their friends.

Appointments at Hulme Hall and in the university did not yet bring Hicks into contact with the social problems of the Manchester area. He was ready to give assistance in parochial work, especially at Birch-in-Rusholme. But Sunday duty did not involve pastoral work in the parish, and offered little outlet for his social concerns. It was the United Kingdom Alliance which drew him into the experience of life outside the academic milieu. He became known in the diocese, and was offered the parish of St Mary's, Crumpsall, within two or three years of moving to Hulme Hall, but did not accept the offer, considering that he had hardly been long enough in the post for which he had come to Manchester. After six years, however, he was offered, and accepted, the living of St Philip's, Salford, combined with a residentiary canonry of Manchester Cathedral, and became once again involved in the working lives of ordinary people, as he had been in Warwickshire.

He was about to embark on the most strenuous and effective stage of his ministry. We can see how all the varied elements in his experience contributed to making him the kind of liberal churchman he had become. He had from his early days thought of the structure of society as manifesting faults and injustices which it was a Christian duty to remedy. The prophetic fervour of Ruskin had confirmed this attitude, without compelling him to underwrite all Ruskin's schemes and opinions. His classical studies, so far from distracting his attention from contemporary society, had encouraged him to look for the human dimension of lifeless relics of the past and made him feel the need to sympathize with those who had struggled then with intractable issues. When he turned his classical learning to the study of the New Testament he found there, not some armoury of texts for dogmatic warfare, but a message which, because it was of eternal validity, needed to be restated and refurbished for contemporary communication. His awareness of social needs in his country parish motivated small-scale experiments to alleviate suffering and to dignify the sufferers with at least some sense of independence. The waste of scarce resources on self-indulgence, which was promoted by the brewing trade, challenged the social reformer in him to find better alternatives, and allied him with like-minded people of other denominations who saw the same problem and wanted to offer the same remedy.

With his innate optimism and the good fortune of having had Liberal friends in Fenny Compton, he had continued to believe that politics could be carried on with tolerance and honesty, and that reforms could be undertaken which would alleviate the sufferings of working people and open up their narrow views of life by education. So when he left the countryside he became more and more committed to a public stance in opposition to those who resisted social reforms and those who exploited the vulnerability of working people. As he joined other reformers in looking for a fuller life for working people in a democratic society, there was an explicit assumption in much of what he said and did that education was one of the agencies of change. If the amount of leisure for the workers and their families increased, there would be opportunities for qualitative change as well.

Looking at this map of attitudes which went to the making of the newly appointed cathedral canon, we begin to notice something which is a precondition of all the rest—that he gave priority to secular men in a secular society and not to churchmen in a sacred community. That is not to imply that he took a detached view of the institutional church. The rest of his life was devoted to its service in important and demanding offices. But nine of his first twenty-two years in orders had been spent in ministries which were not defined by parochial boundaries and which had brought him into daily touch with young men who looked at life through secular spectacles. Personal relationships, work for daily bread, and perhaps the idea of the nation—those were more likely to be the context of his students' thoughts than the framework of liturgy and doctrine which the church provided.

It is important to stress what he did not share with some of the others who count as liberal churchmen. He did not come from a clerical background. The institutional church was not the taken-for-granted context of his childhood. He was not well connected socially. He did not assume the right to occupy a ruling place in society. He had not experienced the social formation provided by the great public schools of the day. He did not have a secure financial base; nor the dismissive attitude to wealth and social position of those who have possessed, and turned their backs on, those things.

Bishop Edward Talbot, who knew him well and had even come to stay with him at Hulme Hall, in writing to Archbishop Davidson after Hicks's appointment to Lincoln, described him, not only as a scholar and a man of most virile and fearless morals, keen for the things of liberty, but also as a gentleman.[26] The evidence of his Lincoln diaries suggests that he would have been pleased by this, had he known it, because 'gentleman' was a term which he sometimes used as a criterion of praise or criticism in recording his opinions of the clergy in his diocese. It was not uncommonly used to describe the typical product of the ancient universities. It became, therefore, a target for the attacks of Newman and others, who treated it as the label of an ideal which they saw to be in conflict with their own ideal of the penitential and submissive churchman bowing before the supernatural majesty of the Catholic Church. When Newman wrote 'Liberal education makes not the Christian, not the Catholic, but the gentleman,'[27] he was in effect contrasting the gentleman's freedom to maintain a degree of detachment from theories and dogmas with the tendency of all religious systems, and most notably the Catholic Church, to claim to possess that absolute truth for which he longed. In a longer perspective we can see that Newman's ideal of submission to authority was an inverted image of the powerful ruler or ruling group which motivates all kinds of authoritarianism, from the former public school relationship of prefect and fag to the religious relationship of infallible pope and obedient Catholic. That ideal never appealed to Hicks. Neither its dominant form, nor its disguise in submissiveness, finds an echo in his thoughts.

---

[26] Lambeth Palace Library, Davidson Papers, 164: Official Letters, fo. 213.
[27] *The Idea of the University* (1852), 120, quoted in J. Coulson, *John Newman* (1970), 90.

It is no accident that in descriptions of his character by others the word which recurs most often is 'courtesy'. For that implies the rejection of both any assumption of superiority and any show of false modesty. Courtesy is the proper relation of equal human beings. Perhaps it is the best outward expression of liberality. It does not in the least diminish a man's confidence in the principles he has worked out for himself; but it allows him to treat others as entitled to hold their own opinions, provided only that they have given their best thought to working them out. Whether in writing about Bazely or in working with nonconformists, Hicks stood firmly upon his own principles, but embraced others within the openness of his own courtesy. This religious kind of liberality, however, was only part of the equipment which Hicks carried into the new environment of the parish and cathedral.

If outward courtesy expresses recognition of the equal humanity of those to whom it is shown, it must normally lead on to imaginative participation in their lives, and particularly the social handicaps under which they labour. Hicks believed that the culture of 'men of learning and thought' could give them imaginative insight into conditions not their own. In Fenny Compton he had had daily converse with men and women whose condition was far removed from the spacious life of the rectory, and had tried to find ways of mitigating their deprivation. The complexity of social life in Manchester and Salford made the small-scale schemes which had been appropriate in Fenny Compton largely irrelevant— the water company and the allotments and the co-operative shop. But one problem, one handicap, which had come to his notice in the country parish was magnified to new proportions: the presence and the threat of the drink trade. Manchester was the home and the powerhouse of the United Kingdom Alliance, and Hicks had begun his work for the Alliance before he moved to Salford. It became the chief outlet for his strong passion for social reform, and extended his horizons to national limits. There was also another cause which carried his thought and his imagination even further: sympathy with the Boers and consequent opposition to the Boer War. He had to grow in stature to respond to these two challenges. In doing so, he made his witness as a Radical churchman.

PART II
The Witness of a Radical Churchman

6

A Slum and a Cathedral: Salford and Manchester (1892–1910)

The over-quoted remark of Archbishop Tait about the liberals being deficient in religion[1] will not stand up to scrutiny as a generalization. Liberals were not all of a kind; and the definition of 'religion' is problematical. Edward Hicks was a liberal in almost all senses of that word; and the records of his life make it clear that he was not deficient in religion, taken to mean both personal devotion and a loving adoption of a disciplined pattern of public worship. Later chapters will examine his witness in social and political questions, but it is important before that to describe his work as a parish priest, not because he thought that work more important than anything else, but because he believed that his social and political convictions arose, no less than his pastoral ministry, from his understanding of the gospel. The peculiar conditions of the appointment of residentiary canons at Manchester, imposing heavy parochial responsibilities on those who were also responsible for the cathedral, corresponded with the two aspects of Hicks's understanding of the Christian faith. It demanded an unsparing personal ministry, together with responsibility in a democratic society for the conditions of communal life. And the political decisions which he believed to be right did not arise from theoretical considerations but were specifically the consequence of his experience of the miseries of the poor in his parishes.

After Hicks had been in Manchester a short time it must have become obvious that he was a man of distinction, fit to play a significant role in the church. He had both intellectual ability and pastoral experience, and he was at the height of his powers. No doubt Bishop James Moorhouse was keen to retain him in the diocese and was looking for an opportunity to present him to a

[1] R. T. Davidson and W. Benham, *Life of Archibald Campbell Tait, Archbishop of Canterbury* (1891), i. 325.

living. Moorhouse was a man with a liberal reputation, who had previously been Bishop of Melbourne. Gladstone had thought of him for the see of Southwell in 1884, but then withdrawn his name when objections were raised. In 1886 Salisbury had persuaded the Queen to approve him for Manchester. He wanted reform in the church and was chairman of the Manchester branch of the Church Reform League. He also wanted to promote a campaign to prove that the advance of science did not mean the retreat of religion.[2] He found Hicks's character congenial, and his wife and Agnes got to know each other well. So when Hicks had been at Hulme Hall only two or three years the bishop offered him the parish of St Mary, Crumpsall. The previous incumbent had been a schoolmaster and a mathematical lecturer at Owens College, and that may have suggested to the bishop the notion of making another academic its rector. But Hicks was looking for a position which would give him full scope for his gifts and energies. He would want to commit himself to his next post for a good stretch of years, and if Crumpsall seemed a rather uninteresting parish he would only have to find a respectable way of declining the bishop's offer. So he completed six years' work at Hulme Hall, and got it on to a workable basis. It soon outgrew its accommodation and was transferred to new premises in Oak Bank, to which extensions were added.

In 1892, when Hicks was forty-eight, his ability was finally recognized by the Dean and Chapter of the cathedral, who appointed him to a residentiary canonry, and the incumbency of St Philip's, Salford—one of the most demanding parishes in the neighbourhood, with a population of over ten thousand.[3] The conditions governing the ministry of the cathedral were unique. The old collegiate church had been transformed into the cathedral when the see of Manchester was inaugurated in 1847. Its Warden and Fellows, who became the Dean and Canons of the cathedral, had previously enjoyed easy lives and large incomes. Local criticism eventually led to the formation of an 'Association for Promoting a Reform in the Ecclesiastical Provisions of the Parish of Manchester', and the passing of the Manchester Parish Divisions

---

[2] Palmer, *High and Mitred*, 104; *Commonwealth* (July 1900), 192–3; James M. Wilson, *An Autobiography* (1932), 177.

[3] He was not installed by Dean Oakley, as Fowler says (103), but by Dean Maclure, who had succeeded Oakley in 1890.

Act of 1850.[4] By its provisions each canonry had attached to it the incumbency of one of the largest and poorest parishes in the locality, three in Manchester and one in Salford. No houses were provided for the canons, but they were free to live wherever they chose within the ancient parish of Manchester. So the 'residence' of each of the canons involved the duty of attending services and preaching on one Sunday in four and attending weekday services twice a day during three months in the year, no two of which might be consecutive. Even if a canon did no more than his bare duty at the cathedral (and that certainly was not usually the case) this arrangement necessitated the appointment of at least one assistant curate for his parish, to be paid by him from the joint income derived from the parish and the canonry. The stipends of the canons were unequal, and Hicks, as the fourth canon, only received £600 a year. The benefice income of St Philip's was only £250. Pew rents had been abolished. From his joint income of £850 he had to pay the stipend of one assistant curate (£150) and sometimes two, support the Church Army work (£70), and meet various other expenses. The church people of Manchester had struck a hard bargain, though the arrangement scarcely deserved the description later given to it by a church paper: 'a peculiarly vicious type of finance'.[5]

In his new appointment Hicks took up again the concerns which had marked his incumbency at Fenny Compton, but with the inevitable differences imposed by the urban setting. He wanted to build up the church; and he wanted to change society. The church building, its services, and its witness in the parish were even more in need of development than they had been in Fenny Compton. His immediate predecessor at St Philip's, Canon Julius Lloyd, had died within a year of his appointment. His predecessor was Canon Nathaniel Woodard, the moving spirit in the establishment of the 'Woodard Schools', whose interests were certainly not focused on St Philip's. He had been appointed to a residentiary canonry over twenty years before, with the intention that he should become Rector of St Philip's, in accordance with the requirements of the Manchester Parish Division Act, when the living became

---

[4] The provisions of the Act remained in force until the 1920s, when the canons were allowed to resign their parishes, although Canon Peter Green at his own request retained St Philip's, Salford.

[5] *Guardian*, 24 Feb. 1911.

vacant.[6] But the sitting incumbent, who had been appointed just before the Act was passed, survived until 1887. In his declining years he suffered from paralysis and earned the unenviable nickname of 'The Old Figurehead'. Woodard continued to live in Sussex, coming to Manchester for his periods of residence, and waiting (with no great impatience) for the living to fall vacant. When it did, he was instituted, but left the parish to be worked by two curates, and died three years later. He is said to have preached only once in his parish. One incumbency covering forty years and ending when the incumbent died at the age of eighty, another held by a non-resident incumbent, and a third terminated when it had hardly begun, could not have left the parish in good shape. It was with good reason that the Centenary Brochure later commented that with Canon Hicks the ancient history of St Philip's ended and its modern history began.[7] Dr Hicks,[8] it said, was the first who attempted to grapple with the many problems which the parish presented. The character of the district had changed, and the life of the parish had sunk low. Nearly all its distinctive features in the centenary year of 1925 owed their existence to his encouragement and inspiration and he had achieved the entire renovation of the interior of the church building.

During his time at Hulme Hall, Hicks had not stopped thinking about parish work. Indeed it seems that he had been trying to sum up the experience of thirteen years in a country parish and to apply that experience to the urban situation. The Church Congress met in Manchester in October 1888, and he read a paper at it with the title, 'How to Supply the Defects of the Parochial System by Means of Evangelizing Work'. The first defect he mentioned was the 'peculiar independence' of the parish priest, which had certainly helped many salutary changes, but had also sheltered indolence, incompetence, eccentricity, and even scandal. The remedy for this was not, he thought, legislation to change the parson's freehold, but improved episcopal oversight, the subdivision of dioceses, and the development of a stronger Christian public opinion. The second defect was the tendency for the parish to be

---

[6] On this and other details, see Michael Hennell, *The Deans and Canons of Manchester 1840–1948* (Manchester n.d.).

[7] *St Philip's Centenary Brochure 1825–1925* (author evidently Canon Peter Green).

[8] Hicks did not receive a Doctorate (Litt.D.) until July 1910, when it was conferred by Manchester University.

forgotten in concern for the congregation. Here we see a continuance of the theme of his ordination sermon of 1883: the call to be fishers of men. Where, he asked, were the working classes or the unemployed, or the handicapped, or the idlers? Not at church, certainly. 'Are they at Chapel? I wish they were.' He was sceptical about the sufficiency of the ordinary parochial mission. Perpetual pressure was needed, not an extraordinary effort. He looked to the Salvation Army as a model of 'self-adapting versatility', and to lay and clerical brotherhoods, as leaders in mission in the dark places where the life of the parsonage was not the fittest agency. He advocated open-air work: 'When shall we hear of the open-air celebration of the Blessed Sacrament on Easter Day, at the camp service of our volunteers?' And, of course, he urged the need for temperance work, praising the Church of England Temperance Society for attacking vice in its strongholds, and quoting with unconscious foresight a sale advertisement in the *Manchester Guardian*: 'Good public-house; first class drinking locality; off Chapel Street, Salford: ingoing £200'.

We may note here Hicks's association with the Church Army, which developed later and was one expression of his determination to reach beyond the established congregations of the church. In Salford he worked closely with Captain Rowlands, a 'happy little Welshman', who gave twenty-eight years' service to the Church Army, mainly in Salford, but also on 'Pioneer and Tent Missions' in various parts of the country. When the Church Army set up a Pioneer and Tent Mission Department in 1898, it had special missioners in the Manchester diocese and two others, and Hicks was one of only two 'Pioneer Mission Advisers'. Its prospectus has a period flavour, carefully phrased so as not to antagonize members of the clergy, with references to meetings conducted on 'earnest, discreet Church lines, introducing evangelistic adaptation of the Prayer Book' and 'Lantern services, with magnificent art pictures, both in the open-air and inside'. Tents were supplied, 'which are especially attractive in summer, as men can stand round and smoke'. These details suggest an image of seaside missions, and certainly the Blackpool Mission, fostered by Bishop Knox, fits into that category. But a later prospectus (1909–10) includes services conducted at factory gates and among the girls employed at large laundries. A tent mission would not have been possible in St Philip's parish in Salford, but Hicks did a lot of open-air work with Captain

Rowlands in the courts and alleys of the district where they even had to risk physical violence.[9] He continued to advocate, and indeed to practise, open-air preaching after he went to be Bishop of Lincoln.

With his appointment to St Philip's, he had the opportunity he wanted to put at least some of his ideas into practice. Others, such as his advocacy of closer episcopal oversight, would have to wait many years. But the outward look of the church, the concern for working people, the struggle against drunkenness—these at least could find expression in his new sphere of work. In the year following his induction he put out an appeal, in which he described the state of the parish and listed what he saw to be its needs. His appeal is an informative document, describing the parish as he found it in 1893.

The population is 10,225, almost wholly of the working class. I doubt if we have a score of households that keep a servant. We have comparatively few retail tradesmen, but we comprise all kinds and grades of working folk, from the skilled electrician, or joiner, or fitter, down to the coal-heaver, the hawker, and the casual labourer. We live among mills and works of every sort—flax mills, cotton mills, bleach works, fustian-cutting shops, box-making shops, ironworks, coopers' yards, builders' yards, medical plaister works, printing offices, sawmills, coalyards, railway goods yards, and others. Besides the mills and works, hundreds of my people pour into town to every kind of warehouse or place of business. I may meet my parishioners in every part of Manchester.

This appeal letter presents first and foremost a secular community, a world of work, with all its complexity, in which Hicks describes his people (and almost exclusively the men) by their trades, not their religious affiliations. The next section of the letter then describes the church building, dignified without and miserable within. It is an appeal for beauty in the midst of squalor. 'In our grimy Parish . . . where the one pleasant view (from the Crescent over Peel Park and the Irwell) has been spoiled by the smoke above and the stinking river below, our Church, within, should form at least one beautiful object for rich and poor alike: and it shall always stand open.'

Schools and an Institute follow next in the appeal; but there is a feeling of climax as Hicks goes on to describe his hopes of social

[9] Letters from his mother in 1896 and 1897 show her trying to dissuade him from what she saw as risky outdoor work.

work in the parish. First he gives a bleak picture of the state of church life as it had been in the past:

Up to ten or twelve years ago the Church had been chiefly notable as a Garrison Church: hither the regiments stationed in Salford came for Church parade every Sunday. A rabble of parishioners followed them to the Church door, and then dispersed. No real attempt was made to reach the working classes or make them welcome to the Church. The hideous 'free seats' are a crying testimony on this head.

Then he proceeds to a picture of the social life of the parish which is no less miserable:

The extent to which drunkenness has got hold of the population of Salford is only known to those who work night and day among them. Saturdays and Sundays, and all public holidays, are times of continuous dissipation. The women are as often drunken as the men. If I were asked what excited the widest and deepest interest among the working people of Salford at large, I should reply, 'The state of the odds'. If asked what was their favourite enjoyment, I should say 'Drinking'. Other forms of vice exist, but less openly and in less amount. Against all these evils we do battle day by day.

That judgement might proceed from a censorious observer, living at a distance and feeling little sympathy with people of a different class; but Hicks continues: 'Let me say that nothing could be kinder or gentler than the natural disposition of my people. They give me the friendliest welcome, even the poorest and most degraded.' He is particularly moved by 'the hourly sight of the little shoeless, dirty, naked children—robbed of home, of comfort, of the necessaries of bodily life by the Moloch of drink'. And he describes his unremitting battle against such conditions.

Street preaching, assiduous visiting, Church Army services every evening, Band of Hope and other meetings—these (in addition to ordinary parochial ministrations) are some of the methods we employ. We hope by degrees to create a better public opinion among the people themselves: this can only be done by constant converse with them. It is an uphill struggle.

Those last sentences hint at the policy of the UKA—to get parliament to authorize 'Local Option', to enable people in any locality to prohibit licences for the sale of alcohol in their own area. The effectiveness of the policy would depend on the creation of 'a better public opinion'.

Drink and gambling were not the only social problems in the area. Another was the misery of the homeless. Hicks's awareness of that problem is shown by the short preface he wrote to a little publication put out in 1904 by the Women Guardians and Local Government Association, Manchester, with the cumbrous title, *Five Days and Five Nights as a Tramp among Tramps: A Social Investigation by a Lady.* It gave a factual account of the experiences of two women who spent those few days in lodging houses, a workhouse tramp ward, and a women's shelter. They scarcely survived the filth, the vermin, the inedible food, and the sexual harassment to which they were subjected. 'In the common lodging-house you can wash your clothes, but not yourself; in the workhouse tramp ward you can wash yourself, but not your clothes.' Even in that short time they were forced to pawn their last possession and 'cleanliness lost, clothing dilapidated or dirty—what then?'

The social problems of Salford were very different from those Hicks had met in Fenny Compton. There he lived in a small-scale, structured society, in which the agricultural depression had set workers against employers, and in which partial remedies were to hand: bringing back land into profitable use through the allotments system, co-operative methods to make food and clothing and coal more cheaply available, education to occupy the minds and raise the self-respect of working people, temperance to channel available income away from useless expenditure. The parish of St Philip's was not a structured society of that kind. There was no land lying idle, ready for profitable use. Co-operation, if it was to be developed, would not be on a parochial basis. It would not fall to the local clergy to promote the kind of general educational work which in Fenny Compton Hicks had sponsored in the evenings. The church's work must necessarily focus on individual and family life; and there the threats of drunkenness and gambling became the targets to attack. The activities Peter Green specified in the centenary brochure as deriving from his predecessor's encouragement and inspiration were the Barrow Street Mission, temperance work, work among lads and girls, and the Whitsun camp; in fact, just the sort of activities which fulfilled the call to be 'fishers of men'. As we go on to consider Hicks's second great concern—to change society—it is important to remember that the continuing basis of all his activities was his work as a parish priest. Half of the list of needs in his appeal brochure is concerned with getting people to do things, particularly on the cultural frontiers beyond which were to be found the 'un-churched masses' in the teeming parish. Those helpers were, of course, mainly lay people, whose role in the church he never underestimated. He did not usually have more than one assistant curate at a time, until the last few years of his eighteen-year stint, though he also had the greatly valued co-operation of Captain Rowlands of the Church Army and some recognized women workers. The most important of them was Ruth Chamberlain, who took over the running of the Girls' Club in Encombe Place in 1895 and remained in charge till Hicks left Salford, and was a friend to the end of his life.[10] St Philip's gave him his first real opportunity to encourage the contribution of women to the church's ministry. In Salford he clearly recognized the limitations of a ministry exercised exclusively by men. From that point onwards he was an advocate of women's ministry.

It was an awkward parish to work, because it included some formerly well-to-do areas, already socially reduced, with houses let out in tenements, as well as areas of slum dwellings, such as Islington Street. The inhabitants were almost all working people, but that did not mean that they thought of each other as social equals. There could be deeply felt distinctions between different levels of manual work—or lack of it. Whatever ideals of class reconciliation a parish priest might nurture came up against resistance, on both sides of every divide. It was not unknown for the incumbent of a parish with divergent social groups to hand over the care of the poorest to a curate and confine his own ministry to those who were better off. It might seem a sensible division of labour. When Ralph Inge was Vicar of All Saints', Ennismore Gardens, a few years later, he moved in the circles in which dinner parties were the accepted mode of social intercourse; his curates worked the parish—and came to supper with him on Sundays.[11] Hicks had his own duties among the well-to-do at the cathedral, and he might have left the poor of Salford to the ministry of assistants. But even if it had not been his own inclination to work with the poor, he would have recognized that the curates would normally stay with him for only a few years. His cathedral duties, however, made the assistance of other priests essential to the maintenance of services at St Philip's.

---

[10] Other parish workers were Deaconess Stapley and Sister Nora, mentioned in a letter to Dr Guppy (John Rylands Library archives 25 March 1904).

[11] Adam Fox, *Dean Inge* (1960), 72.

He evidently preferred university men as curates, for they were
nearly all Cambridge graduates, with the exception of the curate
he inherited from his predecessor and the most remarkable and
most difficult of them all, Conrad Noel, whom Hicks accepted
at the request of Canon (later Bishop) Charles Gore.[12]

In his sketchy autobiography, Noel refers briefly to his relations
with Hicks during his short time at St Philip's, with a mixture of
appreciation and criticism. The criticism was of the sort Hicks had
to face all his life for his temperance principles. Noel relates an
improbable story of Hicks deliberately knocking a jug of beer out
of the hand of a woman in the street, though he admits that she
was compensated for the loss. It is difficult to believe that it was
a deliberate action. More significantly Noel bears witness to Hicks's
toleration of his own socialist propaganda, and to his devotion in
pastoral work:

In spite of his own teetotal ardour, Canon Hicks was a devoted parish
priest. One day I went into the church school, where he was teaching,
and there is sharply defined in my mind the vivid manner in which he
held the children's attention, while he told them one of the Gospel stories. He made it glow with life, and the scholars felt that he was telling
them a story of their own days and within their own experience.[13]

This bears out other testimonies of Hicks's rapport with children,
notably from his youngest son, Ned, who long remembered the
catechism addresses which his father insisted on maintaining, even
when he was in residence at the cathedral and had to hurry from
them to the morning service. 'As an instructor he was in his element.'[14] Noel seems almost unaware of the remarkable tolerance
of the older priest for a tearaway curate who seemed to be more
interested in the stage, good restaurants and socialist meetings on
Boggart Hole Clough than the poor of Salford. Noel moved on
after a year, with his complaints of poverty, and his occasional fat
cheques from rich relations, and his rector looked for another man
to succeed him.

---

[12] A letter preserved in the Bodleian shows that Hicks had been in correspondence with
Hastings Rashdall, because he was about to lose a 'good and promising man' who had
been unsettled by theological difficulties, and hoped Rashdall could recommend someone
to him (Ms. Eng. Lett. d. 181, 18 June 1895).

[13] Conrad Noel, *An Autobiography*, ed. Sidney Dark (1945), 64. It is curious that Noel
assumed that a teetotaller could hardly be a devoted parish priest. Had he not heard of
Peter Green?

[14] Fowler, 163.

The parish was, of course, not an Anglican enclave, nor free from the stresses common to the Church of England at that period. Both nonconformists and Roman Catholics had a substantial presence. And the relations between ritualists and their opponents were particularly bitter in the area. At an earlier period Salford had been the scene of Canon Hugh Stowell's evangelical ministry and anti-ritualist activity,[15] and a previous bishop of Manchester, James Fraser, had become embroiled in controversy when he applied the sanctions of the Public Worship Regulation Act of 1874 to S. F. Green, Vicar of Miles Platting, on account of his ritualistic practices. The dean of the cathedral at the time, B. M. Cowie, rather ostentatiously visited the imprisoned priest, and there was much opposition to his own developments of ritual. These quarrels do not seem to have had their echo in St Philip's, where Hicks's moderate line and his strenuous pastoral activity prevented any split in the congregation. He was, moreover, drawn into close relations with some of the nonconformists through his temperance work.[16] He also seems to have worked peaceably with Roman Catholics on the Salford Schools Board. He avoided controversy over ritualism, making only moderate changes at St Philip's (unlike his immediate successor, Canon Simpson); but his churchmanship was put to the test when he was offered the deanery of Manchester, and there was no doubt that he stood on the catholic side.

He soon became known for his political interests, but he was not just a 'political parson', and he did not equate his role as parish priest with his role as social reformer. He revealed something of himself when he preached one of the memorial sermons for Archdeacon George Anson in February 1898 in the church of St James, Birch-in-Rusholme. He gave it the title 'The Pastoral Ideal' and spoke of his friend as of one who had embodied that ideal. Anson had formed his understanding of it 'amid the fervour of the Oxford Movement'. He was a conscientious visitor, gentle, sympathetic, courteous, tender and persuasive. He was also careful in scholarship, and had learnt by heart all the Epistles of St Paul in the original Greek. He saw visions of better things, but was no mere optimist, being a shrewd judge of human character.

[15] James Bentley, *Ritualism and Politics in Victorian Britain* (Oxford 1978), 10, 32–3. Stowell was the author of *Tractarianism Tested* (2 vols.).
[16] It was a pleasant sign of friendship that a nonconformist joiner presented St Philip's with a lectern for its chapel when Hicks was furnishing it.

He stood in the sacred succession of parish priests which num-
bered among its exemplars George Herbert, Isaac Williams, and
John Keble. Hicks, who had never served an assistant curacy, knew
that he had learnt valuable lessons from his regular ministry at Birch
while he was at Hulme Hall. At St Philip's he tried to put his
pastoral ideal before his reforming zeal.

Hicks's incumbency in Salford was, from one point of view, just
another example of the kind of active, socially responsible ministry being exercised in many of the large industrial centres of the
country in the latter part of the nineteenth century by men who
came from a very different social background. He raised money,
sponsored clubs, sustained the work of schools, visited the homes
and the hospitals, undertook open-air evangelism, and played an
active role in local good causes. The distinctiveness of his ministry, however, lay in a number of activities which were not common to all his fellow clergymen. Outside his parish he became
actively involved in local and national politics, but he made a clear
distinction between his unpolitical role in his parish and his wider
responsibility as a leading churchman—or perhaps we should better say, as a prominent Christian—in the district. In making this
distinction between his role as a parish priest and his activities in
the wider world he was possibly influenced by the fact that in Manchester and Salford working people were overwhelmingly Conservative in their voting practice. It was more important to change
their social habits than their party allegiance, and to elevate their
self-esteem than to fight against their political misunderstandings.

When he was installed as a residentiary canon the dean was
Edward Maclure, a lifelong Liberal in politics, who retained the
deanery until 1906. There was a strong tradition of social concern
among the clergy of the cathedral, combined with a moderate Anglo-
catholicism in worship. The closing decades of the nineteenth century had seen cross-fertilization between the legacies of the Oxford
Movement and the Maurician school of social Christianity, and
the deans and canons of Manchester exemplified corporately, if
not individually, the resultant combination. Hicks seems to have
found that environment congenial, and had good relations with
his fellow canons. There were important opportunities for him to
exercise his teaching ministry, notably in giving series of Lenten
addresses.[17] In due course he was also given responsibility for the

---

[17] One series was published, with the title *Addresses on the Temptations* (1905).

cathedral finances, which he handled with success. When he left Manchester, the *Manchester Guardian* commented: 'His husbandry of the capitular revenues has been masterly.'

But even parish and cathedral did not occupy all his energies. He continued to contribute to the world of learning with publications on classical epigraphy, and earned some extra money by lighter articles in popular journals. His educational work included teaching in the Diocesan Clergy Training School, Scholae Episcopi, which had been founded by Bishop Moorhouse, and which survived until after Hicks's move to Lincoln. Here again his skill as a teacher was remembered by some of his students.

No student ever had a more sympathetic or brilliant tutor than Dr Hicks. His lecture was the event of the week . . . The fifteen poor men before him inspired him to his best work just as much as a brilliant company of Oxford undergraduates would have done—nay, some of us imagined that of the two he preferred to teach us. His lectures were like the man, full of vitality, thought, suggestiveness and power . . . The Bible, under treatment of this master mind, became to us a revelation indeed, but a revelation of personality. Evolution, Modernism, German Criticism, all had been assimilated by the lecturer, and these only served to illuminate that which the Bible stood for: the supreme expression of the way of life. Verbal inspiration and all other literalisms passed away from us as the mist before the sun. He made us realize that God's interest was the human interest, and we learned to love the Bible by loving Canon Hicks.[18]

There is in this testimony something of over-enthusiasm, but it speaks of a genuine impact of teacher upon student.

When Hicks had carried on his double duty as parish priest and residentiary canon for fourteen years, Dean Maclure died and the nomination of his successor fell to the Prime Minister, Sir Henry Campbell-Bannerman. He had only recently taken office, and was determined to do the thing properly according to his own lights. He was himself a Presbyterian and in favour of disestablishment, at least for Scotland and Wales. In addition to an antipathy to the idea of a mediating priesthood ('claiming to have a right of introducing the laity to the Deity as if they were a privileged caste'), he also disliked the assumption that bishops should be 'gentlemen' and therefore almost certainly Tories. 'I have no patience with professors of a religion founded by fishermen who think that the higher posts in the Church must be preserved for the highly born and

---

[18] *MG* 30 August 1912, quoted in Fowler, 121.

the highly educated. I have little doubt that St Peter dropped his h's and that our Saviour's Sermon on the Mount was uttered in the broadest Galilean dialect.' He was initially disposed to make Liberalism and Broad views the test for all promotions—though he did not manage to apply it consistently. He had a realistic view of the needs of Manchester. When Lord Althorp wrote suggesting a name for the deanery, he set the suggestion aside and wrote, 'The man for Manchester should be a man of energy, accustomed to work among the poor, etc. Also, as it is my first big appointment, he must be (to say the least) a non-Ritualist. That quarrel runs very high on the spot.'[19] Hicks was an obvious candidate. He was politically suitable, he had the right kind of experience, and he was not a 'Tory gentleman'. Moreover some years before he had been in correspondence with Campbell-Bannerman following one of his speeches which dealt with temperance legislation. Of all the Liberal Prime Ministers, he was probably the most congenial to Hicks.[20] It cannot have been altogether a surprise when he received an invitation to accept nomination for the vacant deanery.

But there was a difficulty. Campbell-Bannerman had evidently been lobbied by 'Protestant' elements in Manchester, as is shown by his remark about the quarrel which ran high there. It was probably not clear to the Prime Minister exactly who were the parties to the quarrel. Its most public manifestations had been in meetings of the vestry which were notorious for their disorder, but vestries were open to all parishioners, including those who never worshipped in the church. Dean Maclure was not an extremist. Indeed he was once described as being 'deeply imbued with Low Church ideals', though the same author also said he had a 'love of aesthetics and fancy ritual'.[21] Campbell-Bannerman's suspicions may not have been discouraged by the bishop; for in 1903 Dr Moorhouse had been succeeded by E. A. Knox, the suffragan bishop of Coventry, who was certainly no friend of Anglo-catholicism. The standard of ritual in the cathedral had in the past been proposed as a yardstick for acceptability by Bishop Fraser, when he was in the throes

---

[19] On all this see John Wilson, *C.B.: a Life of Sir Henry Campbell-Bannerman* (1973), ch. 37: 'Bishops and Peerages', esp. 573–6 quoting British Library, Campbell-Bannerman papers.

[20] British Library, Campbell-Bannerman papers 41235/fo. 160, 21 Dec. 1899.

[21] Andrew Boutflower, *Personal Reminiscences of Manchester Cathedral*, 2nd edn. (Manchester n.d.), 70, 73.

of the Miles Platting controversy, and there had probably been little development since then. The niceties of the situation would not have been obvious to the Prime Minister; but he was persuaded to attach to his offer of the deanery the condition that no further ritual development should take place. It may indeed have been represented to him that, though Edward Hicks was a man of learning, an excellent pastor, and thoroughly reliable politically, he was rather too friendly to the ritualists. Had he not recently officiated at a Three Hours' Service in the church of St John the Evangelist, Miles Platting, the storm-centre of controversy over the Public Worship Regulation Act?[22]

There was another question, too. Was the dean paid too much? It was over half a century since this value-for-money question had led to the passage of the Manchester Parish Divisions Act, which ensured that the residentiary canons should be overworked. But the dean had been unaffected, and even the equalization of the canons' stipends in Dean Maclure's time had not touched his own stipend. Someone must have suggested to the Prime Minister that the vacancy in the deanery provided an opportunity to divert some of the dean's stipend to other purposes. The offer to Hicks, therefore, was conditional, not only on an undertaking to restrain 'the unduly ritualistic ceremonial favoured by the late Dean', but also on his agreement that the sum of £1,100 a year, derived from the lease of the old deanery in Deansgate, should be withdrawn from the dean's income and placed at the disposal of the Ecclesiastical Commissioners for other purposes, under a scheme to be formed at a future date. In compensation, the dean would be given free residence in a modern deanery.[23] Hicks replied to the Prime Minister:

I have worshipped daily, and often several times a day, in our Cathedral as a Residentiary Canon for the last fourteen years, and I have grown to love its simple and dignified services. I am sure that nothing but strife and confusion could come from any attempt, such as you suggest, to alter their character. I am a tolerant but real Churchman, in close touch with Churchmen of all complexions and views in Lancashire, and accustomed to work in hearty co-operation with all sorts of Nonconformists; and I feel strongly that it is neither wise nor reverent to make arbitrary

[22] Notes by the Revd E. Glanfield, Bodleian Library MS. Top Oxon e.554, 21 April 1905.
[23] For this, and other details of the correspondence, see Fowler, 122 ff.

changes in the long-established usages of a Church, especially of a Church
so much beloved, and so well frequented, as this Cathedral. Its ritual
(which is moderate) has remained practically unaltered for many years,
certainly for half a century. And some of the old customs—like the turning to the East at all the Glorias—go back for centuries. The late Dean
was no innovator, and I should be sorry to see innovations made in either
direction—upward or downward. Apart from the question of my nomination, but as an average Lancashire Churchman, I would beg of you
to avoid needless friction and collision in such a delicate matter as this.
I am confident that you have been seriously misinformed as to the facts
of the case. I am not aware of any ritual usage connected with the Cathedral
which could be counted illegal.

In this letter Hicks stands upon the principle that, within the bounds
of legality, it must be for the clergy and congregation to make a
decision. It is significant for its implicit, as well as its explicit, content. It reveals Hicks's stance as a liberal churchman. In worship
he valued dignity and order within limits which the church had
accepted.[24] His doctrinal beliefs did not restrain his co-operation
for social ends with those who chose to stand outside his church.
That was how he could be a 'tolerant but real' churchman. There
were, clearly, limits to his tolerance. He did not approve deliberate breaking of the bounds of legality in public worship; nor did
he easily co-operate with those who believed that the Christian
faith had no implications for social reform.

His reply to the Prime Minister also rejected the second proposed condition of acceptance, the diversion of part of the stipend
to other unspecified objects:

You will find the Churchmen, and especially the laymen of Manchester,
very jealous of any diversion of funds, without good reason, and without a definite plan which meets with their approval . . . If such a thing
is to be done at all, a definite scheme for the employment of the money
should be prepared, and should be approved by the chief laymen of the
city, and (so it seems to me) an Act should be passed during the life of
the next dean, to take effect upon the vacancy.

Again, the answer relies upon the principle of local accountability;
the local people, and especially the lay people, should be consulted
and a formal public decision taken, not some private agreement
between the dean and the Commissioners.

---

[24] See Nockles, *Oxford Movement in Context*, 211 and note, for 'conservative practice'
at collegiate churches.

It is surprising that Campbell-Bannerman proposed such high-handed interference, since he was in favour of disestablishment, which must involve the handing over of decisions about appointments from the government to the church itself. But he had opposed the 1874 Scottish Church Patronage Bill which replaced private patronage with election by parishes and confirmation by presbyteries, though that would be entirely suitable for a disestablished church. He thought it would bolster up the Church of Scotland at the cost of the other presbyterian bodies, which he wanted to see reunited as a strong counterweight to the established church. He later claimed that he had shown a 'more catholic (with a small c) spirit' in having appointed 'at Truro a broad and liberal Bishop, at Newcastle an avowed Evangelical, at Manchester a Low Church Dean, at Ely an Academical Scholarly Right Centre Dean, each suited to his locality'.[25] But his appointments were criticized in some quarters for lowering the standard of leadership in the church. Percy Dearmer wrote a bitterly critical article in the *Commonwealth* in October 1907 following the appointment of N. D. Straton to Newcastle. He claimed to be voicing the opinion of many churchmen, that a serious situation had arisen. His indictment was chiefly concerned with the failure to appoint 'strong and progressive men'. 'Oddly enough, under the last two Conservative Governments it was rare for any one to be made a bishop who was not keen about social reform; and oddly enough under the present Liberal Government it is rare for anyone to be appointed to anything whatever who *is* keen.'

The problem for the Prime Minister was to find leading churchmen who looked for social change and were not tainted, in his eyes, with a tendency to favour ritualism. Hicks was as near to the Anglo-catholic wing as he was prepared to go. Campbell-Bannerman was nettled by Hicks's refusal and his polite but definite rebuke for having overstepped the reasonable limits of royal patronage, and so he offered the deanery to a more compliant man. This was Bishop Welldon, who had been a canon of Westminster for four years after returning from India, where he had been an energetic but not wholly effective Bishop of Calcutta. Judged by some of Campbell-Bannerman's criteria, in his letter to Lord

[25] British Library Campbell-Bannerman papers CB 41242 fo. 254, quoted in Wilson, *Campbell-Bannerman*, 576. These were C. W. Stubbs, N. D. Straton, J. E. C. Welldon, and A. F. Kirkpatrick.

Althorp, Welldon seemed suitable. He was certainly a non-ritualist, and a man of energy. But his experience as headmaster success-ively of Dulwich and Harrow and as a bishop in India hardly pre-pared him for work among the poor of Manchester. He would readily have agreed to restrain ritual; and he was not troubled by the proposed reduction of stipend, since he had private financial resources. For Hicks, it had been a final argument against accept-ance of the Prime Minister's offer that he could not face greater expenses without any increase in income.

Hicks accepted the arrival of the new dean with his customary courtesy. They found various common interests, for Welldon had been a classical scholar of distinction, and shared Hicks's dislike of doctrinal rigidity, his social concern, and his hopes of international reconciliation. He had once preached a sermon at Oxford in which he had defended 'conscientious objection' to some current dog-mas concerning eternal punishment, the inspiration of the scrip-tures, and the doctrine of the church—much to the disgust of some of the clergy in the congregation.[26] He supported the aims of the CSU, and took a leading part in the Manchester District Peace and Arbitration Committee, which fostered a rather pretentious idea of a 'Great Conference representing the various religions of the world', and was the chairman of a committee concerned with drafting an 'Appeal of the Churches for Peace' in 1907.[27] But in spite of all this, there was something immature about him. Hensley Henson, who knew him well at Durham after 1920, thought he had never really grown up and that beneath his blustering man-ner there was a sentimental sensitiveness. Henson did not trust him (but whom did he trust?) and, in one of his most biting phrases, said that 'he would never fail to sacrifice a friend to a cheer'. It is only relevant to mention this because Welldon was the source of two tales about Hicks which friendship might have censored before they were spoken, one certainly untrue and the other an improbable old chestnut about teetotallers and sherry trifle.[28] Nevertheless Hicks was always complimentary about the man who had brushed aside his objections to Campbell-Bannerman's ill-judged proposals, and in due course he invited Welldon to preach at his own consecration in Westminster Abbey. His stand upon

---

[26] Henson, *Retrospect*, 23–4.   [27] Lambeth Palace, Davidson Papers, 336.
[28] Kathleen Nugent Hicks, *From Rock to Tower* (1947), 70, 145.

principle earned him the admiration of greater men.[29] It also seemed to have shut him out, at the age of sixty-two, from further chances of preferment.

There had also been a change of bishop. James Moorhouse was an intellectual, with broad theological views, who devoted himself to the visitation of his diocese and gave strong support to its many church schools. When he retired in 1903, he was succeeded by E. A. Knox. The new bishop matched some of Campbell-Bannerman's preferences very well. He was a leading evangelical, and he had shown a capacity for hard work in the Birmingham diocese. But he was much more like a Tory gentleman than his predecessor, and in due course became, with Bishop Chavasse of Liverpool, one of the acknowledged leaders of Conservative churchmanship in Lancashire. He was also more rigid in matters of ritual than his predecessors. Peter Green said he had a domineering personality, and banned parishes or withdrew licences of curates for moderate teaching and practice. The Christian Socialist priest, P. E. T. Widdrington, during a short ministry in Manchester diocese, also found Knox unhelpful.[30] But he was a scholar of some distinction, and Hicks did not let strong political and doctrinal differences between them prevent the development of friendship. Eventually, after Hicks left Manchester, their families were linked by marriage.

Hicks continued with his manifold activities in Salford, in the cathedral, and more widely through a variety of organizations, with little expectation that the Prime Minister or one of his successors would call him to any other field of work. He had made his home in Manchester. Two of his sons went to the Grammar School and then into the world of commerce. His elder daughter married a local clergyman, and he welcomed his first grandchild with all the interest in childhood which came so naturally to him.[31] His long ministry in a centre of manufacture, of civic life, and of political and intellectual vigour, made him the great churchman he became.

---

[29] See e.g. E. S. Talbot to Abp. Davidson, Lambeth Palace, Davidson Papers 164: Official Letters, fo. 213.

[30] H. E. Sheen, *Canon Peter Green: A Biography of a Great Parish Priest* (1965), 39; Maurice B. Reckitt, *P. E. T. Widdrington: A Study in Vocation and Versatility* (1961), 39.

[31] Mary Hicks married the Revd H. D. Lockett, Vicar of St Luke's, Weaste 1907–12, Rector of Holy Innocents, Fallowfield 1912–30. Before 1907 he was Lecturer on (*sic*) the History of Doctrine in the Faculty of Theology, Manchester University, and Principal of Ordsall Hall, a short-lived clergy training school.

His episcopate was in some sense a postscript. Neither the episcopal hierarchy nor the self-concern of the capital city into which
he was inevitably drawn chimed in with his developed interests.
He always felt a visitor in London (though still at home in the
British Museum) and a stranger at Lambeth Palace. He tried to
take Lincolnshire to his heart, but he thought it never trusted him.
He was incapable of being bored or uninterested in new experiences and gave himself unselfishly to the new diocesan responsibilities. But his claim to honoured memory rests upon his life in
Salford and Manchester, and it is at that period, the period of the
renewal of political Liberalism, that his personal history ties in with
its wider context. For a short time a scattered group of churchmen drew together and shared some of their hopes for a renewal
of society through their support of the Liberal Party. His role in
this episode requires a special consideration of his social, political,
and journalistic work. And since his attitudes were remarkably
consistent from the Salford period to the end of his life, it will be
convenient to make use of material which, properly speaking,
belongs to his episcopate.

7

Fighting the Trade

Through all the years preceding Hicks's appointment to St Philip's, Salford, we can trace his increasing concern with social and national affairs. He can stand as a good example of those Christians for whom the devotional and sacramental life of the church, so far from preoccupying their energies, acts rather as a motive for all they do outside the church. Just as no balanced church history can be written without its secular setting, because in due perspective that may be more significant than the details of its internal debates or party rivalries; so the life of a socially aware churchman cannot be told without reference to the particular social or national issues which evoked his commitment. Ecclesiastical biography can sometimes imply, by omission or a lack of balance, that the institutional church was the all-absorbing interest of its ministers. That has seldom been less true than in the case of Edward Hicks. He had developed, apparently without much inward debate, into a moderate and liberal High-Churchman, but it would be misleading to say that he gave himself wholeheartedly to his church work, for there was room in his heart for much else.

The full extent of his abounding energy and his wide human sympathies can be indicated by a consideration of the range of organizations, outside the institutional church, in which he played a part. These included the United Kingdom Alliance and other temperance organizations, the Christian Social Union, the Manchester Transvaal Committee, the Liberal Party, the Classical Association and the John Rylands Library, and among publishing enterprises the *Manchester Guardian* and some minor journals such as the *Optimist*. These extraneous activities were most fully developed during his Manchester period. In the last phase of his life, his Lincoln episcopate, many of them were maintained, but at a lower level of intensity. It is convenient to begin with his earliest involvement with a large organization: the United Kingdom Alliance. That dated back, as has been seen, to his Fenny Compton days, and to the early years of his marriage. His conversion to the temperance cause was due, he said, to his friendship with Prebendary Grier, which he maintained after he had moved to Manchester; but it is probable that his wife's influence was also important. He began to range outside his parish in Warwickshire as a speaker for the UKA, and from Manchester he was given a wide constituency in which to exercise his influence. Combining his support for temperance with his enjoyment of the company of children, he became a leading figure in the Lancashire and Cheshire Band of Hope Union. It was unfortunate that his temperance work was sometimes all that was remembered about him, not only because those who had little sympathy with teetotalism were tempted to attribute to him what they thought they knew about all kinds of odd exponents of that practice, but also because a closer acquaintance with his other interests would have shown that his attitude to the 'drink question' was part of a wider critique of capitalist exploitation of working people.

It is important to hear what he himself actually had to say about temperance, for a better understanding of his character, and not as a contribution to the history of the temperance movement. In 1912 he went back from Lincoln to Manchester to deliver one of the series of lectures which had been founded to commemorate two of the leading lights of the temperance movement, J. H. Raper and F. R. Lees. Its title was 'The Church and the Liquor Traffic'. He began with a picture of slum life which was far from being merely condemnatory. 'Though in slumdom there is no hope, and dirt, disease and hunger abound, yet there is much excitement and good fellowship, and life has its humours and its mirth . . . Nobody seems to remain in these slummy streets except the failures, and these failures are almost always due somehow to drink.' The social situation in the slums, he believed, was dominated by the drink trade. And who owned the pubs? 'City councillors, magistrates, breweries held in shares by titled shareholders and people of either sex of the most honourable traditions.' That was the ground of his campaigning opposition. The 'trade' was an organized exploitation of working people. Shareholders of breweries were guilty of unethical investment. Few had any idea of the conditions under which the poor lived in the slums, and took their dividends without scruple. The slow progress of the temperance cause was due to the enormous profitability of drink. Supply created demand, not vice versa.

The chief problem for the church was that temperance had become a party issue. It was impossible to be adopted as a Conservative or Unionist candidate without the drink trade's permission. Churchmen might set out to vote against socialism or revolution or secularism or disendowment but in doing so they effectively voted for the liquor trade. But the reciprocal influences of drink and politics could have the opposite effect. Hicks declared that he had been kept faithful to the cause of progress by his commitment to temperance reform. This had even led to his voting for those who supported disestablishment because they supported temperance. That left him undismayed. The church was to serve and save others, not herself. But the church had been helpful to the cause only through some of its members, not as a body. The government's Licensing Bill of 1908 had shown up the church's divided witness. 'The Trade' had threatened the withdrawal of gifts and subscriptions, and the Representative House of Laymen 'with its ingrained Toryism' had condemned the Bill. Yet it was encouraging that no bishop had voted against it in the Lords, and two, Chavasse and Gore, had voted in its favour.

This is a rather defensive presentation before a predominantly nonconformist audience, and may reflect the discouragement which Hicks felt when he had been brought into closer touch with the corporate confusions of the church through his experience of Bishops' Meetings and central church bodies. Seventeen years earlier, in November 1895, he had read a paper to a Temperance Conference in Manchester on 'The Duty of the Church in relation to the Temperance Movement' in which he had declared that it was the plain duty of the church to give a lead. The church's handicap, however, was that its members commonly belonged to the highest and the lowest in the social scale, and these were least inclined to temperance. The movement was least effective in clubland and slumland, among 'the half employed rich and the half employed poor'. Even earlier, just before he left Hulme Hall in 1892, he had written to Gladstone, trying to meet his criticism of the attitude of the church and the clergy towards the Liberal Party in recent elections and of their alliance with the liquor traders. 'A very considerable number of the Clergy are in favour of Direct Veto, but were deterred from voting on our side by fear of Home Rule & of Disestablishment. Apart from these, and even apart from Home Rule alone, large numbers of Churchmen, *and especially clergymen,* are ready and anxious for Direct Veto and NO *compensation.*' To back up his claim he enclosed a Declaration 'which three of us (a Liberal, a Tory, and a Unionist) issued' before the elections, and which had been signed by 150 clergymen, including Dean Kitchin, Canon Henry Scott Holland, the Revd Hudson Shaw, and many others. He then proceeded, with great gusto, to dramatize the crisis.

The Trade is organizing its defence in the most thorough manner: the whole country is divided into Districts, with agents and lecturers, etc. The walls are covered with its literature, able pens are engaged, & every bar is [a] centre of agitation: and all in bitter opposition to *the Liberal party* . . . On the lowest grounds of Political expediency, as well as the highest ground of national righteousness, *time presses* . . . There is an enormous moral enthusiasm in the nation which has never been stirred since the Bulgarian atrocities . . .[1]

This was Hicks in his most ebullient and optimistic mood. Gladstone was hardly in a receptive frame of mind, we may suppose, having recently seen his electoral expectations wither, and on top of everything else having to face the threat of the loss of his eyesight. He took no steps to give the reformers what they wanted.

It is important to emphasize the essentially social case which Hicks was making. He saw the temperance movement as one which had originated among working people and was a defence against their degradation. He had first met it in Fenny Compton as an organization of labouring men. He upheld its work in the slums of Salford, and he was glad to meet working-class temperance groups when he moved to the diocese of Lincoln. He also became involved with many other temperance organizations, some national and others regional. In Salford itself he was a moving spirit in the Salford Anti-Footing League. He was a regular visitor of Salford Hospital, and had been deeply disturbed by one particular incident there, when three teenage girls were brought in dead drunk, as a consequence of the local custom of 'footing'. This was a widespread practice in mills and factories, and involved the celebration of all kinds of events, from national holidays to birthdays and weddings, with compulsory contributions from all the workers towards the provision of drink. The girls' club in St Philip's parish

---

[1] British Library, Gladstone correspondence, 46,053 fo. 222, letter from Hulme Hall dated 21 July 1892.

became the centre of the League, which joined other groups in bringing the practice to an end. But it was not only in Salford and Manchester that Hicks worked for temperance. He travelled to many other Lancashire towns in support of the UKA and other organizations. In doing so, he inevitably faced criticism from those who disliked his advocacy of teetotalism.

There were, and still are, two commonly expressed criticisms of it which would have left him entirely unmoved. The first was an accusation of 'heresy', though the particular heresy involved varied from writer to writer. His former curate, Conrad Noel, declared that teetotalism was a 'Moslem' heresy. Hensley Henson declared that it was 'Manichaean'.[2] Whatever the truth about other temperance advocates, Hicks never argued a doctrinal case against alcohol. His whole attitude to creation and human culture was the very opposite of Manichaean. In his Lees and Raper lecture he certainly mentioned both Hindus and Muslims, together with the Society of Friends, but only to indicate that millions of people could live good lives without resort to alcohol. Moreover the brandishing of the charge of heresy, which was one of the more unpleasant marks of the second stage of the Anglo-catholic revival, was itself something which Hicks did his best to discountenance. That put him, later in his life, in a minority among the bishops. It was no sudden development; he had long been convinced that truth was to be defended by argument, not by anathemas. In rational discussion it would have been apparent that he, at any rate, was not guilty of Manichaeism, let alone adherence to the faith of Muslims.

The other criticism which still has currency is that the temperance movement was out of touch with the realities of working-class life.[3] No doubt many of the patrons of the various temperance societies saw those realities only through a social telescope. But it is hard to believe that men like Hicks or his successor Peter Green

---

[2] Conrad Noel, *Socialism in Church History*, which Hicks reviewed in the *MG* 10 March 1910; *Letters of Herbert Hensley Henson* (1924), ed. E. F. Braley (1950), 35: 'the policy of Manichaean intolerance'. Bishop Christopher Wordsworth had even addressed a pastoral letter to the Diocese of Lincoln against teetotalism in 1873, and used the argument that it was a Manichaean heresy. Noel was very free with imprecise charges of heresy. He also aimed them at avarice and extreme communism. See Wagner, *Church of England*, 280, quoting the *Church Socialist* 4 June 1914.

[3] e.g. Brian Harrison, *Drink and the Victorians: The Temperance Question in England 1815–1872* (1971), 183: but here the object of criticism is the *Church of England Temperance Magazine* in the 1860s. Hicks worked along with the CETS, particularly in Lincoln, where he was *ex officio* diocesan president, but the UKA and the Band of Hope were his preferred societies.

were out of touch. The realities of working-class life were multi-farious. As Hicks said, there was excitement and good fellowship, and humour and mirth in the slums; but there were also failures, not to say brutalities, and those failures and brutalities were often due somehow to drink. And drink was readily available, because it made profits for respectable people who were indeed out of touch with the effects of their profit-making. In 1905 Hicks wrote a long letter to the *Manchester Guardian* reviewing a report on child health in slum areas of Salford, such as Greengate. He supported public expenditure to improve the environment, but said it was hopeless to dream of reclaiming the worst homes by spending millions on drains or parks or baths and washhouses. 'You will not prevent their existence by converting Greengate into a garden city.' The worst families would just move elsewhere. Two things were needed. The first was education by public authorities and the church to raise the tone of public opinion about such things as diet, cleanliness, and regular patterns of life. The second was control of the drink trade. He quoted evidence that the great majority of undernour-ished children came from homes where the parents were drunken and dissolute. Local option would enable the local community to control a particular threat to its well-being. It was part of the devel-opment of community self-government.

One further criticism of the movement was, and is, freely used: that its supporters were single-issue extremists, who believed that their chosen remedy would usher in utopia.[4] There certainly were those who made extravagant claims for the benefits of prohibi-tion; for example, that it would solve the problem of unemploy-ment by releasing vast amounts of capital currently invested in the drink trade, but hypothetically available after prohibition for pro-moting other, more healthy types of production, and therefore employment.[5] But neither Hicks nor the leading men with whom he associated in the UKA were in any real sense single-issue fad-dists. The two best known were Sir Wilfrid Lawson and Leif Jones. Lawson was a close friend, and Hicks retained a collection of their

[4] Hamer, *Electoral Pressure*, 3: 'The mental world of someone who believed passionately that the key to the transformation of society was the prohibition of liquor is very difficult for us now to enter.' That was surely not the mentality of Hicks or Gilbert Murray or T. H. Green—nor is Hamer saying that it was.

[5] See, for instance, the criticism and response by J. A. Hobson and James Whyte in the *Commonwealth* 1/6–9 (June–Aug. 1896).

correspondence to the end of his life. They had corresponded when Hicks was in Warwickshire and campaigned together in parliamentary elections after he moved to Manchester. On one occasion in 1897 they appeared together at an eve-of-the-poll meeting in Stretford organized by the UKA at which Tom Mann was also to speak. Mann was at the time an ardent prohibitionist, and Lawson was afraid his extreme views might cut across the UKA policy of Local Option.[6] Lawson was indeed the continual promoter of temperance legislation in parliament; but he was also a man of wide interests. He was once described by an admirer, with a touch of satire, as 'pro-Boer and anti-everything else; a little Englander, a Peace-at-any-Price Man, a would-be destroyer of the Established Church, the House of Lords, the Liquor-traffic, and several other institutions scarcely less robust.'[7] The description, and any close knowledge of his career, reveals a cluster of reforming interests, of which temperance was only one component; and it does not even mention his support for women's suffrage.

A better case for single-issue myopia might be made in relation to Leif Jones, who succeeded Lawson as President of the UKA and the champion of the UKA policy in parliament. But no Member of Parliament could avoid involvement in a variety of issues; and it is worth recalling that in 1908 he had initiated a parliamentary debate on a quite different question—the Belgian Congo. A third supporter of the UKA and its policies was Charles Roberts, MP for Lincoln from 1900 to 1918. Among his other distinctions he became Under-Secretary of State for India and Chairman of the National Health Insurance Committee set up in 1915. Perhaps, like Gilbert Murray, he was pushed into support of the UKA by their formidable mother-in-law, Lady Carlisle; but it is hardly possible to maintain that he was a single-issue fanatic. The truth is that there were some men within the temperance movement who saw it as one element in a progressive programme. Some of them believed that there were sinister forces at work which frustrated the development of society towards a more humane condition. The most obvious of these was represented by the money-making capitalist at home and abroad. The result of their activities was exploitation of working people, whether on the Rand or in sweated industries

---

[6] Letter in Honnold Library collection dated 25 February 1897.
[7] Russell, *Wilfrid Lawson*, 256, quoting an article in the *Pilot* 13 Oct. 1900.

in England or through promoting drink and gambling among those who had few other opportunities of leisure. If attack on the temperance front seemed most likely to succeed, it was justifiable to concentrate attention there.

It is clear that Hicks was one of those who regarded temperance reform as part of something much bigger. In 1899 he contributed to the *Contemporary Review* an article on 'The Present Phase of the Temperance Question', which consisted of an extended review of a book with the title *The Temperance Problem and Social Reform*.[8] He welcomed the composite title, in view of the recoil of many social reformers from the temperance movement. He admitted that earlier temperance advocates 'in their wonder at a great discovery and in the ardour of a new faith, pictured temperance as the one cure of all social evils, rather than as the indispensable condition of social reform'. They had also given the impression that they were the devotees of individualism, whereas in his own view the movement for Local Option was 'the first and early blossom of English collectivism'. Now, he argued, temperance reform was seen as only part of the great move towards social amelioration. Cobden had been right in claiming that it was the foundation of all social and political reform. The present phase was an important time of change within the movement itself.

One final criticism which should be noticed is that the temperance movement, at least in its later phases, was part of a panic reaction to evidence of physical deterioration, coinciding with interest in eugenics among the intelligentsia. Hicks has been specifically mentioned in this context.[9] It is true that he had rather different things to say after the outbreak of war in 1914. But his earlier statements cannot be fitted into either of the two 'histories' of the temperance movement which S. P. Mews has offered: (1) a series of moral reform crusades, or (2) a ferocious right-wing reaction in Edwardian times. 'The desire to deprive women and workers of drink was part of an attempt to put the clock back, to clean up Britain, to make England worth fighting for.' In almost every statement Hicks made, he attacked the capitalists, not the working

---

[8] July 1899, 51 ff.; by Joseph Rowntree and Arthur Sherwell.
[9] Stuart P. Mews, 'Urban Problems and Rural Solutions: Drink and Disestablishment in the First World War', in Derek Baker (ed.), *The Church and the Countryside*, papers read at the seventeenth summer meeting and the eighteenth winter meeting of the Ecclesiastical History Society (Oxford 1979), 475.

people. From the beginning of his work for the temperance cause he had claimed the spirit of the Good Samaritan, not the self-righteous Pharisee. If he saw his temperance work as a moral crusade, it was a crusade against exploitation on behalf of the exploited. He certainly never became right-wing; indeed if anything he moved politically further to the left.

If the case were made out against the degrading effects of drink, what action ought to be taken? Hicks's 1895 paper indicated various kinds of effort which were required: individual abstinence, vigilance in enforcing existing liquor laws, and further restriction of the drink traffic by legislation. It was part of the daily duty of the parish priest to promote personal abstinence, and Hicks believed that this could only be done effectively by those who had themselves renounced the use of alcohol. He did not refuse to work with others who believed they could promote the cause while themselves continuing to drink alcohol in moderation. He just thought they were mistaken. Again, there was no reason for reformers to disagree with each other over the enforcement of existing laws. But major differences within the temperance movement related to the choice of methods for further restrictions.

The United Kingdom Alliance had been founded in 1853, and early meetings were held in Manchester and Salford.[10] In coming to Manchester from Warwickshire, Hicks had moved from the periphery to the centre of the temperance movement. It was always stronger in some of the industrial towns in the provinces than in London, and from its Manchester headquarters it regarded the capital with some distrust. But from the very beginning it had aimed at parliamentary action. Its first title had been 'The National League for the Total and Legal Suppression of Intemperance'. It soon moved to adopt the policy with which it continued to be identified throughout Hicks's life. The substance of the policy remained the same, although it was described from time to time in different ways. Lawson had first introduced a 'Permissive Bill' on the principle of Local Option, and the same proposal was sometimes called 'Local Veto'.[11] It aimed to give local communities the right to vote

---

[10] On UKA history see M. H. C. Hayler, *Vision of a Century: The United Kingdom Alliance in Retrospect* (1953).

[11] The idea of Local Option had been put forward for the provision of religious education many years before by Lord Brougham. See Richard Brent, *Liberal Anglican Politics* (1987), 232.

on a proposal to prohibit licensed premises within their own areas, and to enforce prohibition if there were a two-thirds majority in favour of doing so. The cause was taken up by Sir William Harcourt and for a time won a fair measure of support in the Commons. It even became law in Scotland, where it was not finally repealed until the 1960s. The advocates of Local Option were encouraged by the action of temperance-minded landowners who had prohibited the sale of liquor on their land, as well as the examples of legislation in Australia, New Zealand, and the United States.[12]

The question posed by Hicks's advocacy of the UKA programme is important for understanding his particular kind of liberalism. Why did he support a policy which could be represented by its opponents as a denial of freedom, as a form of compulsion? The answer is that it depended upon several prior facts or assumptions. First, there was the existence of a social problem. Drinking caused widespread suffering to innocent people. Hardly anyone denied that. Then there was the obvious ineffectiveness of existing restraints, due to the vested interests of those who promoted the sale of alcohol. It was not just a matter of individual free choice; it was a social problem which could not be solved except by organizing equally powerful interests on the other side. Informed public opinion must have the opportunity to regulate the conditions of its own life. In a controversial matter it would be wrong to coerce a minority on a national scale. So let the decision rest with villages, towns, or city wards, whether or not licensed premises should continue within the neighbourhood of those who voted. ' "The public house", we are told, "is the working-man's wine-cellar"; then let him have the key and lock it if he pleases.'[13] The policy would be 'an automatic register of local opinion', and it was 'based upon reason, upon constitutional law, and upon political experience'.[14] Here is the same conviction that society ought to be changed, and could be changed, which had been an unquestioned

[12] The *Alliance News* carried a correspondence in 1897 about existing prohibition areas. These included the Trevelyans' estates in Northumberland and the properties of the Artizans' Labourers' and General Dwellings Co. Ltd as well as the parishes in the Brixworth Union. But surely Hicks must have been carried away by his own enthusiasm to claim that there were 'thousands of villages' where the sale of alcohol was prohibited. See the *Commonwealth* (Aug. 1903), 258–9.
[13] E. L. Hicks, Jubilee sermon of the Lancashire and Cheshire Band of Hope and Temperance Union, 21 November 1897.
[14] *Commonwealth* (Aug. 1903), 258–9.

assumption in Hicks's outlook from very early days. The movement for change could be enhanced by the mission of the church
and the mechanisms of social organization, from the local vestry
to parliament itself. And one thing more was assumed in the policy of Local Option: that on balance there were more good-hearted
men and women than evil, so that democracy would bring about
its own reformation. Politics, and even political agitation, must be
the concern of church people as much as any others. 'I hold it
is no disgrace for a Christian man to be a politician . . . For what
are politics? They are the employment of our vote for the promotion of national righteousness. And what is political agitation?
Sir Robert Peel shall tell us: "Agitation is the marshalling of the
conscience of a nation for the moulding of its laws." '[15]
Before pursuing the wider implications of this belief, we need
to consider two observations about Hicks's temperance convictions.
The first relates to the 'extremism' of the UKA policy which he
supported. It is true that the Alliance had its distant sights trained
on a land in which the drink trade would be outlawed. That did
not prevent its members, including Hicks, from supporting lesser
proposals if they seemed to be steps in the right direction. The
historian of the UKA in 1953 was happy to list, as achievements
of the temperance movement, a variety of changes which tended
to lessen the influence of the trade. These included the control
of habitual drunkards, and the prohibition of the sale of liquor to
children and of the use of licensed premises as election committee rooms or for district or parish meetings. The acceptance of
lesser objectives by Hicks is demonstrated by a letter which he
wrote to Campbell-Bannerman in 1899, urging him not to go back
on the definite position he had assumed in Manchester: 'Peel's
Report, plus Scotch and Welsh Veto—English Veto to wait awhile'.
He was aware that some temperance reformers would think he
and those who thought with him had betrayed the veto, but he
wanted to persuade Campbell-Bannerman that it was better to
achieve it outside England first of all, even if for the time being
the only gains in England itself were the comparatively uncontroversial provisions of Peel's Bill. The combination of two issues
in one bill would sustain the coalition of different temperance groups.
If Campbell-Bannerman abandoned Scotch and Welsh Veto

the combination of all Temperance organizations which is now taking place on the basis of Ld Peel's Report (as emphasized by your Manchester speech) would at once be shattered. The advanced Temperance *organizations*—certainly the Alliance—could not be reckoned upon to work for such a meagre scheme (of only licence-reform) at the General Election, though individuals might work and vote for it. And an enormous loss would be suffered by the Liberal Party both in help, in enthusiasm, and in moral sympathy.[16]

This reveals that by 1899 at least Hicks could take on the role of UKA spokesman and that he saw the need for the temperance movement to work the political machinery for its own purposes.

The second observation about his temperance convictions is that they were affected by his move to Lincoln in two ways. He now felt responsible for the whole range of temperance witness within the diocese; and he had to face, after a few years, the changes forced on the country by the outbreak of war. At first it seemed that the old campaigns could continue. Lincolnshire had a long-established temperance movement when Hicks came to the diocese. The 1830s had seen the beginnings of the teetotal campaign in Lindsey, and there had been a sudden expansion between 1837 and 1857, with thousands of pledges being signed by men and women. Work among children, too, was organized through Bands of Hope, although this development may indicate some decline in the effectiveness of the movement among adults. Temperance Halls had been built in a number of villages and towns, and there were, for a time, great annual gatherings at Thornton Abbey, attended by many thousands of supporters, with the encouragement of the Earl of Yarborough. In 1877 a Permissive Bill Association was formed in Lincoln, following a canvass of voters to obtain pledges not to vote for candidates who refused to support a Bill proposed by Sir Wilfrid Lawson.[17]

The attitudes of the churches varied during the earlier years of the century. Few Church of England clergymen were directly concerned with organizing the campaigns, though sermons were preached in a number of parish churches. One particular leader was the Revd John Mussendine Holt, Vicar of Fulstow from 1848

---

[16] British Library, Campbell-Bannerman papers 41235 fo. 160. Letter dated 21 Dec. 1899 from Hicks's rectory at Pendleton.

[17] See Rex C. Russell, *The Water-Drinkers in Lindsey: 1837–1860* (Barton Branch, WEA, 1987); Hamer, *Electoral Pressure*, 213.

to 1860, who was described as 'The Lincolnshire Father Mathew' after the celebrated Irish temperance priest. Holt attained some national standing when he was elected High Chief Ruler of the Female Rechabites in 1841. Wesleyan congregations and ministers were divided over teetotalism, though generally favourable to temperance. The strongest support for the Rechabite movement came from Primitive Methodists and Independents. During the episcopate of Bishop Christopher Wordsworth relations between the Church of England and nonconformity deteriorated, and the churchmanship of Bishop Edward King was regarded with suspicion by many nonconformists, however much they might find him attractive as a person. King had been a great encourager of diocesan organizations, and had presided over the diocesan branch of the Church of England Temperance Society. Hicks naturally succeeded him in that position. But the CETS was a very moderate society which catered for a variety of attitudes. It offered alternative pledges which might be taken by its members: either 'by God's help, to abstain from all intoxicating liquors, except at my midday and evening meals', or 'by God's help to abstain from all intoxicating liquors, except while a medical order is in force'.

Initially Hicks's preoccupation with temperance was uncongenial to many of his clergy, who were often happy to promote the Church of England Temperance Society, but mistrusted initiatives which required them to treat dissenters on equal terms. This suspicion was to some extent tempered as the new bishop became known, and he had begun to feel that he was making progress, when the war broke out. He certainly believed there was a great need of temperance work in the diocese. Lincolnshire was quoted as the sixth most drunken county in England; Boston and Grimsby were reckoned the fourteenth and fifteenth in the league of 156 English boroughs for drunkenness.[18] In 1910 there were a number of different temperance organizations at work, including the Lincolnshire Labourers' Temperance League, and Hicks did his best to draw them together into a United Temperance Association. Some of the clergy rallied to his support, though it was not unknown for him to find himself the only minister of the established church present at a temperance meeting.[19]

---

[18] *LDM* (1910), 25.
[19] *Diary*, 18 Apr. 1918. But it was probably significant that this meeting in Gainsborough was held in the Primitive Methodist chapel.

A new aspect of temperance work opened to him as diocesan bishop. He found himself exercising the role of father-in-God to alcoholic clergymen, of whom there were a number in the diocese. He was already aware that alcoholism was a problem of the 'respectable classes'. Several of his relatives had suffered from the addiction. Indeed it is remarkable how often it is mentioned in personal histories of the period. T. H. Green's support of temperance was no doubt stimulated in part by the alcoholism of his brother. The habits of university Common Rooms and the recommendations of doctors to their patients were probably contributory factors among the clergy, but so were the isolation and idleness of many Lincolnshire benefices, and the poverty of many of them, restricting travel and the development of wider interests. Whatever the predisposing causes, the problem of inebriate clergymen was serious enough to be discussed at Bishops' Meetings at Lambeth. A CETS report in October 1910 stated that there were several hundred cases of clergy being inhibited from taking duty, of which about half were due to intemperance, and some others were indirectly related to alcohol.[20] In addition to this new responsibility, Hicks continued his national work with the UKA, chiefly centred on Manchester, where a 'Hicks Lecture' had been founded in his honour, and he accepted invitations to address temperance meetings in different parts of the country. He was also concerned with the running of the Homes for Inebriates managed by the CETS.

This continuity, however, must not conceal the change both in the terms of the national debate and Hicks's own attitude. A key figure in these changes was David Lloyd George. The temperance reformers had seen their hopes disappointed by one Liberal leader after another. Neither Gladstone nor Campbell-Bannerman had lived up to their hopes, and Asquith, it seemed, was going to prove no better. Lloyd George had his own complicated reasons for taking up the temperance banner. Without denying that he had some inbred dislike of the use and abuse of alcohol, we can see that it was politically convenient to have an issue which he could make his own, and especially one which attached to him in personal loyalty a considerable block of voters. When he became responsible, as Minister for Munitions in wartime, for the efficiency of

[20] Lambeth Papers, Reports of Bishops' Committees, 25 Oct, 1910.

the armaments industry, he was able to combine his appeal to temperance voters with the far more potent appeal to patriotism. The country was ready for restrictions in time of war which it would have stigmatized as an invasion of liberty in time of peace. Hicks's personal knowledge of Lloyd George probably went back at least to 1890, when he addressed the UKA at a meeting in Manchester at the Free Trade Hall, and in a characteristic purple passage declared that the liquor trade 'reeked with human misery, vice and squalor, destitution, crime and death'.[21] Lloyd George had also taken the chair at the annual meeting of the UKA in 1907.

Hicks did not suffer from the snobbery which wrote off Lloyd George as a 'low fellow', nor did he regard his nonconformist origins with suspicion, as many churchmen did. The most significant influence, however, in forming his attitude to the Liberal leaders, and indeed to politics generally, was that of C. P. Scott, the editor of the *Manchester Guardian*. They had many interests in common, including temperance. Scott did not altogether agree with the very strong views of the paper's owner, John Edward Taylor, who had once written to him, asking 'Could you not find a clever fanatic and let him keep all the temperance and licensing matters alive?' Taylor was an advocate of Local Veto.[22] Scott did not push that policy, but under his editorship the paper did keep temperance matters alive. Hicks kept up his friendship with Scott after his move to Lincoln, and was very pleased with the line the paper was taking on temperance matters. In May 1915 he wrote to Scott:

May I thank you for the firm and honourable line the M.G. has taken right through these devious and dangerous proposals about the Drink? The Cabinet would have done wisely for itself & for the Country (& wider still) by supporting Lloyd George at first & throughout. He is the biggest and best man of them all. What a touchstone the 'Drink' question is! Asquith will not give up his liquor: this is the bottom of it. Then the Irish party! We always knew how it depended on the Whisky trade: now the cloven foot is exposed indeed.

I liked especially the article of yesterday (Th. 6th) on the Wastefulness, the miserable unthrift of the 'Trade' in its effects upon the general life of the people. This is the real point to lay stress upon.

As for the remedies, I pray you not to press for 'Disinterested Managements' in preference to 'Direct Popular Local Veto'. We do *not* want

[21] Peter Rowland, *Lloyd George* (1975), 80.
[22] Sept. 1890; see David Ayerst, *Guardian: Biography of a Newspaper* (1971), 222.

either to continue the sale of liquor needlessly or where the locality is willing to exclude it, or to place the *people* in the hands of superior persons who are philanthropic at 5 per cent.[23]

This letter tells us quite a lot about Hicks, though we should remember that it was a private communication to a familiar friend. His verdict on Asquith has been stigmatized as 'less than Liberal',[24] though perhaps that verdict lacks understanding. It was never part of Hicks's Liberalism to soft-pedal what he saw as moral issues, nor to withhold personal judgements in private (as his Lincoln diaries show in no uncertain manner). He was opposed to Asquith on other matters, such as women's suffrage, and found it hard to believe that temperance questions could be approached in an open-minded way by someone who was reputed not to be temperate in his personal habits. A more significant criticism is that he tended to see the drink trade at work in every move opposing progress.

The temperance cause had moved into a new phase with the outbreak of war and the increasing regimentation of national life. Once Hicks had reluctantly accepted the necessity of fighting the war against Germany, he too looked at temperance policy rather differently. New factors affected temperance reformers and new questions were posed. Were German atrocities drink-induced? Was Russia transforming its efficiency by prohibiting alcohol? Why did England lag behind France in introducing stringent regulation of alcoholic drink? Was it true, as Lloyd George had said, that there were three enemies—Germany, Austria, and drink? Was the war effort seriously hampered by drunkenness? Almost inevitably the idea of government interference with the freedom of the individual became more acceptable to serious-minded citizens. Indeed, those among them who were not serving under military discipline felt, perhaps unconsciously, that they could satisfy their consciences by allowing restrictions to be imposed upon themselves. Already in 1914 Hicks had been able to list government actions in Russia, France and England restricting the use of alcohol, and continued:

None of these facts are likely to be lost on temperance reformers. Social reformers of another type, who desire to see the State take stronger steps

---

[23] British Library, C. P. Scott papers, letter dated 7 May 1915.

[24] Michael Bentley, *The Liberal Mind 1914–1929* (Cambridge 1977), 196. An undergraduate visitor of the Asquith household was 'frankly amazed at Asquith's consumption of alcohol' (David Newsome, *On the Edge of Paradise: A. C. Benson, The Diarist* (1980), 326).

in the direction of collectivism, have been startled by the freedom with which the Government has dealt with economic difficulties. Paper currency has been extended, the banks have received all kinds of assistance, our railways have in a sense been taken over by the State, the supply of sugar and foodstuffs has been secured by large Government purchases, and the prices of commodities have been regulated by law. In a word, before we knew where we were we found ourselves living under conditions of State Socialism. And nobody complains: rather everybody praises the Government for its courage and skill in meeting all emergencies. It seems unlikely that we shall ever be willing to go back again to a situation in which grave social evils were allowed to thrive because we were too timid or too dull to employ State interference for their redress. We have had a taste of Socialism, and we like it.[25]

In the new situation Hicks had to review his attitude to the control of the liquor trade. He had consistently supported the UKA policy, which aimed to use the central authority of parliament to put democratic power into the hands of local communities. He justified that as an extension of local democracy. Although he was not given to using the terminology of T. H. Green and his followers, he might have defended it as promoting 'positive freedom'. The sale of liquor, Green argued, interfered with the development of the type of character which it was the goal of society to create.[26] Hicks would not have put it like that, but he certainly saw temperance reform as challenging the freedom of the drink trade to create moral degradation in the slums he knew. Local Option would provide the opportunity to create a healthy public opinion which could then take control of its own environment. That was different from arguing that reform should be imposed in order to create a desirable type of character. Local Option as a policy presupposed an optimistic view of human nature and assumed the probability, or even the inevitability, of social improvement. But now things were different.

The pressure for positive governmental action brought into new prominence various schemes of control for the liquor trade. One proposal was to extend the existing development of 'disinterested management'. A number of 'trust houses' had been set up, with the intention of satisfying the social purposes of public houses while

---

[25] 'The Church and the War', the *Political Quarterly* (Dec. 1914), reprinted in *Oxford Pamphlets 1914–1915*, 14–15.
[26] See e.g. Richter, *Politics of Conscience*, 258.

reducing the incentive to drink alcohol, by providing food and non-alcoholic drinks, and ending the connection between the income of the licensee and the quantity of beer sold. Hicks became involved in a public debate over one particular instance of this kind soon after he went to Lincoln. In his diary for 23 January 1911 he recorded that the secretary of the UKA, George B. Wilson, came to help him in a protest against the establishment of a Trust Public House in Lincoln. His position was made difficult by the fact that the proposal had been supported by H. J. Torr, one of the most prominent Liberal laymen in the diocese, and by the incumbent and curate of the parish concerned. Clearly, if he had to choose between a badly run public house with its attendant vices and a well-run house which put a brake on drinking habits, he could not hesitate in his choice. But he thought it mistaken to give licensed houses the respectability which would come from the backing of 'superior persons who are philanthropic at 5 per cent'.[27] Such public houses would create a vested interest among those who previously had no stake in the drink trade and make it more difficult to create the kind of public opinion without which Local Option would not achieve its object.

That was before the war, at a time when the hopes of temperance reformers were high. The type of control which came to the fore in wartime was public ownership, either by municipal corporations or by the state. Even the brewers were inclined to look with favour on some such scheme, because it would give them the best possible security against partial or total prohibition. It would 'establish the drink trade for ever'. Both types were open to the same criticism, of creating vested interests in the trade. The idea of state purchase, however, found a notable supporter in Lloyd George, and in April 1915 Hicks was invited to call on him at the Treasury, as one of the temperance leaders, to discuss possible legislation.

He wants to suppress all sales of spirits, & to buy up the Beer trade: this the Brewers themselves had suggested to him in their interview last week. I asked him if he thought he could carry such large measures through the House: he thought he could. 'Did I object, as a Temperance man,

---

[27] An advertisement in the *Commonwealth* in 1917 ran as follows: 'The People's Refreshment House Association Ltd, founded by the Bishop of Chester. Manages 140 Inns. Ask for Report. TAKE £1 SHARES. 5 per Cent. paid regularly since 1899.'

to such measures?' I said: 'These were emergency and War measures, not Temperance reforms. As such I did not venture to criticize them. As a Temp. Reformer my only question would be, How far do these measures help or hinder what I, as a Temp. Reformer, really want? I could not see that national purchase, as things are, could do other than facilitate the obtaining of Local Veto.' This was the sum and substance of our talk.[28]

The diary entry reflects the problem which the UKA had to face in wartime. In times of crisis all the hopes of reformers were pushed aside by the nation's need of survival. That was a complaint they had voiced during the Boer War. Now facing an even greater danger they tried to keep separate two related issues: the campaign against the drink trade and the campaign for national efficiency. In parliament Leif Jones, the President of the UKA, made speeches 'safeguarding the advanced temperance position while at the same time supporting those emergency measures which were designed to and likely to restrict this traffic'.[29] Lloyd George made no promises about a further step after nationalization; but neither did he suggest that it was the end of the road for temperance reform. Some reformers believed that national ownership would facilitate prohibition. For example, the leading Methodist reformer, Henry Carter, who was well known to Hicks, appealed to the example of Russia, where he argued that:

the vodka traffic was State-owned, and the Russian government had but to convince itself of the wisdom of prohibition and it was free to act. In Britain the case was reversed. The whole liquor business was in private not public hands; and the 'Trade' had built up an unrivalled defensive organization against restrictive legislation, and again and again had worsted reformers.[30]

The question of prohibition was emotive and confusing. Some of the UKA supporters argued, rather sophistically, that the general production and sale of liquor was 'prohibited'; it was only allowed under licence. They saw Local Option (or Veto) as a way of enabling communities of various sizes to prohibit the granting of licences, at least as one of the options open to them (municipal

---

[28] *Diary*, 12 Apr. 1915. It goes beyond reasonable interpretation to suppose that Hicks was 'mesmerized by Lloyd George' (Mews, 'Urban Problems', 471).
[29] Hayler, *Vision of a Century*, 107–8.
[30] E. C. Urwin, *Henry Carter, CBE* (1955), 40.

control might be another). But wartime regimentation and the arguments about industrial inefficiency and the submarine menace to food supplies inclined some surprising groups, such as the Shipbuilding Employers' Federation, to support the idea of prohibition for the duration of the war, and the time-limit was sometimes extended to include the period of demobilization. There was strong support for prohibition in Scotland, from all parties and all churches. Hicks himself advocated this procedure at a number of meetings towards the end of the war. He evidently believed that the national mood had changed, and that there was an opportunity to break the power of the drink trade for good and all. Events proved him wrong.

Our present generation, battered into acquiescence in the omnipresence of alcohol by the ceaseless advertising of what Hicks would have called 'the drink trade', may find it hard to reach a balanced judgement on his attitude. We need to bear in mind some important facts. First, he did not develop his concern in the study or the lecture room, but in the poverty of his rural parish and the slums of Salford. Then again, the churches in general gave a high priority to temperance. It was not just the fad of the few. He stood out, however, in two respects. He himself had adopted total abstinence as his personal rule. And his advocacy of this uncompromising stance brought him into close contact with organizations chiefly supported by nonconformists. That was held against him by many rigid churchmen. But few Christians of any kind would have questioned the need for a temperance movement. Finally, control of the drink trade was part of national policy. Even Conservative governments gave thought to the best methods of control. In the Liberal Party leading radicals constantly urged legislation to restrict drinking. Men of intellectual standing, such as Gilbert Murray and G. M. Trevelyan, were strong supporters of the temperance cause. Hicks belonged to that particular section of the Liberal Party which moved away from the individualism of the Manchester school and adopted a more interventionist programme for social reform; but the policy of Local Option enabled him to do so without entirely giving way to the temptation to plan reform from above after the fashion of those who favoured state socialism.

The temperance question illustrates a number of choices facing the church and individual Christians in applying their faith to a particular social issue. The 'drink' problem might be defined as a problem of individual self-control; or alternatively in more sociological terms as a culture encouraged by commercial interests. The general tradition of Christian thought through long centuries had emphasized individual salvation, with the implicate of individual responsibility for moral self-control. There was consequently a tendency among Christians to condemn particular kinds of moral evil and hope for their elimination without disturbing the social patterns which made them all but inevitable. The experience of poverty in the countryside and misery in the slums showed Hicks that individuals simply lacked the freedom to act responsibly in oppressive circumstances. But Christian morality demanded that responsibility should be displaced, not denied. He saw blame as falling on those who set up or operated the system. Yet they were often 'good' people, by ordinary standards of judgement. So the responsibility must fall upon the operation of impersonal forces. In a presidential address to the Lincoln Diocesan Conference in 1912, relating to a different issue, he said:

I have been taken severely to task for saying that the Church has to help Labour to protect its Sunday rest from the tremendous pressure of Capital. I believe that statement to be entirely true. By 'capital' I do not refer to particular business men, but to the impersonal, unseen, but overwhelming impulse, which requires money to be made and invested capital to earn its due increment.

The problem of drink, then, was not simply one of personal morality, though it certainly was that. It involved responsibility shared by a whole host of people all of whom had a vested interest in maintaining the trade. The first step towards a solution must be to increase awareness of this responsibility. After that, in Hicks's view, would come the exercise of democratic control.

Another issue turned on the choice of starting-point for thinking about the solution of social problems. There were two options which Christians might adopt. One was to begin with the teaching of the Bible; the other, to develop traditional Christian moral and social teaching. Most of Hicks's contemporaries, if they thought about temperance, would take the first option and extract advice about repentance and self-control from the text of scripture. Others, within the catholic tradition, were beginning to adapt pre-industrial moral teaching to new situations.[31] Neither of these approaches appealed to Hicks. He believed that the New Testament contained little that was directly applicable to contemporary life; nor could teaching developed within a medieval or post-Reformation framework be adapted to the commercial society which had emerged from the industrial revolution.[32]

If the problem of drink was considered simply in individual terms, and the starting-point was moral teaching about self-control, policy would concentrate on practicalities such as enforcement of restrictive laws, licence control, and the provision of rescue agencies. This was the general line of the CETS. But if the definition of the issue was sociological rather than individual, and if there were no suitable guidelines for mass society to be found in the Bible or in traditional social teaching, then the practical solution must arise from recognizing the actual stage of development of society and the sources of power within it and using them to promote the health and well-being of people generally. The stage of development reached in Great Britain at the time of Hicks's involvement in public life was marked by the emergence of large-scale urban society regulated by law, locally administered. The sources of power were located in a democratically elected parliament and subordinate local authorities. The solution, he believed, must be found through the increased awareness of responsibility among ordinary people, bringing pressure on parliament to authorize permissive local action in restraint of commercial interests which were damaging personal and family life. The response of many people to this kind of programme was to repeat the saying that 'you cannot make men moral by act of parliament' or to characterize restrictive legislation as 'grandmotherly'. To these objections Henry Scott Holland had replied that you cannot make men moral by any other method either, but you can make it easier for them to be moral;

---

[31] For a later Anglo-catholic attempt to find an 'autochthonous' theological base for social criticism, see Cyril E. Hudson and Maurice B. Reckitt, *The Church and the World, Being Materials for the Historical Study of Christian Sociology*, iii: *Church and Society in England from 1800* (1940).

[32] In his Introduction to Richard Baxter, *Chapters from a Christian Directory*, selected by Jeanette Tawney (1925) Gore wrote: 'Its particular injunctions are naturally determined by the economic environment of the period in which it was written . . . Its conceptions of the relations between employer and employed are patriarchal, and Weber's remark that Baxter comes singularly near identifying the interests of the former with those of God are not unjustified.'

and that a democracy meant 'every man his own grandmother'.[33] Hicks would have accepted those replies, perhaps more completely than Scott Holland himself, who never supported the proposal of Local Option.

It is important to recognize, however, what Hicks understood to be the system which produced the evil effects of alcoholism. He looked beyond the kind of detailed restraints which satisfied moderate reformers and which were largely embodied in the 1899 report of the Peel Commission. He wanted to bring the entire drink trade under the regulation of local government, without establishing a new vested interest by public or municipal ownership of the trade. He optimistically believed Local Option would lead in many cases to local prohibition. The system would be to that extent changed. What he did not look for was the transformation of the entire capitalist system. On this issue he stood, therefore, midway between Liberals like Scott Holland and the emergent Anglo-catholic socialists, who believed that the whole system must be changed. When he thought about other social issues he recognized the same immoral forces at work under different guises and hoped for similar democratic methods to oppose them; but he was never attracted by a socialist utopia.

[33] e.g. H. Scott Holland, *Our Neighbours: A Handbook for the C.S.U.* (1911), 133; 'our old debate about the Grandmother', etc.

8

Social Issues

The United Kingdom Alliance was not a church organization, but it posed a question to the church. What was its duty in relation to the question of temperance? Hicks had met the difficulty that the church was too closely associated with the Tories, and they too friendly with the brewers. But this was only a particular illustration of the problem of relating the church to movements of reform in society. At the time of the Reformation the church had been virtually an agency of the state, not only in its teaching function but even in the discipline of society. That had gradually ceased to be so, however much it might still seem to be the case to those who were hauled up before clerical justices, like the poor women of Ascott-under-Wychwood. The interaction of two forces had transformed the relation of church and state, not at the formal level which occupied so much attention during the nineteenth century, but as a matter of day-to-day practice. Those two forces were the drive to pluralism in society, marked by the gradual process of disestablishment to which Bishop Woodford referred in 1881, and the greatly accelerated rate of change in society produced by the industrial revolution. It had never been true that there was uniformity of belief or that the condition of society was static. But varieties of belief and unbelief increased to the point of diversity revealed by the Census of 1851, with the Church of England shown to be at most one of three major constituents of society, along with dissent and the mass of the indifferent. And the social changes required to sustain rapid industrialization were of a kind that had never been experienced before in British society and of so radical a nature that all previous Christian moral teaching about human relationships had to be recast. The result was that the established church progressively lost authority to advise and criticize in the field of social ethics; and its members became more and more divided in trying to recast its teaching for a changing society.

In that situation individual members of the church with an active social conscience had various options. One was to band together with other like-minded people, whether members of the church or not, to tackle particular abuses or advocate particular changes. That was the basis of the UKA. Another option was to band together with other like-minded members of the church to survey the scene and try to work out an agreed programme of necessary reforms. That was the basis of the CSU. A third option was to combine church membership with a specific objective, making the target of propaganda the church itself rather than society at large, and co-operating with other groups outside the church for secular object-ives. That was the basis of the Church League for Women's Suffrage. It was much more in accord with Hicks's nature and background to go for the first option, with the UKA. But the specific nature of its objectives was, for him, related to a wider criticism of com-mercial society, and so it is not surprising that in Salford and Man-chester he was drawn into the CSU. He later saw that his status as a diocesan bishop carried with it the possibility of giving official recognition to church organizations of the third type. He threw his energies into the support of all three types, though with vary-ing degrees of commitment.

Hicks had a 'crusading spirit',[1] and for him the UKA was a specially suitable organization. It was devoted to a moral campaign with a very specific object. It operated locally, but had a national organization, with headquarters in Manchester and an office in London set up to facilitate access to Parliament. Its aim was clearly defined as the achievement of national legislation which would empower local communities. Its basis was untheological, and its constituency therefore interdenominational. It even managed to appeal to a cross-section of the social classes, from working-class teetotallers to cabinet ministers and aristocrats, and although min-isters and clergy played an important part in its work, its real leaders were lay people. At almost every point it stood in marked contrast to the Christian Social Union, which was theologically based, dominated by Anglican clergy, diffuse in its interests, and therefore unable to unify its members into a forceful campaign-ing body.

---

[1] See letter by Samuel Proudfoot in the *Modern Churchman* (Feb. 1923), 695–8.

It would perhaps be too simplistic to say that the basis of the CSU was Henry Scott Holland; but that may be taken as a convenient symbol of a more complex reality. Scott Holland was a unique, attractive, forceful character who drew into his company a number of other notable personalities, such as Percy Dearmer, C. F. G. Masterman, Hastings Rashdall, C. L. Marson, and Conrad Noel, as well as lesser lights among the clergy such as T. C. Fry and John Wakeford, who were to feature awkwardly in Hicks's Lincoln experience. There were also significant lay people who became involved with the CSU, such as Lord Beauchamp, the young peer who had transferred his allegiance to the Liberals on the issue of Free Trade, and Gertrude Tuckwell, President of the Women's Trade Union League, whose father was the radical parson, W. Tuckwell. They did not all coincide in theological outlook, any more than they agreed on all points of practical policy, but it was Scott Holland, through his editorship of the *Commonwealth*, whose attitudes permeated the whole Union.

This may appear to underrate the influence of its first two Presidents, Bishop Westcott (from the foundation of the CSU in 1889 until his death in 1901) and Bishop Gore, who resigned the presidency at the end of 1911. Westcott's theology was a constant point of reference to the exponents of the Union's position; but it was his passionate concern rather than the details of his teaching which established his lasting influence. Describing his effect on his hearers, Scott Holland said:

The real and vital impression made came from the intensity of the spiritual passion, which forced its way out through that strangely knotted brow, and lit up those wonderful grey eyes, and shook that thin high voice into some ringing clang as of a trumpet. There was a famous address, at the founding of the Christian Social Union, delivered to us in Sion College, which none who were present can ever forget. Yet none of us can ever recall, in the least, what was said. No one knows. Only we know that we were lifted, kindled, transformed. We pledged ourselves; we committed ourselves; we were ready to die for the Cause; but if you asked us why, and for what, we could not tell you.[2]

It is also significant that Westcott sided with those who saw the role of the CSU as study rather than action. In 1898, in a letter

    [2] Arthur Westcott (ed.), *Life and Letters of Brooke Foss Westcott* (1903), ii. 16, quoting H. Scott Holland from the *Commonwealth*.

to his daughter, he wrote: 'I tried to set out the duties of members in a paper contained in *Christian Aspects of Life*. The central one is quiet study. It is worse than vain to attempt to "do" anything before you are master of the subject.'[3] No doubt it was wise to give priority to understanding a subject, provided that kind of study was explicitly directed towards decision and action. In politics, however, the notion of mastering a subject is less appropriate than in academic studies. Politics deals with issues which change their aspect almost from day to day, and impotence can only be avoided by fastening on some axiom or principle and working out, often under pressure, how to apply it to the changing situation.

Gore, the second President of the CSU, was slightly younger than Scott Holland and Hicks, and outlived them both and continued to be influential in the inter-war period and beyond. But he had many other interests beside the CSU and, like Westcott before him, appeared as keynote speaker at significant meetings rather than busying himself with its day-to-day maintenance. Nor did his relationship with the CSU, any more than with other organizations, involve firm and unambiguous direction. As a theologian he gained a liberal reputation with the publication of *Lux Mundi* in the year in which the CSU was founded; but there were clear limits to his liberalism, even in critical study of the Bible, and he was more at home in exercising authority in the church than in promoting democratic action in the political sphere.

It was therefore Scott Holland's sustained output of fresh and stimulating journalism which settled the tone of CSU and provided some theological underpinning. In his thought two inheritances coexisted: those of the Oxford Movement and those of the tradition which derived from F. D. Maurice. It is debatable how far they ever fused into a coherent theology. The Maurician tradition asserted that in Christ the world was redeemed and the church was called to witness to that fact. In the Tractarian tradition the church was the supreme spiritual reality and was called to conform the lives of its members to a pattern of discipline and devotion which might work in worldly society to effect its transformation, though it was in fact an end in itself. In relation to home politics, the 'church', in that tradition, meant without question the Church of England, to the exclusion of other religious

---

[3] Westcott, *Brooke Foss Westcott*, ii. 261.

bodies. The tension between the two traditions shows in the title and contents of the journal which Scott Holland edited. The *Commonwealth* speaks of the total society; the contents are concerned with political and social matters almost exclusively in relation to the members of the Church of England, as though the other denominational bodies, comprising perhaps half of the country's practising Christians, might reasonably be left to their own devices. When the Roman Catholic Church features at all noticeably it is regarded as part of the continental scene. Such references were interesting, but essentially peripheral to national affairs. The concern of the CSU was almost exclusively with Great Britain, indeed with England.

In one of the Christian Social Union Handbooks which Scott Holland wrote, with the title *Our Neighbours*, he made a brief reference to the wider Christian context, declaring that members of particular denominations would be anxious 'to bring to bear upon the problem of the duties which we owe to our Neighbour the full light of the Creed as that denomination understands it'. But he did not conceal the fact that in his view the members of the Church of England had 'a special contribution to make towards the interpretation of Social Life by the Name of Jesus Christ, in that our Church Creed starts from the conception of Fellowship'. The church exists first, and then members are admitted into its life by faith. This belief should bring with it 'an instinctive understanding of the corporate existence of the Civic Community'. Moreover the creed of the church, being sacramental, declared that the bodily and social life of Man was the seat of the mystery of the Incarnation. This 'applicable and effectual' creed ought to be the special and privileged contribution of the church's members. But it had been largely betrayed, and it was the purpose of the CSU, with its full membership open only to communicants, to compel fellow-churchmen to face the meaning of the principles which they professed.[4]

The controlling concept in Scott Holland's theology, then, was the idea of corporate unity which was focused in the sacraments of union, baptism and the eucharist. This (as he had learnt from the Mauricians) was a witness to the corporate unity of apparently 'secular' society, of the nation and, beyond that, of mankind. There-

[4] Holland, *Our Neighbours*, 54–9.

fore the Christian body must concern itself with social morality
no less than personal morality. Scott Holland referred every practical issue back to the doctrine of the Incarnation.[5] Concern for
social morality was, of course, no new thing; and might be based
upon a different kind of theology. Even J. R. Seeley, author of
Ecce Homo, who was no sacramentalist, had declared more than forty
years before, that the province of religion was 'much more national
and political, much less personal than is commonly supposed'.[6] But
Scott Holland had embraced democratic ideals whereas Seeley
had inclined to right-wing authoritarianism. He did not adopt the
eucharistic socialism of the Guild of St Matthew or the Church
Socialist League, and there was never any doubt that for him
doctrine came first and social or political policies followed. Specific policies were much less important to him than his theology.
The Christian Social Union had a theological centre and a socio-
political circumference. Hicks's distrust of theological dogmatism
and his commitment to political activism permitted him to support the CSU, but with less than complete approval.

It is suggestive to take a snapshot of the CSU at an important
moment in Edwardian political life, February 1906. The Liberal
government, which had come to office when the Conservative Prime
Minister, Balfour, took the calculated risk of resignation in the
previous December, had gone to the country and been returned
with a commanding majority. The issue of the *Commonwealth* for
that month contained a leader by Scott Holland, headed 'The Arrival
of Democracy'. That apparently prosaic title introduced a dithy-
rambic outburst which exceeded even his usual level of enthusiasm.

We are all, I suppose, dazed, and staggered. Such overwhelming moments
carry with them so much reproach. Why were we ever afraid? Why was
there so little faith? Why was hope so faint-hearted? And, then, there is
the trembling sense of inadequacy: of unreadiness: of doubt. Is there anything that humiliates, as the free gift of everything that you had ever
desired? Long ago, at some such moment of unlooked-for boons, a man
whose net shook in his strong hands with the rush of fish, could only
fall on his knees and cry, 'I am a sinful man.'

[5] See e.g. Paget, *Henry Scott Holland*, 286: 'The more you believe in the Incarnation,
the more you care about drains.'
[6] Quoted by Kitson Clark, *Churchmen*, 235, from R. T. Shannon, 'John Robert Seeley
and the Idea of a National Church', in R. Robson (ed.), *Ideas and Institutions of Victorian
England* (1967).

There were three contributions on the question, 'What I want to get by my Vote at this Election'. The Conservative view was briefly put (by Hugh Legge): try to stop the Liberals doing too much harm before the Unionists come back to 'maintain the dignity of our country and the unity of the Empire before the world, continue the worship of God as a national duty, and evolve by natural process into the Constitutional Party of Socialistic Imperialists of the future'. It was clearly the high-water mark of largely meaningless rhetoric about 'socialism' when it could be appropriated to serve the Conservative and imperialist cause.

The Liberal view was put by T. C. Fry. He wanted the government to deal with land, housing, and taxation. Next in importance was the question of the unemployed. 'The severance of the unemployable; the distinguishing of the merely ineffective, though not unwilling, from the wilfully idle; disciplinary dealing with the latter, and a statesmanlike revision of the Poor Law; the organisation of labour, of military service in the militia, of public works, with a view to seasonal depression.' He hoped, too, for a just settlement of the education question. But he had voted largely to stop Mr Chamberlain. The condition of the people was so supremely dependent on free imports that 'the risks of details in an Educational policy that I may not wholly like must be accepted'.

A Labour view was put by Conrad Noel, Hicks's one-time curate. He wanted a future of real socialism: 'the common ownership of land, mines, railways, etc., extinction of unearned incomes, transference of unearned capital from the individual to the national pocket'. But in the immediate future he wanted recognition by the state of the right to work, a minimum wage, free meals for school-children, a graduated income tax. He foresaw that there would ultimately be only two parties, the Socialist and the Plutocratic. The workers could not see any difference between the Tory capitalist and the Radical capitalist. There were some prophetic ideas here. Another contribution, by Constance Smith, stressed the need to remedy the evils of bad housing, sweated industries, unjust fines (by employers) and illegal overtime, and injurious conditions and poisonous materials in industry. In the movement towards International Labour Legislation the government should stop dragging its heels and play a decided part. This sample of CSU writing reveals something of the scatter of interests and variability of political stance to be found in its membership. Hicks shared many beliefs with leading members of the CSU, but he never spoke or wrote as though social policy could somehow be deduced from theological pre-suppositions, though he did believe that the power of ideas ruled life. A few years later, addressing the students at the theological college in Lincoln, he said: 'Be assured that in the long run it is *ideas* that conquer the world.'[7] But that was not the same as a developed doctrinal scheme. The basis of his social concern was something much simpler: his abhorrence of the degrading conditions in which men and women were expected to live and work. A simple love of other human beings was enough to make any sensitive man a social reformer.

In Manchester he was a leading member of the thriving local branch, but he did not confine his interest in the CSU to Manchester alone. He addressed the Macclesfield branch on methods of dealing with unemployment, and spoke to the Liverpool branch on temperance reform. He even went to London in 1897 to contribute an address on 'trusts, syndicates, and commercial rings' in a series of Lent addresses at St Edmund's, Lombard Street, in which the other speakers included some of the more radical members of the CSU such as James Adderley and Thomas Hancock. In Manchester he spoke, as might be expected, on temperance questions, but on other occasions introduced other subjects, such as the industrial history of England,[8] and the communistic experiments described in the early chapters of the Acts of the Apostles. He preached at services sponsored by the CSU in St Ann's Church, which was for a time the focal point of CSU activity in Manchester, and evidently attracted the attention of members of other denominations, for one of his sermons there inspired a leader in the *Primitive Methodist World* on Christian Socialism. In 1895 he was vice-chairman of the branch, with Bishop James Moorhouse as the chairman; and he succeeded to the chairmanship after the bishop's retirement. Hicks was in the chair when it was resolved to make an enquiry into commercial morality as well as to emphasize the religious side of the branch's work.[9]

Its programme covered much the same subjects as other branches, such as temperance, imperialism, poverty, wages, unemployment, the land question, education policy, economic socialism, Ruskin's

---

[7] *LDM* (July 1912).

[8] This address was avowedly based on H. de B. Gibbins, *The Industrial History of England* (1892).

[9] Details of the branch's activities were recorded from time to time in the regular issues of the *Commonwealth*.

Unto This Last, women's suffrage, and a subject which commanded a great deal of attention in the CSU, the effect of using leaded glazes in the manufacture of china and earthenware. The CSU branch never had a wide appeal among church members, but it had a vigorous and active membership, and at one stage promoted groups in different parts of the district.[10] It set up various sub-committees, which examined the Poor Law, the industrial use of white lead, piecers' wages, and municipal representation. Its members joined with the Anti-Sweating League in an inquiry into conditions of home-workers, and took a great part in a sweated industry exhibition in the Cooperative Hall. They investigated alleged sweating in the Bible-binding industry, about which they were naturally sensitive. The branch also published a list of shops supplying china and earthenware with leadless glaze. Their concern over unemployment led them to support the 'St James the Less Labour Yard'. The subcommittee on municipal representation persuaded the branch to take part in municipal elections. They vetted candidates, asking whether they supported a programme which they proposed, and gave their selective approval to some of them. This programme included the revision of by-laws so as to demand greater air space in housing, the acquisition of land by the local council both for housing and for public open spaces, and the extension of municipal trading. But they also protested against the increasing practice of introducing questions of a partisan political nature into municipal elections to the disadvantage of urgent matters of local importance such as housing reform, the control of street-trading, and fair wages for council employees. In general, the branch concentrated on local issues, or issues which could be tackled locally, rather than on parliamentary affairs; though in 1905 it did send a resolution to Balfour in support of the Unemployed Bill.

It is clear that Hicks played a leading role in the CSU in Manchester, and even episcopal duties at Lincoln did not put an end to his sympathetic support. In one of his early pastoral letters, commenting on the 1910 transport strike, he urged clergy and laity alike to make themselves acquainted with the aims and practice

---

[10] The CSU report for 1908 showed that Manchester had a membership of 188, which included 47 new members enrolled that year. That was roughly the high-water mark. In 1905 there had been 180 members. At that time the Oxford branch had over 1,000 members.

of the CSU.[11] The local branch in Lincoln was quite small, with only fifty-four members in 1905. The outbreak of war in 1914 threw general questions of social reform into the background. The arrival of T. C. Fry as dean had provided alternative leadership for the local branch and enabled Hicks to play a less important role in its management.

Before moving to Lincoln, he had used his column in the *Manchester Guardian* to draw the readers' attention to the CSU. He said that its leading spirits were more inclined to socialism than to radicalism, although many Liberals were members. Labour, he thought, for the majority of the CSU, would be represented more by Mr Keir Hardie than by Mr Will Crooks; that is to say, more by an exponent of political socialism than by a practical leader of working-class politics.[12] But his most interesting comment on the CSU was in his article on 16 December 1909, in which he wrote of the difficulty that hampered the Union: 'It is wholly unpolitical.' This seems a curious verdict, in the light of the evidence already presented that there were a number of political issues on which it campaigned. In Hicks's view 'political' covered only what was aimed at specific decisions, whether in national or local government. At the national level 'political' meant 'party-political'. It had become increasingly obvious that problems like bad housing, injurious industrial practices, and the evil effects of the drink trade, were national problems. To mitigate or even solve them at the local level was not enough. Possibly that would merely displace them elsewhere. In any case, local communities lacked power and authority to promote the necessary reforms without parliamentary backing. When the CSU set itself to oppose dangerous industrial practices, it soon learnt the necessity of legislation. Boycott by conscientious customers was valuable only as propaganda. What was needed was a system of factory inspection; and nothing but parliamentary legislation could set up and enforce the powers of an inspectorate. In parliament everything was subordinate to party advantage. In the strife of parties, the influence of a body, like the CSU, claiming members of all parties and of none, was minimal.

Local politics were not yet dominated by party allegiances, and there the only effective forms of action were through groups which espoused specific objectives, such as temperance or housing

---

[11] *LDM* (Sep. 1911). [12] *MG* 8 Dec. 1904.

improvement. It was not enough to study social problems and make general pronouncements on them. Practical actions must be resolved upon; parliamentary bills must be promoted. Hicks had not hesitated to play an active part in municipal affairs. He was for a time the chairman of the Manchester Citizens' Association. This association was specially concerned about the standards of housing for poorer people, and aimed to draw the attention of the City Council to cases where existing powers might be wisely used, and 'to appeal to Parliament for extension or modification of such powers when desirable'. In furtherance of a campaign against the influence of 'the trade' he had shared authorship of an 'Anti-Holt Manifesto' in which he had the support of J. H. Moulton in opposing the election of Alderman Holt, a prominent brewer, to the Lord Mayoralty of Manchester in 1907. The absurdly biased nature of local journalism at that time is shown by the description of the Citizens' Association in an evening paper, presumably because some of its members supported this campaign, as having been established 'for the purpose of hounding publicans and brewers out of public life'.[13]

The year 1910, in which Hicks left Salford for Lincoln, was a critical year in the existence of the CSU. There had been a growing swell of church opinion in favour of some kind of socialism, at least since the Church Congress of 1898, when social questions began to occupy a prominent place in the programme. Ten years later the Pan-Anglican Congress included a great meeting in the Albert Hall, London, on socialism, at which, according to Scott Holland, speaker after speaker declared himself a socialist.

Mr Keir Hardie, as he sat there softly smiling, must have gone away [*sic*] believing that there is nothing more to be done, so far as the speeches went. But his eye, as it reviewed the audience, will not have been deceived . . . The Church's heart is open: the winds blow over it: voices reach it: it has come under the sway of the forces, which are at work in the industrial arena. Is not this what CSU has always laboured to bring about?[14]

The Pan-Anglican Congress certainly heard many speeches in favour of socialism. But there were discordant voices. One of the preparatory booklets, on *Christianity and Socialism*, included a highly

---

[13] *Manchester Evening Chronicle* 16 Sep. 1907.
[14] *Commonwealth* 13/7 (July 1908), 208.

critical paper by Clement F. Rogers with the title 'Socialism, Abstract and Actual'. Two sections of the paper were headed 'Modern Popular Socialism UnChristian' and 'This Socialism to be Opposed because of the Harm it Does to the Poor'. The writer equated socialism with dole-giving administered by an omni-competent state—a common attitude among many Christians who had never listened to the kind of indictment of contemporary competitive society which Charles Gore and Henry Scott Holland and others had been pronouncing for many years. Within the next few months it became apparent that socialist opinions might be a disruptive force within the CSU. James Adderley wrote to the *Commonwealth* in February 1910 claiming that he had been compelled to leave the CSU because he had been removed from the executive and told that it was undesirable that any socialists should hold office in it. The Oxford branch, he said, had issued a leaflet 'of which the keynote was a sigh of relief that two socialists had been got rid of'.

There were other tensions, between the London branch and the Oxford branch, and between those who saw the function of the CSU as essentially that of study and those who wanted it to adopt a more active role. A special council meeting was called later in the year, and afterwards Scott Holland was able to declare that perfect peace reigned. Hicks's conciliatory nature had apparently aided the process of reconciliation. The bishops of Birmingham (Gore), Southwark (Talbot), and Liverpool (Chavasse), as President and Vice-Presidents, issued a statement on the relation of the Union to 'various political parties and propaganda', reaffirming the freedom of individuals 'to take action with any political party, or to join in any declaration of political or economic principles with those with whom they are in agreement. The Union remains entirely uncommitted by such action of its individual members.' Hicks considered that the work of the CSU, in promoting study of social problems within a Christian understanding of society, was to be encouraged; but the task of changing society was beyond it. It had too dispersed an aim, and it tried to keep together too motley a crew. The better alternative was to work through single-issue organizations; not because their supporters had only one thing in mind (that was the mistaken assumption of those who cried 'faddist!'), but because energies could be concentrated instead of being dissipated in a dozen different directions.

Reformers had in mind the triumphant example of the Anti-Corn-Law League, which had given the young Edward Hicks an early memory and an early hope. Its effectiveness had depended on its ability to unite a whole variety of people to achieve a clearly defined aim. The appeal of the UKA was that it defined its aim clearly enough, as parliamentary legislation to empower communities to exercise Local Option. But because of the multiplicity of temperance organizations, it could not gather into itself all temperance advocates, and its impact was consequently blunted. In that other campaign the landed interest had been defeated by a coalition of other interests. But temperance supporters had only a moral interest in victory, whereas the brewers and publicans stood to lose financially. But right up to the end of Hicks's life it did not seem hopeless to campaign for permissive legislation; for no government, whatever its complexion, denied the need for laws to restrict the sale and use of alcohol. The mood of patriotic discipline in wartime encouraged temperance reformers to think their goal was within reach. Hicks did not live to witness the reaction which followed the armistice. That killed the temperance cause, at least in the form it had taken for many decades. When the campaign against alcohol revived, it took new guises, concentrating on addictive alcoholism, drunken driving, or aggressive advertising of drink. We may be sure that, whatever sympathy Hicks would have felt for action on these issues, he would not have hesitated to declare that the evils which were exposed were only the new symptoms of the exploitative hold which the drink trade still exercised.

Another 'single-issue' movement which commanded Hicks's support was women's suffrage. It did appear from time to time among the causes which CSU members considered, and Scott Holland supported the extension of the franchise, though he seemed almost as concerned to criticize the methods of the militant suffragettes as to promote their cause. A number of outstanding women featured in the pages of the *Commonwealth*: people like Gertrude Tuckwell, Constance Smith, Mary Macarthur, and Louise Creighton, of whom it was ridiculous to think that they were unfit for the vote. Scott Holland did not hesitate to say that they were more competent and more interesting than most of the male speakers at Church Congresses. But women's suffrage did not occupy a central place in the interests of CSU members. The very fact that those competent women were finding much to do in the field of social reform without having access to parliament or even the ballot box possibly took the edge off their campaign for the vote.

That was not a line of thought congenial to Hicks. It is easy to see the predisposing influences in his life and ministry which led to his support for women's suffrage. Here he was not much influenced by Ruskin, whose view of the complementarity of the sexes could have been used as an argument against admitting women to political life.[15] When he was at Fenny Compton, the subject was already being favourably canvassed in the district, and one local paper, with journalistic simplification, declared in the year in which Hicks moved to Manchester that Warwickshire was 'in favour of women's suffrage'.[16] He valued the women who shared his parish work in Salford. His home life, and especially his relationship with his wife and his daughter Christina, reinforced his sense of partnership and equality with women. It must have been obvious to him, even earlier, that his mother was quite as politically minded as his father. His work with the UKA brought him into contact with a number of influential women, such as the Countess of Carlisle, Mrs Margaret Wintringham, Lady Henry Somerset, and Lady Barlow. Owens College was involved at an early stage in the development of higher education for women, and the majority of those who supported this development also supported women's franchise.[17] Manchester was an important focus of interest, a source of propaganda, and a centre of organization. A Manchester Woman Suffrage Committee had been formed as early as the 1860s. The Women's Social and Political Union was founded in Manchester in 1903, with Dr Richard Pankhurst among its influential members.[18] Dr Pankhurst was a friend of C. P. Scott, who was himself enthusiastic about women's suffrage.

Hicks's friendship with Scott reinforced his own support for 'the cause', which received favourable notices in the *Manchester Guardian*. And although some Liberals were afraid that women were by nature conservative, and therefore their admission to the electorate would tip the political balance on the wrong side, it is more

[15] Cf. Frederic Harrison, *John Ruskin* (1903), 112: 'In words of exquisite grace he sketches for the girl an education, and for the woman a career, which his Socialist admirers have found perilously akin to that of Auguste Comte.'

[16] *Leamington, Warwick and County Chronicle* 27 Feb. 1886.

[17] But not all. Mrs Humphry Ward was a notable exception.

[18] David Morgan, *Suffragists and Liberals* (1975), 8, 11.

likely that Hicks would have been influenced by another consideration: that women voters would give stronger support to temperance reform than men. Indeed a CSU leaflet (no. 41) claimed
that New Zealand, Western Australia, and South Australia had
enfranchised women as 'a measure of political expediency carried
out by men for other motives, e.g. in the interests of the Temperance Party'. Hicks did not use that argument, though Maude
Royden thought he was influenced by it.[19] In fact, the question
seemed hardly to deserve argumentation. There was no reason why
women should not be voters. As G. W. E. Russell once said, it
was absurd to look with more alarm on the political woman than
the drunken bricklayer. To exclude women from the vote was as
stupid as a proposal Hicks held up to ridicule in one of his 'Quartus'
articles, that 'women and reporters' should be excluded from a
series of meetings on social questions.[20]

Women's suffrage was not specifically a religious or Christian
issue. It was a question which turned on simple equity, if only
cultural stereotypes could be seen for what they were. It was therefore doubtful whether church people should form an independent
organization to campaign for the extension of the franchise. Hicks
had written: 'I know how a Christian or a moral man should view
such matters as the opium traffic or the regulation of vice in Indian
or South African cantonments, or the presence of liquor sellers on
watch committees, but I fail to see what is meant by a specifically
"Churchman's view".' The same might be said about women's
suffrage; it was not a church question. Not everyone agreed with
this attitude. When a great deputation, including members of
the National Union of Women's Suffrage Societies, waited on the
Prime Minister in 1906, the report in the *Commonwealth* noted
with regret that no church society was represented on the deputation. Then in 1908 some opponents of the vote for women, mostly
church people, formed a Committee for Opposing Female Suffrage. They included the Bishop of Peterborough (E. Carr Glyn),
Hilaire Belloc, G. K. Chesterton (still an Anglican and a Liberal),
Montague James, Rudyard Kipling, and Professor Charles Oman:
some weighty names, if not exactly leading figures in church
circles. It later dignified itself with the title of the National League
for Opposing Women's Suffrage and obtained Lord Curzon as its

[19] See Fowler, 218.   [20] *MG* 5 Oct. 1905.

President.[21] Church opinion became polarized, and in 1909 the Church League for Women's Suffrage (CLWS) was founded by the Revd Claude Hinscliff.[22]

The following year a fringe meeting was held in a church school-room during the Church Congress at Cambridge, under the chairmanship of A. S. Duncan Jones (later one of Hicks's examining chaplains at Lincoln). The CLWS had been refused a hearing at the Congress because it was considered 'political', though its official programme included a discussion of compulsory military service, which was quite as much a political question. The main speaker at the meeting was Maude Royden, and she and others put the CLWS in the public eye. Though never a large group, in national terms, it increased its membership to 5,000, including 500 clergy. Other religious groups were formed, and by 1913 it was possible to organize a National Week of Prayer supported by the united religious leagues, including the Catholic Women's Suffrage League and Leagues of the Free Churches, the Scottish Churches, the Friends and the Jews. The following year there was a grand procession of the Leagues from the Embankment to Hyde Park with bands and banners.[23]

It was during this climacteric that Hicks was appointed Bishop of Lincoln. The CLWS needed an episcopal President, to establish its right to be recognized as a church society. Fowler quotes Maude Royden's testimony to Hicks's boldness in accepting the invitation to take on the presidency:

The Churches as a whole, and the Church of England in particular, have stood aloof from the Women's Movement, but there have always been some individuals who saw both its ethical and religious significance, and were not alarmed either by the bitterness of its opponents, or by the eccentricities of some of its supporters. The Bishop of Lincoln was, in the Church of England, the first and the boldest of these. I well remember our—rather faint!—hope that the Church League for Women's Suffrage might, when it was founded, secure a Bishop for its President. We asked Dr. Hicks, and he consented. I doubt if there was another Bishop on the bench who would have done so, though there were some who sympathized. They felt, for the most part, that they ought not to commit

[21] Lambeth Palace Library, Davidson Papers, 515.

[22] The date is wrongly given as 1912 in A. Marrin, *The Last Crusade* (1974), 56, and so quoted in A. Wilkinson, *The Church of England and the First World War* (1978), 91.

[23] *Commonwealth* 19/225 (Sept. 1914), 274–5.

themselves officially to a highly controversial movement. One can understand their difficulty, without ceasing to wish that the representatives of so revolutionary a religion as that of Jesus Christ might have overcome it: without ceasing either to feel passionate gratitude to Dr. Hicks, who carried his accustomed boldness of spirit into so controversial a movement as ours.[24]

His role as episcopal president was very different from his participation in the work of the UKA or of the CSU. He could not participate to any great extent in its regular activities, but gave it the encouragement of his status as bishop. His episcopal diaries reveal, however, that he was more than a mere figurehead. He travelled to meetings in London, and attended those which were held in Lincoln, where he had the support of leading churchmen such as Dean Fry and the Precentor, John Wakeford. Services in the Old Palace chapel were arranged for special occasions, such as the day in January 1913 when the Electoral Reform Bill was taken into committee in the House. In November 1912 he went to Oxford to preach a University Sermon and found that the local branch of the League had arranged a special service in the church of St Peter-in-the-East and he had to sit down and compose a sermon 'after luncheon'.[25] In July 1913 he left a meeting of Convocation and travelled to Brighton to take the chair at an important conference of the League at which the exclusion of militants was debated. It was rejected, partly because of the difficulty of defining militancy. There were, in Hicks's opinion, many members of the League who were militants or approved of the militants' action. The original constitution had aimed to 'band together, on a nonparty basis, suffragists of every shade of opinion who are Church people', and it would have been difficult to alter that basis.[26]

Under the vigorous leadership of Maude Royden, the League strayed outside the limits which its title suggested. Indeed its original statement of objects envisaged this. They put first the securing of the parliamentary vote, but included using 'the power thus obtained to establish equality of rights and opportunities between the sexes'. In 1913 the League issued a pamphlet written by the Bishop of Kensington, J. P. Maud, who gave valuable support to Hicks, with the title, 'The Moral Issues Involved in the Women's Movement'. He spoke of the vote as 'mainly a symbol' in a move-

[24] Fowler, 217–18.   [25] *Diary*, 3 Nov. 1912.   [26] *Diary*, 2 July 1913.

ment which was concerned with moral issues such as the double standard of morality for women and men, sweated wages which drove women to prostitution, and the systematized white slave traffic. In February 1917 the League organized a public conference in the Church House, Westminster, on the subject of 'The Laywoman in the Church of England'. Hicks was recovering from a severe illness at the time, and the chair was taken by the Bishop of Willesden, W. W. Perrin. The meeting passed a resolution welcoming the statement on the aims of the Women's Movement adopted by the Central Council of the National Mission in the previous year in favour of throwing open to churchwomen all opportunities for service already enjoyed by laymen.[27]

In the later stages of the war the CLWS, like some other suffrage societies, resolved to abandon in great measure its suffrage work and put itself 'at the disposal of the authorities to render any service for which it can be utilized'.[28] In May and June 1917 the League organized processions in London which were acts of witness without specific relevance to the Women's Movement. Hicks did not take part in these. When the League's primary object had been achieved, with the granting of the parliamentary vote to most women in 1918, opinions differed about its future. In January 1919 its secretary, Miss Corben, came to see Hicks to discuss a new Constitution, but he disliked its vagueness and its ambitious aims. The League of the Church Militant was formed, but without his support. Within three months he succumbed to his final illness, and perhaps he had no strength for another campaign. The new League was intent on pressing the claim of women to the priesthood, and although Maude Royden believed Hicks would have come to support that claim, he never committed himself to doing so. The ordination of women was a bridge too far. Yet no other bishop would have dared to go to the City Temple and sit at Maude Royden's feet and be blessed by her.[29] There was enough difficulty in getting the church to concede equal status to women as

---

[27] *Commonwealth* (March 1917), 90. The resolution was sent to 'the Archbishops, Bishops, Prolocutors of Convocation and leaders of the Houses of Laymen in Canterbury and York'.

[28] For this and other details of the CLWS work, see papers in The Fawcett Library.

[29] But Maude Royden may have been right. If both Inge and Henson could come round to accepting in principle the ordination of women, Hicks would not have lagged behind. See Brian Heeney, *The Women's Movement in the Church of England 1850–1930* (Oxford 1988), 136, 138; Chadwick, *Hensley Henson*, 329–30.

lay members. His final illness was troubled by the typically authoritarian action of his archdeacon, John Wakeford, in dispute with
his friend and disciple, Samuel Proudfoot, over allowing a woman,
Edith Picton-Turbervill, to speak in church at North Somercotes.

His motivation in accepting the presidency of the CLWS was
in great part his sense of the wrong done to women in their exclusion from an equal place in political life. Maude Royden, having
suggested that Hicks may have seen women's suffrage as a support for temperance reform, went on to say, as though correcting
herself:

He realized, almost more than any man I know, the bitterness of *waste*
which we Suffragists felt so keenly, the waste of our time and energy
and money, not so much in *doing work*, as in agitating to be *allowed* to
work. He looked forward to our release from the work of getting political power to our full and deliberate use of it. But he was not a Suffragist
at second hand, so to speak; he did not want to set us free only because
he believed we should be with the causes he cared for. He believed in
freedom for its own sake, and for those who were not with him as well
as those who were on his side.[30]

Hicks was concerned with society more than with the church,
with freedom more than with orthodoxy, and so he was not first
and foremost a 'church reformer'. Unlike Dean Fry, he was not
active within the Church Reform League. The League was a fore-
runner of the Life and Liberty movement, aiming to give the church
freedom to act for itself, by a reformation of the procedures by
which bishops were appointed, reform of the convocations with
new authority for houses of laity, a role for the laity in appointments to livings, and reform of patronage. Though it did not aim
at disestablishment, some critics, such as Hensley Henson, believed
its proposals distorted the proper relation of church and state. Self-
government, he said, was an expedient which might be all right
for railways and charities, but not a national church.[31] Hicks's attitude was more friendly, and yet the Life and Liberty movement
hardly features in his diary. He was wary of the kind of reform
which would give the church stronger powers to restrict the freedom of thought which he valued as one of the great marks of the
Church of England.

[30] Fowler, 218.
[31] H. H. Henson, *Cross-Bench Views of Current Church Questions* (1902), 15.

It was characteristic of Hicks to see all church questions in the perspective of social reform. He declared his own priorities at the diocesan conference in 1913, when he said that his great fear was that questions of social reform would be carried through without much consultation with the church, and without much endeavour on the part of church members to contribute to their solution. The clergy had the duty to lead their people to heaven, but they were not properly doing so if they left all kinds of iniquities to exist round about them, and allowed vested interests to batten on their neglect and on the weakness of their flock. When church reform came under discussion at the diocesan conference in 1916, he said that he wanted to see her far more efficient, far more enterprising, far more serviceable to mankind. For that purpose the church needed greater freedom to devise her own means, to regulate her own forms, to go her own way. In particular he wanted the voice of labour, the voice of women, and the voice of teachers to be heard in church conferences, for that would provide elements of strength which the church needed.

Other instances of his subordination of church questions to social questions appear in the Chronicle of Convocation during the discussion of Prayer Book revision in 1914 and 1915. He had two issues in mind. The first was women's place in society. Not only did he argue, in discussion of the marriage service, for a lesson from 1 Corinthians 13 in preference to Ephesians 5 to avoid the implication about the subjection of the wife; but he also moved an amendment for equal vows in the marriage service.[32] This was an issue which he had to face personally when a bride and bridegroom requested equal vows and the omission of 'giving away' at a service he was to take, in spite of the bride's father saying he would not attend the service if it did not include the Prayer Book vows.[33] He tried to persuade the bishops to include women's place in the church as an issue to be addressed by one of the committees of the National Mission, but was fobbed off with the reply that it was the concern of them all, and in any case a committee had already been appointed to consider the question historically.

---

[32] Hicks's diary entries for February 1914 show Gore in an indecisive frame of mind, first supporting equal vows, then begging Hicks to withdraw his amendments, and finally regretting the withdrawal, in spite of 'his mass of proofs that "obey" occurred nowhere in Xtendom save in our service'.

[33] *Diary*, 2 Sep. 1914.

The other issue related to militarism. He wanted the wording of
a proposed petition in the Litany either deleted or changed from
'the King's forces' to 'all servants of the King', which he saw as
including those engaged in the arts of peace and commerce. It
gave him the chance to draw attention to the railwaymen ('a thousand killed last year'), the colliers, the foundrymen, and sailors, as
those who gave their lives for the country. 'The wealth of the Empire
was not built up by the Army any more than the wealth of London
was built up by the police.' Temperance reform was inevitably a
subject on which he spoke at length, though he seems to have lost
his composure ('He could hardly trust himself to speak') when faced
with what he regarded as the feebleness of his fellow bishops in
dealing with it. In 1915, for instance, they discussed the question
of drink, especially among women, and proposed a motion 'to
investigate facts'. He burst out, 'the time for enquiry was long past'.
They hankered after state purchase, which he rejected in principle.

One of his last speeches in Convocation was in 1918 in a debate
on 'The Reconstruction of Social Life' (after the war). He urged
his fellow bishops to make a sympathetic response to the labour
movement. Manual workers, he said,

did not merely want more wages, greater comfort and a better supply
of necessities, but they wanted a recognition of their personality. They
wanted to be live men and women, not tools and instruments in the
hands of others. One of the great dangers of wealth was that it put into
the hands of a few control over the lives of others. It was an immense
responsibility, and that was its social danger. It was a most comforting
thing to find that what our workers desired was not merely an increase
of material comforts, but opportunity for the development of their personal and spiritual life.

With assumptions only too soon to be disproved, he declared that
the country would not allow its soldiers to fall back into misery
and indigence when they were not employed. He hoped that before
long the trained and disciplined workers of the nation with their
great capacities would, in times of unemployment, be maintained
with all the care and all the regard bestowed on the nation's soldiers. The church must be ready to translate Christianity into the
social, economical, and political institutions of the country, and
not 'to fall back upon the Incarnation and to talk about ultimate
doctrine'. The bishops should commit themselves to new methods

and new movements, and perhaps to new and definite measures of reform. There were other bishops who shared his sense of urgency, but there was little agreement among them all on the necessity of commitments which would be seen as political. It is not surprising that Hicks was never convinced that the episcopate or the convocations or the Representative Church Council could become agencies of social reform.

He was one of a number of church leaders who called for a new relationship between employers and employed, as a result of wartime experience. Even some politicians hoped that a new spirit had been created by the 'brotherhood of the trenches'. The Archbishop of York, C. G. Lang, had been asked by an officer of the Ministry of Labour to make an appeal to churchmen to create a spirit of co-operation in getting the demobilized soldiers back to work and in redeploying those engaged in munition work. A great meeting of the Church of England Men's Society pledged itself to promote better relations between employers and employed. A writer in the *Commonwealth* noted that this followed soon after an ominous Annual Report of the Employers' Parliamentary Council. This body was known to aim at the repeal of the Trades Disputes Act and the restriction of the activities of municipal bodies to purely political affairs. The Annual Report referred to the wartime suspension of 'Acts meddling and interfering with the management and conduct of nearly all the Trades in the Kingdom', such as the Factory Acts, and demanded that there should be no return to the past. Housing must be left to 'that private enterprise which up to 1914 had adequately supplied all the housing wants of the community'.[34] This kind of revelation of what some at least of the employers were thinking would not have escaped Hicks's notice, and he could hardly have had much hope that even the united influence of the whole episcopate would carry much weight. His image of society had long been that of a community riven by the effects of wealth; and his image of the Church of England was of a body too closely identified with the wealthy.

The most coherent exposition of these views is to be found in his University Sermon preached at Cambridge on 20 April 1913, and later published by the *Christian Commonwealth* with the title 'Christianity and Riches'. The text of the sermon was Mark 10: 25:

[34] *Commonwealth* (June 1917), 189–90, quoting the *New Statesman* 17 Feb. 1917.

It is easier for a camel to go through the eye of a needle, than for a rich man to enter into the kingdom of God. In it he glanced at different attitudes to voluntary poverty in the history of the church, but concentrated on the situation created by industrialization and commercialism. The accumulation of wealth had outstripped its distribution, and left extreme wealth and poverty side by side. The intellectual and moral development of the worker dwindled, and the individual counted for less and less. Vast commercial interests exercised tremendous social and political influence, even controlling the action of parliament, and deciding issues of peace and war according to the interests of bond-holders. The development of commercialism now involved a long and unremembered chain connecting the employed and the capitalist. Its immoral influence could be seen in the Congo and in Peru. It had even laid its hand on sport and degraded it. Betting was a business, prostitution a world-wide concern, the liquor trade was allied with the governing classes and narcotized the conscience of the church. The capitalist himself was helpless, a slave of what he created. The church suffered by being accounted the church of the rich. 'The intellectual and ethical standards of our Church are those of the comfortable classes; her political sympathies are prevailingly those of the rich; her aesthetic and social sympathies are those of the affluent.' With an allusion to Ruskin he could say, 'In the Oxford of half a century ago we shrank from all cash values.' What could be done? There could be experiments in community life. Some might follow the example of the first disciples and give up the pursuit of gain. All must refuse to value anyone the more because of his riches.

There were many other Christians who were saying much the same kind of thing; but not many University Sermons took that line. Hicks was a little surprised at his own temerity; his wife even more so. 'AMH did not like the sermon: feared it would do harm. I hope not: but feel anxious.'[35] He need not have worried. The university enfolded him, hurried him across to King's for Evensong, and gave him and Agnes a cup of tea. Then they went to Newnham, to be shown over the college by little Alice Gardner. 'All looks original; all in the best taste, & has the beauty of perfect adaptation to its use.' Then dinner with the Vice-Chancellor, in company with A. C. Benson, and 'Peel (a radical)'. It may have

[35] *Diary*, 20 April 1913.

been reassuring to find at least one radical in the party, as well as one snob. The next day he had a happy hour in the Pepys Library with Stephen Gaselee, and remembered that he was a scholar.

His sermon, however, presents the dilemma of the reforming churchman within the High Church tradition. He was no Erastian. He believed that the church was a body with its own charter of foundation and its own commission as a witness to the gospel. Its task was to be faithful to that commission within the context of secular society; and that society was constantly changing. The great-est change to which it had to respond was the development of democratic institutions. That change, as it came to enfranchise every adult member of society, necessarily meant that every member of the church had a direct responsibility for national well-being. If the members of the church woke up to their responsibilities, the church would become an agent of social reformation. The dilemma was, what to do if that did not happen. Should he con-centrate his attention on changing the church, or abandon all idea of the church as a reforming agency and choose to work through other agencies? The dilemma remained unresolved. His preference was to carry his responsibility as a churchman into groups or agen-cies which had no necessary connection with the church. But his situation was changed when he accepted a bishopric. With it he accepted public responsibility for the corporate life of the church, and renewed his efforts to make it a more credible witness to social righteousness. The other bishops who to some extent shared that hope were few in number. Their attention was diverted away from social questions to the reform of the church's government, and with the democratization of the church it became evident that it was as divided by sectional interests as the nation itself.

9

The Politics of Conscience

The notion of a 'political churchman' could hardly be said to have existed at the Reformation, because leading ecclesiastics were simply integrated into the process of government. The Shakespearean image of bishops and archbishops is of pieces on a chessboard where kings, bishops, and knights have different moves, but all take part in the same contest. After the upheavals of the seventeenth century the situation was different. The presence of powerful and antagonistic groupings in parliament and the exercise of church patronage alternately by differing interests had the effect of dividing prominent churchmen along party lines. All were, to that extent, political. This was true at every level, from the House of Lords, through Crown appointments, down to the parishes, through private patronage of beneficed livings. The balance between parties at the parish level was uneven. There the preponderance of the landed interest ensured the dominance of Tory convictions among the parochial clergy.

It is hard to determine when it began to be supposed that acceptance of the existing order was not a political attitude and only criticism of it was labelled political. The convention must have become established before Hicks reached adulthood, and was possibly connected with the development of the 'science' of political economy. When its so-called laws were regarded as possessing objective validity, the church was almost forced to withhold any comment on the economic aspect of society. So long, therefore, as the Liberal Party remained faithful to those theories the Liberal clergy could simply be regarded as harmlessly allied to one party within the state for purely intellectual reasons, if not merely from family inheritance. When a reaction set in against the heartlessness of those theories, the situation changed. A few churchmen tried to mobilize theological arguments against current theories, but protest chiefly came from prophetic figures outside the church. Carlyle and Ruskin were among them. They were widely regarded as subversive, and members of the clergy who fell in with their criticisms were accused of political interference, while those who continued to bow to current economic theories were exempted from the charge of being political.

But there were other factors beside those of economics which affected the definition of a political churchman. All churchmen were expected to support policies which maintained the position of the established church. When governments began the process of reforming the church by laying hands on its endowments, many members of the church thought it right to oppose such action. That kind of opposition was not stigmatized as political, whereas support for reform was. The situation was further complicated by the conversion of Gladstone to the cause of Irish disestablishment and Home Rule. Nothing but ulterior 'political' motives, it was thought, could justify support for such policies by ecclesiastics. But in the 1880s a new face of Liberalism appeared. The Whig doctrine limiting the function of the state to the preservation of life and property was superseded by a view of the state as an agent for social reforms. In this new guise the Liberal party could command a new respect among churchmen, and though it might still be thought to be a political decision if they abandoned their conservatism in the cause of reform, they could hold their heads high as conscientious Christians and not merely supporters of a parliamentary faction. For the first time Liberal churchmen came together and tried to organize themselves for effective action. That was precisely the period when Hicks began to move from support of the Liberal Party as the best hope of the temperance cause to support of it for broader reasons.

In Manchester Hicks was a political churchman. Not only so, but he was also explicitly a 'party political' churchman, because it seemed obvious to him that there was no other way to play any effective role in political life. He had already met the common assumptions that support of the *status quo* is not a political commitment, and that some specific topics which are the subject of public debate are in some way or other 'not political'. We have seen that the organizers of a Church Congress distinguished between woman suffrage and conscription, treating one as political and the other as non-political. Hicks's friend John Wordsworth felt free to use his influence over Home Rule for Ireland because, for some reason or other, he regarded it as a subject 'transcending

politics'.[1] He and other bishops also used their influence on educational questions, making it quite clear how, in their opinion, church
members ought to vote. There were plenty of people in Manchester who thought that Hicks, but not Bishop Knox, was a
political churchman, though the bishop was as outspoken a Conservative as Hicks was a Liberal. But while Hicks never hid his
political light under a bushel, he was careful to limit the ways in
which he used his position in the church to advance his views.
He kept politics out of the pulpit in his parishes, but freely used
the pulpit in the cathedral and later his position as a diocesan
bishop to address moral issues which affected political decisions.
But most of his campaigning was done through journalism and
through specific organizations with declared aims. In them he could
speak freely as a citizen with as much right to be political as anyone else.

From the time when he was appointed to his fellowship at
Corpus to the end of his life, a period of about half a century, the
government alternated between Conservative and Liberal administrations, each party holding power for roughly the same number
of years overall. During this period Hicks's politics changed with
changing times, but not in a conservative direction as is so often
the case with those who find themselves in responsible positions
in a great institution. His interest in social reform increased rather
than diminished, so that his radicalism tended to push him from
the left wing of the Liberal Party to the support of the Labour
movement, and the old individualism which was the legacy of the
Manchester school to the Liberal Party gave way to the advocacy
of collective solutions of collective problems. But he was never a
political theorist, and stood apart from those members of the
Christian church who saw in some form of political organization
an analogue to the eucharistic community called into being by
the Incarnation. His entry into the political arena was largely the
consequence of his concern for temperance. The effective constituency organization of the United Kingdom Alliance provided
in many places the backbone of the local Liberal Party in the 1880s,
and this helped to cement his relationship with it. But there were
more than merely organizational affinities to draw Hicks from the
UKA to the party.

---

[1] E. W. Watson, *Life of Bishop John Wordsworth* (1915), 349.

Temperance itself was for some, including Hicks, a path to freedom. It offered working people, as well as the middle classes, emancipation from a particular form of exploitation. Here perhaps we
can begin to see what political Liberalism had at its heart's core
—at least the Gladstonian kind of Liberalism. Gladstone's career
shows what G. M. Trevelyan has called the crossing of 'the long
bridge from the old Toryism to the new Liberalism'.[2] His biographer, John Morley, affirmed that he changed his opinions about
everything—except religion. Put very briefly, those changes were
due to his growing conviction of the central value of freedom; and
the word liberal has an obvious etymological connection with liberty. Gladstone's political decisions from the mid-century onwards
were determined by a belief in the supreme importance of individual liberty, but in his own mind that contradicted neither the
importance of limited government action, which was a means of
enabling individuals to act freely, nor the role of authority in the
church, which was a different kind of community from the state.
Hence the paradox of a High-Churchman supported in office by
the majority of nonconformists and free-thinkers. Gladstone promoted the disestablishment of the Church of Ireland, and favoured
disestablishment in England, too, though it never became politically feasible. The ideal which he represents was that of a free
church in a free state—that is to say, a church free to manage its
own affairs within a state which aimed to increase individual freedom. It set him alongside his friend Lord Acton, who held the
same kind of ideal within the Roman Catholic communion.

Hicks, of course, was not a politician in a narrow sense; nor
did he move with ease in the sphere of international affairs as Lord
Acton did. But the early influences of his politically Liberal parents, together with the social conscience learnt from Ruskin, aligned
him with the radical wing of the Liberal Party, without destroy-
ing the moderate High-Churchmanship which he had adopted at
Oxford or his interest in evangelistic work. During his twenty-
four years in Manchester he developed into a particular kind of
Liberal churchman. He became an outspoken opponent of the cap-
italistic imperialism manifested in the Boer War, a supporter of
women's education and woman suffrage, and a believer in international peace by negotiation.

[2] G. M. Trevelyan, *British History in the Nineteenth Century* (1922), 349.

Hicks, then, was in a manner of speaking born a little Liberal, and his early experience clearly influenced his whole outlook, right up to old age. He was fortunate that two early periods of his adult life, at Oxford and at Fenny Compton, enabled him to develop his ideas without a great deal of tension at a time when the focus of his interest was scholarly and religious rather than political. At Oxford, and particularly at Corpus, he had been thrown into the company of liberals. They came in various guises. In 1869, three years into Hicks's fellowship, the Cambridge philosopher, Henry Sidgwick, put Oxford liberals in three categories: Positivists, Broad-Churchmen, and metaphysicians.[3] Of these categories—and there were surely other variants—the one which made some impact was that of the Positivists, the followers of Comte. The metaphysicians, 'either non-religious or with a religion far too unearthly for them to care about operating directly on the public creeds', left no noticeable mark on Hicks, who always displayed an overriding concern with practical issues. The Broad-Churchmen, 'of the mildly comprehensive and cautiously vague type, with innovating tendencies', could not rival in religious influence the evangelical and Anglo-catholic forces to which Hicks was exposed through such different characters as Henry Bazely and Edmund Hobhouse, the Vicar of St Peter-in-the-East at Oxford, later Bishop of Nelson, New Zealand.

The influence of Comte is a curiosity. He is remembered today as much for his eccentricities as for his more coherent views. The absurdity of trying to create a new religion from his study desk, or his apotheosis of woman in the person of his friend, Clothilde de Vaux, reminiscent of J. S. Mill's reverence for his wife, Harriet, have made it hard for later generations to understand how influential he was for a time in the 1860s even among Christian writers, just when Hicks was beginning to explore new intellectual worlds.[4] He had already commanded the attention of F. D. Maurice, and merited an extended discussion in his lectures, subsequently published with the title *Social Morality*; and Westcott wrote an article for the *Contemporary Review*, with the title 'Aspects of Positivism in Relation to Christianity', which he considered of sufficient

---

[3] Letter to James Martineau, quoted in A. M. G. Stephenson, *The Rise and Decline of English Modernism* (1984), 28.

[4] See T. R. Wright, *The Religion of Humanity: The Impact of Comtean Positivism on Victorian Britain* (1986), esp. 127–9.

importance to have reprinted as an appendix to his *The Gospel of the Resurrection*. There seems today little in common between the founder of sociology (as Comte is sometimes described) and the tradition of Christian social thought which traces its origins back to Maurice. It is also puzzling that his name was sometimes coupled with that of Ruskin.[5] Hicks later mentioned him along with Ruskin as providing an example of the way that thoughts could be 'in the air'. This was in a Long Vacation Lecture to the clergy at Oxford and was apropos of similarities of thought in Paul and Seneca. 'I know not how much Mr Ruskin has ever read of Comte: but I know that some of his lectures, when I heard them, seemed inspired by all that is best in the Positive Ethics.'[6] The reasons why Comte was taken seriously in some Christian circles were principally that he provided a way of escape from the tyranny of political economy as commonly understood; that he held out the expectation of future progress in the condition of human society; that he treated society as an organism instead of a collocation of essentially independent, and therefore competitive, units; and that he allowed a proper place for moral and emotional elements in social organization.

F. D. Maurice, in a characteristic fashion, looked for the good elements in Positivism, and found them largely by restating them in his own words. Comte, he said, had 'explained to our generation the desire of former teachers to build up a Universal Society, and a Morality which should be adapted to it; their eagerness to associate this Human Society and Human Morality with physical studies; their impatience of theology'. Comte had compelled theologians to admit that 'if what we have called the Kingdom of Heaven is not concerned about the reformation or regeneration of the earth . . . we have been walking in a dream, or have been deliberately imposing a lie upon our fellow creatures'. And further, Comtists 'suppose the human characteristic, that which they are to strive for because it is human, to be not selfishness but love; only when each man seeks not his own interest, but the interest of the whole society, is he truly human . . . Great as the intellect is, it must bow to the heart.'[7]

[5] Harrison, *John Ruskin*, 97–8.
[6] 'St Paul and Hellenism', in *Studia Biblica et Ecclesiastica: Essays Chiefly in Biblical and Patristic Criticism by Members of the University of Oxford*, iv (1896).
[7] *Social Morality* (1886 edn.), 355 ff.

Westcott picked out other elements in Positivism to praise. He claimed that it was 'more in harmony with a *historic* religion than any other philosophy' and had 'vindicated the social dimension'. Moreover, its scheme of successive stages or eras—the theological, the metaphysical, and the Positivist—embodies the conviction that there is progress in human history. No one can fail to detect a general advance of humanity, even though periods of devastation have been needed to prepare future growth. Progress means the harmonious elevation of our whole complex being. 'To transfer a form of one age unaltered into another is in most cases to be faithless to the very principle by which we claim to be children of the first century or the fourth or the thirteenth.' Positivism suggested ideas of continuity, solidarity, and totality, which were congenial to Christian faith.

But both Maurice and Westcott believed that, in the last analysis, Positivism was wanting. Comte, Maurice said, calls us still to 'believe in Humanity, only in a headless Humanity'; it is to be adored in ourselves and our fellow-creatures. He has given us 'the most clear and complete Philosophy of Idolatry that exists in the world'. Westcott's criticism is similar. Any doctrine which is based upon the Incarnation or the Resurrection must be progressive, organic, and total, as Positivism also seeks to be. But a perfect religion must take account of three entities: the individual, the world, and God. The Comtist omits God. Evangelical religion omits the world, as in Newman's 'two only supreme and luminously self-evident beings, myself and my Creator'. One leads to secularism; the other to mysticism. Most of these appreciations and criticisms would have found an echo in Hicks's thoughts, for they did indeed correspond to certain ideas propounded by Ruskin. He, too, could be said to be in favour of continuity, solidarity, and totality. He, too, argued for a Human Society and a Human Morality. And he would have agreed with Maurice and Westcott that the missing dimension in Positivism was a God who was something other than idealized humanity. But it must be said that both Ruskin and Comte saw their ideals as realizable only through the action of an élite. And that was also true of the 'metaphysicians'. Hicks showed little sign of this kind of élitism. He would have agreed with Gladstone's memorable remark to Queen Victoria, that 'on all the great questions dependent mainly on broad considerations of humanity and justice, wealth, station, and rank had been wrong and the masses right'.[8]

In the latter part of Hicks's time at Oxford the influence of Positivism was yielding to the newer school of 'metaphysicians' to which Sidgwick referred in his description of the liberals, but there is hardly any evidence in the surviving records of his life that he had an interest in the foremost Oxford metaphysician of his generation, T. H. Green. That is surprising, in view of Green's support of the Liberal Party. He was an admirer of John Bright, and had proposed a motion eulogistic of him in the Oxford Union in 1858 and had been in a minority of two who voted in its favour.[9] He also had a strong interest in temperance and in social action by municipalities, and he exercised a formative influence on people whom Hicks admired, such as Henry Scott Holland. Churchmen of such disparate theological positions as Edward King and F. J. Chavasse saw in him something like a saviour of the Christian cause. The explanation of Hicks's indifference may be simply that he never came under Green's personal influence. Even in the small community which was Oxford University in the mid-nineteenth century there were various coteries whose members could pass each other in the streets without acknowledgement. That may explain why Green could be described both as becoming predominant in the intellectual life of Oxford and also as an embattled figure.

It is, however, possible that Hicks already saw some of the less welcome implications of Green's philosophy and deliberately turned his back upon it. He may already have taken into account Mark Pattison's verdict, which he quoted in his 1903 recollections of Corpus, and been alienated from a philosophy which he saw to be ultimately inimical to the reformation of society, or at least open to a variety of political applications. Green himself told Scott Holland that his philosophy could supply intellectual formulae for different styles of religious life, whether for an orthodox clergyman or for a follower of Mazzini, that is, for one who undertook small-scale activity for the good of individuals, or one who aimed to use the spirit of nationalism for the benefit of society as a whole. In his own case, he attached to his philosophy a conscientious view

---

[8] J. L. Hammond, 'Gladstone and the League of Nations Mind', in J. A. K. Thompson and A. J. Toynbee (eds), *Essays in Honour of Gilbert Murray* (1936), 117.

[9] Trevelyan, *Life of John Bright*, 268.

of his civic duties and acted upon the formula of 'positive freedom', which demanded legislative interference to remove ob-
stacles to free and responsible citizenship. But, as has already been
noticed, it was not long before F. H. Bradley was building upon
Green's foundation an ethic of 'my station and its duties' which
could easily become the excuse for acquiescing even in the cor-
ruptness of a rotten society,[10] and certainly undermined the resolve
of privileged academics whose conscience was stirring them to go
down into the slums created by industrialism. Not all those who
responded to the teaching of Green and his followers set about
founding university settlements. Not all the exponents of Idealism
remained idealists.

Initially Hicks's own idealism found an outlet in commitment
to the parochial ministry. He decided that scholarship should take
second place to mission; and at that stage politics came third in
his priorities. His parish was predominantly Liberal, and politics
were in all probability a matter of occasional interest to him as to
most of his parishioners. He later referred to his uncertainties at
this period. While he was in Warwickshire he had refused to vote
for a Home Ruler, because he was not sure that Home Rule for
Ireland would be wise; and he had equally refused to vote for a
Unionist who was no friend of temperance reform.[11] He said that
later, in the year in which he moved to Manchester, he was persuaded to support Home Rule 'by the example of Lord Spencer
and the curious policy of Lord Randolph Churchill'. He had a
slight acquaintance with Lord Spencer, who was Lord of the Manor
of neighbouring Wormleighton and had contributed to the support of the Fenny Compton school.[12] His reference was to the
fact that Lord Spencer had tried, as Irish viceroy, to apply a policy of firmness in Ireland but after it had been discarded by the
incoming Conservative administration, had come to agree with
Gladstone's aim of Home Rule. The reference to Lord Randolph
Churchill is unclear, but certainly expresses mistrust of a politician whose attitude to Ireland (as of other matters) was determined
by passing political advantage rather than principle.

---

[10] John Bowle, *Politics and Opinion in the Nineteenth Century* (1954), 296. For a critical
estimate of Green's influence see Michael Freeden, *The New Liberalism: An Ideology of Social
Reform* (Oxford 1978), esp. 55–60: 'Green's Idealism Eclipsed'.

[11] 'The Church and the Liquor Traffic' (Lees and Raper Lecture 1912).

[12] Correspondence in Honnold Library, 18 June 1874.

It is evident, however, that Hicks was beginning to take a closer interest in politics, and by 1887 he was corresponding with Sir Wilfrid Lawson on political questions.[13] But there was a period when his political allegiance wavered, while temperance remained the overriding concern. Like many others, Hicks was looking for a candidate who presented precisely the same range of convictions as those which he himself held. In doing so, he embodied within himself the conflict of ideas which led to the Home Rule split of the Liberal Party and six years of Conservative government. But it was temperance reform which was closer to him in his daily life than the administration of Ireland. Home Rule was a debatable issue. Temperance reform was not negotiable. And if it had not quite settled down as an element of Liberal policy, it was clear that the reformers' best hopes were definitely with the Liberals.

At this stage Hicks came under the influence of Sir Wilfrid Lawson. For many years he had been calling on the government to promote legislation for Local Option, and even Gladstone had voted in favour of a resolution to that effect in 1883. He had been active in Warwickshire as well as other areas, and Hicks made his first contact with him there, though it was later that they became personal friends and fellow-workers in the cause. It is clear, at any rate, that Hicks's political awakening was connected with his involvement with the UKA. Fowler quotes a note (now lost) which Hicks included with a collection of Lawson's letters which he had bound together after Lawson's death. After explaining that he had joined the United Kingdom Alliance while at Fenny Compton, he continued:

From the first I read diligently the articles in *The Alliance News*, and especially the clear, humorous, but always argumentative speeches of Sir Wilfrid himself. In reading these I was often annoyed by the sarcasms and jokes that he loved to hurl at the Bishops and Clergy. Very soon I found myself so much vexed, that I wrote from my country rectory to remonstrate with him: 'Why make enemies of the Church and the Clergy, who might

---

[13] In one of Sir Wilfrid Lawson's versified letters to Hicks there occur these words: 'Best thanks for your lines upon Randolph's career. | I have got them today, they were forwarded here. | He's a "rum un" if ever there was one, no doubt, | And no one can tell what, at last, he'll turn out. | He may pose as a Tory or "stump" as a Rad, | As to serve his own interest he thinks good or bad. | Only one thing is sure of that wonderful elf, | Whatever he does, he'll be *true to himself*' (Timothy Hicks papers).

perhaps be converted into valuable friends? etc., etc.' His reply was highly characteristic. I wish now I had kept it. I remember its purport. He assured me that he had the deepest respect for the Church: indeed, he added, unless the Church had been under some signal and supernatural protection, it must long ago have come to naught through the stupidity and blindness of the clergy. This was his way of conciliating a clerical convert![14]

This was an inaccurate memory, for, strangely enough, the letter which he thought he had mislaid has survived in the family papers. It is dated 25 February 1881, from the House of Commons. Hicks had evidently sent Lawson a copy of a sermon which he had preached. Lawson thanked him for it, and continued:

I am very glad to hear what you say about the views of the Anglican clergy. I hope that I do not misunderstand them, although I often attack the *system* of a State Church. I am well convinced in my own mind that if the clergy themselves were not estimable and worthy men, the system could not maintain its popularity. But whether they are 'established' or not makes no difference to the desirability of all of us uniting against the great evils of the day.

The UKA had a political purpose, and Hicks's interest in politics came alive. When it did, it focused on the Radical wing of the Liberal Party. That was where he located the real opposition to the drink trade. Then came the move to Manchester, which had a crucial effect on his involvement with politics. There were few other places in the country where political life was so much part of the air that people breathed—Birmingham, perhaps, or Liverpool might have had the same effect on an intelligent and socially minded churchman, though ecclesiastical life in the one was too much dominated by Unitarian and Congregationalist influences, and in the other too divided between the large Roman Catholic population and the self-consciously Protestant opposition.

Manchester church life was not biased in either of these ways. More importantly, its secular life had special features which set it apart. They could be summed up in the existence of the *Manchester Guardian*. For that paper not only espoused causes which appealed to Hicks, but had its own particular connections with Oxford, and, by chance, with Hicks's own college. Its great editor, C. P. Scott,

<hr>

[14] Fowler, 193–4.

was a graduate of Corpus Christi, and one whose conversion to Home Rule precisely coincided with that of Hicks.[15] One of its most able leader writers, L. T. Hobhouse, had been a fellow of the same college. There was a kind of affinity between the political and intellectual ambience of its editorial office and Hicks's own cast of mind. At its best estimate, it was conscience-driven, fostering a kind of secular evangelism; in the words of Lord Robert Cecil, it had 'made righteousness readable'.[16] A less favourable verdict is implied in the memorable, but unfair, vignette of Colin Cross, who said that the growth of the *Manchester Guardian* was

largely due to the talents of an anonymous, ill-paid band of leader-writers, who in their shabby suits and wing-collars travelled into the office by tram and bicycle from the Manchester suburbs. Almost entirely lacking in first-hand contact with the world outside Manchester, they felt no qualms about issuing the most trenchant advice to international statesmen. Late every night, conscious that they had set the world to rights, they journeyed humbly back to their homes. They were readable and persuasive, vital allies of the brilliant ministers at Westminster.[17]

The strong Oxford connection is itself something of a refutation of the charge of provincialism, and the names of the paper's contributors certainly included men of experience. Scott was himself for a time an MP, with the access to information and the availability of the experience of others which that implied, and his house and his office were located at the centre of a political spider's web. It remains true, however, that Hicks was ready to fall in with the habit of passing judgement on world affairs which grows inexorably in those who adopt a 'politics of conscience' and have a ready outlet for their opinions. His period of residence in Manchester and Salford was a time of transition from the individualism of the Manchester School to the age of social reform. It was the time of the disruption of the Liberal Party and its reintegration on a different basis after the South African War. Through these upheavals the *Manchester Guardian*, edited but not owned by Scott, followed a line which Hicks approved, and shortly before Scott took over its ownership in 1905 Hicks was invited to become a regular contributor.

---

[15] Ayerst, *Guardian*, 204.   [16] Hammond, *Scott of the Manchester Guardian*, 299.
[17] Colin Cross, *The Liberals in Power (1905–1914)* (1963), 77.

It was not an easy time for Manchester Liberalism. During the six years that Hicks spent at Hulme Hall, the Conservatives were in power. The extension of the borough franchise in 1868 may have strengthened the Liberal Party elsewhere, but it did not have that effect in Manchester, and further extensions strengthened Conservatism yet more.[18] There was a strong local element of working-class Conservatism, to which Bishop Knox was able to appeal in his fight for church schools. In any case Hicks's six years at Hulme Hall may not have included much specifically political activity, apart from such as was incidental to his work for the UKA. But that work soon caught him up into national politics, and he felt able to speak for Liberal churchmen to a Liberal Prime Minister. The letter, already quoted, was written from Hulme Hall in July 1892, just after he had been appointed to the Manchester canonry. Its burden was a plea to Gladstone to prosecute the fight against the 'liquor interest', for the sake of the Liberal Party. But it indicated the principles which he would continue to express in other situations in the years to come. In speaking of what he saw as 'enormous moral enthusiasm' in 1892 he referred back to the Bulgarian atrocities, committed by the Turks in 1876 and denounced in unmeasured terms by Gladstone. This comparison shows that he felt deeply about all kinds of oppressive behaviour and believed it was the duty of government to check it, whether at home or abroad. The same sensitivity of conscience made him the critic of the home government when he believed it was itself the agent of oppressive imperialism. Alongside this principled opposition to oppression we may place a certain degree of argumentative skill. He had carefully chosen to remind the great statesman of an episode from the past when he had been stirred by deep emotion and had won the support of excited crowds.

Hicks was also developing a style of preaching which emphasized social and political issues. This was not the norm for his sermons at St Philip's, where he aimed to exclude politics from the pulpit. He had declared in his appeal that 'in our parish church we know *no* political colour'. When he became a residentiary canon, he saw his preaching in the cathedral in a different light; and even before that he had occasional opportunities to preach on themes which related his religious beliefs to the state of society. While he

---

[18] P. F. Clarke, *Lancashire and the New Liberalism* (Cambridge 1971), 38.

was still at Hulme Hall he had been invited to preach a Founder's Day sermon for the Grammar School in the cathedral.[19] He chose to preach extempore, but was afterwards asked to provide a script for publication. He took the text 'Man shall not live by bread alone' and urged his hearers to be aware of their intellectual and spiritual needs. But he began with the need for bread. 'In a land like ours that supports nearly a million paupers, and in a town like ours where more than one in every six of the population dies a pauper's death,' it was part of the duty of a good man to support his family by honestly earning a living. Even greater was the importance of recognizing other needs and their sustenance. The greatness of a nation was to be estimated by the possession of ideas. Hicks's own experience and scholarly interests spoke out. 'The greatness of Germany is not measured by her armies, but rather by the concentrated learning which makes all the world of scholarship seek to her Universities.' Then, quoting his favourite Ruskin, he declared that the dignity of knowledge itself depended on the motives for which it was sought and the ends to which it was put.

All the sympathies, all the interests, all the energies of mankind are today converging and are being concentrated upon the social problem of this modern time . . . To us it is given for the first time to study the problem of misery, to deal with the science of human life. To us the task is committed of learning how to elevate and purify the social state of our large towns, to equalise human conditions, to help the worker to more leisure, and (yet more) to help him to the virtue and wisdom to use the leisure aright, to aid every cause of freedom and of goodness, to help in making the democracy of England . . . a democracy great because generous and strong because pure.

Here he was speaking in generalities. But later, with his official position established in the cathedral, he was not afraid to stir up political feeling and even alienate some of his hearers. It is not surprising to learn that at least one member of the congregation walked out of the building during one of his sermons.[20]

The end of Hicks's six years at Hulme Hall coincided with an important change in the situation of the Liberal Party. There were

[19] 'The Bread by which Man Lives', a Founder's Day sermon preached in the Cathedral Church of St Mary the Virgin Manchester before the Grammar School, 2 May 1890.
[20] J. M. Elvy, *Recollections of the Cathedral and Parish Church of Manchester* (Manchester 1913), 32. Elvy says that Hicks was 'always worth hearing, even when you least agreed with him'.

those who already spoke of a 'new Liberalism'. G. W. E. Russell, for example, was a regular contributor to the *Manchester Guardian* and shared many of Hicks's attitudes. In an article in 1889 he contrasted the position of the party with its situation four years before. The fall of the Turkish tyranny, he said, had freed them for a programme of social reform. It had given them an ennobling ambition, to make lives healthier, sweeter, brighter, and more humane. 'To some of us it was much more; for it meant the application of the Gospel of Christ to the practical business of modern life.' The old Whig doctrine had limited the function of the state to the preservation of life and property. Modern Liberalism saw the state as the agent for all moral, material, and social reforms. The old Liberals, including Gladstone, had snubbed the plan for social reform. But it would succeed. It would help to enlarge the boundaries of the Kingdom of God.[21] Russell's connection of social reform with the gospel was not shared by all Liberals; nor was his optimism immediately justified. The Liberals were returned to power in 1892; but this administration, the last to be headed by Gladstone, was ineffective and short-lived. Gladstone retired in 1894, and in the following year the Conservatives regained power. But the changing attitude towards social reform within the Liberal Party coincided with the increase in Hicks's concern with social problems as he undertook the double duties of his new post, as parish priest of a slum area and residentiary canon in the cathedral which stood at the heart of Manchester's civic life. Hicks continued to keep an eye on the public speeches of Liberal leaders. An example of this vigilance on behalf of the UKA and other temperance reformers has already been mentioned. That letter to Campbell-Bannerman included some detailed arguments about parliamentary tactics, which showed at least that Hicks, through his association with the UKA and with people like Lawson, had come to study the details of political life. But the Liberal Party did not regain power for another six years, and many questions of social reform were thrust aside by the outbreak of war. This was the event which brought Hicks to the attention of a wider audience.

Temperance was a 'single-issue' campaign to which Hicks gave vigorous support; a social issue with objectives he hoped would

[21] G. W. E. Russell, 'The New Liberalism: A Response', *Nineteenth Century* 26 (1889), 492–9.

be achieved through political action. The next campaign in which he played an active role was opposition to the Boer War. Though it may appear to be a completely unrelated issue, that was not how it seemed to him. The 'pro-Boers' and their critics became involved in a range of arguments which included assessments of the Boers and their religion, the relative treatment of the native races by Dutch and British colonialists, conditions in concentration camps, and indeed the whole rationale of imperial expansion by European nations. But the heart of the matter, for social reformers like Hicks, was the dominance of unprincipled capitalists. If the brewers were among the agents of exploitation at home, the diamond and gold interests were the principal exploiters in South Africa. They carried the double guilt of having provoked the sufferings in wartime of combatants and non-combatants alike, and having checked the advance of social reform at home while all the nation's energies were devoted to an unjustified war.

Just as Manchester was the centre of the organization of the UKA, so also it was, outside London, the centre of opposition to imperialism in South Africa. Britain's annexation of the Transvaal in 1877, after having previously recognized its independence, led to the rebellion (or First Boer War) in 1881. The Transvaal Independence Committee was formed and its supporters included some of the temperance societies.[22] That committee became inactive after 1884, while Hicks was still at Fenny Compton. Kruger's ultimatum of 1899 led to the outbreak of the Second Boer War,[23] and the opposition movement again became active. In London the Transvaal Committee was under the chairmanship of G. W. E. Russell, and its members included Henry Scott Holland. In Manchester the association of Hicks with C. P. Scott was particularly important. Opposition to the Boer War brought them closer together as they shared the opprobrium of being unpatriotic. The *Manchester Guardian* suffered in circulation, and Scott received abusive letters, calling him a traitor and a dirty Fenian and saying that he had made the name of Manchester stink in the nostrils of all loyal people.[24]

Hicks was not exposed to that kind of abuse, though his preaching in the cathedral provoked strong reactions. His prominence

---

[22] See Arthur Davey, *The British Pro-Boers 1877–1902* (Cape Town 1978), 28.

[23] Though, as Hicks later said in one of his sermons, 'He is really responsible for war who makes war inevitable'; clearly he did not put all the blame on Kruger.

[24] Ayerst, *Guardian*, 225.

in Manchester in the opposition to the war is indicated by the fact that he took the chair at the formation of the Manchester Transvaal Peace Committee in November 1899.[25] A letter to 'My dear Scott', dated 23 August of that year, shows that he was not just a convenient figurehead but that he had, in fact, been instrumental in calling the meeting together, that he was in touch with sympathetic groups in Manchester, and was trying to get Gore to throw his weight into the agitation in London. He wrote:

In arranging for the meeting it would be important to secure the sympathy and help—which would be readily given—of the '95 Club' and the Native Races Committee . . . I wrote to Gore nearly three weeks ago, offering to preach a strong sermon in Manchester if he would do the same in London. He replied by saying he was in doubt as to the rights of the question as Balfour had told him one story but his Church friends in S. Africa spoke quite differently: he was perplexed: uneasy etc. etc. But he seems to have been stirred up by my letter, or something, for he spoke pretty well last Sunday. I am writing to him again, and will sound him about the Manchester meeting. I feel sure the Bp. of Hereford would come. I will write to him also. I intend to preach a straight sermon at the Cathedral on Sunday morning next.[26]

Two of his cathedral sermons on South Africa have been recorded. The first was preached on 27 August, and subsequently published as a leaflet of the Manchester Transvaal Committee, with the title 'The Duty of England'. He took an appropriate text from Ahab's question to the prophets in 1 Kings 22: 6: 'Shall I go to battle, or shall I forbear?' But this was no sermon couched in generalities and spiced with scriptural parallels. Platform, pulpit, and press, he said, seemed to conspire in recommending war. How was it that a whole nation seemed to acquiesce or even to approve if it was about to commit a great political blunder or a grave international crime? As in the case of Ahab, a lying spirit was abroad.

Prejudice and passion have prevailed instead of calm and collected reason. Few have examined the official records, the actual facts. Statements of the wildest sort, pleas wholly groundless, have taken hold of the popular mind. And, what is worse, the public press has been deluged with telegrams and paragraphs from the Transvaal and the Cape designed to mislead British opinion or excite animosity against the Boers. Literally

[25] Davey, *British Pro-Boers*, 148.
[26] Manchester University John Rylands Library, Manchester Guardian archive, 122/78. In fact, Bishop Percival was on holiday and unable to come (letter in Honnold Library).

a lying spirit has been at work. Listen to the words of General Sir F. W. Butler, in a letter to Mr. Chamberlain on January 11th last. After noting the insolent behaviour of the officials of the [South Africa] League, he goes on:—'Be that as it may, I am convinced by the knowledge of facts which it is impossible to ignore that it is necessary to receive with caution, and even with a large measure of suspicion, statements emanating from the officers of this organisation.' In other words, the capitalists of South Africa have been using the telegraph and the press to mislead the judgment and abuse the patriotism of the British people.

He appealed to memories of the mistakes of the past when prophetic voices had spoken their warnings—at the time of the Bulgarian atrocities the voice of Gladstone, and at the time of the Crimean war the voice of John Bright, whose burning in effigy in Manchester evidently stirred some childhood memory in him. Those who loved liberty must respect the independence of the Boers, whose faults and virtues recalled in some degree the qualities of those who followed Hampden and Cromwell in their stand for freedom.

Five months later he took up the theme again. He and those who shared his views had been maligned and ridiculed by the irresponsible writers of the hysterical war press; but he would continue to associate himself with 'that band of noble and not undistinguished men who, drawn together from every political party' had all along deprecated the war. He spelt out the cost already incurred, in casualties, in production lost from peaceful industry, in the paralysis of South African trade. And what was the country aiming at? 'What is to be the settlement when the war is over? Do we want to create a Dutch Ireland 6000 miles away? Do we dream of keeping the Afrikanders under, like another India, with a permanent garrison of men in Arms?' The Dutch and English populations should be uniting together to face the situation created by the fact that they were together far outnumbered by the black population. And above all, the world needed more freedom, not less. 'The Empire grew because we left our colonies free to work out their independent life . . . Let us hold fast to these grand old traditions. They are based on the experience of history; they are true to human nature; they harmonise with the dictates of the Gospel.'

The great majority of Christians in England, of all denominations, rallied to the support of the government. The 'khaki election' of 1900 was sprung on the nation, and Hicks played a prominent part in it, in support of Liberal candidates; to no avail.[27] Everyone who hesitated to support the war was labelled a traitor. But the mood changed, when details of mortality in the concentration camps, particularly among children, were made public. John Percival, the Liberal Bishop of Hereford, who had written personally to Lord Salisbury to oppose a declaration of war in September 1899, continued to criticize government policy. He wrote a long letter to *The Times* in October 1901, asking 'Are we reduced to such a depth of impotence that our Government can do nothing to stop such a holocaust of child-life?'[28] Opposition to the war was virtually limited to elements within the Liberal Party, but criticism of government policy after the end of the war became more widespread, particularly with the introduction of Chinese labour into the Transvaal mines. Hicks was later to write that 'the whole significance of the South African war, the whole issue between the Jingo and the anti-Jingo policy', was gathered up into this question. It was a touchstone for parties, groups and churches. It offered no possibility of compromise.[29] The encouragement of Chinese indentured labour was a desperate expedient to provide cheap labour when it became apparent that there were not enough British immigrants and that Africans were not willing, in sufficient numbers, to work in the deep mines for low pay. Hicks took it as confirmation of the opinion he had held all along, that the war had been provoked by 'sordid capitalism'.

The importance of the pro-Boer episode in Hicks's life cannot easily be overstated. Perhaps its most important personal effect was to cement the friendship between him and C. P. Scott. They continued to hold slightly different opinions about temperance policy; but otherwise a description of Scott's political stance can often be taken as equally true of the attitude of Hicks. As a 'pro-Boer' he became one of a select band who had suffered opprobrium together.[30] It is not difficult to guess what he thought of

[27] Clarke, *Lancashire and New Liberalism*, 71–2.
[28] Margaret Blunden, 'The Anglican Church during the War', in Peter Warwick (ed.), *The South African War: The Anglo-Boer War 1899–1902* (1980); Stephen Koss (ed.), *The Pro-Boers: The Anatomy of an Anti-war Movement* (Chicago/London 1973), 228 ff.
[29] *MG* 1 March 1906.
[30] Hammond, *Scott of the Manchester Guardian*, 185: 'It is difficult to realise how close a bond agreement in that struggle created between public men . . . [Scott] had no intimate political friend who had taken the other view of the Boer War.'

the archbishop's action when he issued in January 1900, in response
to a direction from the Privy Council, a Form of Intercession 'on
behalf of Her Majesty's Naval and Military Forces now in South
Africa' which included in one of the prayers, as it were for the
information of the Almighty, the words, 'We believe that our cause
is just.' He surely agreed with Gore that he could not use those
words in prayer.[31] The attitude which Hicks adopted also made
him a notably political churchman. Temperance might be regarded
as a matter of individual choice; but rejection of government policy in a matter of war and peace put him on the public stage; in
the eyes of others it made him a politician. It also showed his commitment to a particular kind of politics, the politics of conscience.

To define politics as the art of the possible is to give priority
to expedience in public policy. It allows political life in parliamentary
democracy to be seen as an elaborate game in which the prizes
are positions of power or wealth and the culture which wealth
makes possible. It does not exclude benevolence, since benevolence itself may result from the calculation of how to avoid revolutionary upheavals in social life. But it stands in strong contrast to
the kind of politics which is driven by conscience. Hicks was no
political theorist, but he and Scott and those with whom they sympathized began with convictions about morality in public life; their
political activity was conscience-driven. Of course, they did not
stand alone. It can indeed be argued that, like the congruence of
Ruskin and Comte noted above, this attitude revealed itself in different ways in the thought of different men who had no obvious
contact with each other. Of this, two examples have been offered
to us.

The first is T. H. Green. It has already been noticed that Hicks
does not seem to have been influenced by him. But Green is a
good example of the politics of conscience.[32] Melvin Richter has
argued that a generation brought up under the discipline of evangelical piety, even when it had lost faith in the dogmatic religion
of its forebears, needed a justification for its moral code and a new
objective for its moral endeavour. There was a crisis of conscience.
Green adapted Idealism to provide that code, and redirected that
endeavour to political objectives. Richter quotes from Green: 'We

---

[31] G. L. Prestige, *The Life of Charles Gore* (1935), 224–5.
[32] See Richter, *Politics of Conscience*, passim.

are reason of [God's] reason and spirit of his spirit; who lives in our moral life, and for whom we live in living for the brethren, even as in so living we live freely, because in obedience to a spirit which is our self.' This seems not far away from Comte's Religion of Humanity, though Green wanted to emphasize the difference between Comte's image of God, a mere abstraction created by the intellect, and his own description of God as a personal and living reality, the ideal self which is the presupposition of human knowledge and experience. But as Hicks would have rejected the former, on the lines of the critique developed by Maurice and Westcott outlined above; so he would have repudiated the ideal self as a true image of the God he worshipped. It is true that some of Green's disciples were spurred to go out and undertake a strenuous life in the cause of social reform; but others, of a more orthodox faith at either end of the Anglican spectrum, such as Edward King and F. J. Chavasse, accepted the reinstatement of the spiritual dimension of human life without feeling the need to take political action.[33]

A second example of the politics of conscience is provided by Lord Acton.[34] John Nurser has illustrated the fact that Acton placed morality above religion as a guide for life.

If you are guided by any object, then that object must be the highest. Men may then say, the highest object is religion. Therefore persecution is the right thing. To counter that, you must have some object higher even than religion. That is, either politics [are] an affair of morality or the purposes of religion transcend it. If politics transcend religion, that is, if you are a Liberal, it is because the ethical purposes are supreme.[35]

Acton not only argued for the supreme place of morality in political decisions; he also demanded that moral judgements must be brought to bear in historical studies. In this he differed from the Anglican historian, Mandell Creighton, who was scrupulous in avoiding what he regarded as anachronistic moral judgements on people from the past. It is interesting to set this contrast alongside the other difference between the two historians: that Creighton

[33] Edward King, *The Love and Wisdom of God* (1910), 307; on Chavasse, see J. B. Lancelot, *Francis James Chavasse, Bishop of Liverpool* (Oxford 1929), 26: Green 'seemed to have more of the prophet about him than any man I have had the honour of meeting'.

[34] See John Nurser, *The Reign of Conscience: Individual, Church and State in Lord Acton's History of Liberty* (New York 1987).

[35] Cambridge University Library, Add. MS 4908, quoted in Nurser, 29. Many other quotations reinforce this presentation.

moved away from his early Liberalism to a more Conservative position whereas Acton, who was naturally conservative, continued to
assert a Liberal faith. Indeed, as Nurser argues, Acton's view was
that 'a man's standing in the sight of God was to be measured
by his politics rather than his religion. As early as 1877 he had
noted, "Christianity without Liberality will not take us far towards
heaven".'[36]

There is nothing here which is alien to Hicks's own attitude.
But he may have been restrained by two factors. In the first place,
observation would have shown him that most men could hardly
be said to think out either their religion or their politics until they
were roused or challenged to question the standards offered by
their social milieu. His daily contact with the ordinary people of
Salford revealed how limited was their capacity for thinking at a
theoretical level. They were subject to exploitation of both mind
and body; their attitudes were more like reflexes than rationality.
And secondly, the geniality of his nature prevented him judging
anyone's ultimate salvation by his or her political creed. He could
never have written, as Acton did, that 'Disraeli is a criminal'. It
was a true assessment by Dean Fry, after Hicks's death, that he
was 'tolerant beyond the most tolerant that I have known'. He
felt that even the exploiters in society suffered from the methods
they used.

Within the church he found himself surrounded by clergy who
openly worked for the Conservative Party, appearing on Conservative platforms, organizing special meetings for their congregations
and even speaking from their pulpits in favour of the Conservative
cause. The basis of their action was concern about the church's
place in education and the threat of disestablishment. 'Free Trade
in our markets, but no God in our schools.'[37] Both the Lancastrian
bishops, Knox and Chavasse, were stalwart evangelicals and quite
open in their support of the Conservative Party. Knox wrote a
letter which was published in the *Lancashire Daily Post*, in which he
went so far as to say, 'Churchmen who value the security of the
Church on all important issues . . . will naturally throw their whole
and undivided strength into the support of the two excellent

[36] Nurser, *Reign of Conscience*, 170, quoting Cambridge University Library, Add. MS
5552, p. 9
[37] The Vicar of St George's, Stockport, in the *Manchester Courier* 1 Jan. 1906, quoted
in Clarke, *Lancashire and New Liberalism*, 261.

Unionist candidates who are before the constituency [of Preston].'[38] Years earlier, the evangelicals had rallied to the support of the Conservative administration over the Public Worship Regulation Act of 1874. Ritualism and Romanism were indistinguishable in the minds of many. 'Home Rule means Rome Rule' could be a telling slogan. Now they had other reasons for continuing that support. It was no longer to oppose ritualism or Home Rule but to maintain church schools or resist disestablishment. But it was not only the evangelicals who kept aloof from the Liberal Party. The ritualistic phase of the Anglo-catholic movement merged into the phase of slum missions and socialistic theory, of the discovery of the realities of working-class life and the development of catholic socialism. That change did not provide friends for the Liberal Party, which was thought to be irretrievably tainted with individualism and middle-class values. In politics some of the Anglo-catholics turned to the Independent Labour Party (ILP) or even the Social Democratic Federation (SDF). Others, more eccentrically, became extreme Tories, like Archdeacon Denison who nevertheless thanked God that he had never been a Conservative. Nonconformists, on the other hand, were still usually supporters of Liberal candidates —even Hilaire Belloc, the belligerent Roman Catholic candidate, who was backed by the Salford South and West Free Church Council in 1906.

During the last seven years of his ministry in Salford and Manchester it was a problem for Hicks that he found himself owing canonical obedience to a bishop of very different ecclesiastical and political principles from his own. He never spoke a word of criticism of that appointment, but it must have been an unwelcome change after the liberal regime of Bishop James Moorhouse. Knox fitted well into the life of Manchester, with its pronounced strain of working-class Toryism. He was also, in Peter Green's words, a domineering personality.[39] But it was his political activities which brought him into conflict with Hicks, particularly over church schools. At the time of the election in 1906 Knox took part in a demonstration in support of them in the Free Trade Hall and then organized a great show of strength in London which he led with

[38] 6 Jan. 1910, quoted by Clarke, *Lancashire and New Liberalism*, 262. The two sections of Clarke's book, 261–73, provide a valuable background to the last phase of Hicks's activities in Manchester and Salford.

[39] Sheen, *Canon Peter Green*, 39. See also Reckitt, *P. E. T. Widdrington*, 39.

Winnington Ingram, having laid on thirty-three special trains from Manchester for the purpose.

It was a critical issue for Hicks, as for other churchmen who supported the Liberal Party. He was certainly no enemy of church schools, but he was prepared to back Liberal Party policy with its overriding concern for a national system of education within which there could, he believed, be room for religious education as requested by parents. In a letter of December 1905 he wrote:

I am convinced that the safe and solid ground on which we ought to take our stand is the right of all parents, however poor, to have their children taught religion according to the creed which they profess. I am not careful to specify the methods by which this claim would best be satisfied. Let the Government see to that. I observe that the President of the Board of Education starts from the same point, and has repeatedly and explicitly declared himself in favour of an honourable compromise on these lines.

I therefore think it unwise to hasten a conflict with the new Government, or to hold public meetings. I believe far more in private approaches. I fear the only outcome of this sort of conflict—if continued —is strictly secular education. Moreover, I do not want our Churchmen and Clergy, who have been the trusted and impartial administrators of the various Education Acts, to be so committed by a premature agitation to a partisan attitude, as to be disqualified from serving the Church under a new or amended Act.[40]

He was not the only churchman to take up this position. In February 1906 a conference had been held at Scott Holland's house from which a resolution had been sent to Birrell, declaring that the signatories accepted public control over the whole system of secular education, but urging that religious teaching according to the requests of parents should be provided by the religious bodies concerned and given within school hours. A similar line was taken by Hicks's future colleague at Lincoln, T. C. Fry, who argued that the church could not afford all it wanted and should seek a compromise: public control of all schools, with right of entry for religious teaching.[41]

All this was anathema to Bishop Knox, who set out to rally support for church schools and appealed to Conservatives and Unionists to defend them. He put out a Manifesto in 1906 in which

---

[40] Fowler, 131; see also Clarke, *Lancashire and the New Liberalism*, 72–3.
[41] Paget, *Henry Scott Holland*, 227; *Commonwealth* (Jan. 1909), 3.

he called on churchmen to organize a political agitation against Birrell's Education Bill. Hicks wrote a vigorous reply in the *Manchester Guardian*. It was chiefly concerned to explain his own views: that the dual system should be ended and a secular solution should be found. But it concluded on a political note: 'To my mind one of the worst things that could happen to the Church is for it to serve as the rallying-point of a defeated and discredited political party, and for its sacred claims to be placed under the patronage of all those forces of reaction, privilege and militarism from which the democracy has just set itself free.'[42] The political disagreement between Hicks and his bishop continued and reached a climax in another letter from Hicks, published with the heading: 'The Church of England as Electioneer'. Hicks took strong exception to the fact that he was receiving repeated appeals, circulars, and messages from the diocesan office urging him to see that his parishioners were canvassed from house to house and every elector pressed to vote only 'for Church and schools'. It was, he said, a misguided policy to tell churchmen that they must not, on peril of their churchmanship, give weight to the momentous issues of free trade, the rights of the House of Commons, or the menacing power of selfish wealth or the bloated tyranny of the liquor trade. But what he most feared was a widening gulf between the church and the politics of the people, as in France and Italy. 'The sacred cause of freedom has become associated with unbelief and irreligion; the church has shrunk in numbers and in moral influence, until it is regarded (and with justice) as a mere interest or party, the enemy of the nation, and concerned only with manipulating politics to serve its own advantages.' Let it not happen in England.

It is a semantic curiosity that Knox was not called a political churchman but Hicks undoubtedly was. A profile in the *Manchester Evening Chronicle* in 1907 can be taken to show how he was generally regarded:

Parsons nowadays may be roughly divided politically into Conservatives and Christian Socialists. Canon Hicks, Rector of St. Philip's, Salford, is that comparatively rare bird—A Radical clergyman. He makes no secret of the fact. Rather he glories in it, for he loses no time in identifying himself with what is good or bad in Liberalism. He was against the war

[42] *MG* 23 April 1906.

in South Africa, against his own Bishop in the education controversy last year, and now he is against the election of Alderman Holt to the Lord Mayoralty of Manchester . . . Years ago he was tutor to Bishop Welldon, now Dean of Manchester, a post for which the Canon himself was a strong candidate. But his day will come, for the Liberal Government can scarcely overlook its debt to one who has been faithful to its doctrines and ardent in their advocacy.[43]

Yet in spite of his clear support for the Liberal Party during his time in Manchester, his radicalism was deeper than his Liberalism. If the cause of democratic reform found a better advocate than the Liberal Party, his loyalty to it would be strained.

[43] 'Men of Mark', *Manchester Evening Chronicle* No. 48, 16 Sep. 1907.

10

In Favour of Democracy

The position of churchmen who supported the Liberal Party always seemed paradoxical to their critics, because the Liberals drew much of their support from nonconformists and espoused causes such as disestablishment and non-denominational schooling which appeared threatening to the church. During most of Gladstone's political lifetime they could point to him as an undoubted High-Churchman, though that would not commend the Liberal cause to people of moderate churchmanship. In fact he polarized opinion among church people, who tended to see him either as the great leader or as the great betrayer. Differences of opinion about him were also found among Liberal supporters, because the party was, like all political parties, a coalition of different interest-groups, and their comparative influence fluctuated with the passage of time. After Gladstone's death, churchmen who were supporters of the Liberal Party felt embattled, and this feeling persisted right up to the outbreak of war in 1914. When appointed Bishop of Lincoln, Hicks wrote: 'I have had *dismal* letters from the Bp. of Hereford & of Birmingham, lamenting the attitude of the Church towards progressives, & the awful difficulty of being a Bishop & a Liberal!'[1] In his Lincoln diary he mentions a meeting in 1911 with someone who came all the way from Oxford to have his courage as a Liberal fortified by a bishop's assurances. Many church people certainly felt less than wholehearted loyalty to the party. It is noticeable that Scott Holland and other contributors to the *Commonwealth* often express the feeling that their support for the party is not in serious doubt, but neither is it unconditional.

In trying to describe Hicks's political commitment, we need to place it against the background of developments within the party from about 1886 onwards; that is, from that year's General Election, which was the beginning of almost twenty years of rule by

---

[1] Letter to C. P. Scott, 11 April 1910, Manchester Guardian Archives, 128/157.

Conservatives and Unionists, a period broken only by the brief Liberal administrations of 1892–5. G. W. E. Russell's assessment of the change in Liberalism during that period has already been mentioned. Something of Hicks's retrospective view of the same period has also been noticed, with particular reference to his 1889 article on 'The Present Phase of the Temperance Question'. It shows his awareness of the inadequacy of the individualism of the old Manchester school, the need for a programme of social reform, and the possibilities of municipal management—though not in the drink trade. If matters like these were at the top of his agenda and the agenda of other churchmen, and if they acknowledged that such objects could be achieved only through parliamentary action, then they would have to settle for supporting a particular party, even if elements in its programme were uncongenial to churchmen generally. It was also becoming clear that the party would have to take the measure of the reactionary House of Lords.

Hicks was certainly not alone in forming these opinions, and he was drawn into the company of other churchmen who supported the Liberals in parliament, yet felt the difficulty of their situation. In January 1897 he was one of a group which had met under the chairmanship of Scott Holland and drafted a letter to the Liberal whip, Thomas Ellis, in an attempt to influence party policy following the resignation of Lord Rosebery from the leadership. The signatories claimed to represent many others; and they may be taken as a good sample of Liberal churchmen at that date. The list, as published, is headed by Scott Holland and includes, in addition to Hicks, Charles Stubbs (Dean of Ely and later Bishop of Truro), Charles Gore (then Canon of Westminster and later Bishop successively of Worcester, Birmingham, and Oxford), T. C. Fry (headmaster of Berkhamsted School and later Dean of Lincoln), James Adderley (first head of Oxford House), G. W. Kitchin (Dean of Durham and formerly of Winchester), W. R. W. Stephens (Dean of Winchester), E. C. Wickham (Dean of Lincoln), H. J. Torr (Lincolnshire landowner and Liberal parliamentary candidate, and a leading member of the Church Reform League), and H. Russell Wakefield (future Dean of Norwich and Bishop of Birmingham). There was a fair weight of intelligence, learning, and ecclesiastical stature here, but the group contained only two or three lay persons, no diocesan bishops, and therefore no one with a voice in the Lords. The most avowedly Liberal of the bishops, John Percival, appointed by Lord Rosebery to Hereford two years earlier, was perhaps too much of a Low-Churchman to be gathered under Scott Holland's wing.

They believed that the old policy of Liberalism was practically fulfilled and that future policy must concentrate on social questions. The reform of the Lords was important chiefly as bearing on the solution of social difficulties. Even temperance should be seen as part of a wider programme of reform; 'effectively to control drink, powers must be given which will control much else as well'. Disestablishment should be accepted, if it were evidently the will of the nation; but it would contribute nothing to the solution of social problems. The main issue was what they called 'the social pressure on Labour'—a comprehensive term hardly veiling their criticism of exploitation by the capitalists, whether through repressive action against trade unions or through imposition of inhuman conditions in sweated trades. Yet official Liberalism, they said, was out of touch with labour and failed to recognize that workers saw no difference between a rich Liberal capitalist and a rich Tory capitalist. The signatories referred to two matters specifically related to the church. On education, they favoured the fullest popular representation on boards of managers, only requiring that church teaching should be secured to the children of churchmen. On church reform they said it would be 'little less than immoral' to refuse it on the tactical ground that a reformed church would be less easy to disestablish.[2]

Scott Holland's enthusiastic but eirenic personality had conjured agreement out of a group of distinct individuals, but the group had no lasting coherence. They went their different ways, developing different interests, which in later life ranged from the foundation of a religious community (Gore) to presidency of the Christian Counter-Communist Crusade (Russell Wakefield). There were attempts to create a Liberal churchmen's pressure-group, but they led to nothing. The 'new social earnestness' which the signatories claimed to have found among church people found many kinds of outlet; but not in an organized phalanx within the Liberal Party. The South African war not only postponed the movement towards social reform but also divided churchmen of all political persuasions. In May 1904 the *Commonwealth* recorded 'another attempt'

---

[2] *Commonwealth* (Feb. 1897), 58.

to unite Liberal churchmen in a Union. The committee consisted largely of CSU members, but there were notable omissions: Fry and G. W. E. Russell, for instance. In December an advertisement appeared inviting readers to join a Church of England Liberal and Progressive Union. The chairman was the seventh Earl Beauchamp, who had broken the political tradition of his family and joined the Liberals on the issue of Free Trade, but continued the firm churchmanship of his father. Though the sixth Earl was always a Conservative, he had been a friend of Percy Dearmer at Oxford; and Dearmer persuaded the seventh Earl to support him in some of his work for the Christian Social Union, which was largely Liberal in membership. There were other points of contact between the Earl and Liberal churchmen, such as the movement for Church Reform, in which prominent parts were played by Fry and H. J. Torr, and protests against the treatment of conscientious objectors in the 1914–18 war, which also greatly exercised Bishop Hicks. Lord Beauchamp continued to represent the Liberals in the House of Lords and became Lord President of the Council in 1914, but had evidently lost interest in the newly formed Liberal and Progressive Union. In 1906 another advertisement for it, claiming branches in Oxford, South Wales, Liverpool, and Rochester, revealed that the presidency had been taken over by Lord Aberdare. It seems to have left little mark on the history of the time.

The reason why no effective organization of Liberal churchmen arose is simply that there was no adequate basis of agreement between them. What has been said of Dean Inge was true of most of the others. 'He was convinced that he was a Liberal, and that all the opinions he had formed were liberal.'[3] It was a big achievement of Scott Holland to get even a select group to make an agreed statement: 'it is a social policy that we want, and the leader who believes in it'. But exactly what kind of social policy? There are a number of questions which may be taken not only to indicate disagreements between different kinds of Liberals, but also to show what kind of Liberal Hicks was. They all have to do with 'the social pressure on Labour'. There is the question of strikes and labour unrest. There is the question of the relation of the church to secular society. There is the question of the meaning of democracy. The first of these questions is perhaps the most revealing.

[3] Fox, *Dean Inge*, 116.

For although it may superficially be seen as a tactical question concerned with the relation of employer and employed or the nature of the contract underlying industrial relations, it is a touchstone by which to judge how someone sees his or her social situation. Is it on a level with the employed, or with the employer? The second question, concerning the relation of the church to secular society, is unavoidably obscure, but it is useful for the purposes of analysis to divide social reformers into those who see the church as a contributory element within society and those who envisage it as a separate organism, nearer to God than the secular order, and even capable, if necessary, of offering an alternative kind of society to its members, a kingdom of Christ set apart from the kingdoms of the world. At the deepest level lies the third question, of the meaning of democracy. Who constitute the 'demos' and what powers may it legitimately exercise?

These questions have a special importance in the present context because they help to bring out in greater detail Hicks's attitude to social reform. For he wrote no political testament, but had something to say about each of them, chiefly as a journalist and as a frequent correspondent with the papers. He was invited to become a contributor to the *Manchester Guardian* in 1904 and continued to contribute as 'Quartus' until 1910. This was almost the last period before the transformation which overtook the press when newspapers which had formerly prospered or failed through close political associations shook themselves free in order to respond the better to commercial considerations.[4] This kind of journalism was something which Hicks enjoyed. In his letter to C. P. Scott on his appointment to Lincoln, he referred to his last contribution and said, 'Another "Quartus" will be a happy morning for me.' Although his articles dealt mainly with church affairs, he did not hesitate to raise political questions in which the church ought to be involved. Indeed the distinction between political questions and those of a moral or religious nature was not one which had much meaning to him. The politics of conscience determined that questions of conscience were often those that were labelled political. He also wrote frequent signed letters to the *Manchester Guardian* (about seventy in the period 1892–1910), and he evidently

---

[4] See Stephen Koss, *The Rise and Fall of the Political Press in Britain* (1981). Koss is chiefly concerned, however, with the London situation rather than that at Manchester.

drew a distinction between his comments as 'Quartus' and his personal letters, though the basis of that distinction is not obvious.

Other comments of a political nature were contributed to the *Optimist*. This small-circulation journal, founded directly under Hicks's influence and edited by his disciple, Samuel Proudfoot, set out to answer the question, Does the church care for bodies as well as spirits? In 1908 it described itself as 'A Review dealing with practical theology, literature, and social questions in a Christian spirit'. Surprisingly, it survived for a number of years and attracted some interesting contributors. These ranged from the Archbishop of Canterbury's Chaplain, G. K. A. Bell, through various kinds of traditional Liberal churchmen, for example Russell and Fry, to such colourful characters as G. K. Chesterton and the Countess of Warwick, and on to a varied group of committed socialists including Conrad Noel and the leftwardly mobile Hewlett Johnson. It did a balancing act on the borderline between the Liberalism of the CSU and the socialism of the Church Socialist League, and its two changes of name, already mentioned, show the difficulty of doing so. Hicks was happy to consort with such a goodly company of contributors.

He also just occasionally contributed to other journals such as the *Political Quarterly* and the *Contemporary Review*. But his contributions to the *Manchester Guardian* were those which reached the widest readership, though it was read more by so-called opinion-formers than by working people. Hicks, like most members of the educated class, had a poor opinion of the cheap press, which, he said, had been used by millionaires to lead the masses away from a sane view of national interests and political duties and to delude them into reactionary courses. After his move to Lincoln his journalistic output declined; but he did not hesitate to touch on political matters in his regular letters in the monthly *Lincoln Diocesan Magazine* and in presidential addresses to the diocesan conference. There are, therefore, various sources from which we can assess his opinions on the questions mentioned above.

The organization of workers' strikes elicited extreme reactions from some churchmen. The worst responses date from a much later period and are related to the General Strike of 1926.[5] The

---

[5] For example, Inge thought that all his class might then be ruined by civil war (Fox, *Dean Inge*, 188).

sympathies of churchmen could be strongly biased by their social distance from industrial workers, so that they overlooked the misery which led to strikes and thought only of those who suffered as a consequence of their action. The humane Francis Kilvert, in the 1870s, could only see a miners' strike as leading to the suffering of the poor who were left without heating in their homes, and thought the union men were intimidating their fellow workers who wanted to go to work. But then he never had any close experience of industrial areas. After the end of the First World War the Bishop of Liverpool, F. J. Chavasse, urged both mine-owners and miners to forgo some profits or wages, as though they both had something to spare.[6] It is noticeable that the *Commonwealth* and those associated with it generally supported the strikers or those who were locked out, by their comments and sometimes by their actions. One of the first actions of the newly founded CSU in August 1889 was to persuade Frederick Temple, then Bishop of London, to become involved, even though rather ineffectually, in conciliation during the Dockers' Strike.[7] Several successive issues of the *Commonwealth* commented on the engineering dispute in 1898, and castigated the Liberal leaders for failing to say a word for the men because they were in terror of the great nonconformist capitalists. The period before the outbreak of war was a time of bitter industrial unrest, and strikes were frequent. They included some which seem now surprising, such as a strike of professional cricketers (1896) and of organ builders (1914).

We can presume that Hicks would regard the actions of the capitalists with suspicion and would try to understand the problems and the miseries of the workers. An editorial comment in the *Commonwealth*, probably by Scott Holland, repudiated the common assumption that the blacklegs stood for freedom of labour, and asserted that unorganized labour means labour that is never free. Hicks was certainly not bound to old-fashioned Liberal individualism, and would not have disagreed.[8] As bishop he tried to be very careful in any public comments on industrial disputes,

---

[6] Frederick Grice, *Francis Kilvert and his World* (Horsham n.d.), 247–8; Lancelot, *Francis James Chavasse*, 210. Kilvert approved of a proposal to import Chinese coolies to work in British mines.

[7] Paget, *Henry Scott Holland*, 170; E. G. Sandford (ed.), *Memoirs of Archbishop Temple by Seven Friends* (1906), 142 ff.

[8] *Commonwealth* (July 1912), 211.

without taking the easy way out and saying nothing. In August 1911, just over a year after his enthronement, there was a great railway strike, and in Lincoln this somehow gave rise to a riot. Hicks responded in a sermon which he preached in the cathedral and in a pastoral letter in the *Lincoln Diocesan Magazine* in the following month. He made a firm distinction between the genuine workpeople on strike and the lawless element which was always ready to take advantage of any unrest. That element had to be cowed by the exhibition of force, but force was no remedy in dealing with honest working people. He was glad to be able to say that employers and employed 'are now conferring upon terms of perfect equality'. That must imply that the workers were acting as an organized union, without which there could be no possibility of equality. In a longer perspective, the lawless element in society should be lessened by education, by religion, by better housing, by temperance reform. But, more generally, he urged his readers to ask themselves some questions:

Can any of us feel satisfied with the condition of our working classes? Which of us would be willing to exchange lots with them? Are we satisfied with their housing, their average health, their average conditions of toil? If not, let us set ourselves resolutely to amend them. Be assured that the way of social peace and national prosperity lies through social reform and the improvement of industrial conditions.

It is noticeable that he assumed, as many were unwilling to do, that working people had the same basic needs as middle-class families. His sermon made some of the same points, with more emotive force.

In the following year there was a great coal strike and Hicks preached another sermon, reported at length in the *Lincoln Diocesan Magazine* for April 1912, in which he sketched the historical background of what he called the 'labour war'. England had been developing for centuries from a feudal aristocracy into an industrial democracy.

The education of the workers, their voluntary organisations, their collective intelligence, have combined to make them feel acutely the disadvantages under which they live. They perceive how the vast scale of modern industry, the recent developments of capitalized trade and manufacture, tend continually to make the workman a mere hireling, or even a machine, employed to create wealth which his class does not enjoy, divorced as they are from the ownership of land and any other instruments of production. They perceive also that while the wealth of modern England is almost incalculable, it ministers to the luxuries comparatively of a few, while millions of the toilers exist on less than £1 per week per family, though the purchasing power of the £1 grows less.

He went on to declare his belief that the workers' desires were not merely for better material conditions of life but also for a better intellectual and moral life, for thought, for culture. That, he said, accorded with the purpose of God and the gospel of his Son. It was a nice irony that the report of his sermon in the *Lincoln Diocesan Magazine* was followed by a review of G. W. E. Russell's memoir of Bishop King, whose 'character approached as near to faultlessness as any we are likely to meet upon earth'. Hicks's predecessor had never been stirred to declaim against the structural evils of industrial society; and he had even been mildly rebuked by his friend Scott Holland for failing to intervene in an earlier strike in Grimsby. It was clear, then, where Hicks's sympathies lay, though he stopped short of sympathizing with each and every strike. In 1918 he privately referred to a strike which involved railwaymen along with miners as 'absurd', perhaps because he thought secondary action unreasonable, or perhaps because he thought the demands of the war effort altered the situation.[9] But the main point is clear: that he tried to see strike action from the position of the honest worker, badly paid, badly housed, badly treated at work. That sympathy pushed him from radicalism to the support of the Labour movement.

The second test question about Hicks's kind of Liberalism is: How did he see the relation of the church to society? He served the church in its ministry for almost fifty years, and with eminent faithfulness. Yet it never became the be-all and end-all of his life. He saw it as an agency of God within the life of society. But the relationship of church and society during his active ministry was inevitably seen in terms of establishment or disestablishment. His Liberal upbringing would have familiarized him with Gladstone's change of opinion from something like Hooker's equation of citizen and churchman to the ideal of a free church in a free state.[10] The ideal relationship of church and state, Gladstone had argued, was that of two coextensive societies; but this was no longer practicable, because of the degree of religious pluralism which had

---

[9] *Diary*, 25 Sept. 1918.   [10] See Butler, *Gladstone*, 105, 124–5.

arisen. The autonomy of the state, however, did not give it the right to dominate the church in the manner of old-fashioned Whig Erastianism. It should enable the church to develop according to its own nature and its own commission. The state should also continue to exercise a moral responsibility in government. The logic of this development led to disestablishment, and Gladstone in his first ministry in 1869 carried through the disestablishment of the Church of Ireland. There were, of course, special reasons, apart from the acceptance of the ideal of religious liberty, which made this both desirable and possible. By the time that Hicks became politically active that was past history, and the debate had turned to further acts of disestablishment. Gladstone had begun to prepare the way for disestablishing the Welsh and Scottish churches. Campbell Bannerman, the first effective Liberal leader after Gladstone, was strongly in favour of disestablishment, but it was left to Asquith in 1912 to take the next decisive action by the introduction of the Bill to disestablish the Welsh church. That is the background against which Hicks expressed his thoughts about church and state.

From the first his attitude was given a particular slant by his overriding concern for temperance legislation. Temperance had been his way into political life, and it inevitably affected other political issues. For one thing, it brought him into familiarity with leading nonconformists. He was quite willing to stand alongside the predominantly nonconformist members of the UKA for the sake of temperance, though it strained his loyalty to the UKA when they endorsed the candidature of a Conservative whose views on temperance they approved. This dilemma did not face him in Salford itself, where in 1900 the UKA opposed the Conservative candidate, J. G. Groves, who was a brewer. But there were problems when Liberals deserted the cause of temperance. Hilaire Belloc, who was no sort of temperance advocate, represented Salford South as a Liberal from 1906 to 1910 and tried to enlist the support of publicans who had their own reasons for disliking the brewers. In his overriding concern for temperance Hicks was at first inclined to take a neutral attitude to disestablishment, and to prefer that it should not be part of Liberal policy. So in 1892 in the letter to Gladstone already quoted he declared that fear of disestablishment had made many churchmen vote against the Liberals rather than for the Conservatives, and in doing so had defeated hopes for temperance reform.

As the years went by he began to regard disestablishment with a more friendly eye. In 1905, in one of his articles in the *Manchester Guardian*, he made it clear that he did not want just any kind of established church:

> One had thought that Dr Arnold's notions of Church reform were as extinct as the dodo . . . I thought his ideas of State-made uniformity were imported by Chevalier Bunsen from the Court of Prussia, and belonged to the same exotic influence which gave us the Jerusalem Bishopric . . . All the living forces in the Church today are making for her independence of the State . . . In the person of W. E. Gladstone and his friend Lord Acton . . . we have surely learned that a devotion to historical Christianity, and to its more Catholic type, is at least compatible with the most ardent and modern love of liberty.

At one stage he saw disestablishment as loss, as humiliation, with probable disendowment; not as release into freedom. It stood for the repudiation by secular society of what the church stood for. It meant that society was to be organized on secular lines. But still the church could serve and save.

By the time he moved to Lincoln, nonconformist pressure for the disestablishment of the Church of England had diminished and the focus was on the very different situation in Wales, with its predominance of chapel-goers. In his Primary Charge he referred to the issue, saying that he had been brought up in Oxford to regard the church's connection with the state not as essential but as accidental, and quoted Liddon after the Purchas judgment in support of his attitude. There was, he believed, a contradiction between establishment and the principle of popular representation which had come to rule in political life and was winning its way in church organization, too. His emphasis here was not on any theoretical arguments about church and state, but rather on the question of 'church defence', at a time when there were efforts to organize church members to oppose the Welsh Church Bill— efforts in which the dean of his cathedral was playing a leading part. Hicks argued, as Anglo-catholic leaders had in the past, that effective church work was the best and indeed the only church defence. In April 1912 he refused to vote for a resolution, supported by the archbishop and almost all the other bishops, calling upon all church people to oppose the Bill. He had not actually spoken against it, and in a letter to Scott he said, 'I had to give a *silent* vote in Convocation, restraining myself with difficulty, because everything I say is passed on to the Lincolnshire local papers and commented upon . . . so as to make me as odious as possible to the Churchfolk of the Diocese.'[11] Later he wrote:

I am not a devotee of Establishment; I feel keenly the disadvantages of union with the State. But the Church is Established, and the vast majority of Churchmen today—clerical and lay—appear to delight in Establishment. If so, while we are an Established Church we must make the best of our position, and be content with some laxity of discipline and with a certain give-and-take in the matter of legislation.[12]

The reference in the last sentence was to the question of the remarriage of the divorced. He had urged the clergy not to solemnize such marriages, but his refusal to take up the cudgels against permissive legislation had left him open to a charge of Erastianism. It points to the fact that there were two different kinds of issue raised by the establishment debate: doctrinal and moral. On moral issues, a disestablished church could bear its witness but not dictate to the state. On doctrinal issues, and related liturgical matters, the state could not interfere with the decisions of a disestablished church.[13]

There were certainly many complications in the question of disestablishment, but Hicks's general line was to accept the decision of the democratically elected representatives of the people, and get on with the work which the church had to do. The situation was, however, further complicated by the outbreak of war and the National Mission which will be discussed later. It was as though the increasing pluralism of the pre-war years had been halted, and there was now a single body to be addressed, a nation unified by a common purpose, and the proper agent to carry the call to repentance and reform was the Established Church. Hicks felt that the criticism and the rivalry of the nonconformist churches had fallen away. The relation of church and state seemed to have been transformed. In his presidential address to his diocesan conference in 1916 he said:

I have been cheered by receiving resolutions from several Synods of the Wesleyan Methodists, who wish God-speed to the National Mission

---

[11] *MG* archives, 332.   [12] *LDM* (Nov. 1912), 179–80.
[13] But doctrinal questions might enter into legal disputes, as in the case of Scottish 'Disruption'.

. . . It is noteworthy today that few attacks upon the Church come from Nonconformity. Dissenters may desire Disestablishment and even Disendowment; they may question Episcopacy; they may disapprove of our Sacramental teaching; but they have feelings of sympathy for the Church as a preacher of the Gospel of Christ, and words of praise for the devotion and effectual zeal of her Ministers.

He went on to argue that in order to be more effective the church needed freedom to regulate its own life; but denied that that would necessarily involve disestablishment, pointing to the example of the Church of Scotland.

He spoke in this instance with an optimism which he did not always feel. But his words reveal that to him the church mattered a great deal, but the nation mattered even more. Two years later, in his presidential address the emphasis had changed. He spoke about the Life and Liberty movement, whose champions were 'bravely battling against apathy and ignorance'. The essence of the movement was the conviction that the church could not be alive and alert and active unless it was permitted by the state, within certain safe limits, to reform itself, to 'adapt her rules, her formularies, her worship, to the needs of the time'. His earlier optimism seemed to have been eroded by wartime experiences, or perhaps just by advancing years, for he was well on in his seventies and his health was not robust. He continued:

If the Church makes this challenge to the State: if she asks for a liberty which is essential to her life, and is denied it, what, then, is the Church to do? I can see no honourable alternative, except to ask for voluntary Disestablishment. If Liberty is of vital importance, and no other means are available for obtaining it, then Disestablish. Better Disestablishment and even some loss of endowments than a moral and spiritual Death. It is because this alternative presents itself so clearly to my mind, that I have been less strenuous than some others in pressing forward the 'Life and Liberty' movement.

Here, and indeed throughout Hicks's recorded statements about the role of the church, there is little trace of the image of the ark of salvation or the eucharistic community living the redeemed life in the midst of an unredeemed world. For him, the church was above all a witness to the world for righteousness. He believed it ought to be 'a mighty engine for moral and social reformation'. He loved its history, he valued its stores of learning, and he treasured its tradition of worship. But the men he admired were those he regarded as prophets, whether or not they had been churchmen: Carlyle, Maurice, Kingsley, Browning, Tennyson, 'and Ruskin the greatest of them'. With them he coupled great political leaders, Peel, Cobden, and Gladstone.

If we try to answer the question concerning the relation of the church to secular society, as Hicks understood it, we must put him on the side of those who saw it as a contributory element within society rather than on the side of those who envisaged it as a separate organism offering an alternative kind of society to its members. It was endowed with great treasures, but it could not claim any kind of infallibility. It was too evidently faulted by its failure to witness to social righteousness, and not least by its subservience to conservative politics. That prevented it exercising what ought to have been its prophetic role. At the same time, it needed some degree of freedom to carry out its own reform. That might be achieved by the measures proposed by the Life and Liberty movement. But Hicks was less than a wholehearted supporter, because he mistrusted the politically conservative tendencies of existing representative bodies, and probably foresaw the development of organized partisan groups within the Church Assembly. He was always an independent churchman, without the backing of a group of like-minded ecclesiastical politicians. In his view the state connection, with all its disadvantages, had preserved precious freedoms. In 1905, in a 'Quartus' article, he had reviewed Gore's opinions about the parson's freehold, and stressed the dangers inherent in its abolition. It would not be wise, he said, 'to add to the autocracy of the bishop' whatever power was taken from the freehold. The bishops' influence was conservative, a drag on the wheels of reform. Both the evangelical revival and the Oxford Movement would have been stifled at birth, but for that freehold. If it had to go, it would be necessary to 'call into life the corporate authority of the Church'.[14]

Here, too, as in his address to his diocesan conference in 1918, he avoided committing himself to a particular policy for church reform. He wanted to combine effectiveness with freedom. A church free from state interference could not be guaranteed to preserve within its own life the freedom it had in fact enjoyed while the

---

[14] *MG* 16 Feb. 1905.

state, for whatever reasons, frustrated heresy hunts. The contemporary Free Churches and the Roman Catholic Church supplied cautionary examples of the tendency of self-governing bodies to maintain unity by the repression of speculative thought. Yet the Church of England's comparative toleration of theological speculation coexisted with a degree of political servitude which led to ineffectiveness in the field of social reform. The favourable and unfavourable aspects of Establishment matched each other. In the time of his episcopate Hicks found himself inevitably caught up in discussions of ecclesiastical discipline and authority, and striving to maintain the maximum degree of freedom of thought for individuals within the church. He also believed it was necessary, for the coherence of the church, to limit individual freedom in public worship and in moral action. The often-quoted phrase concerning 'the right of the individual, which is to be free, and the duty of the institution, which is to be something'[15] appropriately describes the assumptions underlying much of Hicks's activity.

The problem which seems to have been at the back of his mind was the danger of the institution becoming oppressive. It was a problem which had exercised Acton. 'The Church, left to herself, to her own laws and penalties, her own legislative and judicial powers, will govern by fire and torture. The very principle of liberty is: the Church curbs the State, and the State the Church.'[16] There is no evidence to show that Hicks knew Acton's opinion (though it is not impossible), but his hesitations indicate a similar train of thought. It may be significant that when he met J. N. Figgis at Lincoln they did not seem very sympathetic to each other. His diary entry for 30 December 1913 includes a brief record of their meeting at one of the Lincoln vicarages. Although Figgis shared with Hicks a highly critical attitude to the contemporary worship of mammon, they were very different from each other, both temperamentally and in their view of the way society was constituted and ought to develop. Figgis had a romantic view of the Middle Ages, thought ideas of progress hollow, and espoused a syndicalist view of the nature of society, as a set of interlocking

[15] *Amiel's Journal: The Journal Intime of Henri-Frédéric Amiel*, trans. Mrs Humphry Ward (1901), 156.
[16] Cambridge University Library, Add. MS 4915, quoted in Nurser, *Reign of Conscience*, 45.

corporations.[17] Hicks, on the other hand, took a more Maurician view of the nation, as part of God's constitution for mankind; he believed that there had been genuine progress in political life and that further progress waited upon further political action; and he found no inspiration in medieval society. The purpose of the church as an institution, in Hicks's view, was primarily to witness to social righteousness; and while working out his position on church reform he was also adjusting his political position to changing circumstances. He was edging towards the nascent Labour Party.

So we can proceed to the third test question. What was his attitude to democracy? The idea of democracy was not popular among churchmen and intellectuals. Churchmen were committed to an organization which had developed on lines inimical to democracy. As Mandell Creighton once said, 'The state tends to become more democratic; the church is monarchical or oligarchic.'[18] But it was not only by their acceptance of the church's organizational tradition that churchmen were restrained from welcoming democratic ideas. They could appeal to much in the Bible in favour of monarchy or oligarchy. That was a stumbling block to biblical literalists, of course; but it was a problem also for F. D. Maurice, the fountain-head of much social thinking for churchmen of Hicks's generation. Maurice had written to J. M. Ludlow during the American civil war.

The horror of democracy which you impute to me is a horror in the interest of the people . . . If they grasp at any power merely as a power, I believe the voice of the Demos will be the devil's voice and not God's. I apply no different rule to one set of men from that which I apply to another. I look on the tyranny of the one, the few, or the majority, with like abhorrence.

The tyranny of the majority, he believed, was the surest step to the tyranny of the one.[19] Much had changed since 1865, when this letter was written. Above all the reform of parliamentary franchise had incorporated into one electoral body, along with an educated

[17] See David Newsome, 'The Assault on Mammon: Charles Gore and John Neville Figgis', *Journal of Ecclesiastical History* 17/2 (Oct. 1966), 227–41.
[18] Creighton, *Life and Letters*, 432.
[19] F. Maurice (ed.), *The Life of Frederick Denison Maurice, Chiefly Told in his Own Letters*, 2 vols. (1884), ii. 497.

middle class, many of those whose extra-parliamentary activity in 1848 had so alarmed Maurice and his friends. Moreover, the widening of the franchise had not had the revolutionary effect many had prophesied. This restructuring of British society really undermined much of Maurice's theological interpretation of the constitution of the nation. Monarchy was enervated; nobility was coming to appear a merely reactionary element, resisting the changes necessitated by industrialization; and Demos approximated more nearly to the total nation as the franchise expanded. At the same time the use of scripture as a quarry for political ideas became less acceptable, as critical method began to dissolve its apparent unity, and historical study relegated the structures of Israelite society to the status of stages on the road of human development.

The other group resistant to the appeal of democracy was a certain element within the intelligentsia. Dean Inge once wrote that Conservatives wished the country to be governed by intelligence, and therefore they could not really be in favour of democracy.[20] It was a strange statement about Conservatives in general, but it could have been applied more justly to some intellectuals. There was already at work in late-Victorian and Edwardian times the élitist view which found expression in H. G. Wells's utopia of the rule of the Samurai, and in various writers' advocacy of eugenics. This kind of attitude arose from the idea that government was a technical activity which could be handled simply by the use of intelligence. But intellectuals who had a firm grasp of the moral nature of government could not be seduced by that kind of pseudo-scientific élitism. Lord Acton, who might have had every excuse, religious and intellectual, for opposing democracy, was not so deluded.

The danger is not that a particular class is unfit to govern. Every class is unfit to govern. The law of liberty tends to abolish the reign of race over race, of faith over faith, of class over class. It is not the realisation of a political ideal: it is the discharge of a moral obligation . . . Almost all that has been done for the good of the people has been done since the rich lost the monopoly of power, since the rights of property were discovered to be not quite unlimited.[21]

---

[20] W. R. Inge, *Assessments and Anticipations* (1929), 135.
[21] Lord Acton, *Letters to Mary, Daughter of the Right Hon. W. E. Gladstone*, ed. Herbert Paul (1904), 93–4.

Hicks was both a churchman and an intellectual. He looked up to Maurice as a great teacher, and he respected intellectual gifts. But he was exempted from the temptation to reject democracy on religious or intellectual grounds by his adoption of a critical attitude towards the Bible and Christian tradition, by his interest in the historical development of human societies, and by his conviction that good government depended on sensitive morality and not on clever manipulation. All this is explicitly borne out by his public pronouncements. He was far from being unaware of the dangers and failures of democracy, but he would not let them destroy his hopes of democratic reform. In a sermon in 1906 he admitted that the old faith in democracy, the faith of Mazzini and de Tocqueville, had lost its spell, partly through the evident corruption of American municipal life and the blundering development of democracy in the colonies. But democracy had not committed one thousandth part of the crimes of oligarchy and tyranny. He declared that he remained an invincible and unwearying optimist.[22] As for the silence of the New Testament on political issues, it was necessary to recognize the difference between the political situation of the early church and that of the contemporary church.

The ethical teaching of the New Testament is limited in its precepts (not its principles) by the range of circumstances with which it deals . . . Today you and I are members of a Christian democracy. We have, or shall have, the power of voting on all sorts of issues, and thereby shall play a part in governing not only ourselves but also a large portion of mankind. It would seem that no small part of the duty of a Christian gathers round his status as a free citizen of a Christian democracy . . . It is clear that the area of moral obligation has been vastly widened by this enfranchisement.[23]

In a sermon preached to a congregation of men in 1913 he declared that 'Demos' had come of age; let him beware, and avoid flatterers, be virtuous and do his duty by home, his class, his country, and his God.[24] Given his acceptance of democracy and his concern for the condition of life of working people, it was inevitable that he would turn his attention to the Labour movement, and in due course to the Labour Party.

[22] *Optimist* (Apr. 1906).
[23] *Christianity and the Drink Trade*, quoted in Fowler, 190–1.
[24] *Diary*, 19 Oct. 1913.

The main period of Hicks's involvement with political ideas coincided with a critical time in the development of trade-unionism and labour representation in parliament. The 1880s saw the rise of the 'new unionism', in which the emphasis shifted from more-skilled workers and the provision of benefits to the less-skilled and to more militant tactics inspired by increasing acceptance of socialist ideas. Strong reaction from the employers and, later on, the Taff Vale judgment of 1900, which made unions liable for damages resulting from official union actions, increased workers' resolve to obtain parliamentary representation to ensure the reversal of this judgment and the passing of other legislation to protect and encourage trade-unionism. The co-operation of the Parliamentary Committee of the TUC with the Labour Representation Committee in the election of January 1906 resulted in the presence of over fifty members in parliament and the formation of the Parliamentary Labour Party. The divisions within the Liberal Party after 1910 encouraged Labour supporters to envisage the formation of a Labour government in the near future.

Hicks's temperance interests had made him a sharp critic of capitalists and he was ready to see the need for workers' organizations to resist inhuman treatment by employers. By 1905 he was looking for the creation of a parliamentary force to champion the cause of working people. In a 'Quartus' article (26 January) he commented on the situation in Russia, where the national church had shown not the slightest sympathy with the people's aspirations towards liberty and right government, and continued: 'Our progress is proceeding peaceably but slowly. Progress will be quickened if Liberalism and Labour avoid quarreling. The Church of England has many sons whose sympathies and convictions lie wholly on the side of democracy and labour.' And it was not only in the Church of England that these sympathies were at work. In a later article (9 March) he expressed the hope that the day would come when Church and Dissent would 'vie with each other in practical sympathy with the righteous aims of labour'. His attitude was evidently in strong contrast to that of his bishop. Bishop Knox drew severe criticism from a labour correspondent in the *Commonwealth*, who accused him and other bishops of trying to defeat the Progressive cause and going to the utmost extreme in identifying the church with Toryism and Protection. Hicks did not single out his bishop for criticism, but he was particularly outspoken in his criticism of Tory influence in the church at the time of Lloyd George's budget of 1909, which embodied a scheme of land taxes, strongly resisted in the House of Lords. 'Every organisation of churchmen in certain dioceses', he wrote, 'is being drilled and engineered for the Tory party.' Nevertheless not a few of the clergy would be found definitely on the side of the people as against the peers, and on the side of democratic finance as against the plutocratic domination of the land and liquor monopolies. In Hicks's view the achievement of the righteous aims of labour would not come mainly through the sympathy of the churches. His close association with Sir Wilfrid Lawson had taught him otherwise. At the unveiling of the statue to Lawson on the Embankment in 1909, he made a short speech, as Honorary Secretary of the UKA, and said:

One homely sentence of his came again and again in his speeches, and I cannot help recording it. He said, 'Working-men, you must help yourselves; no-one can help you unless you help yourselves.' It appears to me that that homely phrase of his is prophetic of developments which we shall see in the social and political progress of our country in the coming years.[25]

When he was appointed bishop in 1910 he believed, rightly or wrongly, that unlike the majority of bishops he had the support of working people. In his letter of thanks to C. P. Scott for his good wishes, he said that 'the friendship which lies behind is more precious than all else', and went on to mention warm-hearted letters which he had received from working men. 'These assurances that I am understood by the industrial class and Labour are comforting to me.' The dismal letters from Percival and Gore had not entirely discouraged him. 'Neither of them, I reflect, finds that he has the backing which I have, and *hope to retain*, in the sympathy and convictions and approval of a vast industrial population such as Lancashire.'[26] One of his last articles for the *Manchester Guardian* before leaving Salford (3 May 1910) was on the question of 'Morality and Politics'. In it he referred to a sermon of the Revd John Wakeford, which had apparently attacked the dishonesty of politicians as contributing to the weakened influence of Great Britain in international affairs. Hicks declared that this diagnosis was

---

[25] Russell, *Wilfrid Lawson*, 386.   [26] *MG* Archives, 128/157, 11 April 1910.

wrong. The fault lay in the weakness of a coalition government and in the divided state of English counsels. It was obvious that the Labour Party and the Radicals were far more keen than the Whigs on moral issues in international life, such as Chinese slavery on the Rand, Armenian massacres, and the evils of the Congo. The disgraceful story of the Chinese Opium Wars and the intrigues by which the British became owners of the Kimberley mines proved that our own hands were not clean. But Radicals at least were ashamed of such misdeeds. It was not a question of the moral honesty and dignity of politicians, but of their outlook on life and their sensitiveness to moral obligations. Hicks's politics of conscience, which had kept him on the Radical wing of the Liberals, was now pushing him into the arms of the Labour Party.

After his move to Lincoln he continued to press the cause of the working population, though he tried to avoid laying himself open to the criticism that he was telling the diocese which party they should vote for. There had already been a debate in the diocesan conference in 1907 in Bishop King's time on the question of 'The Attitude of the Church towards the Changing Conditions of Labour', with T. C. Fry as an invited speaker giving a forthright address in which he described trade unions as 'a dyke to resist the flood of unmoralised capital', and the Magnificat as 'the anthem of the labour movement'. We do not know how Bishop King would have responded to this strong stuff. He was ill and unable to attend, but his prepared address was read out. In it he appealed to the law of love to guide commercial and economic relations, and urged that the subject should be treated 'without the narrowing influence of party politics and without prejudice or partiality to any class'. The resolutions proposed at the conference recommended that ordinands should study social relations, that church workers should be taught the elements of 'industrial and sanitary law', and that there should be more public teaching on duty to one's neighbour. All this was in line with the usual eirenic procedure of representative church conferences.[27] At Hicks's first diocesan conference he reversed the procedure. Instead of taking off the edge of a speaker's rhetoric with an anodyne set of resolutions, he picked

[27] The Lincoln resolutions were largely an echo of those which had been proposed by a Joint Committee of the Canterbury Convocation and House of Laymen on which Dean Wickham served. Wagner (*Church of England*, 243 ff.) comments that they were 'singularly moderate in view of the Report'.

up a discussion of 'Religion and Amusements', probably program-
med before his arrival in Lincoln, and gave it a cutting edge by
saying, in an extempore intervention: 'We have organised capital
trying to encroach upon the rest and the quiet of the Sunday, and
on the other hand we have Labour; and our business is not to
organise amusement, but to take part in the great conflict on behalf
of Labour against the encroachment of Capital.' He returned to
the topic again in 1912, because he had been taken severely to
task for what he had said. His comment then was that he had not
referred to particular business men but to 'the impersonal, unseen,
but overwhelming impulse, which requires money to be made and
invested capital to earn its due increment'. It was an important
consequence of his genial human relations with all kinds of individuals that he adopted what we might now call a sociological
approach to political questions.

In discussions about the need of the church to have greater
freedom to manage its own affairs, he urged the importance of
letting the voice of labour be heard in church conferences, along
with the voice of women and the voice of the teachers. They were
elements of strength which the church could not afford to miss.
He responded gladly when invited to chair a special Ruri-decanal
Conference at Scunthorpe on 'Labour and Organised Christianity' in 1916, in which representatives of the ILP and the trade
unions participated. He was already telling church people to look
forward to the possible formation of a Labour government within
the next ten years. If that came about, he said, they would perhaps wish that more churchmen had been found in the ranks of
progress. In 1918, despite the discouragements of the war, his hopes
seemed to rise. In a Lenten Pastoral he tried to assess the impact
of the reform of the franchise. He wrote of the new role of women
and its effect on the church, and then continued:

Great Britain presents now to the world at large perhaps the greatest and
completest Democracy that ever yet had being. The experience of the last
three years has rapidly trained our manual workers and wage earners of
either sex to enjoy a standard of comfort not reached before, and to
think out anew the great problems of Labour and Capital, and the trend
of our industrial development. It is conceivable that a Labour Ministry
may be in power within a very few years; and we may well ask whether
the Democracy of Britain is ready—in education, in character, in a sense
of responsibility—for the great task that may have to be undertaken.

He had already taken the unusual step, for a bishop, of promoting the formation of a branch of the Labour Party within his diocese. He was the chief speaker at the first public meeting under the auspices of the Spalding and District Labour Party in February 1918, being supported on the platform by two of the Spalding clergy. In his speech he maintained that they were at a point of great importance in the history of their country. The recent increase in the electorate had made a kind of revolution in England. Each Reform Act had changed the temper and character of the House of Commons. Now it was time to take counsel about the probability of a Labour government, and the grave responsibility attached to government in a democracy. In particular, they must abolish all secret diplomacy and ensure that the enfranchised millions knew what their rulers were doing. The Labour Party must open its membership to all and work for the good of the whole country.[28] It was an optimistic speech, designed to raise hopes and to call the hearers to a sense of responsibility. The last parliamentary election before his death left him struggling against disillusionment. But then he had never shared what has been called 'the nineteenth century hope of a single progression which simultaneously explains and validates the final product'.[29] There were doubts and problems in the progress of social reform. Although he recognized the need to change the structures which produced exploitation, he believed that the motive power for that change derived from significant individuals. When he accepted the bishopric of Lincoln he hoped to be able to put his shoulder to the wheel of change.

[28] Report in the *Lincolnshire, Boston and Spalding Free Press* 19 Feb. 1918.
[29] Ernest Gellner, 'What do we Need Now?', *Times Literary Supplement* 16 July 1993.

II

A Liberal Bishop

In spite of the opinion of Randall Davidson, Asquith recommended Edward Hicks to the king for appointment to Lincoln in 1910. In retrospect some commentators on church affairs thought the choice of see unsuitable. Hastings Rashdall wished Hicks had gone to London in 1901, to save that diocese from chaos. It is doubtful if that would have suited him, for he was no Londoner. London, to him, meant the British Museum and not much else. A writer in the *Church Times* thought he should have gone to Durham in 1890.[1] Each of these notions reveals, beneath the obvious respect in which Hicks was held, a hidden agenda. To Rashdall, Hicks was a defender of theological liberty; to the *Church Times* he was a more reliable churchman than Westcott, not to mention Moule. In its obituary notice it spoke of 'grave anxieties' about the succession to Edward King at Lincoln which had been set at rest by Hicks's appointment. Durham would certainly have been attractive because of its combination of scholarship and industrial life. It would have been a proper climax to a ministry which had been marked by those two interests. But it is never the way of Prime Ministers to consider how a particular priest's ministry should be developed; discussion starts from the vacancy, not from the individual.

So it was to be Lincoln, however unsuitable, and in his usual optimistic way Hicks told himself that his thirteen years in rural Warwickshire had not been irrelevant. In fact it was mainly the interests of his twenty-four years in Manchester and Salford which influenced his distinctive work as a bishop. His pastoral care matched that of other bishops. His political and social concern, which had been only germinal in the Fenny Compton days, now had to be set in new directions. It is convenient to divide his epis-copate into two almost equal periods, the period up to August 1914 and the period of the war. He lived less than a year after the

---

[1] P. E. Matheson, *The Life of Hastings Rashdall D.D.* (1928), 220; Fowler, 226.

armistice, and in those few months he was enfeebled by illness. In some ways the wartime period of his episcopate showed him at his best. In the preceding years he had seemed in danger of being dominated by the routine of office, but the war demanded adaptations and initiatives and he responded to those demands with vigour.

The diocese of Lincoln is one of the largest in the country, but one of the most sparsely inhabited. Some of its farms were almost totally cut off from the media of communication which were taken for granted in urban society. It was actually possible in November 1914 for a servant working on a farm 'in the marshes near the river Humber' to be unaware that war had broken out three months earlier.[2] It was a complete change for Hicks from the populous parish of Salford. The pastoral responsibility of a bishop was also a great change from that of a parish priest and residentiary canon. Hicks found that he had to relate much more to the clergy than to lay members of the church, although as Rural Dean he had already assumed a pastoral role in relation to his fellow clergy in Salford.[3] Pastoral visiting in Lincolnshire meant, for the bishop, mostly visiting the clergy and their families. He began a big programme, aiming to reach every parish in the diocese (some 580 in all, including about 40 held in plurality) during the period of ten years which he hoped to be able to devote to it. It was a formidable undertaking for a man who was already sixty-seven years old at the time of his appointment.

Sometimes he found that his visit was the first time within living memory that a bishop had been seen in a particular parish. His visits were rather different from those of Bishop King, who usually arranged, on his confirmation tours, to spend two nights in a country house and to have two meals, one with the 'squires' of the neighbourhood and the other with the clergy.[4] Hicks had few such dinner parties. When he stayed with the Earl of Yarborough, no dinner party is mentioned, and his diaries give the impression that his relations with some of the county magnates were distant. No doubt some of the strongly Conservative, or even Liberal

[2] 'Recollections of the Great War 1914–1918' by Olive Mary Taylor, in Imperial War Museum archives 83/17/1; see also, for depopulation and poor quality of the work-force, H. Rider Haggard, *Rural England* (New York and Bombay 1902), ii, esp. 159–61.

[3] See the anecdote in Fowler, 133–4.

[4] Lord Elton, *Edward King and Our Times* (1958), 125.

Unionist, landowners were hesitant to offer hospitality to such a radical bishop. But of course the county magnates were often away from Lincolnshire,[5] and in the wartime years entertainment of that kind was severely restricted. In any case, his demanding programme of visits required him to move on each day, or at least to make a foray into a neighbouring parish and then to return to his host, usually one of the clergy, for a second night. He was not greatly interested in visiting socially prominent laymen, though he counted some of them among his friends. Sometimes he felt himself surrounded by political opponents, and it was true that the political temper of the county and the intransigent attitude of many of the clergy were burdens to be borne. The judgement of the *Manchester Guardian* was that when Edward King was bishop there were few dioceses where there was less co-operation between Anglicans and Free Churchmen and few in which the lines of division were drawn on more purely political principles.[6]

But in fact there were some leading supporters of the Liberal Party among the churchmen in the diocese. The most notable was the Liberal MP for Lincoln, C. H. Roberts. In spite of differences in family background and a difference of age of almost twenty years, they had much in common. Roberts was an Oxford man, the son of a clergyman, had been a fellow and tutor of Exeter College, and shared Hicks's concern for temperance reform. They met frequently and evidently enjoyed each other's company. Roberts had been elected to represent Lincoln in 1906, but his connection with the city ended when he lost his seat in 1918, just before Hicks's death. His wife, Lady Cecilia, was the daughter of the ninth Earl of Carlisle, and sister-in-law of Gilbert Murray. More significantly, her mother was the redoubtable Rosalind, Countess of Carlisle, who was a tower of strength to the UKA, maintained Leif Jones for a time as a personal assistant at Naworth Castle, and ensured that her sons-in-law toed the temperance line. Lord and Lady Carlisle had operated 'Local Option' and brought about the closure of the pubs on their estates. Roberts was an expert on licensing laws, and made his maiden speech in the House on a Pure Beer Bill in 1906.[7] There could hardly have been a more congenial MP for Hicks to have at hand for discussions of political matters.

---

[5] R. J. Olney, *Rural Society and County Government in Nineteenth-Century Lincolnshire* (Lincoln 1979), 173.

[6] *MG* 16 Aug. 1919.   [7] Hayler, *Vision of a Century*, 94.

In Lincoln, therefore, Hicks was in touch with the Liberal intelligentsia, and that element in it which favoured his temperance work.

Another leading layman in the diocese whose general political views Hicks shared was Herbert J. Torr, who had stood unsuccessfully as a Liberal for the parliamentary seat of Horncastle in a by-election in 1894. Torr had forfeited some votes by refusing to pledge himself for the full programme of disestablishment and disendowment demanded by the Liberation Society.[8] He was active in the CSU, serving on its council, and speaking at some of its branches on a variety of topics. It was in this connection that he got to know T. C. Fry, and so later welcomed him when he came to the deanery. Like Roberts, he was regarded as an expert on temperance legislation, and in the Church Reform League he was much in demand for his mastery of issues connected with the establishment of parochial church councils and representative diocesan bodies. Charles Gore invited him to contribute a chapter on 'Parochial Church Councils' to a volume of *Essays in Aid of the Reform of the Church*, published in 1902, to which Fry also contributed. He took an interest in the Social Service Committees which were sponsored by some bishops, notably Bishop Percival of Hereford. He moved familiarly among the hierarchy of the church, and it is no surprise that he was invited by Archbishop Davidson to serve on some central committees. In Lincoln he was a key member of the diocesan conference and earned Hicks's admiration for his contributions to its debates.

That was more than could be said of some other prominent laymen. Hicks's attitude to Lord Heneage, for example, was decidedly critical. Heneage was politically a Liberal Unionist, but his distance from his radically minded bishop might be gauged from his speech at the laying of a church foundation stone in Grimsby, in which he described 'the new Socialism' as having three chief aims: 'the abolition of the Ten Commandments, the denial of our Lord, and the degradation of men and women to the level of brute beasts'. This was reported in January 1908 in an editorial in the *Optimist*, and would have been noticed by Hicks. There was no open breach between them, and Hicks recognized that Heneage was an important supporter of the work of the diocese. But his

[8] D. W. Bebbington, *The Nonconformist Conscience: Chapel and Politics 1870–1914* (1982), 23.

diary entry (25 July 1917) about a meeting of the Grimsby Church Extension Fund is critical enough: 'Lord Heneage came in very late, like a Hurricane, but quite good tempered. He left early in the same extraordinary style. Perhaps he thinks it the grand style. But the County folk regard him as an old blunderer: of course he is a good old dear, only absurdly vain and egotistical.'

Two other prominent laymen were Thomas Cheney Garfit and Christopher Turnor. Cheney Garfit was one of the Boston dynasty which had in the past achieved leadership in a borough with a reputation for political corruption.[9] His politics do not seem to have troubled Hicks, but he was a nuisance in the diocesan conference, especially when he tried to get it to pass a resolution in 1916 calling for the repeal of the Act for the disestablishment of the Welsh church, though he certainly knew that his bishop would not support the resolution. This was brushed aside by the conference, and Hicks saw it as Cheney Garfit's nemesis, which he had been inviting for years by his egotism and overbearing manners.

Christopher Turnor was very different. Hicks did not approve of his brand of churchmanship, noting in his diary, 'The Turnors very PB!'[10] His parents had indeed been ardent members of the Plymouth Brethren, but Christopher did not dissociate himself from the Church of England. He was an interesting man: a large landowner with property in Wragby as well as at Stoke Rochford, where his family had lived since the seventeenth century and his grandfather had built a 'Jacobethan' residence of huge proportions in rivalry with nearby Harlaxton, yet he was once described as having no sense of class or other distinctions. There is an attractive portrait of his household by the pioneer of the Workers' Educational Association, Albert Mansbridge:

Stoke Rochford, in his time, must have been unique amongst English country houses. I have seen in it children from the slums, labouring men and women, teachers, squires, noble men and women, and a succession of those whom he was helping over stiles. Everyone seemed to be at home . . . The home atmosphere was unique. I have seen, for example, a ship's steward and a countess arguing together at dinner in perfect amity, the one a left-winger, the other a Tory. There were no rules, the whole house was open and free. Its treasures were manifest . . . He was entirely unambitious, only seeking to do needed work to the utmost of his power.

---

[9] Olney, *Rural Society*, 167.   [10] *Diary*, 28 Feb. 1913.

Even as a quiet stream fertilizes the land and gives rise to life, so did he flow on.[11]

Turnor had studied, and for a short time practised, architecture; he interested himself actively in agricultural questions, including the provision of smallholdings; he devoted much of his time and energies to education, and was a member of the consultative committee of the Board of Education. Later he served on, and hosted at Stoke Rochford, the Archbishops' Committee on Christianity and Industrial Problems—one of the five follow-up committees set up after the wartime National Mission. Its report gave currency to the ideas of R. H. Tawney, who served on it. Turnor's contacts with Hicks were mainly in meetings concerned with rural questions: the Rural Welfare Association, the Wages and Housing of Labourers, and Rural Education.[12] Unlike other prominent laymen, he did not serve on the diocesan conference in Hicks's time, and so did not have regular occasions to meet him.

The bishop's extensive travels in the diocese brought him into touch with all sorts and conditions of men—though not so many women. Unlike the dean and the Archdeacon of Stow, he did not possess a car, although he hired cars when rail travel was impracticable, or impossible—for instance, during a rail strike. In wartime this had the advantage of saving any worry about petrol rationing.[13] He used the railways as much as possible, and recorded in his diary chance meetings with a variety of people, ranging from a party of Freemasons led by Lord Yarborough to a French *poilu* visiting his sister at Woodhall Spa. He was the last Bishop of Lincoln to enjoy on any considerable scale the personal intercourse of the railway compartment. One meeting in a train with a 'rusty-tempered socialistic workman who had some drink' shows that he was not always shut away in the sanctuary of the First Class.

He greatly appreciated the company of intelligent and capable women and the opportunities he had to work with them. His wife, Agnes, continued to be the mainstay of his domestic life, battling on to provide hospitality throughout the difficult wartime years, and supporting his temperance work and other diocesan initiatives.

[11] Albert Mansbridge, *Fellow Men: A Gallery of England 1876–1946* (1948), 93 f.

[12] *Diary*, 27 Jan. 1911; 21 Nov. 1913; 10 Oct. 1916.

[13] Hensley Henson in 1918 regarded as inadequate his monthly ration of 30 gallons. See *Retrospect*, i. 265–6. Herefordshire was poorly served by railways.

His younger daughter, Christina, had graduated from Somerville College, Oxford, and spent much time at Lincoln, both before her marriage and after her husband had been posted to France in the war. She was very close to her father, for they travelled about together in the diocese a good deal, and she undertook much of his correspondence during his last illness. There were other women outside the family with whom Hicks worked and took counsel. He had valued the work of Ruth Chamberlain in Salford, and she spent more than one Christmas in the family at Lincoln. Other fellow workers were Miss Savill, headmistress of the High School, Miss Elliott, the children's work organizer ('very nice, very clever, very good, & *hideously dressed*!'), and (with some reservations) Miss Todhunter, Principal of the Diocesan Training College. His appreciation of the ministry of women was perhaps nowhere more evident than in his going to the City Temple to hear Maude Royden preach.

Yet although he had many appreciative contacts with lay people in the diocese, it was inevitable that the clergy were the main objects of his pastoral care. They were, to him, both a burden and a support. A cursory reading of his diaries may leave the impression that he was less conscious of the support than the burden. His verdicts are often uninhibited. 'Tall, dreary, ineffective, with a ridiculous utterance of the service, reading etc. sometimes largo, sometimes prestissimo.' 'I have had the worst account of him, and I do not like his looks.' Those are but specimens of his private comments to his diary. He had cases of drunkenness and sexual immorality among the clergy to deal with. One priest he had to depose from his orders. 'It was a painful experience, which I hope never to repeat.' He had firm standards of pastoral practice, expecting clergy to say their offices in church, and to be regular in visiting. He told at least one parish priest, whom he believed to be slack, that he must keep a regular diary of visits. He approved of open-air work and set an example, preaching on the sands at Cleethorpes and in a storm of rain in Grantham market-place to a crowd hidden under umbrellas. His standards of churchmanship made it difficult for him to get on with some of the more evangelical clergy whose lack of interest in liturgy had led to slackness in meeting the demands of the Prayer Book. One clergyman was so ill-advised as to defend his failure to say mattins in church by quoting the remark of a former archdeacon, W. J. F. Kaye: 'I don't believe in praying to stone walls.' He received the curt reply that 'it was a wicked & foolish saying, whosesoever it was'.[14] At the other end of the scale of churchmanship, he had little time for those who wanted to push for innovations such as the use of incense, unless he thought they were pastorally efficient. Where he found good spiritual work being done, he was ready to show flexibility, even beyond the bounds of what he considered the true Anglican tradition, and certainly did not expect uniformity of practice.

Against his critical comments on many of the clergy must be set the warmth of his appreciation of those he judged to be faithful and efficient, and whose departure from the diocese he so much regretted. 'Alas!', he wrote in his diary, 'I have lost Heygate, & Carr Smith, & now I am to lose Gough!' There were others who just seem to have become his friends, quite naturally, like old Canon Stephenson, who had retired to Minster Yard from Boston on account of ill-health, and his wife Eliza who was blind until her cataracts were removed.[15] Some were congenial to him for reasons other than their pastoral capability. E. A. Woodruffe Peacock had been vicar of the village of Cadney, near Brigg, for almost twenty years when Hicks went to Lincoln. The church building there was a ruin. 'Roof in great holes, lead blown off in rolls; pigeons and their dung and straw and litter everywhere: lovely oak screens nearly rotten to pieces.'[16] The bishop felt this to be almost a personal affront, and set about ensuring its repair and restoration. But Peacock was a good preacher and his ministry was appreciated elsewhere, at his mission churches. Hicks noted in his diary that he was 'a born and trained naturalist, of the best and most scientific sort: insects, flowers as cross-fertilized by insects; nature of soils (& so geology) as connected with the growth of plants: a friend of Wallace & all other scientific naturalists. Has a good library: I bought his set of Goethe's *Werke*.' Peacock was a fellow of the Linnaean and Geological Societies and had written a critical catalogue of Lincolnshire plants.[17] Hicks's own interest in the natural world had apparently been fostered in part by his friendship with

[14] *Diary*, 22 July 1918.

[15] There is a nice account of their friendship in Marjorie S. Broughall, *A Pastel for Eliza* (1961), 180–1. He pretended that she would get a shock when she saw his face clearly.

[16] *Diary*, 2 Mar. 1912.

[17] Peacock's other interest as an 'additional field observer' of the Grouse Commission and a game specialist may not have appealed to the bishop.

W. Warde Fowler, the Oxford scholar who combined classical learning with skill as an ornithologist. He had maintained a friendship
with Warde Fowler over the years and took great pleasure in inviting him to a 'bird dinner' in the Old Palace at Lincoln, to meet a
group of local people interested in natural science. This included
Peacock, as well as another clergyman, F. L. Blathwayt, who had
taken time from his incumbency at Doddington to watch a cor-
morant perching on a pinnacle of the minster and track down
records of kites soaring round its towers.[18]

Not surprisingly, Hicks took an interest in local archaeology,
as he had in Manchester, and accepted the position of President
of the Lincolnshire Architectural and Archaeological Society, and
this gave him a special interest in members of the clergy who had
undertaken archaeological investigations. His diaries carry many
notes of historical or archaeological interest. One of the most interesting examples is the record of the previous treatment of the
ancient statue of St Hugh on the south-west pinnacle of the cathedral.[19] It is unlikely that we could find anywhere else a record of
the condition of that statue in the time when E. W. Benson was
Chancellor of Lincoln. There are plenty of other such entries—
recording the discovery of a medieval crucifix in a churchyard,
noting conditions laid down by a distinguished architect when asked
to restore a church, describing the origin of the bell on the chapel
of the Old Palace, or noting the sites of demolished country man-
sions. The Lincoln Record Society had just been founded in 1910
when Hicks moved to Lincoln, and he gave his support to its great
worker, Canon C. W. Foster, who found the Alnwick Tower at
the medieval bishops' palace and the Exchequer Gate chambers
in 'filth and disarray', and rescued irreplaceable historical material
for future generations.[20] Hicks's diaries bear out the testimony of
his daughter Christina to his wide-ranging interest in everything
and everyone around him. 'Unless he was ill, I have never seen
him bored, and very rarely then—or perhaps I may make exception to the Chairman's speeches at temperance meetings.' Another
testimony corroborates this. 'Whether in the University, in his
country parish, or in the poor streets of his great Salford parish,
he was never bored, never uninterested, never without something

---

[18] *LDM* (Oct. 1916), 150–1.   [19] *Diary*, 22 Sept. 1912; 6 Dec. 1913.
[20] See Doris M. Stenton, 'Eminent Local Historians: 1. Canon C. W. Foster of Tim-
berland, Lincolnshire, 1866–1935', *Amateur Historian* 6/5 (Autumn 1964).

to awaken his sympathy, his zeal and unselfish devotion to work.'[21] His wide range of interests may be counted among the factors essential in making him the particular kind of liberal churchman that he was. He served religion, but religion was to him an element in the complex activity of social life.

He intended his episcopal ministry to be seen as a continuation of Bishop King's, at least in matters of churchmanship, however different it was in social witness. That is not to say that Bishop King was anything like an uncriticized model for him. When Archdeacon Wakeford expressed to Hicks the opinion that the late bishop was for years before he died weak and in the hand of unwise advisers, and that discipline was bad and appointments poor, Hicks commented in his diary, 'There is *some* truth in this: but . . .'.[22] Bishop King had not been good at restraining those clergy who traded on his reputation as a 'catholic' champion to get him to acquiesce in their more extreme practices.[23] But Hicks may have begun to suspect that Wakeford was one of those whose high opinion of themselves is bolstered by criticism of others, and he never expressed any open criticism of his predecessor. He was regarded as one of the High-Church bishops, but with a difference. Hensley Henson called him (amongst other things) 'an independent High Churchman'.[24] Both churchmanship and independence were important elements in his episcopate. His definite interpretation of churchmanship based on the Prayer Book seemed old-fashioned to the militants of the English Church Union. He was never invited to address their meetings. But he promoted to responsible positions in the diocese not only Wakeford, who was commemorated by the *Church Times* as a 'stalwart of the Catholic faith' (surely its highest accolade),[25] but also J. O. Johnston, the biographer of H. P. Liddon, whom he made Chancellor of Lincoln Cathedral in 1913. In both cases an influential factor was probably their reputation as preachers; for Hicks all his life held preaching to be of equal importance with any other pastoral gift. His churchmanship, however, was restrained by his independence. He never fell into line with the 'catholic' contingent among the bishops, parting company with them on issues like the disestablishment of the Welsh church and the usefulness of censuring supposed 'heretics'.

[21] Fowler, 156; *MG* 16 Aug. 1919.   [22] *Diary*, 30 May 1914.
[23] See e.g. *LDM* (Feb. 1963), 29.   [24] *Retrospect*, i. 290.
[25] Obituary in the *Church Times* 21 Feb. 1930.

His appointment of Johnston was evidently a success and gave Hicks much pleasure. The same could not be said without strong reservations about Wakeford, or about the appointment of Fry to succeed Dean Wickham. Both of them were known to him through their involvement with the CSU. In his Primary Visitation he commended Wakeford to the diocese as a thoughtful and eloquent preacher and a laborious and effective parish priest. Wakeford's later career as archdeacon bore out those remarks, but also brought to light other aspects of his character. His bullying methods as Archdeacon of Stow were in sharp contrast to those of his courteous bishop, and he developed a running feud with Dean Fry which brought scandal on the cathedral chapter. There was a tragic end to Wakeford's apparently brilliant career, when he was accused of adultery during a visit to Peterborough. Hicks was aware of his indiscreet behaviour and had already warned him of his danger, but his diaries give no support to the rumour that anxiety over Wakeford's morals shortened his life.[26] But it is true that his fatal illness while on holiday in Worthing was clouded by a dispute of Wakeford with the Vicar of North Somercotes, Samuel Proudfoot, over his invitation to Edith Picton-Turbervill to speak in his church. Hicks was hardly fit enough even to deal with the correspondence and had to rely on Christina to write his letters.[27] In spite of his connection with the CSU, Wakeford does not seem to have exerted himself much on its behalf in the diocese, and he did not allow any sympathy with the Liberal Party to moderate his opposition to the disestablishment of the Welsh Church. His role in the diocese was that of preacher and administrator, and in these aspects his career, during Hicks's lifetime, fulfilled his bishop's expectations. In his archdeaconry, his authority was accepted; but in the cathedral the situation was very different. It is all too well known that the structure of authority in cathedrals, as between the dean and the chapter, and in relation to the bishop, provides a constant threat of discord. In Lincoln the authoritarian archdeacon came into collision with the authoritarian dean.

Hicks had been delighted to come into the diocese at a time when Dean Wickham was still alive, for he had an established friendship

[26] E. F. R. Woolley, 'Memoirs 1895–1920' (Lincolnshire Archive Office).
[27] The case for a conspiracy against Wakeford by Dean Fry and the Revd C. T. Moore has been argued, to a point short of demonstration, in J. Treherne, *Dangerous Precincts* (1987).

with Wickham and admired him as a scholar and cultured church-man of Liberal sympathies. It was a great blow to him when he received the news of Wickham's death—'Decanus noster dilectis-simus', as his diary entry calls him. He at once sent off a long let-ter to the Prime Minister, saying that he would like a full Anglican Liberal (according to Asquith's own summary) and suggesting Fry.[28] Asquith considered the possibility of offering the deanery to Hensley Henson, but decided it would be 'rather like sending a torpedo destroyer into a land-locked pool'. And so Dr Fry came to Lincoln, and a successful public-school headmaster succeeded an unsuccessful public-school head as Dean of Lincoln. There are few more unsuitable preparations for exercising the confused authority of a dean than twenty-two years of undisputed author-ity in a school. Fry did a great work in raising vast sums of money for the restoration, one might almost say the rescue, of the cathed-ral building. But in retrospect it looks inevitable that he and Wakeford should fall out with each other. Bishop Hicks, who sel-dom fell out with anyone, could hardly have anticipated the con-tinual bickering between the dean and the archdeacon. In many ways he was very happy to have obtained Fry for the cathedral and diocese, but there were odd traits in Fry's character, and his authoritarianism led him into strange pronouncements.

Before the war he advocated all the 'advanced' views on social reform which were congenial in CSU circles; but the war seemed to release in him his aggressive and repressive instincts. He not only became, like many another clergyman, a moral recruiting sergeant, but also gave vent to curious opinions about the use of troops to suppress night-club life and the need to deprive soldiers of their sexual appetites during the war.[29] Indeed sexuality seemed to evoke his worst opinions. Graham Greene's picture of him as a sadistic flogger at Berkhamsted was not based on direct knowledge, since Greene was never a boy at the school during Fry's headmaster-ship; but it is true that in a debate on 'White Slavery' in the dio-cesan conference in 1912 he had referred, with apparent approval, to the example of Australia, where 'the penalty of a hundred lashes and ten years' penal servitude had crushed the evil'. It was, strictly speaking, only in relation to his militaristic behaviour in 1914 that

[28] Lambeth Palace, Davidson papers, 10, 30 Aug. 1910.
[29] Letter to *The Times* 30 Sept. 1915, quoted in K. Gregory (ed.), *The First Cuckoo* (1976), 99; R. P. Graves, *A. E. Housman, the Scholar Poet* (1979), 174 n. 283.

Hicks described him as a 'degenerate Liberal'; but perhaps there was more to that verdict than dislike of his immediate and whole-hearted adoption of the recruiting role. Another theological liberal, Dean Inge, had bitterly criticized one of Fry's manœuvres in Convocation in 1912 when he sabotaged a motion to open divinity degrees at Oxford and Cambridge to nonconformists and laymen: 'a foolish and treasonable act for a Liberal', he noted in his diary.[30] It is difficult to reconcile the less pleasant side of Fry's character with other memories of him which refer to his 'disarming geniality' and 'lively sense of humour',[31] and his continuing friendship with men like Henry Scott Holland. Perhaps part of the truth about him is that he was a man of moods. That much is suggested by Hicks's comment in his diary, when a committee on 'Purity and Rescue' had been set up: 'The Dean was made convenor. It is safe in his hands—so long as he is in a good temper.'[32] Another verdict might be that he was spoilt by his personal circumstances. He had married a wealthy woman, and had been able to use her money to get his way with the governors at Berkhamsted by simply offering to pay for things he wanted, even when the governors were unenthusiastic. That, and his position as headmaster had given him too many years in which he had not been forced to take criticism seriously. It was not so easy to get his own way in the cathedral.

The presence in the diocese of leading laymen and clergymen with liberal and reforming views meant that Hicks was far from isolated in his opinions and plans. That does not mean that he had universal support, even in the church. He identified his enemies as the Tory press, the brewing interests, the odd exponent of extreme protestantism, and some of the reactionary clergy. These elements did not in fact determine his episcopal policy, or even deflect it from the course he chose. He could brush aside the Kensitite heckler on the sands at Cleethorpes; and ignore the rudeness of a 'Catholic reactionary' incumbent who failed to meet him in the rain at the station and declared he never heard or saw him 'without feeling more of a tory than ever'.[33] The Tory press and

---

[30] W. R. Inge, *Diary of a Dean: St Paul's 1911–1934* (n.d.), 15.
[31] *Church Times* 1930, 182.   [32] *Diary*, 17 Nov. 1916.
[33] *Diary*, 17 Aug. 1913; 1 Aug. 1914. The heckler was the same E. de Lacy Read who, with others, had petitioned Archbishop Benson to try Bishop King for alleged illegal acts in 1888.

the opponents of temperance were part of the secular society he wanted to change, and he could not ignore them.

His Primary Visitation shows what were his hopes for the church as opposed to secular society; but those hopes included the church's pressure for social change.[34] The visitation charge called on the clergy to put out their best powers to counter crass ignorance of church principles and callous insensibility to moral evil. It declared his conviction that establishment was not essential to the church, and that the best defence of the church was the effectiveness of its work. The chief interest, however, of the charge lies in Hicks's assessment of the outlook of the church and the problems it was facing. He believed that there were signs of religious decay and decline in society, but he also thought he saw signs of hope. One of these was the higher education of women, which would strengthen the Christian home and bring into prominence the gentler virtues. The church must face the challenges of a time of tremendous change. Criticism and research, based upon the historical and comparative method, were bringing about the reinterpretation of the scriptures. Applied science was altering the habits of civilized mankind. The factory system was threatening to convert human agents into mere machines. The scramble to exploit distant lands threatened international peace. He also drew attention to the vastness of non-Christian populations, and their inevitable desire for independence. In this new situation there were urgent questions to be addressed: how to prevent war, how to enfranchise women, how to prevent the domination of the plutocrat and the corrupting influence of the millionaire, and, in short, how to Christianize the social order.

For that task there was little direct help in the New Testament. The apostles were men of very limited political outlook. Christ himself never addressed the self-governing citizens of a free country. Church people must undertake social tasks, but whenever this was proposed there were two kinds of dissenting voices. On the one hand, there were persons of deeply pious conviction who declared that only by a true conversion could individuals be brought to do their duty. Such people showed only a tepid sympathy with social reformers, and seldom even exercised their right to vote.

[34] *Building in Troublous Times,* a charge delivered at his Primary Visitation 1912 by the Lord Bishop of Lincoln.

To them he would say, 'It is as pious a work to carry a good law as to enlarge a church or conduct a prayer meeting.' They might look for an example in the Society of Friends. Then again there were those who saw the church as the embodiment of God's will, and argued that it must be extended, to regenerate the world. His answer was that the examples of France, of Spain, of Italy, showed that 'the aggrandisement of the Church was not the salvation of human society'. It was due to Protestant Dissent that in Britain revolt had not led to unbelief. Both groups of Christians who rejected the call to social reform were mistaken. For all church people he proposed three axiomatic rules: to maintain self-discipline, to enlarge and enrich the opportunities of others, to believe in freedom. And he could not resist quoting Ruskin: 'There is no wealth but life'; and 'Life without industry is guilt; industry without art is brutality.' It was a very different kind of charge from any his predecessor would have given.

Bishop King had certainly not given priority to promoting social change. His favourite kind of confirmation candidate was the ploughboy, though he did recognize that even in Lincolnshire industrial change was creating new opportunities for working men. He listened to the tramp of the hobnailed boots of the foundry workers as they walked downhill, when he was still living in Hilton House, and he prayed for them. He knew about their heavy work, but did not ask questions about the industrial relations at the foundries, or whether church people could help to enlarge and enrich their opportunities. It was not the case, however, that the diocese had slumbered in peaceful ignorance of social questions. Indeed, as we have seen, in 1907 the diocesan conference had discussed the attitude of the church towards the changing conditions of labour. It is difficult to judge whether the topics taken for discussion at the diocesan conferences, either during King's episcopate or Hicks's, were due to the direct influence of the bishop, or merely accepted by the bishop at the suggestion of the diocesan conference subjects committee. In 1907 the influence of the staunch Liberal, Dean Wickham, was evident.

Between Hicks's enthronement and the outbreak of war the range of subjects included 'Religion and Amusements', 'Laymen's Work in the Church', 'The Use of Sunday', and 'Parochial Visiting'. They were all certainly matters on which Hicks had definite views; and they may even be taken to express his kind of religion

—as opposed to his views on social reform. He believed that
Christians should enjoy themselves, that lay people had a role in
the church of equal importance with that of the clergy, that Sunday was meant to be a time of rest and recreation for working
people as well as worship, and that the clergy must set themselves
a regular pattern of home-visiting. He spoke in favour of dancing; he referred to the growing sense of equality in society and
pointed to the need for lay influence on a basis of equality; he
urged church people to support the Labour Party in demands for
a day of rest; he reminisced about his own methods of visiting in
Salford and Fenny Compton. Yet somehow he seemed in danger
of being absorbed, for all his energy and prophetic fire, in the mere
business of keeping the diocese going. It was full to overflowing
with organizations. The Diocesan Training School for Mistresses
(later called the Diocesan Training College) had been founded in
1862. During Wordsworth's episcopate the diocesan conference
had been set up, a Brotherhood of Mission Clergy (the 'Novate
Novale') had been established, and two colleges had been founded:
Scholae Cancellarii, or the Bishop's Hostel, for the training of clergy,
and the Missionary College at Burgh-le-Marsh. Edward King, during his episcopate, had taken further initiatives. He had encouraged the establishment of a Home for Penitents, he had set up
Ruri-decanal Conferences, and he had inaugurated the *Diocesan
Magazine*, the Missionary Prize Scheme, the Diocesan Sunday Fund,
retreats for clergy in the cathedral, the Diocesan Association of
Lay Readers, the Diocesan Guilds' Union and the Diocesan Sunday Schools Association. Hicks's only significant additions to this
network of organizations fitted in with his interests in social issues.
They were the co-ordination of various local temperance bodies
on an ecumenical basis in a United Temperance Association, and
the establishment of a Women's Diocesan Council.

   Like every diocesan bishop, he had to devote much of his time
to the structures of his diocese. Undoubtedly he had lost something in his move from Salford and Manchester. His long residence there, his work with ecumenical temperance organizations,
and above all his closeness to C. P. Scott and the readily available
outlet for radical opinions which it had encouraged, all these had
given him a personal standing as a leading churchman and a critical commentator, not just on religious affairs, but on broad moral
and political questions. This recognized status could not simply

be transferred to his new situation. It was only natural that he should keep in touch with family and friends and organizations in Lancashire, but perhaps he also felt some sense of loss. He went back to receive an honorary degree from the university, to visit St Philip's (though he told himself in his diary that he must leave the way clear for Peter Green), to consult with the UKA leaders, and to visit his elder daughter and her family. The family connections were strengthened when his younger daughter married a son of Bishop Knox and his eldest son married into a family which had moved from the Manchester area to Woodhall Spa. He maintained a correspondence with C. P. Scott. But he resolutely turned his attention to the county which was coextensive with his pastoral charge, and he was very soon involved in controversy.

Early in 1911 he used one of his monthly letters in the *Diocesan Magazine* to comment on the moral condition of the county. Lincolnshire was among the six worst counties for the number of convictions for drunkenness. The returns of the Registrar-General revealed a similarly bad condition of morals in the county. It was pilloried, he said, along with two other rural counties as exhibiting a high proportion of illegitimate births. Its death-rate among infants and children was bad. In Grimsby, 'there is a frightfully lax state of morals, especially in the vicinity of the docks: children are being brought up in an atmosphere of moral contagion which constitutes a moral danger'. The rural clergy testified that in some villages a chaste marriage was an exception. The situation in Grimsby had been a matter of deep concern to Bishop King, who had exerted himself to promote the building of new churches there. Hicks, with his strong belief in the ministry of women, followed this with a plan for the appointment either of Church Army sisters or of Greyladies to work there. He also criticized the state of housing in the county. In the villages the social level could be dragged down when housing was so vile that it only attracted the worst type of tenant. In Lincoln itself in wartime he was approached by a Labour Party organizer to support a new housing scheme, but it was suddenly vetoed by the government till after the war. Another particular practice which drew his criticism was the local custom of annual 'flitting'. Annual contracts between farmers and their workers, combined with the provision of tied cottages, meant that the workers' families might be regularly uprooted and moved to another farm. A controversy rumbled on for some months in the

Diocesan Magazine, with Lord Heneage defending the custom and various parish priests testifying to its socially undesirable effects.[35]

So in the years before the outbreak of war Hicks devoted his energies mainly to the two aspects of ministry which had characterized his time in Salford and Manchester, pastoral work and social witness, now focused on conditions within his diocese. But his episcopal status now involved him in meetings of Convocation and Bishops' Meetings, both at Lambeth and in the group of 'East Anglian Bishops' which had met since 1865.[36] One of the central committees which he attended had the odd and question-begging title, 'The Misuse of Marriage', in which the contentious focus of interest was on contraception. The bishops were feeling their way cautiously along the path which led from the resolution of the 1908 Lambeth Conference condemning artificial means of contraception,[37] to the position of the 1958 Lambeth report on 'The Family in Contemporary Society' which declared that the means of family planning 'are in large measure matters of clinical and aesthetic choice'. The records of the committee which met in 1912 and 1913 suggest a shift from emphasis on the 'peril to national morality and welfare' arising from the deliberate restriction of procreation, to a fuller recognition of the social realities of much family life. 'Modern conditions of life' had enlarged the number of cases justifying 'exceptional conduct'. Social conditions were unsound, if pay was not enough to support a family. Inadequate housing was morally wrong and nationally disastrous.[38] It is not possible to tell what role, if any, Hicks may have played in getting the emphasis shifted; but it is certain that he would have welcomed it.

Archbishop Davidson's initial mistrust of him as a 'faddist' prevented a close relationship between them. When he eventually

[35] The annual migration has been represented rather romantically, e.g. in Ursula W. Brighouse, *A Lincolnshire Childhood* (Stroud 1992), 86. But it is clear that its effect on the education of children was disastrous. Hicks made a point of discussing it with his school inspectors (*Diary*, 12 June 1913).

[36] See G. W. Kitchin, *Edward Harold Browne, D.D., Bishop of Winchester: A Memoir* (1895), 282–3. The meetings in Hicks's time involved the bishops of Lincoln, Ely, Norwich, Peterborough, St Alban's, Chelmsford and St Edmundsbury and Ipswich.

[37] 'Resolution 41. The Conference regards with alarm the growing practice of the artificial restriction of the family, and earnestly calls upon all Christian people to discountenance the use of all artificial means of restriction as demoralising to character and hostile to national welfare.'

[38] Lambeth Palace Library papers, Bishops' Committees, 22 May 1912; 21–2 Oct. 1913.

invited Hicks to convene a committee of bishops it was concerned with the future of their official residences. Not only was it, as Hicks noted in his diary, like ploughing the sand, because of the hopelessness of trying to get any agreement among the bishops, but also, by luck or calculation, the archbishop had chosen one of the few topics on which Hicks took a conservative position. The committee was largely a waste of time, could not even present an agreed report and served to neutralize the passion for social reform which Hicks might have expressed through some other committee. His diary bears eloquent testimony to the boredom and isolation which he often felt in the company of his fellow bishops. There were few of them with whom he could feel much affinity. Hereford (Percival) was past his best: disappointed of what he thought had been a promise of the archbishopric of York, and increasingly unable to see any possible objections to plans he elaborated in splendid isolation. Oxford (Gore) was sometimes on Hicks's side; but, like Hereford, too much of an individualist to organize an effective group among the bishops which alone could have pushed them to decisive actions or resolute declarations on social policy. Hicks supported F. T. Woods when he became Bishop of Peterborough in 1916, and they did work together to some extent on temperance questions, but Woods was busy settling in to his diocese, and wartime conditions had put a brake on other ideas of social reform. Henson, another latecomer to the episcopate during Hicks's time, was sometimes to be found on the same side on specific issues, such as the treatment of conscientious objectors, but he made no attempt to understand, let alone befriend, Hicks as one of the few bishops who had stood by him during the storm of controversy which heralded his consecration.

Perhaps his expectations of the Bishops' Meetings were not high. Few of the bishops were, in his eyes, free from the taint of Toryism. But it was a time when ideas of progress and reform had begun to feature even in official pronouncements from church bodies. Hicks would have looked for signs of hope in the work of the 1908 Lambeth Conference, and perhaps been encouraged by the report of the committee appointed to consider the subject of the moral witness of the church in relation to the democratic ideal and social and economic questions. That report spoke of 'the new prominence given to the wage-earners; the growing sense of dissatisfaction with things as they are; the claim, increasing in intensity, for

justice in the distribution of the proceeds of industry'. The democratic movement should be welcomed as 'one of the great developments of human history, which have behind them the authority
of GOD'. The church must set its house in order, embracing the
idea of democracy in its own government; but, more than that,
there should be in every place groups of Christian men and women
determined to bring the sense of justice to bear on everyday life
in commerce and social affairs. The report was a watered down
version of some parts of an earlier report of the Canterbury Convocation. The Lambeth bishops went as far as could reasonably
be expected of such a diverse body. The bishops accepted the view
that Christianity involved a social mission and social principles;
they declared that property ownership was a trust for the benefit
of the community and its right use a religious duty; they declared
that investors had a moral responsibility which extended to the
social effects of their investments, and the treatment of employees
in the businesses in which their money was invested, including the
payment of a just wage. They also declared that the government
must not sanction any forms of trade which involved the degradation of races or peoples under their rule or influence. The church
looked as if it was committed to ideas of social reform.

The experience of Convocation and Bishops' Meetings left
a different impression. Among the dominating questions on the
agenda during Hicks's episcopate were Welsh disestablishment,
Modernism, the reserved sacrament, and Prayer Book revision.
On the first two he had firmly held views. His attitude to disestablishment has already been indicated, and he was content to
accept it as a justifiable enactment for Wales. Modernism, in its
English form, he saw as part of the exploration of theological ideas
which should be handled only by the exercise of argument, not
by anathemas. In a debate on 'The Church's Faith and Order' in
the Upper House of Convocation in April 1914 he supported Percival in an amendment to Winnington Ingram's motion calling for
a fresh declaration of faith by the bishops. Such declarations, he
said, were futile.

There was a declaration in 1905, and there was a declaration in 1908,
but they had made no difference whatever to the progress of inquiry
. . . The best way of dealing with books and arguments like those that
the Bishop of London was so distressed by, was by writing learned and
convincing books on the other side . . . The Church of England had lived

by its freedom, and by its open discussion of the deepest and largest questions. He did not want to unchurch anyone, or to put under ban any reverent seeker after truth within their communion.

When a vote was taken Hicks was in a minority of three, with Percival and the Bishop of Southwark (Burge). He wrote in his diary, 'I know that I shall be grossly misunderstood: but I do not believe in *authority* in the Ch. of E. to declare credenda.'

On matters concerning public worship, including Prayer Book revision and the perpetual reservation of the holy sacrament, he seems to have had less definite views. He found the debates on the Prayer Book interesting and made some contributions to the discussions; but these were concerned with socially relevant issues, such as equality of vows in marriage and international peace, not with liturgical principles. He loved the language of the Prayer Book, and had found its patterns of devotion adequate for his spiritual life. His friendship with Percy Dearmer and A. S. Duncan Jones, probably deriving from CSU contacts, certainly brought him into touch with the strain of liturgical development which owed nothing to the exponents of the 'Western Use', which he would have mistrusted. The comments in his diary, after a visit to Duncan Jones at St Mary's, Primrose Hill, are equivocal:

I attended Mattins (unrobed) beautifully rendered in plainsong: they have re-converted it back into a monastic Hour Office: the plainsong, sung in unison firmly but not aggressively by a good choir, & accompanied *softly* on the organ, was beautiful; but so elaborate that few, if any, of the Congregation, could or did join in. It appeared to me that our Reformers had deliberately & with great skill *transmuted* the old hour offices into congregational services, and that our Mattins & Evensong were marvels of liturgical art. I was convinced that the recent attack upon Mattins is nothing less than the undoing of the Reformation. I was thankful that I had spoken as clearly as I did in my Lecture on Nov. 7.[39]

In that lecture he had urged his hearers to look forward and be led by the free spirit; and he had declared that the Church of Rome, by her devotion to externals, by her ever looking back, and by her excessive legalism, had ended with what he enjoyed calling the 'Petrifaction' of Christianity. But with his missionary spirit he was well aware that the patterns of devotion which met his own

[39] *Diary*, 18 Nov. 1917.

need did not necessarily meet the needs of others. He had earlier written in the *Diocesan Magazine* of the great virtues of 'our common folk in the army', and had continued: 'I wonder whether in our Prayer Book, and within our Acts of Uniformity, and within the customary worship of our parishes, we have found room, or are prepared to find room, for all this native exuberance, these high spirits, this innocent gaiety, this spontaneous enthusiasm.'[40] Because he attached so much importance to public worship, and the need to meet the needs of ordinary people, he found the sessions in which the bishops' discussed Prayer Book revision more interesting than most others. For rather different reasons he paid close attention to their prolonged discussions of the perpetual reservation of the holy sacrament. His diary has a long insertion on 6 July 1917, consisting of typed notes giving the regulations governing perpetual reservation which had been issued by Winnington Ingram for the Diocese of London, and his own detailed notes of the bishops' discussion on that date. This degree of interest belonged rather to his role as Ordinary for his diocese than to his personal scale of religious values. He took his disciplinary functions seriously, however much he disliked them. Happily there were few ritual problems in Lincoln diocese. His first judgement on any such question was directly related to his estimate of the pastoral effectiveness of the clergy concerned.

One other aspect of his episcopal duties seems to have offered him less satisfaction than might have been expected: his membership of the House of Lords. He was certainly committed to political action and here, it might appear, was an opportunity for direct involvement. But there were a number of reasons why he may have felt less than enthusiastic about taking his seat there. He had long regarded the House of Lords as an obstructive body, particularly on questions of temperance reform. A letter which he had received from Sir Wilfrid Lawson back in 1897 had said it was perfectly childish to suggest amendments to 'that monstrosity'. It must be abolished. As a leading member of the UKA Hicks did not forget that they had thrown out the government's Licensing Bill in 1908. Their rejection of Lloyd George's budget in 1909 was not only, from his point of view, deplorable in itself, but it had also precipitated the conflict between the two Houses and led to

---

[40] *LDM* (Sept. 1915), 132.

the General Election of January 1910 which reduced the Liberal majority in the Commons and thus damaged the cause of social reform. As a Liberal in the Lords he would feel the frustration of being in a perpetual minority. More than that, he was there in virtue of his bishopric, and would be constantly under pressure to act as one of the corporate episcopate. These are only conjectures about his feelings. His actions, however, can be called to witness. He obtained his seat in the Lords only in March 1917, at the age of seventy-three. After that his diary records fairly regular attendances when it was his duty to take prayers in the House, but only a few occasions when he went specifically to hear particular debates, though he did not always stay to vote. They concerned wartime reprisals (April 1917), conscientious objectors (May 1917), electoral reform and women's suffrage (December 1917) and *maisons tolerées* (April 1918). These were clearly subjects on which he had strong opinions; but it is also noticeable that each time he went to support Archbishop Davidson. The bishops as a body were inclined to side with the party in power, and fortunately for him that was the Liberal Party during his brief membership of the Lords. It was something of a reversal of fortune that after long experience of opposing Tory rule in the most vigorous period of his ministry, he ended his working life backing the government. It was another reversal to be supporting, with whatever anguish of heart, the waging of a war which he found so hateful.

12

Peace and War

Bishop Hicks was a man of peace, but he did not advocate 'peace at any price'. At the turn of the century no political party actually took that line; they merely disapproved of each other's wars.[1] The issue has been obscured by the ambiguity of the term 'pacifist'. If pacifism is defined as the belief that it is wrong to take part in war or support or condone it in any way, then Hicks was not a pacifist, for he had never taken that position; and did not, therefore, have to reject it in August 1914, as has been suggested.[2] His outspoken opposition to the South African war was not the opposition of a pacifist, but the result of a moral judgement on the motives and aims of the imperialists and capitalists whom he considered to have provoked the conflict for selfish ends.

On previous occasions he had taken a different line. The 'politics of conscience' had led him to support collective European military action to check Turkish massacres in Armenia, and he had preached a sermon to that effect in August 1896. There was, indeed, scarcely any pacifically minded Liberal who would not have made an exception in favour of war with 'Abdul the Damned' for the sake of the Armenians.[3] The continued sufferings of the Armenians led him to join in organizing famine relief for them in Manchester in the following years. In 1897 he used the columns of the *Manchester Guardian* to support mass meetings in protest against the government policy of using British ships on behalf of Turkey against the freedom movement in Crete. His friend and fellow-worker in the UKA, G. B. Wilson, said he was not afraid of war where questions of principle were at stake.[4] He did not reject the

[1] J. A. Spender, *The Life of the Right Hon. Sir Henry Campbell-Bannerman, G.C.B.* (1923), 210.

[2] Martin Ceadel, 'Christian Pacifism in the Era of Two World Wars', in W. J. Sheils (ed.), *The Church and War* (Ecclesiastical History Society 1983).

[3] Spender, *Campbell Bannerman*, 210.

[4] G. B. Wilson, *Looking Back* (UKA 1946), 7.

use of force where there was a moral justification for it. He saw
no such justification for the South African war.

His earliest memory of war had convinced him that no war,
however unjust, could be stopped once it had broken out, and
that therefore every effort must be made to negotiate peace before
the fighting had begun.

Nations have not only their pacific moods; they have their warlike moods
also. I was a boy at the time of the Crimean campaign. But I recollect
distinctly the war-fever of the time. It swept through the country like
a prairie fire. And yet, as we look back on it, what a ridiculous war it
was—how heedless its inception, how incompetent its carrying out!

That is a passage from a paper which Hicks read at a Peace Conference in the Friends' Meeting House, Manchester, in November
1904.[5] He went on to quote Cobden's resolve, after the Crimean
war, that if another war between Britain and some other great power
should break out he would not utter a word on the subject until
peace was made. 'You might as well reason with mad dogs as with
men when they have begun to spill each other's blood in mortal
combat.' In 1904, Hicks said, the cause of peace was fashionable;
but that threw into relief both the opportunity and the difficulty
of the church.

The church's opportunity, he said, arose from the failure of other
agencies which formed public opinion. The press was generally a
follower, rather than a former, of opinion. Politicians were not to
be trusted, because their business was to see how to rally opinion
to their own party. So what of the church?

Would it not be well if those of us who are entrusted with the care of
large industrial populations were to try more regularly to remind the
working men that the great interest of labour is Peace? That war selects
chiefly the workers as its victims in the field and the hospital abroad,
and as its victims in taxation, dear commodities and unemployment at
home?

The preacher should dwell, not only on the hideousness of war,
but on its broader effects: the burden of national debt, the retard-
ing of national progress, the interruption of cultural and spiritual
interchange between nations. 'How much we owe here in England to Italy, to France, to Germany, in the world of letters, of

[5] *Commonwealth* (Jan. 1905), 8–11.

learning, of art!' But the clergy and ministers of the churches were all, in various ways, dependent on the goodwill of their people and judged by the size of their congregations. They could not lead them faster than they would go. In any case, they usually shared their congregations' prejudices on 'the larger morals which involve political, and social, and international issues'. '*The Daily Mail* is a familiar paper in the Country Vicarage.'

At the end of the nineteenth century there were no fewer than 450 national and international peace movements. The Boer War had checked the development in Britain; but by the time of the Manchester Conference the momentum was picking up again.[6] A few years later, in 1907, Hicks would have been aware that the Dean of Manchester, Bishop Welldon, was chairman of a cumbrously named 'Committee for the Appeal of the Churches for Peace' and that Bishop Percival was also involved with it. There developed a Manchester District Peace and Arbitration League, which promoted the idea of a great conference representing the various religions of the world. The notion of reconciliation or co-operation between different world religions seems to have been a fruit of Welldon's time as Bishop of Calcutta.[7] On the international scene, Andrew Carnegie, whom Hicks met when he was given the freedom of the city of Lincoln in June 1914, founded the Carnegie Endowment for International Peace in 1910. The same year saw the foundation of the World Alliance for Promoting International Peace through the Churches. This busy activity indicates a feeling that war in Europe was threatening. British anxiety focused on Germany, and led to the formation of the Associated Councils of Churches in the British and German Empires for Fostering Friendly Relations between the two peoples, and the holding of an Anglo–German Understanding Conference in London in 1912.[8] Hopes of success at this conference were dashed by the insistence of the German delegates that religion and politics must be kept apart. This did not restrain some German theologians from interventions in the political arena. Adolf Harnack, for example, had written a bitter letter declaring that Great Britain

---

[6] Norman Angell, 'Peace Movements', in Edwin R. A. Seligman and Alvin Johnson (eds.), *Encyclopaedia of the Social Sciences*, xii (1934).

[7] He even suggested, at a later date, that the eastern and western worlds might solve their religious difficulties in 'the craft of freemasonry'. *Forty Years On* (1935), 292.

[8] See Davidson papers, 336: Germany 1907–1913.

was plotting against Germany, when the three 'Germanic Empires' (Germany, Britain, and USA) ought to combine in 'friendly rivalry'.

In the midst of all this agitation for peace, Hicks had been elected President of the newly formed Church of England Peace League on his appointment to the see of Lincoln in 1910. He continued to hold that position throughout the war and until his death. The League's membership was always very small, but it included some significant names in the list of Vice-Presidents: Deans Rashdall, Fry, and Moore Ede, and Canon Barnett. It could also call on some effective speakers such as Bishop Gore and J. A. Pease, the President of the Board of Education. Its primary purpose was the education of church members. It aimed to organize church opinion in favour of the peaceful settlement of international differences 'in the face of persistent and defiant clamour for warlike preparations and the tendency to exploit international jealousies for political purposes'. In its manifesto it declared:

The enormous number of arbitration treaties recently made, the frequent and successful resort to Arbitral Tribunals, the rapid growth of international jurisprudence, and the serious attempts to establish a permanent High Court of Judicial Arbitration for the civilized world are matters which require to be brought home to the mind and conscience of all the members of the Church of England.[9]

Hicks persuaded C. H. Roberts to speak at a meeting in Lincoln in 1913, and the League followed the example of the CSU in organizing a course of addresses at a London church the following year. But events soon pushed international arbitration out of the realm of possibilities. The League struggled on. It published a *Little Manual of Prayers for Use in the Time of the Present War*, in which the emphasis on peace and righteousness and the concern for women and civilians contrasted with some other prayers composed for special occasions during the war.[10] Another of its publications, a pamphlet on *Our Common Humanity*, was among the tracts which led to the arrest and sentencing of two women in Hertfordshire for distributing unpatriotic material.[11] It is unlikely that Dean Fry, with his bellicose tendency, continued to support

[9] *Guardian* 10 Feb. 1911.
[10] See Marrin, *Last Crusade*, 215. His list includes prayers at the 'baptism' of tanks, to stop the north-east wind (to prevent the use of gas), and against naval mines.
[11] Samuel Hynes, *A War Imagined* (1990), 147, quoting R. W. Hobhouse, *An Interplay of Life and Art* (Broxbourne 1958).

the League during the war; but others saw its role as holding out a new hope of arbitration in the post-war situation. Hicks noted in his diary in January 1919, only a few months before the onset of his final illness, that the League's annual meeting had heard a fine speech by Gore, and carried a resolution in favour of a League of Nations. Before that, they had all passed through the shadowed valley.

When war seemed imminent in 1914, Hicks still hoped against hope that the country might remain neutral. He wrote in his diary: 'God keep England outside of it!' He was at Cleethorpes on Sunday 2 August, and later wrote in his diary, forgetting how easily the war fever had spread at other times: 'At 3 I preached on the sands, with the Church Army Missioner, to a large crowd. Before my sermon, I spoke of the outbreak of war, & pleaded for *British neutrality* & was applauded. If this Government join in, it will be a really unpopular move, except with the thoughtless and the war party.' The next day the *Daily News* printed a message from him which included the words: 'For England to join in this hideous war would be treason to civilization and disaster to our people. God save us from the war fever.' It was held against him years later, by an anonymous correspondent in the *Lincolnshire Echo*.[12] In reply he quoted the testimony of Asquith in March 1915, which can serve as a brief statement of Hicks's own position: 'The invasion of Belgium made the vital difference, as far as I was concerned, between peace and war. And, I might add, the violation of Belgian neutrality turned our own people from a desire for peace to an insistence for war.' This sounds like a dispassionate judgement; Hicks's own change of mind was more agonizing. On the Sunday after Christmas 1914 he preached in his cathedral on the text 'Blessed are the peacemakers', and lifted the veil a little on his private thoughts. The transformation of Germany, he said, was strange, dreadful, almost unbelievable.

It is a grief to us that the dear old Germany of our childhood that we all so respected and loved, the Germany of our fairy stories, the Germany of our Christmas trees, that gave us such glorious music and musicians, such great poets and philosophers, Goethe, Schiller, Kant and the rest, Germany the organiser of classical archaeology and the builder up of modern physical science, should now be lost to us.

[12] *Diary*, 6 Jan. 1918.

He warned against the newspapers which were preaching their own version of Prussian hate. He warned against bringing an indictment against a whole nation. He declared that the German people did not enjoy a free government or free speech. When peace returned, Europe would not be Europe without Germany. He looked forward to the day when its militarism had been exorcised and it could achieve under God some of that political liberty and democratic spirit with which England was blessed.[13] In December 1914 he wrote a long article for the *Political Quarterly* which set out his position more fully.[14] The war, he said, had destroyed in a moment all the efforts of two generations.

Gradually but surely there had grown up among us an ideal of international brotherhood, of mutual understanding, through which the European nations might cease from being like crouching panthers waiting to spring upon their prey, and might begin to live in amity . . . Was it unreasonable to hope that by degrees the principle of law and the voice of collective humanity (or some organized portion of humanity like the European nations) should be capable of enthroning public law so strongly in the midst as to make appeal to warfare needless, absurd, and impossible?

Such hopes had been destroyed. He had passed through the gloom of the first days of war as if stunned, but then began to open his eyes to the living facts of life.

Those facts included the adoption by the German government of a theory of history and a conception of ethics in violent contrast with the moral ideals of Christian Europe. There was an element of the British press, too, which proclaimed the splendours of war. He had to ask himself how this war differed from the South African war which he had denounced so courageously. The politics of conscience had required him then to condemn the militarism, not of a foreign government, but of his own country. He had seen it as a mask for commercial greed. Now there was no material advantage (as he believed) for the capitalists in going to war. And the guilt of British imperialism had been purged. The loyalty of South Africa was the most convincing justification of the policy pursued after the Boer War, which undid the political

---

[13] Report in the *Lincoln Echo* 28 Dec. 1914; Hicks's comment was 'well reported'.
[14] Reprinted in *Oxford Pamphlets 1914–1915* as 'The Church and the War'.

mischief of the war and gave freedom to the provinces which had
been conquered.

There was much more he had to say: about the nemesis of spiritual deterioration which a bloody war would almost surely bring;
about the common fallacy that war ennobled a nation; about for-
getfulness of the hourly conflict of industrial armies with constant
danger in peace time; about the ready acceptance of government
control in many areas of life, which would make it impossible to
go back to a situation in which 'grave social evils were allowed to
thrive because we were too timid or too dull to employ State interference for their redress'. Nor could he refrain from urging the
need for temperance. So in the early days of the war he struggled
to come to terms with a catastrophe he had thought could never
happen. His initial reaction was not shared by the dean, who was
'eager for war & for fighting Germany'. Later in the month Hicks
noted that 'the Dean has been in a highly warlike mood, & is still.
He goes to drill, & is beating up recruits'. The bishop never saw
that as part of his duty.

The war, however, affected him in ways he might not have
expected. He hated so much about it, yet he was spurred to fresh
initiatives, as he became involved with the unexpected ministry
of the church to the hordes of men and women who flooded into
the diocese. There were also, in the early stages of the war, groups
of Belgian refugees to be welcomed. There is a touching note in
his diary about a little group of them at Thornton-le-Fen who
attended a church service. 'They awaited me in a group at the
Churchyard gate, & knelt around me while I gave them a Bene-
diction, and wished them Godspeed in the best French I could
muster on a sudden.'[15] The plight of the Belgians had already been
brought home to him by the arrival in Lincoln in October 1914
of a number of Belgian refugees. Six were sent to the Old Palace
and often joined the bishop and his wife for meals. One Sunday
he noted: 'All our Belgian lodgers at supper. Such a merry time!
All in French!' The following year they moved out: 'Today our
Belgian guests left our roof, to go into 2 houses on their own. We
were sorry, & they also, at the parting. We have got fond of each
other, & they shed tears, & made beautiful speeches.' One of them
died in 1916 and was buried in the cemetery behind St Nicholas'

[15] *Diary*, 5 Feb. 1915.

Church, Lincoln, and his daughter and grandson returned to France. Old Major Léonard, aged sixty, stayed in Lincoln, often having meals at the Old Palace, and making himself useful. When he left in 1919 with the rest of the refugees they gave him a farewell luncheon and he made a 'very pretty and affectionate speech'.

Even before the refugees' arrival, the wounded had begun to pour into Lincoln. An army hospital (the Fourth Northern Military Hospital) had been quickly set up in the grammar school on Wragby Road. On 9 September 1914 the bishop noted: 'No wounded as yet: only invalids from the great Camp of reservists & recruits at Belton Park.' But six days later he began visiting the wounded there, and soon the number of hospitals multiplied. He mentions visits to hospitals or convalescent homes at Woodhall, Horbling, Boultham, Spilsby, Bourne, and Mablethorpe. The buildings of Bishop's Hostel, the theological college in Lincoln, which had closed in the summer of 1916, became a dormitory for eighty nurses for the 4th Northern Hospital. In 1918 the Old Palace itself was handed over to the Red Cross, and the bishop and his household moved into a vacant house in Vicars' Court, hoping to economize there. Rising prices and increased taxation had hit the bishop's budget, in common with everyone else's. The bishop kept his study in the Old Palace, and continued to use the chapel, except when it was cold and there was no possibility of heating.

On one hospital visit he came upon a shell-shocked RAMC private whom he had known as a choirboy at Manchester Cathedral, 'now over 6 ft'. But the suffering of the wounded came closer still when his son-in-law Eddie Knox, who had been wounded, was transferred from a hospital in Edinburgh to the 4th Northern and recovered there. The bishop's youngest son, Ned, was also wounded and brought home. There was a fair chance of recovery for those who got to England. The bishop's eldest son, Edwin, was not among them. In 1917 the diary has this entry: 'Wed. 16 May: This morning letters came announcing that dear Edwin died on Sat. last in Amiens, of cerebro-spinal meningitis. It is very sad: but people most kind.' The bishop shared the bitter experience of many parents—and got on with his work. He was lucky he had so much to do. Others, he noted, had to find ways of filling an emptiness. Two years before, he had gone out with his younger daughter, Christina, to pay two visits, and wrote in his diary (8 June):

In afternoon with Tina by car to call on Eddie's Orderly's wife at Fulbeck (good people), & on Mrs Gilliat & daughter at Stragglethorpe Hall. She a wealthy widow who has lost a son at the War, & has busied herself restoring & beautifying a lovely old timbered manor-house into a modern mansion. It is really beautiful, including her garden (& especially the herbaceous border!) & it has distracted her from her grief.

He did not allow the war to interrupt his programme of travels and visits; and now there were additional military services and confirmations. The major military camp was in the grounds of Belton Park, near Grantham, where on one occasion in 1915 he enjoyed an open-air confirmation of forty territorials 'in a lovely corner of the park, near the lake, under the trees', followed by tea outside the mess tent with the chaplains. Normally, it seems, Belton Park was a sea of mud.[16] These hospitals and camps needed chaplaincy provision, and behind the episcopal activities recorded in his diaries there was the preparatory work of the chaplains. Cranwell, the naval air station, was particularly well served by its chaplain, and Hicks recorded three confirmations there, including women in the services. There was a large naval presence off Grimsby, with minesweepers and submarines, which he visited. One confirmation took place on board a battleship during a busy Sunday's programme. He had been staying at Riby one Saturday night, and wrote in his diary (3 October 1915):

Rose early & motored to Grimsby: a lovely autumn day! At 8 I consecrated St Stephen's Church with a full service & sermon. We used all proper expedition, but did not get out of Church until 10.15. After a mouthful of breakfast, at 10.45 by car to North pier, & so by a Tug to the *Illustrious* (20 minutes' voyage), where I confirmed 25 men & lads of the crew: a beautiful service. At 2 by the Tug to shore. A car met me at 2.30 & I motored to Bradley, where I preached at 3 pm Evensong. Then by car to Great Cotes, where after a *quiet* interlude & a nod, I preached at 6.30 Evensong.

He was almost seventy-two at the time.

Clergy went off to serve as chaplains with the forces and left problems of pastoral provision behind them. Others fulfilled chap-

[16] See e.g. the facetious entry about Belton in Imperial War Museum papers 87/30/1, *St George's Gazette* 31 Oct. 1914: 'There are rumours that certain men of the Battalion who have been reported absent were not so after all, but were, as a matter of fact, engulfed in the mud and not able to extricate themselves till the next day.'

laincy duties to units stationed in Lincolnshire. Hicks was critical of the inadequacy of pastoral provision for the men in the forces.

No sane man now-a-days, in drawing up a scheme for religious ministration to the troops would regard 'Church parade' as of cardinal importance. Nor would he dream of one chaplain to three battalions as in the least an adequate provision. He would bethink himself of the daily and private ministrations of a wise and sympathetic clergyman as more important than all else, and he would regard opportunities for the reverent Celebration of the Eucharist, and the preparation of the men for Confirmation, and arrangements for the innocent spending of leisure as essential matters.

The bishops, and especially the Bishop of London, argued that the troops at the front constituted a densely populated diocese, requiring episcopal care. Those protests led to the appointment of Bishop Gwynne, the Bishop of Khartoum, as 'bishop at the front'. This was an implicit criticism of the Chaplain General, Bishop John Taylor Smith. At a meeting of bishops early in 1918, according to Hicks's diary entry, they were agreed that the Chaplain General's office 'had entirely broken down'. He had other meetings with the Australian and New Zealand Chaplains General. The former, who came to see him at the House of Lords, said he was tired of lecturing the men on continence.

In the later stages of the war the government, having been persuaded to hold back from conscripting the clergy, directed the bishops to arrange for some to undertake work of national importance. Hicks had argued strongly that the law of the church did not allow them to bear arms, but he combed through the diocesan clergy, to see who could be spared, by a process of temporary pastoral reorganization, for other work. The result was that, including chaplains to the forces, he could list over ninety who had left their parishes and were engaged in a wide variety of occupations, from work in the foundries and in farming to unspecified 'government work' and education.[17] Those who remained in their parishes sometimes undertook other part-time work. The bishop found one of them machining parts for aeroplanes in his workshop; another was helping the local blacksmith in the forge; a third was superintending the supply of hay for the troops. Some of the

[17] *LDM* (May 1917), 67.

clergy were almost pathetically patriotic. One had enlisted and been found unfit for anything better than serving beer in a wet canteen. Hicks must have felt this was real degradation, and the man himself had sunk into an unresponsive spiritual condition as he lay in hospital after an unsuccessful operation, where the bishop visited him, with little hope that he would survive. Another priest, of scholarly habits, came to consult him about going as a chaplain; he said he couldn't speak extempore, couldn't sing a note, and couldn't ride, and his wife was all alone, with no servant. 'But if I send him, he will go.'[18]

Death and suffering on a huge scale made unprecedented demands on the church's pastoral ministry. The bishop had the difficult task of balancing the new demands for chaplains with the proper claims of the parishes. In spite of episcopal advice some of the clergy attested or enlisted—with unfortunate results. On 18 January 1916 the bishop wrote: 'W. W. Leeke, who enlisted in spite of my wishes, is now in difficulties. He attested before the Act, & is now accordingly called up: but the Act exempts the Clergy: how then does he stand?' The diary does not answer the question. But later in the war the clergyman concerned was working with the YMCA in Lincoln. His repugnance at 'this hideous war' did not prevent him from enjoying the company of military men. His sons and his son-in-law had been commissioned and brought fellow officers, including Sacheverell Sitwell, to the Old Palace, and he found them 'quite delightful young folk'. When he dedicated a hut as a chapel at the camp on Wragby Road in Lincoln, he praised the reading of the lesson by the colonel and confided to his diary, 'I wish I knew these military men better. They are admirable.'[19] He had less contact with the 'other ranks', except at confirmations and services and when he visited hospitals. It is difficult to tell how much the realities of the battlefront were brought home to his imagination. Like other people, he would have read the censored news of the fighting. His diary records some occasions on which chaplains on leave told him about their experiences, though conversations of that kind were most probably focused on the specific religious tasks the chaplains undertook.[20] Those who returned from the trenches were understandably unwilling, or unable, to convey

[18] *Diary*, 7 Sept. 1918; 16 Feb. 1918.   [19] *Diary*, 30 Nov. 1915.
[20] e.g. *Diary*, 4 Oct. 1916: 'he sees no sign of spiritual revival among the troops; but they are quite responsive to religious appeal, but *dreadfully ignorant* of religion'.

the full horror of their ordeal. Not all the returned chaplains held their peace. The Rector of Kettlethorpe, J. M. S. Walker, wrote daily letters home, and gave a talk to the clergy about his work at a casualty clearing station.[21] He resigned his commission and returned to Kettlethorpe, feeling unable to cope with the constant round of confessions, administrations of Holy Communion, and blessings of the sick and dying, and oppressed by the prevalence of venereal disease. He 'crawled back into his hole', returning to his country parish. His only recorded contact with the bishop was in 1918, when he told him that he wanted to get a commission as a combatant in the army, and was dissuaded.

Hicks's appreciation of military men and his readiness to find for some of his clergy alternative work of national importance did not lessen his sympathy with conscientious objectors. They posed a new question, because national conscription was a new thing. It was an instance of the conflict between the rights of the individual and the rights of the nation. Discussion between intellectuals could lead to some tortuous answers. Hastings Rashdall, in a letter to C. C. J. Webb in 1917, wrote:

You hardly seem to admit sufficiently that it may sometimes be the duty of one individual to do something which nevertheless it may be the right and the duty of other individuals to shoot him for doing. Of course both parties cannot be objectively right, but when the claim for infallibility on the part of anyone is denied, it must be admitted that it really is the duty of some individuals to do the thing and for other individuals to punish them for doing it.[22]

Conscience seldom allows itself to be compelled. So the question challenged Christians most acutely, not in reference to the right to object, but in reference to the treatment of those who objected.

There were those who were carried away by their patriotism and believed that no treatment was too bad for men who refused to fight for their country. That was not the view of the bishops as a body. Least of all was it Hicks's view; for he himself had been, in a manner of speaking, a conscientious objector in his opposition to the Boer War. He had earned the title of a pro-Boer. Now he saw men of conscience labelled pro-German. There was also

---

[21] Diary of J. M. S. Walker, Imperial War Museum archives P179. 66 ff., printed as 'Slaughter on the Somme', in M. Moynihan (ed.), *People at War* (Newton Abbot 1973), 69–84.

[22] Matheson, *Hastings Rashdall*, 158.

the curious irony that his conscience had led him to object, not specifically on religious grounds, but on the moral ground of his opposition to capitalists and warmongers. He made his own position plain in a letter to *The Times* (4 April 1916). He asserted that the Act under which men were recruited provided in explicit terms that the conscientious objector to war was to be exempt from service. The treatment handed out by some tribunals was a cause of 'painful fears' that the nation was slipping into its old vices of intolerance and persecution. Conscience was a sacred thing. 'Is private judgment to be swept wholly aside in time of war?' He was reminded of Faithful before the court in Vanity Fair, and the heretics before the Inquisition. He quoted Mabel Dearmer, the wife of his friend, writing from Serbia: 'What chance would Christ have today? Crucifixion would be a gentle death for such a dangerous lunatic.'

There were many protests against the actions of the tribunals and military authorities right from the beginning of the operation of the Military Service Act. The tribunals were accused of working sometimes without knowledge of the powers they held or the nature of the jurisdiction they were called upon to exercise.[23] In May 1916 Hicks signed 'An Appeal to Christians', asserting that the letter and the spirit of the Act had been repeatedly violated by those who administered it. They had actually defied the law. That was a threat to the nation's liberties. The treatment of conscientious objectors should be left in the hands of the civil authorities, and sentences already passed should be reconsidered. This appeal was signed by an ecumenical body including John Clifford, Scott Holland, W. E. Orchard, A. S. Peake, and W. Moore Ede (Dean of Worcester). Hicks was the only bishop among the signatories. In the same month Lord Parmoor presented a petition to the Lords. In the following May Hicks went with the archbishop to the Lords to support Lord Parmoor in raising a question about the treatment of the objectors. His name was at the head of a long list of signatories to a protest backing Lord Parmoor's action, and the Church of England Peace League, now including among its Vice-Presidents E. W. Barnes and William Temple, undertook a follow-up enquiry.[24]

---

[23] Lord Parmoor, *A Retrospect; Looking Back over a Life of More Than Eighty Years* (1936), 119.
[24] Davidson Papers, 348.

In spite of these protests 1917 was the year in which the scandal of the persecution of conscientious objectors was most blatant, because the sense of national peril was at its greatest. There was a particularly inhumane case in Hicks's own diocese concerning James Brightmore, who had been refused exemption from military service, enrolled in the Manchester Regiment, and refused to obey orders. He had been sentenced to six months hard labour and on the completion of this sentence had been returned to the regiment. In his statement to a Court Martial held in Cleethorpes he said that when he again refused to obey orders the commanding officer sentenced him to 28 days solitary confinement and he was put in a pit dug in the ground 10 feet deep which contained mud and water to the depth of 2 feet. He was given two planks to stand on, but was exposed to the rain and cold wind. There he was expected to cook his own food. This case, and others, led to questions in the House, and defensive answers by the Under-Secretary at the War Office.[25] Hicks seems not to have intervened directly in this case, but he was in touch with a member of the Society of Friends who was supporting Brightmore. The commanding officer concerned had been relieved of his duties, much to the outrage of one of the clergy. Hicks was visiting Canon Markham, the Vicar of St James, Grimsby, at the time and noted in his diary:

Mrs Markham and the Vicar expressed to me their distress at what had happened at Cleethorpes: the (new) Colonel says 'the Brigadier that has been sent away is the best they ever had there. The men are almost in *mutiny* about the CO being let off: they will not be persuaded to go out on the next draft etc.' They little knew my views, & were astonished when I gently let them know.[26]

In October and November Hicks put his signature to two memorials to the Prime Minister on the subjects of 'absolutists' and COs in prison. Lord Parmoor convened a meeting at the House of Commons in February 1918, to which Hicks was invited. This long list of protests over several years shows how difficult it was to move the government to take any effective action.

With the establishment of military camps and aerodromes Hicks found himself dealing with something like a second community within the diocese, but the regular work of the church was

[25] Reports in the *Grimsby Telegraph* 24–5 July 1917.   [26] *Diary*, 25 July 1917.

sustained with remarkably little alteration. In an important sense, however, the war brought a dramatic change. Diocesan policy was inevitably affected by the launch of the National Mission of Repentance and Hope in 1916. The war seemed to contradict everything Hicks had hoped for in international relations and to set back indefinitely any chance of social reform, as the second Boer War had done in 1899. But the National Mission afforded him some compensation. It is true that he was inclined to regard with some reservations an initiative in mission which arose from the divided counsels of the bishops, was launched without adequate preparation, and lacked warm support among church people generally. Indeed the planning of the Mission went ahead without clear agreement on its nature and even without general conviction about its title.[27] Among those churchmen whom Hicks respected more than most, two were particularly critical of the project. Bishop Gore declared that the church was in such a state, and the clergy so inclined to run away from their spiritual duties, that a mission was impossible. Peter Green had his own reasons for doubting the viability of the Mission. He seems to have thought that it could not be led by clergy whose influence in the community was nil.[28] He saw parochial missions as appropriate only in flourishing parishes and not as desperate remedies for desperate situations, and applied the same criteria to a national mission. He was appointed to the steering committee of the National Mission, but was prevented from attending its first meeting by the pressure of parochial work and then resigned.[29]

Nevertheless the National Mission might offer an opening for the kind of social message which Hicks wanted to promote in the diocese. Other wartime demands were a distraction from what he had hoped to do in his episcopal ministry, but the National Mission was not. He thought its launch had been rushed, but he took it up with enthusiasm and got down to planning preparations in the diocese, and commented:

---

[27] See David M. Thompson, 'War, the Nation and the Kingdom of God: the origins of the National Mission of Repentance and Hope, 1915–16', in W. J. Sheils (ed.), *The Church and the War* (Ecclesiastical History Society 1983), 337–50. This has the advantage of access to the papers of A. W. Robinson, who had been given a leading role in the preparation of the Mission by Archbishop Davidson.

[28] G. K. A. Bell, *Randall Davidson* (1935), ii. 767–8.

[29] M. G. Price, 'Canon Peter Green: A Study of his Pastoral Work in Salford 1901–1951' (Manchester University M.Ph. thesis 1994), 107.

The extraordinary feature of it is that its aims and scope exactly correspond with what I have been always insisting upon as the duty and call
of the Church, viz. to appeal not only to individuals for their conversion to God, but to appeal to the Collective Church to take collective
action in Christ's name in order to remedy the national evils and social
sins of England.[30]

In fact it was chiefly there, in the social message of the church,
that there was a dividing-line between those who actively supported the Mission and those who co-operated grudgingly or merely
sat back and criticized. It evoked extraordinary invective from a
variety of churchmen. The best known and most outspoken was
Hensley Henson. In a personal letter he wrote that it was

a grave political blunder, for the time was inopportune, and there were
none of the conditions of success. Its only permanent consequence to
the Church will be the raising into sudden, and wholly unmerited, importance a number of foolish persons, ardent, bigotted, and ill-informed,
who would not otherwise have gained a hearing.

He complained, in his diary, that 'professed and professional missioners' would determine its temper and method, and that the nation
could not be expected to attend to a religious appeal in wartime.
The extent of needed restatement of the Christian message was
too little realized. His overriding interest, at the time, in the restatement of doctrine could not be satisfied by the mission as planned,
and therefore he derided it.[31] An even less restrained criticism is
to be found in another clerical diary. The Revd Andrew Clark,
Rector of Great Leighs, Essex, recorded this delightful outburst,
in August 1916:

The old women of the Episcopal bench are devising old-womanish
National Missions, and relays of women preachers, but will not move a
finger to lighten the Church service of dreary incrustations of a by-gone
age, or allow reasonable liberty of substituting reasonable alternatives for
intolerably long and weary psalms and lessons for the day.[32]

These examples show how easy it was for members of the clergy
to condemn the National Mission because it was not designed to

---

[30] *Diary*, 22 Apr. 1916.
[31] *Letters*, ed. E. F. Braley (1950), 14–15; *Retrospect* (1942), i. 177.
[32] James Munson (ed.), *Echoes of the Great War: the Diary of the Reverend Andrew Clark
1914–1919* (1985), 150, 160.

promote the causes nearest to their hearts. Henson believed that
the need of the hour was to reformulate the creeds, or at least to
reinterpret them, and so incurred the charge of heresy from those
who thought themselves upholders of orthodoxy. Clark believed
that there was little hope for the church unless it revised its forms
of worship. Another idiosyncratic statement of the purpose of the
Mission was given by A. C. Headlam, at that time editor of the
Church Quarterly Review, who declared that the failure of the church,
which the Mission should set out to remedy, was a failure in 'intellectual keenness'.[33] The objectives proposed by these individuals
could not be incorporated in the plans for the National Mission,
because there was no consensus about them. Neither was there a
consensus about the social application of the Christian message;
but the bishops could not shake off the notion that they ought to
say something to 'the nation'—that was what a national church
ought to do. There were several members of the original planning group, notably William Temple, who believed that social issues
were of the essence of the Mission; but this was never accepted
by Winnington Ingram, the Bishop of London, who became the
church's figure-head in the eyes of the nation and the greatest of
all the clerical recruiting officers.

It was, therefore, true that the cause which Hicks had at heart,
to 'take collective action in Christ's name in order to remedy the
national evils and social sins of England', was just as divisive as any
other emphasis in the promotion of the Mission. But a national
mission could hardly omit all reference to the nation, and the way
was open for Hicks to press on the diocese, and on church people
generally, his own interpretation of its meaning. Even if there had
not been a National Mission he would have interpreted the crisis
as a summons to national self-examination. In his article in the
Political Quarterly, already mentioned, he had been largely concerned
to sustain hopes for the post-war world in spite of the shock which
the war had given to ideas of progress. But he began it with a
positive estimate of the new situation:

The outbreak of a tremendous European war is a challenge to the nation
in every department of its common life: it becomes a touchstone of our
patriotism, our unity, our physical strength, of the intelligence and energy

of our people, of our resources in every kind of wealth. But it is more: it is a challenge to our ideals. Our moral and religious convictions find here a searching and inevitable test.

In 1916 he spoke about the National Mission in his presidential address to the diocesan conference, and gave it his own social meaning:

To shelter the weak, to raise up a barrier against organised selfishness, to storm the citadels of legalised vice, to fight for municipal righteousness, to agitate for wholesome legislation, to use the vote for promoting good government, to help the weak against the strong, and to make the ways of the world a little less thorny for the wayward, the ignorant and the poor, to make England in all her towns and villages a wholesome place to bring up children in—there we have before us a task so grand, so difficult, so menacing to selfish interest, but so splendid and Christlike in its features and in its issues—that it at once inspires and inflames the ardour of Christian souls.

Hicks was reckoned more impressive in extempore speech than when he stuck to a script, and the reporting here reads like a transcript of a speech from brief notes. He evidently found what he himself sometimes called 'liberty'—the flowing of eloquence from a prophetic conviction of the rightness of what he had to say.

He gave up a great deal of his time to the promotion of the Mission by addressing groups of clergy on its meaning wherever he saw an opportunity. It was difficult to raise their eyes above limited horizons. They could only put questions to the bishop about making the harvest festival the climax of the Mission or using it to introduce the eucharist as the main service on Sundays.[34] Hicks knew that he had to proceed gently. When he was invited to address the clergy of the Rural Deanery of North Grantham on 'The Personal Life of the Clergyman in relation to Social Movements', he felt he must take the chance to speak out. He tried to explain why he was so strongly a Progressive, and declared that the church had never woken up to social needs: 'I fear I astonished them. But they needed it. I think the time for reticence is over: we must be frank and fearless—though endlessly kind. The men present raised some feeble protests, and expostulated, but all was kind and courteous: they *tolerated* me, as an oddity.'[35]

[34] *Diary*, 19 July 1916.   [35] *Diary*, 18 Sept. 1916.

Hicks was also keen to make the most of the opportunity which the National Mission presented to develop the contribution of women to the work of the church. In June 1916 he commissioned a group of women to go out into the diocese as 'Pilgrims of Prayer'. They wore a simple uniform and stayed in villagers' cottages, and gave addresses and led prayers. The experiment was successful and was repeated the following year.[36] There had been those who regarded the National Mission almost as a plot to introduce a claim for the ordination of women. Hicks never came out in favour of such a big step in developing women's ministry in the church. He favoured specific moves which he thought no reasonable Christian could refuse, and devoted his advocacy to the establishment of equal rights for women among the laity.

The increased emphasis on women's role in the church was an incidental but positive effect of the outbreak of war. All through his ministry Hicks had shown a special concern for women and their place in society and the church. He was the President of the Church League for Women's Suffrage, as already noted, and was present in the House of Lords on the memorable occasion of the Second Reading of the Electoral Reform Bill, which included votes for some women—doubly memorable, because it took place during an air raid (18 December 1917): 'Upon the Adjournment, we all would gladly have gone home. But, by reason of the battle in the air, & the din of the guns, etc., we obeyed advice & descended into the "cellars" used as a pantry for the tea-rooms. Here we sat & talked for two hours.' The main object of the Church League for Women's Suffrage was achieved, ironically enough, at the end of a period during which suffragist agitation was suspended. The League had redirected its energies to the support of the national effort.

The bishop's concern for the place of women in society, as distinct from the church, also had other outlets. It showed itself during the war in a particular interest in the welfare of women away from home—in the camps and in munition work. In 1917 he paid a visit to Harlaxton Flying Camp:

We learned how careful & strict the War Office is in the discipline of the waitresses. All (now) belong to the Legion of Women, dress in Khaki, are under the governance of a Lady Superintendent, have very strict rules,

---

[36] *Diary*, 19–20 June and 1 July 1916; 15 June 1917.

& are discharged at once, if unruly. They are part of the Army itself. I am well satisfied—if the system is well worked.

The first uniformed women police officers were employed early in the war at the Belton camp, and later the Women's Police Service worked in and around munitions factories.[37] The welfare of the women engaged in munition work was a matter of sufficient importance to occupy the attention of the bishops at one of their regular meetings. In May 1917 Hicks noted: 'We met in the (old) Library. A good deal about looking after the girls whom the Ministry of Munitions has *herded* by thousands in huts away from their homes, untended and uncared for—save in body.' Later he had an opportunity to talk with a granddaughter of Bishop Wordsworth, who had been engaged in the 'Mission to Munition Workers' at Woolwich. In Lincoln he referred the situation to a committee representing the various women's organizations in the diocese. The only practical step he records was the setting up of a hostel for 'munitioner girls' under the YWCA in Castle Square, Lincoln; but that was in 1918, only a few weeks before the armistice.

Nothing brought home to civilians the realities of a new kind of war more forcibly than the experience of air raids. The first occasion on which Hicks refers to them was in October 1914 when he was staying with his daughter Christina Frances in London and enjoying the company of her new baby: 'C. really anxious about the threatened German Zeppelins & bombs. Wonderful searchlights soaring up into the heaven, over the Thames, like horns of fire. London very still a.m., & at night *very dark*. But at 5.30, at dark, vast crowds apparently returning to their homes as fast as they could.' Soon Lincolnshire became the target of raids. The diaries refer to the dropping of bombs at Cleethorpes, Fiskerton, Boston, Scartho, Washingborough, Greetwell, and Saxilby. The bishop and his household were never in real danger, but they had to get used to broken nights. He records how he was going up to dress for dinner (a practice he kept up all through the war, it seems), when:

the BUZZER warned us of ZEPPELINS. So we put out all lights & went down to the Examination room, *all* of us. By 8.30 or 9 we were all hungry, & took food by the light of *one* candle in the dining room. After this we stayed up some time, but by degrees the servants crept off to

---

[37] Diana Condell and Jean Liddiard, *Working for Victory: Images of Women in the First World War 1914–1918* (1987), 67.

bed, though I doubt if they really undressed. Agnes & I stayed up until past midnight, but no buzzer had yet signalled safety. But we heard the trains begin to move again. We were soon asleep. At *2.30* we were awoke by the Buzzer, which announced our safety: the Zepps were gone!

After long, weary years the war was won. Hicks had been one of those who supported Lord Lansdowne's attempt to promote a negotiated peace in 1917.[38] That had led to nothing but uncomprehending vilification. When the end finally came, it seems to have been unexpected by Hicks. At the beginning of October 1918 he had contracted a bad cold while staying at Alford Vicarage and was glad to be able to take an easy weekend. On 14 October he wrote: 'I came home to Lincoln by the 8.59 train. Great news today: *Germany has surrendered*! PEACE is coming!' Armistice Day found the bishop busy as usual, spending most of the day at Bourne. His diary for that day contains no reference to the armistice, but on a later page he summed up his reflections on 1918 in sombre mood:

At the announcement of the Armistice the Churches were crowded with throngs of people who came of their own accord. The troops at home & abroad received the news with a dignified silence—like dazed sleepers, suddenly aroused from a hideous dream, & hardly able to take it all in. In London & Manchester, & elsewhere the nights of Nov. 11 & 12 were spent in the streets in quiet dancing & *sober* merrymaking: but there was no 'mafficking'.

His thoughts were now full of the problems of peace. Already in 1917 he had been one of a distinguished list of speakers, including Bishop Gore, Mrs Creighton, Herbert Samuel, Maude Royden, and Sidney Webb, at a Summer Meeting on the problems of reconstruction held at Hampstead. He accepted an invitation from the Quakers to serve on an Emergency Committee for the assistance of Germans, Austrians, and Hungarians in distress.[39] But he found the political scene disheartening. His friend Charles Roberts, the Liberal MP for Lincoln, lost his seat in the 'Coupon Election', but remained sanguine, saying 'It is the rule in British politics never to give up. Your turn will come.' The bishop did not share his optimism:

[38] Letter in archives at Madresfield Court.
[39] *Commonwealth* (Aug. 1917 and Apr. 1918).

The turn over of the General Election on Dec. 14th, as was seen on the 28 & following when polls were made known, shows that the national mind was still occupied with memories of the War, the baseness of 'Pacifists', who failed in 'patriotism', & fear of Germany or Bolshevism. It was a vote of Reaction, based on fear—joy to be free from War, fear of all sorts of dangers & warnings, & a determination to stick only to 'Patriots'. The national mind had clearly not turned to thoughts of Peace, or the terms of a lasting settlement. All movements for real *Progress* will have to find their course outside the House, in the country.

In 1914 he had asked what were 'the terms and conditions we should desire to secure, if Providence grant us a powerful voice in the settlement of Peace'. His answer had included the exorcism of militarism from Europe, the rejection of all ideas of a balance of power, the independence and neutrality of small states, the democratization of foreign policy in order to avoid secret treaties, and the nationalization of all manufacture of the weapons of war. He had little faith in the elected parliament of 1918.

No doubt he would have devoted himself to those movements, if he had been ten years younger. His last efforts were in support of the formation of a League of Nations. In February 1919 he referred, in his monthly diocesan letter, to the break-up of the Austrian and Turkish Empires, and warned that the smaller units in those empires could easily fall prey to alien aggression or internal strife. They needed the guardianship of a League of Nations and the establishment of mandatory states. At his last diocesan conference, in July 1918, he had praised President Wilson's attitude in peace negotiations, commended the case for a League, and moved a resolution rejoicing at the unity of spirit between Britain and the USA in defence of the principles of civil freedom and national independence. He would have been horrified by the terms of the Versailles treaty and the withdrawal of the USA into isolation; but his days of active concern were drawing to a close. He was taken seriously ill on holiday in Sussex in the following April and never recovered his strength. He died on 14 August 1919. He was seventy-five years old.

PART III

The Meaning of Radical Churchmanship

13
A Practical Theology

'My father had little interest, if any, in theological controversy. He often said that he was no theologian.'[1] That comment by his son Ned Hicks is only superficially true. Ned was too young to have known much about the workings of his father's mind before his appointment to Lincoln, and during the period of Ned's developed theological interest at Oxford he was heavily under the influence of Ronnie Knox, for whom theology had a particular focus at that time on questions of authority and dogma. In fact there are many indications that his father kept himself informed of current theological controversies; and his whole attitude to life was formed upon a religious basis which can only be denied the title of 'theological' by a restriction of its meaning. We can rephrase the comment by saying that Hicks took a detached interest in many of the controversies of the period, and never regarded himself as a systematic or creative theologian. It would do him an injustice, however, to overlook the significance of his belief and its formulation as the rock upon which his life was stabilized.

In his childhood there were both Methodist and Anglican influences. He was baptized as an infant by a Wesleyan minister[2] and later confirmed in the Church of England. His early religious education was evidently unexciting. He described his preparation for confirmation as being 'of a very dry kind'. But he was strongly influenced by the Revd Edmund Hobhouse, the High-Church incumbent of St Peter-in-the-East. The worship in his college chapel was reverent but formal. His undergraduate studies were not specifically theological, and like most clergymen of his generation he had limited theological preparation for ordination. At the age of

[1] Fowler, 167.
[2] His recollection that he was baptized by Dr Jabez Bunting was inaccurate. The certificate produced at the time of his ordination shows that he was in fact baptized by the Revd James P. Dunn, the second minister at the Wesleyan church. Perhaps Dr Bunting was visiting the church at the time.

twenty-six he was ordained deacon at Cuddesdon on the title of his fellowship at Corpus, and licensed as a public preacher, having provided a certificate of attendance at the lectures of Professor Payne Smith and Professor C. A. Heurtley. He spent some time in the country parish of Byfield reading for priest's orders and was ordained priest in 1871. His fellow ordinands were A. H. Sayce, who became a notable scholar in Egyptian and Babylonian studies, and F. J. Jayne, who went on to be a tutor at Keble, Vicar of Leeds, and eventually Bishop of Chester. But the formative influences on Hicks's religious outlook were to be found elsewhere, and they were of various kinds. He referred later to having been brought up in the Oxford Movement. He never forgot what he owed to Ruskin. He had a firm friendship with the evangelist Henry Bazely. Each of these three types of religion, the Anglo-catholic, the Ruskinian, and the evangelical, left its mark on him.

His theological capability, in the eyes of others, is evidenced by his appointment as an examiner in the Honours School of Theology at Oxford in 1888, where one of his colleagues was J. O. Johnston, the biographer of Liddon, whom he later invited to Lincoln Cathedral as Chancellor. For seventeen years he was a lecturer at the Scholae Episcopi in Manchester 'to students whose only fault was their poverty'. As a teacher he mediated the influences he himself had felt. His largely unclerical list of 'prophets' has already been mentioned. On another occasion he put some names together in a sort of calendar of modern saints. They were a mixed bag in terms of churchmanship, and included Henry Martyn, J. C. Patteson, (John) Keble, (Bishop Thomas) Ken, and Robert Nelson. He was equally happy to quote Pusey and Liddon and to praise the witness of the Society of Friends. This is enough to show that he was glad to welcome light from all possible directions. The problem is to determine the central elements in Hicks's personal faith among all the numerous influences to which he kept himself open.

Hicks was reticent about his own spiritual life, and we cannot judge how far he responded to the mystical element in religion. His Lincoln diaries refer to some of the books he read, and they include Evelyn Underhill's *Mysticism*, from which he says he derived much refreshment. When he said that the mystical element in religion and the sensuous element in art were equally abhorrent to Bazely[3] it was a tactful disclaimer of any suggestion that he himself shared that point of view. Wild accusations of 'Manichaeism' aimed at teetotallers entirely miss a target in Hicks, who had a sensitive enjoyment of the natural world and such sociable pleasures as were not made the object of exploitation. He found much pleasure in music and was no mean performer. Poetry, whether in the classical languages or in English, was a source of enjoyment to him. The visual arts often evoked his interest and comment. In an address at the annual meeting of the Manchester Art Museum in 1889 he contrasted the 'leisured' context of art and the squalid surroundings in which a Sister of Charity did her work, and asked, 'Can the two ideals of life be reconciled? Can Art learn self-sacrifice, and can the life of Christian service make the beautiful its end?' He went on to assert that it was a religious duty to give our best to God's poor; and our best was not wealth or even knowledge, but 'the capacity of noble and ennobling enjoyment'.[4]

There are echoes of Ruskin here. Reference has already been made to his inaugural lectures in the Faculty of Theology at Manchester University in which he allowed himself to reflect on the influence of the Oxford Movement 'with its romantic sentiment, its religious zeal, its passionate appeal to an idealised past' and also its retrograde effect on ecclesiastical art. His exaltation of enjoyment to a high place in his scale of values, and his forward-looking attitude to art, are both notable features of his personality. But they are themselves only part of his open responsiveness to all kinds of human experience. And that is not irrelevant to the structure of his theology. It certainly set him apart from some kinds of piety. Baron von Hügel once quoted a friend as saying that Dr Pusey, at least at a particular stage of his life,

was incapable, or had made himself incapable, or deliberately acted as though he were incapable, of taking any interest in anything that was not directly, technically religious, or that was not explicitly connected with religion. And that this was quite uncatholic, quite unlike the greatest of the Catholic saints, quite unlike the Jesus of the Synoptists, with all of whom God is the God of Nature as of Grace—a God deeply interested— if this be not profane—also in not directly religious things—grace things.[5]

[3] *Henry Bazely*, 14.   [4] Fowler, 93–4.
[5] Baron Friedrich von Hügel, *Selected Letters 1896–1924*, ed. Bernard Holland (1927, reissued 1933), 254.

It may be debated in what sense the interest in nature as well as grace is distinctively Catholic; it was quite certainly an essential part of Hicks's liberalism.

His implicit theology may be said to have been controlled by certain leading categories, such as myth, history, morality, and prophecy; and though these are not precisely secular, neither are they necessarily Christian. In presenting an artificially constructed description of his theology, it is necessary to set aside the usual categories and try to identify some keywords and ideas. And always it must be borne in mind that for Hicks theology was not just an intellectual exercise. As he said in an address to the students at Bishop's Hostel, Lincoln, at their festival in 1912: 'Reflect that theology is, after all, a practical science; it deals with living and breathing human beings, as redeemed by the active love of a personal God. Therefore study human nature. Perhaps the best manual is Shakspeare, next to Holy Scripture. But above all test your theology by the touchstone of facts.' This distrust of theories ran through all the areas of life in which he was interested: politics, social reform, church organization, liturgical revision. But pragmatism alone was not enough; it must be based on a limited number of simple principles. Those principles had been declared in the life and teaching of Jesus Christ, who was himself the redeeming presence of 'the active love of a personal God'.

It is important to remember the particular ways in which his classical scholarship developed. His attention was early drawn to two particular aspects of classical studies: to myth and to epigraphy. They both had their implications for his future studies of religion. In his Latin Prize Essay on myth he argued that a people's myths are a sure indication of the gods they worship. In his epigraphical work he felt the excitement of coming into contact with actual historical people from a past age. In the one case it was necessary to understand the form of the language and ritual used, and not to be misled into a kind of fundamentalism which would reduce poetry to prose and imagination to reportage. In the other case the surviving artefact which brought the past to life also revealed a social context greatly different from that of the student, and led him to appreciate the process of historical development.

The implications for biblical interpretation are obvious. They are also inevitable, unless the Bible is put into a category of one, as the single inspired text over against all other literature. There were some who did precisely that, and not only on the evangelical wing of the church. Darwell Stone, for example, although he could be described as 'a true "liberal" in his outlook in the best sense of the word', held a belief about the Bible as the Word of God which required him to affirm that a gulf divided the Bible from all human literature.[6] The kind of textual criticism with which Hicks was familiar in classical studies carried over into his study of the New Testament and made it virtually impossible to isolate the Bible in that way. The biblical text was a treasured and irreplaceable witness to what lay behind it: the personalities and the social life of the first disciples. The study of the text was a developing discipline. So Hicks, in writing of Bishop Ellicott, 'the last of Palmerston's bishops', placed him in 'the older Cambridge school which has given way to the richer and more human but not less scholarly methods of modern criticism'. The growth of archaeology and of sounder historical methods, he said, 'have revolutionised the study of Christian documents'.[7]

He was not afraid of the outcome of these studies. He enjoyed corresponding with J. M. Thompson, the Modernist scholar who later caused such offence to the orthodox. Convalescing after a bout of illness in 1911 he wrote to him, saying that he had been reading C. W. Emmet's book, on the eschatological question in the gospels, and referred to *The Quest of the Historical Jesus*. He was himself confident that Schweitzer was wrong. 'The portrait of the Christ that he produces is—so far as it is distinguishable at all—impossible and absurd.' Apocalyptic should be emphasized, but Schweitzer had 'reduced it *ad absurdum*'. He went on to ask for references in books he could follow up dealing with specific questions of synoptic studies—the tendency to set little store by the third gospel, the limiting effect on Matthew of the needs of the Palestinian church, the possibility that Mark, too, was constrained by the Petrine tradition.[8] Here we see Hicks, released for a while from episcopal duties, engaged in and enjoying detailed study of the gospel texts, and ready to sit at the feet of a young scholar.

[6] F. L. Cross, *Darwell Stone, Churchman and Counsellor* (1943), pp. xix, 42.
[7] *MG* 2 Nov. 1904. Hicks also described an earlier bishop of Lincoln, Christopher Wordsworth, as 'the last of an old era of English scholarship and the harbinger of the new' whose work on the New Testament would not bear the light of newer studies. *LDM* (July 1912).
[8] Bodleian MS.Eng.Lett.d.181.

When he went for a walk with B. H. Streeter in a break during the first general conference of the Student Christian Movement in July 1914 (where he had spoken on 'The Redemption of Society'), it comes as no surprise that they 'talked of many things: N. T. Criticism, Reunion, etc. etc.'.[9] In his Primary Visitation he had included the development of biblical criticism as one of the factors which had created a new situation for the church. As bishop, he tried to accustom his clergy to its principles, was happy to get into discussion with a learned clergyman on the sources of the synoptic gospels, and continued his reading in that field. At the age of seventy he could still describe some new ideas about the text of the New Testament as 'exciting'.[10]

There was no disjunction for Hicks between the classical studies which he had pursued at Oxford and the study of the New Testament which he undertook later, either in method or in aim. They both required close attention to the literature and the surviving artefacts of societies at different stages of development. Hellenism was for him a continuous thread of history running from the ancient world to the New Testament. Alice Gardner, reviewing Fowler's biography of Hicks, remembered how as bishop he had retained and perhaps increased his love of Greek learning:

In 1912, being President of the Classical Association, he delivered a learned and thoughtful and at the same time a heart-warming address to the Association at their Conference in King's College, London. Tracing in a masterly way the history of Hellenism from Alexander the Great down to the present time, he made his audience—mainly of classical teachers—feel thankful for their task of perpetuating its invigorating influence. One realised that there was no hard-and-fast line to be drawn between ancient and modern—even between Christian and Pagan. To him all history was a continuous and fructifying stream, of which the most refreshing powers were due to the influence of Greek ideas.[11]

Her review perceptively fastens on Hicks's understanding of the continuities of history as central to all his teaching. She sums up his contribution to religious thought as consisting in his 'sym-

---

[9] *Diary*, 14 July 1914.   [10] *Diary*, 2 July 1918; 6 May 1914.
[11] 'Hellenism as a Force in History', Presidential Address, *Proceedings of the Classical Association*, ix (1912), 61–76. *Modern Churchman* 12/10 (Jan. 1923), 580–4. Alice Gardner, of Newnham College, Cambridge, knew Hicks personally, and on one occasion gave him a conducted tour of the college (*Diary*, 20 Apr. 1913).

pathetic readiness to trace historical continuity rather than to insist
on authority'. It was the key to his religious attitude. He could never
accept the appeal to authority as a way of terminating a discussion or giving an apparent answer to a difficult problem. Historical
continuity did not preclude change; nor did it justify looking for
precedents where they did not exist. He was deeply suspicious of
those who tried to answer contemporary questions by appealing
to the past.

There were two variants of this appeal which he rejected. One
was the attempt to find patterns of social organization which had
received Christian approval in the past, in order to prove their necessity in the present. In one of his 'Quartus' articles in the *Manchester
Guardian* he reviewed a 'slashing pamphlet' by Conrad Noel, *Socialism in Church History*. Hicks noted that Noel wanted to find collectivism everywhere, for example in the Fathers; though he had
difficulty in finding it in the gospels. This showed a feeble sense
of historical evolution. The point of Hicks's review is not that
socialism is bad or good, to be rejected or welcomed by Christian
people. It is that these questions cannot be decided by criteria drawn
from other periods in the historical development of human society. The study of past history might provide a stimulus to the critic
of modern society, but not patterns to be imposed on situations
which were utterly different. He had surely found such stimuli in
the views about Hellenism of both Ruskin and Charles Newton:
the one emphasizing the Greeks' ability to turn the drudgery of
work into the beauty of craftsmanship, and the other seeing the
Hellenic legacy as exemplifying the emergence of the humane from
the primitive and barbaric.[12] There were not 'values' in the Hellenic heritage which could be transposed unchanged into modern
industrial society. There were responses in the mind and heart of
the student which could issue in prophetic judgements.

The second kind of appeal to the authority of the past which
Hicks rejected was even more common: the appeal to the word
of scripture. With all his reverence for the New Testament he did
not imagine that it contained much that was directly applicable
to the world in which he lived. It provided, at best, principles not
prescriptions. He did not hesitate to describe the apostles as 'men
of very limited outlook' and declared that Christ 'never addressed

[12] See Turner, *Greek Heritage*, 63 ff.

the self-governing citizens of a free country'.[13] Discussing one particular issue at the time of the National Mission, he said that 'the place of woman, in the family and in the Church, cannot have been in St Paul's time and experience what it is in England at this hour'. With a touch of humour he contrasted St Paul's advice to women to consult their husbands quietly at home on points of Christian teaching with the present situation. In most cases the husband would be more likely to ask his wife's opinion on religious questions than she his. There were obvious gaps in New Testament teaching.

Is it not strange that in Ephesians v–vi, where the Apostle goes into much detail in sketching the duties of each member of the Christian family, he omits altogether the duty of the mother, and her vast responsibilities in the home? We feel sure that there are social conditions among us to-day,—conditions for which we may thank God for His good hand upon us,—which were a sealed book to the great apostle, forbidding us to regard his directions upon the social usages of the Churches he addressed as if they were a complete and final code of Christian manners and customs, of perpetual obligation.[14]

Here is the truth which underlay Maude Royden's belief that Hicks would eventually have come to approve the ordination of women. He carefully avoided committing himself on the subject because the urgent necessity was to establish women's common rights as equal members of the laity. It is, however, perfectly clear that he would never have argued that the issue could be settled by attributing universal validity to the decisions of the New Testament church or of any other stage in the church's history.

That did not mean that Hicks wrote off past stages of history as irrelevant; rather that he saw its proper understanding as a preparation for facing the future. Two examples of this approach may be taken to illustrate that fact, one a review and the other a sermon. The review was of Gilbert Murray's *Four Stages of Greek Religion*.[15] In it he began by noticing the great change in classical studies since the idea of development had come to control the study of archaeology. It had become clear that primitive cults and local customs had been little affected by any 'Olympian revolution'. Their study was proper to the understanding of the past; but there

---

[13] See *Building in Troublous Times* (1912), ch. 2.
[14] ' "Women's Work in the Church", A Letter from the Bishop', *LDM* (Sept. 1916).
[15] *Commonwealth* (May 1913).

was another way of looking at them, too. 'Man's religion, like himself, is not degraded but glorified by our knowledge of its lowly
beginnings. "The nature of a thing", said Aristotle, "is that which
it is normally destined to become." ' The study of the stages of
Greek religion showed that during the Hellenistic period the absorp-
tion of the city-states in huge military empires was accompanied
by despair of public and social life. The individual and not the
nation became the centre of spiritual experience. The consequent
spiritual demand was met by mysteries of penitence, new birth
and spiritual illumination. This might be seen as a remarkable
preparation for the gospel, but Murray implied that Christianity
was hardly more than one among many religions of mystery and
redemption. In response, Hicks quoted from 'Mark Rutherford's
Deliverance'. 'Nature is Rhadamanthine, and more so, for she
visits the sins of the fathers upon the children; but there is also in
her an infinite Pity, healing all wounds, softening all calamities,
ever hastening to alleviate and repair. Christianity in strange historical fashion is an expression of Nature, a projection of her into
a biography and a creed.'

In one of his sermons in Manchester Cathedral long before
Hicks had challenged his hearers to face the question whether
Christianity ought to stand in a kind of antagonism to the ordinary conditions of humanity, and make a man feel a stranger in the
midst of ordinary human existence. That thought was evidently
with him still. He continued his review of Murray's book by
distinguishing Christianity from the mystery cults, with their use
of astrology and magic, as both a revelation of truth and a call to
duty. But even in its emphasis on conduct it coincided with the
transfiguration of contemporary paganism, shown by 'the rare
elevation and beauty of character' of Marcus Aurelius. It was not
alien to its time. It belonged to its age. He believed that ideas could
circulate in a whole culture; could be 'in the air', producing coin-
cidences, or bringing together apparently unrelated events. So he
coupled the mystery of the influence of Christianity upon paganism with the mystery of the relations between the Renaissance
and the Reformation, apparently so different, yet both being 'of
their age' and both converging to one end—the evolution of the
modern world.

This, of course, is not a worked-out argument. It is a piece of
journalism; academic perhaps, but journalism nevertheless. The

details of the argument are not as important as its underlying assumption that there is movement in history which obscurely conforms to the divine purpose. That idea is even more clearly conveyed by the university sermon Hicks preached early in 1913.[16] He took as his text, and repeated like a refrain, the words of the Psalmist: 'Instead of thy fathers, thou shalt have children', and worked out his message in relation to the individual, the nation, and the church. In each case it was a plea to 'live in the future'. Let the young man dream dreams that are worthy to become the ideals of the mature man. Let the nation capture a new vision, of reorganizing, amending and purifying the social order. 'Its realization will involve sacrifice: there will be a struggle of classes: some beautiful and precious things that adorned the old order will suffer injury and perhaps destruction: but none can doubt that the evolution of a new order is imminent and inevitable.' Every institution, every element of the social order, every claim of class prerogative, was on trial. The supreme test for each one was whether it rendered real, beneficent, tangible service to the community. It must serve the future, not boast of its past. The church, too, must face the future. Its task was not just to preserve the heritage of the past, but to welcome all that was true and beautiful in the discoveries of the present, and 'to do and suffer all things, so that the people of England may become a great religious and progressive democracy'.

A brief summary of the sermon fails to convey the cumulative force of the repeated assertions that the future, not the past, is the realm of God's will. The kingdom is to come on earth. History is the record of the ways in which society has changed—not always for the good, not always in accordance with some blanket notion of progress, but always within the will of God. That must be the bedrock of any kind of Christian liberalism worthy of the name. It connects with Hicks's declaration: 'We are invincible and unwearying optimists.'[17] It will be necessary to consider how this attitude was affected by the outbreak of war in 1914, but the whole of Hicks's life before then had been conditioned by this conviction about the movement of history.

That conviction also determined his attitude to tradition. In many ways he was a traditionalist. He loved the treasures of the

---

[16] Printed as 'Sermon for the Month' in the *Commonwealth* (June 1913).
[17] Sermon for the CSU reported in the *Optimist* (April 1906).

past, from the Greek and Latin texts which he continued to read for mere enjoyment down to the language and liturgy which Cranmer had given to English Christians. But tradition did not mean something once and for all delivered to the church, ruling with a dead hand from the past. It had developed; it had changed; and it was still a process, not a datum. It must still be open to change, and that change was to be achieved through the interaction of Christian minds in the present and the future. Take the Athanasian Creed, for example. 'Why not honestly confess that this Creed, beautiful and majestic as it is, like a Norman cathedral, was composed in an age when no Christian thought there could be salvation outside of the Church, and that the opinion of Christendom has happily changed in this respect!' The damnatory clauses were wholly out of date. Stripped of them, it would still have its beauty and its value for purposes of instruction.[18] Hicks here appeals to the consensus of the faithful, as something capable of modifying what has been received from the past. It may be debatable whether there is, at any particular moment, such a thing as 'the opinion of Christendom'; we cannot convincingly identify it while a particular controversy is being exercised. In this instance he was right. Most Christians have ceased to believe that there is no salvation outside the church. But he did not claim to know all the answers, and he certainly did not believe that the bench of bishops, or the Convocations, or the Representative Church Council, could be trusted to give correct answers to difficult questions. The consequence was that he vigorously affirmed the right of enquiry and dissent within the church. Perhaps a consensus might emerge from free discussion. It was wholly alien to the character of the Church of England to stifle that freedom.

His concern for the maximum of personal freedom is made clear in his diary, in which he notes discussions in the Bishops' Meetings which determined to a large extent the public policy of the Church of England in the days before the Enabling Act of 1920 and the consequent inauguration of the Church Assembly. There were two particular instances in which he stood up for the freedom of the individual within the church. The first case involved a personal acquaintance, already mentioned: J. M. Thompson, whose book, *The Miracles of the New Testament*, advocated what

---

[18] *MG* 18 May 1905; 18 Nov. 1909.

were regarded as 'very radical and negative conclusions'.[19] Hicks opposed Gore's demand that the bishops should make a pronouncement against it, asserting that such a book could only be dealt with by argument. The history of the Church of England, he said, was 'strewn with the relics of mismanaged controversies'. Hicks did not in fact agree with those who argued *a priori* that miracles were impossible. But he wanted to keep the debate clear of anathemas. After Thompson had called at the Old Palace in Lincoln and thanked him for his support, he noted in his diary, 'he is anxious for other young Oxford theologians, who would feel themselves censured, if he were: & so might come a grave schism'.[20]

It is clear, however, that it was not for friendship's sake that he had stood up for Thompson, for there was no such consideration in the other instance of his controversial stand for freedom of theological debate. That was the case of the consecration of Hensley Henson as Bishop of Hereford. Again Gore was the focus of opposition, and Hicks was amongst those who supported Henson against the charge of heterodoxy. He took part in Henson's consecration in February 1918, but noted in his diary 'Winton and Oxford conspicuous by their absence' (i.e. Edward Stuart Talbot and Charles Gore, Henson's chief critics). Talbot had written a brochure opposing the appointment of Henson, which contained a great list of criticisms culminating in the accusation that he was willing to stretch disbelief to cover the two great miracles of the New Testament —the Virgin Birth and the Resurrection.[21] The question of miracles arose here as in the case of Thompson. Hicks's own view of the Virgin Birth was probably just the same as that which he had expressed in a letter to Hastings Rashdall as long ago as 1895, though that view was, as he said, just put down *currente calamo*. There was no possibility of evidence, but the doctrine 'falls in with the rest of my conceptions of the Incarnation, and of any ideas I can form of the relation of God to man'. He thought the conception of man and nature and their relation to the divine as set forth in scripture led naturally up to some such mystery as that which is termed the miraculous and immaculate birth.[22]

Again Hicks gave his support to someone accused of heterodoxy without agreeing with him. He believed that the church could

---

[19] Bell, *Randall Davidson*, i. 672.   [20] *Diary*, 4–7 and 23 July 1911.
[21] Chadwick, *Hensley Henson*, 143.   [22] Bodleian MS.Eng.Lett.d.181.

only benefit from the stimulating and argumentative presence of Henson on the episcopal bench. He wrote at some length about Henson in his *Diocesan Magazine*. Henson had been criticized especially for a sermon in a volume entitled *The Creed in the Pulpit*. Hicks wrote:

The incriminated sermon in the volume, on The Faith and The Resurrection, was preached on Easter Day 1912; and I read it more than once on Christmas Day of that year. It so impressed me that I pencilled these words in the margin: 'One of the most beautiful sermons I ever read in my life'. I have lately read it again, and find no reason to revise that opinion. My conviction, based on all that I have read of this divine, is that his preaching has been, and is likely to be, a mighty power for good, in convincing gainsayers, in enforcing the Christian gospel, and confirming in hearty belief hundreds of educated and thoughtful men and women who in these days are in danger of 'thinking themselves out' of all allegiance to revealed religion.

He said that he had accepted the archbishop's invitation to take part in Henson's consecration because he was jealous for the breadth and sympathy of the Church of England with its three well-defined schools of opinion. It would not benefit the church to squeeze out any of them from its general comity. As for Henson himself: 'The general aim and argument of a sermon are forgotten in the presence of some unhappy phrase that is thought to reveal heretical bias. I am afraid that few of us would endure such scrutiny. Even in St Paul himself there are careless phrases.' He then made a list of other controversies which had involved Maurice, Pusey, Colenso, Frederick Temple, Farrar, and the writers of *Lux Mundi*, including Gore himself.[23] How mistaken those controversies seemed today! After a final dig at Henson's style of debate and his unprogressive politics, he concluded: 'I cannot see reason for refusing to welcome him to the Episcopate as one of our best and most persuasive exponents of positive Christian belief, and a man of rare eloquence and learning.'[24]

In this verdict we can see the combination of two basic convictions: that the Christian tradition was a living process in which the truth would triumph, but could only be appreciated in retrospect

---

[23] *Lux Mundi* had been denounced at the Birmingham Church Congress by the eccentric Father Ignatius for 'denying Jesus Christ' amid scenes of uproar. See E. A. Knox, *Reminiscences of an Octogenarian 1847–1934* (1935), 151.

[24] *LDM* (Feb. 1918).

when the controversies had run their course; and that the church's task was always to find new language to win new generations to faith, as Paul had done in his own time. In professing this open-minded attitude to theological discussion Hicks ran the danger of being accused of vagueness in belief. That was not the impression he gave. The reason may be that he was firm in his commitment to two other elements in the Christian life, worship and morality. In the liturgy of the Prayer Book he found nourishment for his spirit. There was room for improvement and experimentation, in particular to remedy the Prayer Book's deficiency in Passiontide observances; but the framework must be maintained as the very condition of that freedom. And a distinction should be drawn between the regular pattern of worship within the church building and the need for adventurous experiment outside it for missionary purposes.[25]

The other firm commitment was in the realm of morality. On one occasion he had even said that he was content to adopt Matthew Arnold's words and define religion as 'morality touched with emotion'.[26] That was in a lecture deliberately aimed at a popular audience, and full of anecdote and quotation. He would certainly not have considered it a complete definition, because he was very much aware of the aesthetic dimension, no less than the doctrinal content, of religion. Morality, however, is most often described by him in terms of personal characteristics rather than delineated in sets of rules. So the gospel was a gospel of charity and generosity. The gentler virtues were to be developed. The church was to be a place of brotherhood. The 'golden rule' could be taken as a general principle. All these interpretations of the content of morality could be related to the overriding purpose of creating the maximum amount of freedom. In practice Hicks applied that idea most strenuously in the attempt to prevent oppression abroad and exploitation at home, for they were the most flagrant forms of the denial of freedom to others, and yet the forms most easily connived at, through ignorance or lack of imagination. The application of that golden rule required imagination and a developed sense of responsibility. The shareholders of a brewing

---

[25] See e.g. Hicks's elaboration of an idea for an ἐπιτάφιος πομπή (funeral procession) on a Greek model for Good Friday in his *Diary*, 2 Apr. 1915.

[26] 'The Religious Point of View', in *Is Christianity True? A Series of Lectures Delivered in the Central Hall, Manchester* (1904), ch. 5.

company, for instance, had to be told what it was like to live in a slum and be subject to all kinds of pressure to spend money on drink and so ruin family life. Since there was no prospect of putting the brewers out of business, at least the ordinary people in each locality should be given the chance to shut out the menace of the drink trade from their own neighbourhood. The Christian conscience must find ways of combating the threat to morality arising from overcrowding. The Contagious Diseases Acts, with their legalization of a double standard of morality, must be repealed. There must be education and leisure for the workers so that their lives might be released from oppressive conditions at work. The badges of creed and church were, in these matters, irrelevant because they divided those who might work together for the social good.

He did not agree with those who wanted to make their idea of the rightness of a particular social order depend on a theological basis of a sacramental kind. There were some of these so-called 'Gore's people' among the supporters of the CSU, though in Manchester at least there were many, perhaps a majority, who could be described as 'Low Church'. The perception of the social needs of one's fellow human beings did not depend on a dogmatic faith. He also criticized those church people who retreated from commitment to specific reforms and took refuge in theological generalities. He spoke impatiently to his fellow bishops in Convocation in a debate on the Reconstruction of Social Life in 1918:

He would beg their Lordships not to be content with mere generalities. Several of the members who had spoken had urged the House to deal with principles, and, by all means, let them enunciate general principles, but the matter must not be allowed to end there. What they wanted to find out was what the Church and the Bishops were prepared to do and to advocate. Was the Church the friend of the social reformers or not? Could the social reformer trust the Church at a pinch? He was much afraid that, when definite social reforms came to be agitated in Parliament, or on the platform, the Church would be content still to discuss general principles, and to fall back upon the Incarnation and to talk about ultimate doctrines.[27]

Hicks may seem Quixotic in expecting much support from the bishops for specific social reforms. Yet at much the same time one of the follow-up committees appointed after the National Mission

[27] *Chronicle of Convocation*, Upper House, 1 May 1918.

had produced a report on 'Christianity and Industrial Problems' which had dealt with such topics as over-emphasis on the motive of self-interest, the coexistence of poverty and riches, the evil of insecurity and unemployment, co-operation versus competition in industry, a living wage, and women's employment, as well as related questions of local government and housing. To Hicks it seemed obvious that no one needed theological expertise to see the evil effects of industrialization on human relations or to approve all practical means to remove them. All that was needed was a true love of freedom and a strong belief in brotherhood. In his own case that love and that belief were grounded in his Christian faith, but he would not refuse to accept as companions in the work of reform any others who came to the same position without sharing his religious commitment.

His liberal attitude towards theological debate, then, existed alongside firm commitment to a particular tradition of worship and an unwavering stance on social morality. But he was greatly affected by the outbreak of war in 1914. It terminated the period of optimism which had begun with the return of the Liberal government in the election of 1906. Hicks had thought that western society had moved into an era when arbitration would replace conflict. Shocked by the reported atrocities in the early days of the war,[28] and later by the toll of human life on the battlefields, he had to re-establish his faith. He had never thought progress was automatic or would cost nothing. But he had to take stock of the situation and restate his faith. He confided little of his inner thoughts to his diaries. We can perhaps gauge their drift, as the war proceeded, from two addresses he gave in Lincoln. The first is a paper on 'God the Creator' which he read at a 'Spiritual Convention' in May 1916 and the second is a lecture given in the Chapter House of the cathedral in November 1917. They are unusual among his varied short writings in that they are not directed at a particular issue or problem but contain general reflections on the nature of Christian belief.[29]

The paper on 'God the Creator', read at short notice when the intended speaker was unable to come through illness, shows no

---

[28] But he did not fasten the blame on German Christians, like J. N. Figgis: 'The new Teutonic Christianity . . . is conducting its first mission—with the bonfire of Louvain for its Bethlehem Star' (*The Fellowship of the Mystery* (1914), p. ix).

[29] *LDM* (July 1916 and Dec. 1917).

sign of hasty preparation and must represent thoughts long matured in his mind, and perhaps contains an autobiographical element. It begins with an uncharacteristic lament for the loss of the sense of God's presence in contemporary society. The image of God as an oriental despot directing the universe from a distant throne had been rejected, but no better belief had taken its place in ordinary people's minds. The older orthodoxy, presented in a lively fashion by Paley's *Evidences*, and still held by many religious people, pictured a distant Creator who only ventured to modify his laws at moments of urgent crisis. That view of creation and providence accorded well with a literal reading of scripture. But the great scientific discoveries of the nineteenth century compelled Christians to think of a gradual making of the world. Lyell's study of geology disclosed an evolutionary, not a catastrophic, process; and astronomy had long shown that if man had any unique dignity on this 'eccentric speck' of the universe, it could only be because of 'God's regard'. Then Darwin and Wallace unfolded the doctrines of evolution and natural selection, and popularizing books, often with a controversial bias against the gospel, threw religious minds into confusion.

So far Hicks had just sketched a background for what he saw as the present stage of religious thought about creation. Thoughtful people, he said, including some scientists, reacted against the view of life and the natural order as the result of blind chance. They were led to posit 'mind' behind it all; but if mind, then purpose; and if purpose, then a Person. At this juncture, Hicks said, the argument took a serious turn. In spite of initial claims by Huxley and Herbert Spencer that biological study would help to guide man to right conduct, Huxley later came to admit its bankruptcy in this field. In his Romanes lecture of 1893 he made the 'almost over-vehement avowal' that goodness and virtue 'repudiates the gladiatorial theory of existence'. In the meantime the researches of psychology reinforced religion through the study of the phenomena of man's moral nature, his reason, conscience, and will. That is the region of man's nature where religion has its birth, and the spiritual being of man seemed inexplicable except in relation to God our Creator; and the religious mystics testified to the reality and the joy of converse with God. The result of this long journey of theology from the older conception of creation could be summed up in the words of Aubrey Moore: 'Darwin has conferred upon philosophy and religion an inestimable benefit by showing us that we must choose between two alternatives: either God is everywhere present in Nature, or He is nowhere.' Of course, problems remained; especially the problem of the pain and suffering of the world. Perhaps it was wrong to assume that in the Creator's view suffering was the greatest evil.

Probably the aim of the Creator is fixed on progress—progress through conflict; for indeed our own life is, we confess, a life of conflict, and without conflict—with evil, with difficulties, with our own besetments —there can be no spiritual advance. Let us say further that it does not seem to be the purpose of God to permit us to be absolutely certain of His existence, or of His goodness, without possibility of doubt, or the need of a venture of Faith . . . No sooner have we made this venture, and declared our decision, than we receive abundant confirmation of our conclusion, from the Life and Teaching of Christ, in Whom we find the nature and character of God manifestly disclosed to our gaze. The Son has revealed the Father.

Our beliefs are indeed confirmed by the wonders revealed by physical science, the vast scale of the universe matched by the marvels revealed by microscopic research and the analysis of matter.

Beauties of colour and form, of movement and of texture, challenge us wherever we gaze, and an additional and mysterious wonder accrues when we note that beauty and utility go hand in hand in all the works of God: every graceful curve in plant or animal, every charm of colour and movement, is there, because in some real way they contribute to the welfare and activity of the organism. And so we recover our wonder and delight in Creation, and praise the Creator whom we know also to be the God of Grace.

There is nothing remarkably original in this paper; but it shows a side of Hicks's make-up which has not received emphasis so far: his interest in the developments of science, limited though he knew that to be by his lack of specialist knowledge. Perhaps that is the wrong way to put it, if it suggests a discrete area of interest. It was an essential part of his liberalism that he believed all human activity to be within the purpose of God. That kind of attitude always puts questions to simple orthodoxy, as knowledge expands and poses new conundrums. Without building too much on slight indications, we can guess that towards the end of his life, he may have been reviewing the fairly simple orthodoxy which had been the basis of his ministry. His busy pastoral activities and his vigorous social campaigning in the Manchester period, as well as his continuing interest in classical archaeology and other kinds of scholarship, may have given him little leisure to reflect on the impact of the sciences on theology which he outlined in this paper.

Two factors, unrelated to each other but brought into prominence by the outbreak of war, seem to have influenced his ideas at this last stage of his life. First, the sufferings of wartime raised in an acute form doubts about the purposiveness of human history. That was in part the problem addressed in his paper on God the Creator. There were those who were pushed by the catastrophe of war to consider the idea of a limited God, struggling against the recalcitrance of the human nature he had created. Nothing that Hicks said in public gave expression to this idea, but he cannot have been unaware of it. Perhaps that is the implication of a note in his diary on 26 November 1916:

A restful evening, & read the rest of H. G. Wells' 'Mr Britling sees it through': a very remarkable & clever book. His characters are wholly free from any attachment to organized religion; in Mr Dimple he scorns the English Clergy: he repeatedly notes the existence of Bps as an English stupidity: & yet, in the end, Mr B's confession of faith is virtually the Xtian doctrine of Xt & the Cross. With all his comments on the War & politics I am in complete agreement & sympathy.

Wells attracted a good deal of attention from Christian commentators with his writings in wartime. A few days before this diary entry A. E. J. Rawlinson (later Bishop of Derby) had preached a sermon in Christ Church Cathedral, Oxford, which was largely a discussion of this particular book. Wells had presented the challenge to faith in God which every bereaved person in the war had felt. Mr Britling, the middle-aged academic, has lost his son in the war, and learns of the agonizing death on the eastern front of a German tutor whom he had employed in his family. His young male secretary who had been taken prisoner escapes and returns maimed by the loss of a hand. Mr Britling emerges from a phase of jingoism into belief in God; but it is a limited God he proclaims. When one of the other characters in the book says God must be responsible for all the suffering, Mr Britling denies it and accuses the theologians of false teaching:

They have been extravagant about God. They have had silly absolute ideas—that he is all-powerful. That he's omni-everything. But the common sense of men knows better. Every real religious thought denies it. After all, the real God of the Christians is Christ, not God Almighty; a poor mocked and wounded God nailed on a cross of matter . . . Some day he will triumph . . . But it is not fair to say that he causes all things now. It is not fair to make out a case against him. You have been misled. It is a theologian's folly. God is not absolute; God is finite . . . A finite God who struggles in his great and comprehensive way as we struggle in our weak and silly way—who is *with* us—that is the essence of all real religion.

Wells later repudiated this limited theism; and certainly Hicks cannot be interpreted as endorsing the words put into Mr Britling's mouth. But neither did he fall to criticizing them. He was content to find in Christ the image of the Father, and to leave the problem of suffering with only a few hints at a solution.

The other factor brought particularly to his attention during the war was the unwillingness of church leaders to adopt the kind of programme of social reform which seemed to him implicit in the idea of the National Mission. Just as he came to despair of parliamentary action ('All movements for real *Progress* will have to find their course outside the House, in the country'), so he looked for signs of hope outside the church. In November 1917 he gave an address on 'The work of the Holy Spirit in the World' as one of a series of lectures in the Chapter House. Two years later he wanted to return to this theme, and planned a 'Spiritual Convention' in the diocese on the subject of the Holy Spirit, which he was eventually unable to attend on account of his final illness. The programme of this convention was to begin with 'The Work of the Holy Spirit outside the Church of Christ'. It was, in a sense, his last message to the diocese.

The culmination of his address in 1917, and the key to his choice of subject, had been a denunciation of the church's failures in the recent past. 'Those who abolished the slave trade, and then slavery, found little or no help from the established Churches: the Quakers and Non-conformists were the leaders. It was the same with the drink question, and with Labour ideals.' He had begun with a brief survey of the beginnings of the doctrine of the Holy Spirit in the Bible, and its careful definition in the fourth century. Then he had proceeded to his real subject. He declared that the Spirit was at work upon the conscience and the will wherever human souls were to be found. More than that, it was the Holy Spirit who invested nature with the mystery and the beauty which made created things a sacrament of the divine presence. Christians need not be afraid of pantheism, for there was a true, as well as a false, pantheism, as Wordsworth knew. It would be a terrible mistake to confine the work of the Holy Spirit within the limits of orthodoxy. That was what the orthodox had done in our Lord's time when they attributed his power over devils to complicity with Satan. 'Wherever we see moral excellence, let us recognise it as the work of the Holy Spirit.' The difficulty of the church was that, like all organizations, it felt the impulse to self-defence, self-preservation, and self-aggrandizement. Its task was to be led by the free spirit to apply the principles of the gospel to the new circumstances of the time.

That can perhaps stand as a summary of Hicks's religion, with its three keywords: the gospel, freedom, applicability. The gospel was that which was given in the continuing tradition of the Christian community, which included criticism and reinterpretation, of texts, of documents, of liturgical practices. Freedom was the gift of Christ, to be enjoyed in the life of the individual. That freedom was to be 'applied' and made available increasingly in the life of society and the world at large. Each of these concepts indicated enemies to be fought. The gospel was threatened by 'petrifaction', by legalism, by enslavement to the past. The freedom of the individual was threatened by fear of the future, by fear of new knowledge, by fear of the unknown. Its availability within society was threatened by distrust of others, by the acceptance of distorted images of other groups and classes within society, by the desire to dominate and exploit. The role of the church was not to create or sustain values within a self-sufficient organism, but to feed and support the lives of those whose task was the transformation of society. The touchstone for all theology, however, was its practicality. It dealt with living and breathing human beings, as redeemed by God's active love. It must be put to the test of the experience of a life spent in the service of man, which is the service of God.

Hicks's pattern of beliefs was one particular form of liberal Christianity, and other forms will be considered in the next chapter. It is evident, however, that it took its shape, as did other forms of liberalism, in response to forces acting from outside upon a core of personal commitment established before those forces gathered strength. It was true not only of political Liberalism, but of religious liberalism as well, that its character during the period of Hicks's ministry differed radically from anything that bore the same label in a previous period. Its form was the result of social, scholarly and scientific changes: the emergence of a democratic stage in industrial society, the development of critical disciplines, and the provision through scientific methods of alternative sources of information and authority to set alongside or supersede the simpler sources of revelation. But liberals who remained church men and women did so because they believed that these changes could be made to carry forward into the future the Christian tradition embodied in the church's creeds and patterns of worship. The very fact that individual commitment, not conformity to unchanging tradition, was at the heart of liberal churchmanship meant that the liberals interpreted the tradition in markedly different ways. There were many varieties of liberalism.

14

A Radical among Liberals

To describe in detail a particular liberal churchman is also to establish a point of reference from which other liberal churchmen may be more clearly understood. Liberalism is a word with a great variety of possible meanings, and it is not surprising that churchmen who claimed the title of liberal for themselves frequently failed to see how the title could be applied to others from whom they differed. Hensley Henson, for example, did not think of Hicks as a liberal, but found other categories to put him in. His dismissive description of Hicks ('a feminist, a total abstainer, and three parts a pacifist') is both an injustice and, paradoxically, an indication of his merit. The injustice lies in representing him as an oddity, a sort of amalgam of fads. Yet there was, though his critic could not see it, a coherent basis which gave rise to his particular social and political commitments.

The epithets, condescending if not quite contemptuous, bear unintended witness to his passionate concern to change the quality of life of ordinary people. He saw that the full potential of half the human race was left unrealized so long as women were denied equal education, or excluded from work they could perfectly well do, except for a prejudice against their whole sex. He believed that great numbers of working people were shut up within the cultural ghettoes of the slums and deprived of decent family life, not only by the conditions of their work but also by the pressures applied through moneymaking brewers and the bookies' runners. He saw that political and commercial aims involved thousands of men and their families in the sufferings of war, nurturing and then exploiting a patriotic sentiment which seemed to lift them out of the dreariness of daily life but finally left them with no tangible reward when the fighting was over. And though the forms in which his concerns were expressed were of their age, those concerns themselves are not irrelevant to later generations. Today we may speak differently, of sexism, of the social effects of poverty and unemployment, of the causes of war and the search for peace, but we are in reality articulating the same concerns in a different language.

Henson had no personal knowledge of Hicks and picked up his notion of what he was like by extracting a compound quintessence of the societies to which he lent his name. He did not see him as a real person but as a kind of caricature. The feminist cause was smothered in the post-war concern to find jobs for the demobilized soldiers. The church resumed its conventional practice of allocating a restricted role to women. In reaction to the austerities of wartime many young people took on a frenetic search for enjoyment, and drink and drugs were seen as a mode of release and not enslavement. The mask of unity in a nation at war, with all its miseries, was put aside and revealed deep divisions, so that the social conscience was dulled, and individuals and groups averted their eyes from the sufferings of others. Perhaps above all the catastrophe of 'world war' seemed to destroy the basis for believing in progress. Theology itself abandoned hope, except in an ultimate consummation dependent only on God's inscrutable will. Ideas of human progress were indicted as Pelagian or criticized for avoiding the note of divine judgement on history. Christian optimism went out of fashion in theological circles. Toleration, too, was challenged by those who upheld the importance of dogma or looked for the reassertion of authority in religion.

Yet this is only part of the picture. There were liberals still within the churches. The problem was that they had not inherited a coherent tradition from their predecessors in the pre-war world. The life of Edward Lee Hicks touches the lives of a distinguished company of men, and a small number of women, who upheld liberal traditions in the Church of England, as well as some who might be called fellow-travellers outside its limits. There was Gore, with his supporters in the CSU. There was Scott Holland, with those who responded to his electric personality. There were Modernist theologians like B. H. Streeter and Hastings Rashdall. There were women active in 'the cause'—Maude Royden and Louise Creighton and others—and intellectuals like Alice Gardner. There were churchmen of some eminence, like C. W. Stubbs and F. T. Woods and John Gott, who became bishops, and W. Moore Ede, who held a deanery. There were men with a creative flair for liturgy, like Percy Dearmer and A. S. Duncan Jones. There were laymen

like H. J. Torr and C. H. Roberts, and Free-Churchmen such as
A. S. Peake and J. H. Moulton. The trouble was that, if it was a
company, it was certainly not a regiment. They met, they corresponded with each other, they wrote their articles and their books;
but their relegation of dogma to a subordinate place made it impossible to establish a countervailing force to match the dogmatic
squadrons on either wing of the church. The Modern Churchmen's
Union was never more than a talking-shop for individualists. The
coalition of forces within the Christian Social Union, under internal stresses throughout its existence, lost its heart with the death
of Scott Holland, and its current ran into the sand of shop-floor
evangelism when it took on the guise of the Industrial Christian
Fellowship and recruited Woodbine Willie as its missioner. Hicks's
verdict, that it was wholly unpolitical, may not have been true always
and everywhere, but it was prophetic of its final destination.

Liberal churchmanship, then, was as fissiparous as protestantism,
but in a different way. The groups or sects into which protestantism
split did not lose their dogmatic nature in doing so; indeed a specific
dogmatic scheme was what held each of them together. They may
sometimes have looked to outsiders like cults of personality, but
their claim was always a claim to truth in doctrine. The disagreements of the liberals were often converted into agreements to differ, though the degree of mutual toleration varied. Liberals were
usually engaged in reinterpreting traditional doctrine and therefore
found it easier to accept theological differences than disagreements
about social or political policy. Henson thought Hicks a faddist.
Inge disliked Christians who called themselves socialists. But if disagreements could be kept at a theoretical level, even when they
might have ultimate political implications, personal friendships could
remain undamaged. A good example of this is the friendship and
intellectual opposition between the two deans, Inge and Hastings
Rashdall, both of whom were given preferment by the Liberal Prime
Minister, H. H. Asquith.

Hicks did not have much contact with Inge, but he was personally acquainted with Rashdall and evidently won his admiration.
When Rashdall was given Fowler's biography of Hicks by his mother
in 1922, he wrote: 'He is a man after my own heart. He ought
to have been a bishop 20 years before. If he had been Bishop of
London all these years, it might have made a vast difference to the
Church.' They had a good deal in common, including experience

of the life of an Oxford Common Room and membership of the CSU. But Rashdall had nothing to match Hicks's long and demanding parochial experience. After various other academic posts he was successively Tutor and Sub-warden of New College, Oxford, Canon Residentiary of Hereford Cathedral, and Dean of Carlisle. Although he wrote extensively on ethical and social questions, and was for eighteen years a joint editor of the CSU journal, the *Economic Review*, he always seemed to speak with a degree of academic detachment. He was not a social crusader like Hicks.[1] But he was politically Liberal in outlook and this produced a skirmish with Inge over one of the central convictions of many liberals: the idea of progress. Inge had delivered a Romanes Lecture[2] attacking the belief that there was a 'law of progress' in human affairs. Rashdall replied with 'two modest propositions': '(1) On the whole there has been progress on this planet—no doubt with many lapses, periods of stagnation, and periods of regression. (2) There is a reasonable expectation of such progress being continued for a considerable period in the future.' These ideas of progress are far removed from notions of inevitability often credited to liberal theologians, and they are evidently meant to conciliate Inge. But Rashdall does not hesitate to accuse him of looking at the whole human panorama from an aristocratic point of view (in other words, of a kind of élitism or even snobbery) and failing to understand the Middle Ages (in other words, of academic superficiality). The two men remained on good terms with each other, and Inge was always ready to defend his friend from the attacks of those who were in no sense liberal. But there was no possibility of their co-operation in influencing either church or society. They were divided on this central issue of 'progress', which affected so many other aspects of social policy. The focus of their religious interests, too, was so different as to make them inevitably opponents in theological debate. In particular Inge's interest in mysticism was deeply mistrusted by Rashdall.

Rashdall's theological liberalism had two aspects. First, it involved a careful restatement of traditional beliefs. What remained believable was summed up in an article in the *Modern Churchman* in 1911 like this:

---

[1] For a valuable guide to his writings, see: Margaret Marsh (ed.), *Hastings Rashdall, Bibliography of the Published Writings* (Leysters, Herefordshire 1993).

[2] Reprinted in *Outspoken Essays*, second series. Rashdall's reply is included in H. D. A. Major and F. L. Cross (eds.), *Ideas and Ideals* (Oxford 1928), 78–93.

(1) The indwelling of God in Christ must be not wholly isolated or differentiated from that indwelling of God in every man which is itself part of the teaching of historical Christianity;

(2) The indwelling of God in Christ must be recognized as a unique or supreme indwelling—a supreme realization of the true relation of God to man;

(3) The proof (if such a word is to be used) of Christ's Divinity must be sought in the appeal which He makes to the moral and religious consciousness of mankind.

There is a critical limit implied in the second of these points—the unique and supreme indwelling of God in Christ. To maintain that, it was not necessary to break off all courteous relations with Unitarians, as the fiercer exponents of orthodoxy seemed to think, but it was necessary to draw a theological line, even while giving full appreciation to many aspects of belief in which they occupied common ground. Probably Hicks would not have disagreed with this position, and he would certainly have maintained Rashdall's right to hold it, for he agreed with the other main emphasis in Rashdall's theological liberalism. That was his insistence that the clergy must be able to enjoy freedom of thought and discussion without fear of persecution.

Here we meet one of the few substantial changes which the liberals effected in the life of the church. In a letter to *The Times* in November 1901 Rashdall wrote: 'No thoughtful man will take orders if he is expected to abandon his profession the moment he finds himself at issue with traditional views on any single point of history or doctrine.'[3] Those words are a reflection upon the theological battles of the nineteenth century, not just in the Church of England, but in all the churches in Great Britain. Those battles were fought with particular bitterness because they were fought between opponents all of whom were convinced that they stood for the same thing: honesty. On one side were the theological conservatives (or so they saw themselves) who accused liberal theologians of dishonesty for drawing their pay as ministers though they had abandoned the faith of the churches which paid them. On the other side were the liberals, of a variety of colours, who saw themselves as the only true guardians of honesty in claiming the right to investigate the historical origins of Christian belief without determining

---

[3] For these quotations, see Matheson, *Hastings Rashdall*, 220, 134, 102.

in advance the conclusions of such an enquiry. Although there were still some skirmishes in the twentieth century, notably in the case of Hensley Henson's appointment as bishop, the real battles belonged to the past.

The conservatives had achieved almost nothing in the heresy hunts which had been attempted in attacking the authors of *Essays and Reviews*, Bishop Colenso, and even Charles Gore in the Church of England, Professor Robertson Smith in the Free Church of Scotland, and the Congregationalist divine, Dr Samuel Davidson. The results of that procedure had not been to silence the views expressed by the liberals, but at most to divert their proponents' energies into educational channels. Academics and educationalists, even if they were ordained ministers, might pursue their studies and develop their speculations largely unhindered. Lay people were not called to account. Even in the Roman Catholic Church lay thinkers such as Lord Acton or Baron von Hügel were permitted great freedom, so long as they were seen to conform in practice. Hicks argued for openness to fresh interpretations of the gospel. That inevitably involved the clergy, who were its main students and exponents. They must not be inhibited by restrictions which no longer promoted the contemporary mission of the church.

The prevalence of the changed attitude towards subscription is well illustrated in a statement of Neville Figgis in 1914:

Is there not borne in upon each of us, whether conservative or liberal, the sense that loyalty to a great religious society with a complex organisation and a long past is not the formal acceptance of so many propositions, and that it depends upon what sense we put upon the whole, what value we give to each of the parts? Loyalty to the idea of the Church, to its living Lord, to its earthly membership, to its multitudinous life, to the many-coloured richness of its sanctity, to the romance of its origin, to the treasures of its present inheritance, but above all loyalty to the splendour of its future glory;—that is the root of the matter. When a man feels that he has that, who are we that we should lightly charge him with dishonour, merely because he applies in one place methods of exegesis which each one of us applies elsewhere?[4]

Figgis was certainly no enemy of dogma. One of his heroes was Newman, whose lifelong opposition to what he saw as the undog-

---

[4] J. N. Figgis, Appendix B: 'Modernism *versus* Modernity', in *The Fellowship of the Mystery* (1914), 270.

matic character of liberalism in religion was a central feature of his whole outlook. Perhaps those like Figgis who treasured the Tractarian tradition had their own reasons for favouring reinterpretation of the church's formularies, but here his statement goes beyond that to an emotional description of the church's tradition, with an emphasis on 'feeling', and an awareness that it can only be appreciated in retrospect. This can be taken as very near to Hicks's own position, in spite of the temperamental distance which separated him from Figgis, who was in no sense a liberal in theology.

The general agreement among liberal churchmen that the definition of orthodoxy must be loosened to accommodate insights derived from historical and scientific research was not matched by agreement on political change. The disjunction is well illustrated by the case of Inge. It has been said that Inge's contribution to theology was 'himself'.[5] That is perhaps a polite way of saying that he was an egoist. He always had a deep concern for the spiritual life of the individual, but he saw no reason to adopt a particular critique of society and call it Christian. He did at one time show an interest in the CSU, but quickly abandoned it. His political attitude of contempt for the Labour movement set him apart from many liberally minded churchmen, and certainly from Hicks. It was fortunate that his vague hope in 1910 that he would succeed E. C. Wickham as Dean of Lincoln was not fulfilled. Hicks was warm in his appreciation of Inge as a preacher, but makes no record in his episcopal diary of having read any of his books.

Inge had not been brought by his limited parochial experience into much contact with working people. He had spent only a few years as incumbent of a West End parish in London. From there he went to be a Cambridge professor, and then on to the deanery of St Paul's. His particular interest in the mystical tradition encouraged him to treat dogma with a large degree of freedom. He was, therefore, drawn into the liberal camp, as far as theology was concerned. It did not follow that his opinions on other matters were liberal, though he deceived himself into thinking they were. More than that, in the judgement of his biographer, Adam Fox, he felt entitled to think those who disagreed with him were illiberal.[6] That is a hard saying, but it fits in with Rashdall's criticism of his friend.

[5] C. C. J. Webb, quoted in Fox, *Dean Inge*, 269.   [6] Fox, *Dean Inge*, 116.

His 'aristocratic' point of view led him to pass confident judgements on others. Like many politically conservative churchmen Inge had a particular dislike of those who wanted to deduce revolutionary, or even reformist, social ideas from the gospel. So in commenting on the philosophy of Plotinus he said that 'It is an escapist philosophy; but so is Christianity'; or, during the war, 'The gospel of detachment is the only one that brings any comfort at a time of universal ruin.' Much of his character and his attitude can be related to his personal circumstances. He had enjoyed the comforts of privileged life in his early manhood, saw the barbarities of the 'Great War' as a sign of the collapse of civilization, and was confirmed in his pessimism by the social conflicts of the post-war period. In contrast, Hicks had not enjoyed a comfortable childhood and was saved from many illusions about the quality of life in the closing decades of the nineteenth century by his long ministry to the poor. The outbreak of war was in a sense just another instance of the selfishness and stupidity of the human race, a set-back in the struggle, not an apocalyptic judgement which destroyed hope.

Liberal churchmen can be separated into those who denied and those who believed that there was a necessary connection between the Christian faith and political action. That division sometimes made them more bitter in criticism of other liberals than of more rigid theologians who shared their political propensities. They might even get on better with unbelievers of similar political opinions than with those who professed the same religious faith. Hicks was prepared to keep political and theological judgements separate. He was not much interested in trying to correct the implicit assumptions of those with whom he campaigned for social reform through political action. His opponents were mainly Christians of two different kinds who rejected his political Liberalism, but for different reasons. There were those who believed that the Christian tradition supported a different political stance; and there were those who thought it could not be used to support any political stance at all. They all tended to support the Tories, some through a kind of inertia, or unpolitical acceptance of the *status quo*, and others as a matter of conviction. Most evangelicals fell into the first group; the second included people like Inge. Believing that religion, and specifically Christianity, was primarily, if not exclusively, concerned with the individual and his inner life, he maintained that interest in social problems distracted the clergy from their proper work. It was only in the post-war period that he turned his attention to problems of conduct, and even then he exhibited the prejudices typical of an educated élite, both fearful and contemptuous of the masses. It is no surprise that he toyed with eugenic notions, as did Bishop Welldon. He never became the centre of any effective group. Even the Modern Churchmen's Union, of which he was for a time the President, eventually came under his condemnation for harbouring those who wanted to commit it to 'a kind of sloppy socialism, totally alien to the objects for which it was founded'.[7] His idea of freedom was individualistic and could not accommodate the insight shared by liberals like Scott Holland and Hicks, that working people in industrial society could not negotiate their freedom individually.

There was a different kind of contrast between theological liberalism and political conservatism in the case of Hensley Henson. Inge and Henson were both, in their different ways, essentially individualists. Neither of them appreciated the importance of group pressures in social life, the weakness of ordinary men and women as isolated units in society, the unreality of freedom in the lives of all who had no special skills to sell. Inge simply had no idea what working-class life was like. Henson's background was more middle-class, but he soon achieved the distinction of the Common Room at All Souls and moved among the leaders of political and religious life. Oxford House (for a few months) and the parish of Barking (for seven years) gave him the direct experience which Inge never had. But it failed to nurture in him a sense of the need to change society for the sake of those who had no choice but to live in what he described as 'the streets of this ancient Christian town' which 'have become as the highways of the City of the Plains'. He was later to display considerable courage in denouncing from the pulpit of Westminster Abbey the atrocities of the Putumayo Company in the upper Amazon which had been shown, chiefly on the evidence of Roger Casement, to be guilty of terrible inhumanities in the exploitation of the rubber trade. The company had intimidated the Dean of Hereford with threats of libel; but they failed to intimidate Henson. He declared the guilt of the directors of the company, some of whom were British, and ensured

[7] Fox, *Dean Inge*, 249.

that the issue was taken up in parliament. But in Barking he does not seem to have stopped to consider the guilt of those who had made it, in his own words, like Sodom and Gomorrah.

Without any doubt Henson was theologically liberal, and would not even have disowned the label of Modernist. Owen Chadwick writes:

> He wished to be a Modernist bishop, thus far at least, to show that a man who was agnostic about the great miracles of the creed might lawfully be not only a priest but a high priest, and that such agnosticism had in it nothing either insincere or disloyal. He distrusted the Anglo-Catholic movement headed by bishops like Charles Gore and Cosmo Gordon Lang, and wanted to counter its influence which he thought disastrous.[8]

He distrusted Gore and Lang for different reasons. They shared the taint of Anglo-catholicism, but whereas Lang might be described as a Tory democrat, Gore compounded the error of his Anglo-catholicism, in Henson's eyes, by arguing for what he saw as its socialistic corollaries. Henson did not have much time for evangelicals either. We can safely locate him in the liberal camp, theologically speaking; but not politically, whatever he may have thought about his own attitudes. The Warden of All Souls, Sir William Anson, who was a Liberal, described him as 'a Jacobin lacquered over to look like a Tory',[9] but others might have called him a Tory lacquered over to look like a liberal. Even the lacquer looks thin sometimes. Perhaps he was just trying to shock the clergy at a meeting at the Stepney Mission House, back in 1894, when he criticized the objects of the CSU, declaring that God's law and will for human society were unknown and apparently would ever remain so; and then went on to declare: 'Many Christians today believe that some form of slavery is probably the type of social organisation best adapted to the needs of backward areas.'[10] He was careful not to make that opinion (if anyone actually held it) explicitly his own, but it was an extraordinary thing to say, at a time when attention was already directed to conditions in South Africa, and it put him outside any possible definition of 'liberal' at that time in his life. His preferment by leaders of the Liberal Party was to some extent facilitated by his friendly attitude to

---

[8] Chadwick, *Hensley Henson*, 134.   [9] Ibid., 29.
[10] *Church Times* report 4 Jan. 1895.

dissenters. But he remained largely uncommitted in terms of party politics. He neither accepted the consequences of the existing industrial system, nor believed that there was any real possibility of change. The sufferings of the poor, he said, disgusted him with industrialism 'in spite of my failure to discover any satisfying alternative'.[11] His dislike of socialist policies and hostility towards the methods of militant trade-unionism left him to drift into support of the *status quo.*

What he shared with Inge was a particular devotion to an idea of the English (rather than the British) nation, which included a spiritual dimension best expressed through a recognized institution, the established church. Because it was in principle national, it must be comprehensive. In his early days he was a doughty opponent of disestablishment. He changed his mind about this (one of a number of changes during his long life—1863 to 1947) and argued in favour of disestablishment after the rejection by parliament of the proposed revision of the Prayer Book in 1927 and 1928, but he still held that the Church of England, though it needed broadening to make room for nonconformists, was an ineradicable part of British history and British life. For all his liberal pretensions, he remained a Tory in outlook. That means, at least, that he saw society as a regulated structure of social classes, which it would be perilous to change. Early experience in parish work in Liverpool and in Barking had developed in him a genuine sympathy with working people, and he retained even as Bishop of Durham, strolling in his own park, the ability to chat on even terms with the miners he met there. This did not restrain his denunciation of what he saw as the evils of concerted action by the miners through their trade union.

There was no lack of churchmen who could claim to be liberal during the late-Victorian and the Edwardian periods, but they were all liberal in their own ways. In some the social conscience was awake, stirred by people like Ruskin, and Green, and Toynbee. Others saw that scholarship and science had superannuated many of the old assumptions of religion and opened the way to reinterpretation of doctrine. There were overlaps between the two kinds of liberals, but it could not be presumed that anyone among them would be equally sympathetic to change in both aspects of religion:

---

[11] *Retrospect,* i. 29–30.

social concern and doctrinal expression. Indeed those who were primarily concerned to assert freedom of religious speculation were drawn away from all ideas of authority in religion; and this led to rejection of collectivism in social theory, which could be seen as the imposition of another form of authority. At the same time, they needed to identify themselves with some larger social entity and, like Inge and Henson, they tended to emphasize the national community, accepting with greater or less complaisance its structures of economic life and class organization, and even deriving the church's validity as an institution from its role in the national life. Among those who had learnt anything from the Oxford Movement, this did not lead to a form of Erastianism, because the church universal was acknowledged to be a spiritual entity with its own inherent life, though the particular expression of that life depended for its authority on its capacity to relate itself to the life of the nation. The attitudes of liberal churchmen to the institutional church varied. Henson was more inclined than Inge to see its significance. This may have been related, in practical terms, to his preferment in its hierarchy, but his acceptance of preferment itself increased his sense of the historic tradition of the church as the nation in its spiritual aspect.

Another interest common among theological liberals was the liturgical tradition of the church. Many of them, perhaps because they lacked a sense of unity in dogma with their fellow Christians, valued the support which could be found in sharing their devotional life with others. That was certainly true of Bishop Hicks. Dean Inge stands out as an obvious exception. It is not surprising to learn that after the Coronation in 1911 he noted in his diary, 'I prudently brought in a book, but the boredom of the six hours in the Abbey was extreme.' But his repeated groanings about the tedium of cathedral services was unworthy in a dean. The centre of his personal faith was elsewhere, not in dogmatic religion, nor in liturgical worship, but in his own particular combination of religious philosophy and mysticism. He saw his position as Dean of St Paul's as that of a religious teacher in a public place, not of a sacramental person representing the corporate life of the church. He would have made a disastrous bishop. But however much liberal churchmen may have valued common worship, they could not give the same kind of dogmatic status to their proposals for

liturgical reform, or their demand for liturgical fixity, as the Anglo-
catholics and evangelicals.

All this makes it apparent that leading liberal churchmen, however different, had something in common, if only that they did
not accede to either of the organized parties in the church. It was
not so much that they rejected the dogmas of others as that they
gave dogma a much lower value. In every case they found their
inspiration somewhere else; but it might be in a whole variety of
places. Dean Inge found it in Christian Platonism and the mystical
tradition. Rashdall was almost the antithesis of Inge, in his philosophic creed, which emphasized 'the absolute, unqualified reality
of individual persons, minds or spirits';[12] but he was akin to Inge
in being committed first and foremost to the mind and heart of
religious belief and not primarily to the institutional church.
Hensley Henson found his inspiration in

surrender to the historic Christ who still lives among men; more a surrender to a person than to a creed, but always a crucified person, through
whom men found pardon and peace; a person of whom the convincing evidence was the life and faith of his best disciples, both then and
through the centuries and now; in whose light Henson saw purpose and
providence in history.[13]

He cared little about churches—their dogmas and their hierarchies
—in comparison with this crucified Lord. But this personal devotion was matched by a strong historical sense. As far as outward
interests were concerned, he gave the primacy to the nation.

One could go through a list of liberal churchmen, noting the
variety of their primary interests, and observing that primacy was
seldom accorded to organized religion or the institutional church.
Of course, that would also be the case if we were looking at evangelical churchmen. So it is necessary to add that the evangelical,
unlike the liberal, finds the controlling feature of his religion in
his experience of the word of scripture and a particular scheme
of doctrine arising from it. It follows that evangelicals, like catholics, can form a far more cohesive phalanx on the religious scene
than liberals, whose closest allies may be those who share their

---

[12] C. C. J. Webb in Matheson, *Hastings Rashdall*, 240.
[13] Chadwick, *Hensley Henson*, 327.

dominant interest without sharing their churchmanship. The theological liberal is one who has something else to distract him from
total commitment to what is called 'organized religion'. In its
extreme form that phrase implies a firm structure of dogma underpinning and justifying the exercise of authority within a visible
community. The vision of that structure in its ideal form and the
mission to bring that ideal to realization have inspired some saints
and many sinners. But it does not inspire the liberal. His inspiration is to be found elsewhere—his, or hers; for we may set alongside these clerical liberals women of the stature of Maude Royden.
In the case of Hicks, the centre of interest was in the political realities which determined the conditions of life for ordinary people.
If they were better served by some form of collectivism, then that
cause must be promoted, but not because of any theory that it
was a necessary correlate of incarnational doctrine.

There were, however, others who not only welcomed collectivism in social life pragmatically but claimed it as derivative from
the collectivism of the church, the exponents of what has been
called sacramental socialism.[14] If the liberals did not cohere as a
force in the church, what about these socialist Christians? If the
liberals failed to leave a legacy, did the socialists? And what was
the relation of Hicks to them? In general he was sympathetic, but
wary. His sympathy was for collectivism; his wariness was over the
dogmatic underpinning which these various exponents tried to provide. In a paper read to a temperance conference in 1895 he had
distinguished between the individualism of the old Manchester
school, which had frowned on legislation for temperance, and the
development of collectivist ideas by the early Christian Socialists
which were in line, he believed, with the policy of local control
of licensing as advocated by the UKA. In 1912 his Lees and Raper
Lecture on 'The Church and the Liquor Traffic' made the same
point, that Local Veto would afford opportunity for collective social
experiment. This was appropriate at a time when 'the collectivist
ideal is superseding the old individualism'. These arguments were
clearly opportunist, and would certainly not have appealed to men
like Conrad Noel and G. K. Chesterton, for whom the consumption of wine was almost an article of the creed. They indicate,

[14] See Peter d'A. Jones, *The Christian Socialist Revival 1877–1914; Religion, Class, and Social Conscience in Late-Victorian England* (Princeton, NJ 1968), pt. ii.

however, that Hicks did not accept the view expressed, notably by Inge, that Christianity was individual and universal.

He had no fear of collectivism, though he saw through the tendentiousness of arguments which tried to find evidence for its Christian credentials in the Fathers. His historical interests made him regard the past as a challenge to the understanding and not a source of precedents. Each age must work out the application of Christian principles to its own problems. Christians in industrial society could not simply read off solutions from the dicta of Christian teachers in another age, or even from those of Jesus. Here he agreed with Henry Scott Holland. Neither of them put much trust in systems of any kind. After Holland's death there were commemorative articles in the *Commonwealth* by Gore and F. L. Donaldson.[15] Gore mentioned Holland's debt to T. H. Green but asserted that he was never enslaved by his philosophy; Donaldson said that he was 'not beguiled by any mere scheme of collectivist intellectualism from the path of practical reform'.[16]

There were plenty of such schemes about, each differing from the others, but all assuming that there was a divinely ordained pattern of society which had been revealed in the Bible and (usually) in the tradition of the Catholic Church. The list of mainly Anglican societies looks impressive: the Guild of St Matthew, the Church Socialist League, the Catholic Crusade, the League of the Kingdom of God. Within these societies, sometimes moving from one to another, were Fabian advocates of state socialism, campaigners for a new society based on producers' co-operatives, guild socialists, and those who were attracted by such panaceas as Single Tax or Social Credit. The Christian socialists were as varied and disunited as the theological liberals. Many of them tried to justify their political utopias on theological grounds; just as their opponents did. Generally speaking, they have left no progeny. What did survive was the Labour movement. To these socialists in the churches Hicks must have appeared, if they were aware of him, as someone who had not really seen the light. He had begun with the idea of Local Option and he had not moved much beyond ideas of municipalization, of gas-and-water socialism. But at least he had backed the Labour movement in its beginnings, and the

---

[15] Donaldson was the radical vicar of St Mark's Leicester, who had led a famous march of unemployed men to London in 1904.

[16] *Commonwealth* (Sept. and Nov. 1918).

future held more blessings in Britain for that movement than for the varieties of socialist theory which burgeoned during the period of his active ministry.

The difference between a social reformer such as Hicks and those who joined the various Christian groups committed to a socialist programme appears at first sight to have been entirely a difference of view about the proper organization of society. But it went deeper than that. Even in political terms there was a prior question about whether there actually existed an ideal form of organization which was capable of realization. The socialist groups proclaimed that there was such an ideal and that it could be realized. The adoption of a panacea for social ills was the very thing that held a group together. Such groups were always at risk, because their members could easily start disagreeing about policy. But beneath all surface agreements and disagreements there was often a feeling of desperation about the state of industrial society. Revolutionary politics can be the secular equivalent of apocalyptic theology. There will be an 'end of history' when the ideal is realized, not through divine intervention but through human action or the working out of the historical process. Hicks's own attitude was more cautious, gradualist, practical, and it seems to have originated from his interest in a developmental view of history, perhaps even from his early epigraphical studies. He believed in continuities: of Hellenism, of the Christian tradition, of the Liberal inheritance. So in the future there would be changes: towards greater social justice, towards various forms of collectivism, towards fuller realization of democracy. He conceded only grudgingly that there were apocalyptic elements in the gospels, and he never indulged in apocalyptic interpretation of the 'Great War'. The Labour movement won his adherence because it was a movement, with a past and a future. He did not try to work out where it was going. That would depend on future circumstances.

There was another difference between the social reformer and the socialist Christian. It had to do with their different images of the church. It is often true that the members of the church, as of other organizations, project upon its confusing realities a vision of what they believe it ought to be. That was particularly true of those who embraced a socialist ideal in some form or other. They might describe the church as 'God's co-operative society' or a eucharistic fellowship of the poor or a militant crusade against

found a star for its wandering bark. The disillusionment and the hedonism of the post-war period and even the great depression of the thirties failed to extinguish the flickering flame of hope. After another and greater war it flared up again, not only in the return of a Labour government, but in much talk of Christian reconstruction. It seemed as if the ideal society of the radical Christian socialists was still a possibility. Mere reformers were seen, by the enthusiasts, as conniving at the continuance of an unjust social system. But Temple, popular as he was, never succeeded in persuading the generality of church people to think of the Church of England as a force for political change, and he himself drew back from the demand for radical change in industrial society. Now, after the experience of more recent decades, few churchpeople any longer nourish the hope of that kind of change. It is arguable that, since Hicks's death in 1919, the future has been with the liberal reformers and not with the socialist visionaries. That, of course, is not a value-judgement; but it justifies a new evaluation of what he stood for as a liberal churchman.

First of all, he was unquestionably committed to the church. He had deliberately chosen to be ordained and then to exercise a long parochial ministry in preference to leading the life of a classical scholar at Oxford. He had more than thirty years' experience of parish life, eighteen years' connection with a cathedral, and just under ten years as a bishop. His commitment to the institutional church cannot be doubted; and yet his deepest motivation was not to be found in serving an ecclesiastical institution. Nor was it to be found in championing a doctrinal cause. Because his first study had been of the classics and not theology, he had learnt as a scholar to champion freedom of enquiry and discussion, and he maintained the same openness in questions of doctrine. In that sense he was a liberal theologian. If doctrine is seen as the interpretation of manifold experience it must not be rigid. But his most ardent convictions, kindled by Ruskin's hatred of industrial capitalism, were social and even political without ceasing to be religious. He passionately desired the liberation of working people from subjection. He did not, however, see subjection in what we think of as Marxist terms—the oppression of the employed by the employer, the wage-slave by the capitalist. In his parish experience he found other, and perhaps more pervasive, methods by which the wealthy kept the poor in permanent subjection. Those methods were both negative and positive: negative, in the denial of decent housing and fuller education to working people, and positive in the active promotion of ultimately self-defeating forms of enjoyment, most obviously drink and gambling. This exploitation was more than a hindrance to preaching; it was also a reproach to all who, consciously or unconsciously, connived at it. It was a Christian duty to fight against it. But it was not enough to call people to temperance, to offer them the pledge. It was not enough to reproach the shareholders in breweries and the 'superior persons who are philanthropic at 5 per cent'. Legislation was required, and the Liberal Party alone offered the hope of enacting adequate measures of social reform. Hicks did not hesitate, therefore, to give it his open support. It was not a perfect agent in the cause, and its programme from time to time contained elements which he would not have chosen. The meaning of political liberalism was continually changing throughout Hicks's life, but he was prepared to accept the changes which it underwent, because he saw the Tories as a party too heavily influenced by those whom he held responsible for the misery of working-class life. He was, therefore, liberal on two counts. He stood for freedom within the church—freedom to ask all possible questions and re-examine all established attitudes. He also stood for freedom in social life—freedom which he knew, from his Salford experiences, was denied to great numbers of ordinary people. In this he was different from some of those accounted liberal churchmen who confined their liberalism to the freedom of the mind; but not from all.

There certainly were others who coupled theological and political liberalism together. Prominent among them was Dean Fry. Fowler, in his biography of Hicks, comparing bishop and dean, comments that: 'it was curious to observe how the one seemed here and the other there the more advanced in his views. But they thoroughly understood and trusted one another, and it was a satisfaction to the Bishop to be able to count on intelligent sympathy and unfailing support from the Dean and the Cathedral body.'[19] The only honest comment on those words is to observe how difficult it is to write a frank biography while some of the leading actors are still alive. The bishop's diary tells another story. The dean's moods were incalculable, and he maintained a running feud with

[19] Fowler, 244.

the precentor. It is certainly true that Fry was what Hicks had asked Asquith to provide, 'a full Anglican Liberal'. But, as Fowler himself says, 'the two men were by no means cast in the same mould'. At the risk of sounding dismissive, we may say that Fry believed in all the right things and supported all the right causes. He supported co-operation and the trade unions. He was a great participator and became prominent in the CSU, the Liberal Churchman's League, and the Church Reform League. He was active in the Representative Church Council and later in the Church Assembly. He not only supported the *Commonwealth* financially, but also wrote many articles for it. He was a friend of Scott Holland, Charles Gore, and other leading churchmen. He was more out-spoken than Hicks on questions of biblical criticism. And yet there was something about him which was very different from Hicks.

Perhaps it was due to his different career. The headmasterly strain of authoritarianism was always there, patently or below the surface. There was some likeness between him and another headmaster, Bishop Percival. According to his biographer, William Temple, 'With all his liberalism, he feared liberty. He wanted to see the whole day mapped out and to know what every boy was doing at any moment.'[20] In that, Percival resembled the archetypal headmaster, Dr Arnold, of whom A. C. Benson said, 'He did not wish others to be free on their own lines, but upon his own.'[21] Another char-acteristic of Percival, which may have been shared by Fry, was his inability to understand why other people did not see that his own view of any subject was the right one. That kind of attitude would be disruptive in any cathedral close, and the troubles at Lincoln arose from the conflict of two men who were over-endowed with self-esteem, Fry and Wakeford. It was possible for social reform and Liberal political policies to be supported by men who were, at base, authoritarian. Fry's advocacy of forced labour colonies for the unemployable, and the use of troops to suppress night clubs, indicate just such a flaw in his liberalism. The true liberal must respond to personalities and to opinions which are not his own, and must resist the temptation to look for authoritarian ways of overcoming opposition.

[20] William Temple, *Life of Bishop Percival* (1921), 116.
[21] A. C. Benson, *The Leaves of the Tree* (1911), 291.

Consideration of leading liberals among churchmen certainly does not lead to any clear definition of the meaning of liberalism in religion. Its meaning will be explored at greater length in a final chapter. At this point it may be useful, however, to provide a general perspective. Perhaps the most that can be learnt from the discussion so far is the need to recognize distinct spheres in which the word 'liberal' may be used. There are obviously the spheres of politics, theology, and church order. In politics, the formal use of the word 'liberal' needs further definition in view of the changing nature of the Liberal Party, and particularly its move from an earlier to a later phase. In both phases the dominant idea was that of freedom. At first freedom was seen as involving an attack on privileges and vested interests, coupled with a dogmatic individualism which ignored the reality of social groupings and failed to recognize that individual liberty needed forms of community for its own fulfilment. Liberal churchmen found much in Christian teaching which taught the value and the responsibility of the individual, and they could see much merit in attacks on vested interests, even if the objects of those attacks included the established church. The institution existed, they thought, for the benefit of the individual, and if it did not provide benefits it must be reformed. In the later phase of political Liberalism ideas of 'positive freedom' of the kind approved by T. H. Green deeply modified the earlier individualism. Great numbers of individuals were seen to be denied freedom by the structures of society which permitted exploitation. The capitalist and the worker did not face each other on equal terms. What came under attack at this stage was not privilege in the old sense but accumulation of power in the hands of the few to exploit the many. Liberal churchmen then might be comparatively indifferent to the maintenance of Establishment, not because they saw the church as a privileged body in need of reform but because they began to hope that a disestablished church might use in the cause of social reform the freedom it would gain.

Theological liberalism was quite another matter. It arose, not from a social conscience, but from an intellectual revolution. That was brought about by the impact of historical and scientific studies. It also had its phases and its modes. The first shock created by critical studies of the documents and formularies of religion produced in some students that kind of liberalism which Newman abhorred, an attitude in which men and women not only questioned apparently established truths but also doubted whether there was such a thing as truth in religion. The shock sometimes produced the panic reaction of asserting ever more fiercely the unassailable truth of one particular religious position among the many. The liberals refused to do so, but adopted a variety of alternative attitudes. Those who did not lose faith altogether fell into two main categories. First there were liberal Anglo-catholics and liberal evangelicals who drew a line at some particular point beyond which they did not allow questioning or relativism to go. Then there were those who acknowledged no such limit but looked for other unassailable foundations of belief in human experience. The turn of the century was a time of great interest in the developing discipline of psychology, and religious interest in mysticism coincided with this. If the enemy of liberalism was seen by liberals to be restrictive dogmatism, the mystical element in religion seemed to offer a way out of its restrictions into a new kind of freedom and a new kind of certainty. When the philosophical arguments of T. H. Green in favour of a spiritual interpretation of life began to wear thin, what better than to find another basis which had all the attraction of being part of a new scientific discipline?

The last enemy of liberalism to be set alongside institutional or corporate oppression and unscientific or unhistorical dogmatic claims was denominationalism in its rigid forms. In fact the challenge to ecclesiastical exclusivity had been an element of political Liberalism since the early days. It could trace its history back at least to the Glorious Revolution. Towards the end of the nineteenth century there were opposed forces within the Church of England, some asserting the rights of the church, particularly in education, against vociferous nonconformity, and others beginning to recognize the need for Christians of different persuasions to find common cause against common enemies at home and abroad. The Liberation Society had been a symbol of the adversarial forces, but it had progressively lost momentum. The other forces were represented by Dr Arnold's plan for a comprehensive church, but that was in a form unacceptable to many churchmen of the time, and it became progressively more so with the revival of catholic ideas in the aftermath of the Oxford Movement. Eventually there followed another phase in denominational relations when the very churchmen who made the greatest claim for the Church of England's catholicity, in asserting its rights to independence from the state, began to recognize the logical right of other Christian groups to exist in equal independence; and from there it was a step, or perhaps a leap, to the position of those who looked for increasing co-operation, particularly in social work and in some forms of mission.

The significance of Hicks's story in this context is that he came to embrace some form of liberalism in each of these three areas. He came from a Liberal background, politically speaking, and found his own political identity in the Liberalism represented by the *Manchester Guardian* of C. P. Scott. But he did not adopt any theoretical views of a socialist kind about an ideal society. He was led by his scholarship in secular studies to appreciate the force of the impact of historical and scientific studies on the documents and traditions of the Christian church. But he preserved a centre of personal faith from which to appraise theological developments. And he worked alongside other kinds of believer and unbeliever in promoting the social causes which he had at heart, but he did not question the value of the Anglican tradition in worship and pastoral care.

No man can be a liberal in all things. There has to be some rock in the swirling waters, some base of certainty from which to view with sympathy the movement of thought and history into the unknown. His motto which he had inscribed on his book-plates at an early stage was *EYΣEBEIN KAI EYEPΓETEIN*. The two supports of his adventuring faith were just those two things: worshipping and well-doing. He was slow to modify moral values, particularly in family life; and he was anxious that the ways of worship in the Church of England should not revert to mere medievalism but, on the other hand, that if there were to be changes in the patterns of worship they should conform to social realities and not to liturgical fashions. So in all three areas—politics, theology, and church order—he expected change, yet kept in mind the limits beyond which he believed continuity would be lost.

15

Churchmen and the New Liberalism

The life and ministry of Edward Lee Hicks was in an obvious sense unique; yet it may also be taken as a representative example of churchmanship at a particular moment in the development of English society. That was the time of the New Liberalism, and Hicks was fortunate in living in the very home of the *Manchester Guardian* which became one of its best advocates. Students of political thought can quite well describe the emergent ideology of the period without any regard for the participation of churchmen.[1] They were not to the fore in promoting that development. Yet it is useful to identify the participation of churchmen such as Hicks in supporting it, not in order to add significantly to the description of the New Liberalism, but to indicate that the development of Christian social thought was as closely linked to that political development as to the emergence of socialism. As usual in modern times the pace of Christian social ideas was largely set by general changes in secular thought, and only added a theological commentary to a text already drafted by others. In both the new movement within Liberalism and the new phase in Christian social thought the figure of Ruskin was significant, and can be seen as a link between them.

The political context of Hicks's mature ministry is all-important. The meaning of the title 'liberal churchman' during that period can be understood only by relating it to the fortunes of the Liberal Party. The word 'liberal' is in itself so protean that it is scarcely helpful to use it without some such anchorage in factuality. The title does not here include other kinds of liberal Christian, whether nonconformist or Roman Catholic, but refers explicitly to churchmen, that is, to convinced members of the established church. Their membership inescapably involved a relation to the public realm,

---

[1] See Freeden, *New Liberalism*; David Powell, 'The New Liberalism and the Rise of Labour, 1886–1906', *Historical Journal* 29/2 (1986), 369–93.

and by sympathy or reaction they were affected by the organization of parliamentary life, since it was parliament which acted as the agent of the royal supremacy. It was hardly possible that someone could be described, or describe another, as a liberal churchman without some awareness of what liberal meant in the political context. Of course, many churchmen, particularly among the clergy, would have seen themselves as unpolitical. That implied reasonable contentment with the *status quo*. Those, however, who were described, or described themselves, as liberals could not be unaffected by the shifting nature of political Liberalism. It always implied a desire for some change in society, some kind of liberation; but the kind of change was itself subject to change. To know what a liberal churchman was, we have to know what date we are talking about.

The Liberal Party had emerged from its Whig antecedents and taken definite form before Hicks left Fenny Compton, and that form was largely determined by the leadership of Gladstone. It could not assume the anticlerical guise of continental liberalism as long as its leader was so strong a churchman. Equally, Gladstone himself would not have been a Liberal politician if Liberalism had been still what it was in the eyes of Keble, Newman, and the Tractarians.[2] But even this new kind of Liberalism had to undergo a further transformation. The Home Rule crisis and the electoral defeat of the Liberals in 1886 (the year when Hicks moved to Manchester) signalled a redirection of emphasis in the party. In opposition various reforming causes made the party their home, and the new Liberalism began to see the state much more clearly as an agent for social reform.[3] Not that there was any lack of disagreements among the Liberals. There were still imperialists and opponents of imperialism. There were those who looked for the extension of democracy and those who feared any such extension. There were those who hoped that the development of voluntary co-operatives would sufficiently alleviate the sufferings of the poor,[4] and those who wanted more direct action by the government. There were divisions of opinion over disestablishment, the

[2] See Butler, *Gladstone*, esp. 124–5.
[3] See Russell, 'New Liberalism', already quoted.
[4] Backstrom, *Christian Socialism*, 194. Rosebery addressing the Cooperative Congress in 1890 praised co-operation as a voluntary means of uplifting labour with only the benevolent neutrality of the state.

House of Lords, women's suffrage, temperance, and education. Liberal churchmen, like other Liberals, were not all of one mind.

To understand how this motley crew could hold together and work their way back to power in parliament, as they did, we have to consider whether there were general characteristics or assumptions which underlay the differences, gave them some kind of unity and predisposed them to adopt policies of social reform. Later critics have not been slow to suggest what they were. Optimism and belief in progress come high on the list. Optimism in the age of democracy must depend upon belief in the rationality of the ordinary voter. The idea of progress need not involve the belief, of which its exponents were commonly accused, that progress was inevitable; but it did depend on the assumption that change for the better was possible, if only people set their minds and wills on bringing it about. Good government, as Ruskin said, must be expectant. If it ceased to be hopeful of better things, it ceased to be a wise guardian of present things.[5] Another basic assumption was that freedom was supremely valuable; but in the last quarter of the century that old Liberal tenet was increasingly modified by the awareness of freedom's necessary preconditions. The old individualism was yielding to a sense of the importance of community in giving the individual the opportunity to be free. As R. L. Nettleship said of T. H. Green:

The idea of the free personality, exercising its freedom under conditions which it has itself created, formed the meeting-point for his political and religious aspirations. In the light of this idea he interpreted to himself the problems of history, of morality, of theology. In the approximation to it he saw political and moral progress, and in the eternal realisation of it the life of God.[6]

Green was just one of those who turned their attention from the freedom of the individual to the creation of the conditions under which it could be exercised. Here, then, are some of the positive attitudes which were shared also at the time by churchmen who were politically Liberal. But there also existed in their minds at least mistrust and at most detestation of commercialism, of money-grubbing, of Chesterton's 'Kingdom of Mammon'.[7]

---

[5] John Ruskin, *The Political Economy of Art* (1857), lecture 1.

[6] R. L. Nettleship (ed.), *Works of Thomas Hill Green*, iii (1891), Memoir, pp. xxix–xxx.

[7] Chesterton on Gladstone: 'Yea, this one thing is known of you, | We know that not till you were dumb, | Not till your course was thundered through, | Did Mammon see his kingdom come.'

This brief indication of what a writer in 1913[8] called 'the uncriticized assumptions' of the Liberals is set out in order to consider how far Hicks fitted the stereotype and how far he and, by implication at least, others left such assumptions uncriticized. To begin with optimism, it may be conceded at once that there were many signs and sorts of optimism in the Victorian period,[9] but as the substance of a general charge, it can carry little weight. In every society there are those who have reason for optimism, and others who have none. In our present context the issue is whether it was justifiable for churchmen to share in an attitude commonly displayed by liberals of all kinds. If it is made into a theological issue, it can only be said that optimists and pessimists are equally good at finding grounds for their attitudes in scripture and tradition. Although we may suspect that the division has more to do with psychology than theology, it is also the case that in theology it corresponds with the division between those who put the greatest emphasis on Incarnation and those who emphasize the doctrine of Redemption. Certainly in the period after *Lux Mundi* the former had a higher profile.

Declarations or accusations of optimism need to be set carefully in time and place. For Liberal churchmen the date was important, because in the period during which the Liberal Party was in opposition their optimism naturally received a set-back. They regarded the dominance of the Conservatives as a drag on necessary social reform at home, and the so-called pro-Boers among them deplored the rampant imperialism of the national mood during the Boer War as a threat to international peace. Optimism returned with the rise in the fortunes of the Liberal Party after that war, and when Hicks's disciple Proudfoot founded the *Optimist* in 1905, it was a response to a change in mood. When in the following year, in his sermon to the CSU in Manchester, Hicks declared firmly that he was an invincible and unwearying optimist, the grounds he gave were nothing to do with theological gradualism. They were purely political. He spoke of 'the crumbling of the colossal military despotism in Eastern Europe', the birth of free nations, the re-enfranchisement of Finland. The triumph of the Liberal Party with a programme of social reform then changed the situation at home. It was not a time for a theology of crisis.

---

[8] Neville Talbot, *Foundations* (1913), 5.
[9] See e.g. Walter E. Houghton, *The Victorian Frame of Mind 1830–1870* (New Haven and London 1957), pt. i: 'Emotional Attitudes', ch. 2: 'Optimism', 27–53.

If the date was important, so also was the place. The article in the *Commonwealth* welcoming the first number of the *Optimist* referred in passing to 'the hopeful north'. Hicks knew the slums of Salford all too well, but he also experienced something of the confidence in municipal reforming enterprise which particularly marked the Birmingham of Joseph Chamberlain, but was not absent in Manchester. In 1858 it had been described as 'the very symbol of civilization, foremost in the march of improvement, a grand incarnation of progress'.[10] And although it had yielded that palm, its leading citizens were men of enterprise and culture. T. C. Horsfall, the chief promoter of the Manchester Art Museum, was a friend of Hicks, and art and archaeology were among the cultural interests which he helped to foster. Provincial cities were confident of their standing in national life. The ascendancy of London over the provinces was not fully established until the turn of the century.[11] The problems of the metropolis were too distant to overshadow the vigour of municipal pride. The optimism of the Victorians has been pilloried as a reflection of the success of capitalism in raising the standard of life of the more comfortable classes. But in a limited fashion the working classes, or at least some sections of them, also experienced a rise in living standards, and English society, at least outside London, became far more ordered and law-abiding in the second half of the nineteenth century.[12] No optimist could deny the miseries of the poorest, but it was possible for conscientious people to feel some confidence that a start had been made in overcoming them. In Manchester the Citizens' Association for the Improvement of Unwholesome Dwellings and Surroundings of the People, and the local branch of the CSU, in exercising pressure on the municipal authority, were just two of the organizations with which Hicks and other church-men were involved. Optimism arises from an assessment of the direction of movement, not from an unrealistic view of the present state of things. That is what the idea of progress means. Liberals did not have to be simple-minded about that idea. It was only too obvious that there were repeated set-backs to improvement in human society, and the churches were not always on the right side.

---

[10] *Chambers Edinburgh Journal* (1858), quoted in Asa Briggs, *Victorian Cities* (1963), 83.

[11] Briggs, *Victorian Cities*, 370–2.

[12] José Harris, *Private Lives, Public Spirit: A Social History of Britain 1870–1914* (Oxford 1993), 208 ff.

In 1905 Hicks, writing in the *Manchester Guardian*,[13] referred to the failure of the national church of Russia to show even the slightest sympathy with the people's aspirations towards liberty and right government. That was just one example of the failures and frustrations which marked human history. But there were successes as well. It is not surprising that theology fell into step with the general self-confidence of late-Victorian society, or that it found it difficult to understand disaster when it struck.

The greatest challenge to the liberal faith in progress during our period was, of course, the First World War. Among the many agonized responses to its horrors one, which was not untypical, was the publication in 1915 of *The Faith and the War*, edited by F. J. Foakes-Jackson.[14] It consisted of a series of essays by church members who would have seen themselves as liberals. Of special relevance are two contrasting contributions. Alice Gardner, of Newnham College, writes on 'The Idea of Providence in History', and particularly points out that there were various versions of the idea of progress. Sometimes it was connected with the growth of human knowledge, at other times with the growth of human liberty, or more power over nature, or the increase of the spirit of mutual understanding and co-operation. The average man had come to expect God to be on the side of regular steady progress. Now it was obvious that there was nothing inevitable about it, and Christians were having to learn that God shared suffering with his creatures. The implication of the essay was not, however, that progress was an illusion. There had been advances in education, in democratic institutions, in better surroundings for the working classes, and even in understanding between nations. It was not necessary to abandon hope.

There was a considerable contrast between this essay and another in the same volume by Dean Inge. It can hardly be described as coherent, for he seems successively to affirm and deny the idea of progress. The title, 'Hope, Temporal and Eternal', gives a clue to its apparent contradictions. He wants to affirm the supreme reality of the eternal in which there can be no change, no progress. But something obviously happens in time, which was created as

---

[13] 'Quartus' article 26 Jan. 1905.

[14] F. J. Foakes-Jackson (ed.), *The Faith and the War: A Series of Essays by Members of the Churchmen's Union and Others on the Religious Difficulties Aroused by the Present Condition of the World* (1915).

a sphere 'for the working out of God's finite purpose', and so he throws out ideas of recurrence and of eugenic realization of a racial type along with forebodings of a great reversion to barbarism. But all the possibilities of the future are swept aside by Inge. Nothing of absolutely vital importance is at stake in any earthly conflict. 'Earth's success may be heaven's failure, and earth's failure heaven's success.'

This essay, and the whole publication, shows how deeply disturbed and confused liberal Christians were at the recession into barbarism of the apparently cultured civilization of Europe, and how they struggled to maintain hope and faith in the future. It was still possible for them, even for Inge, to cling to the idea of the advance of social democracy. The hope of progress was encouraged by the spin-off from scientific developments. Liberals found support for their ideas of inevitability in their readings of Darwin and, even more, of Herbert Spencer. Facing the catastrophe of world war they turned to another aspect of scientific thought: the immense extension of horizons demanded for evolutionary processes. Inge wrote patronizingly of 'many well-meaning persons' who 'say that Christianity stands for faith in progress'; but then accepted that there had been some progress from the savage state, and went on to invoke the long dimensions of evolutionary time as the grounds of a distant hope. 'The race is probably much nearer the beginning than the end of its human development.' In spite of all his reputation for gloom, he rejected forecasts of apocalypse.

Among all the variations of the theme of progress, Hicks gave priority to a particular emphasis which had first been permitted a secure place in the attitudes of the Liberal Party by Gladstone, and was shared with him, and indeed even taught to him, by Lord Acton. The essential element in progress was the extension of liberty. In the list of possible meanings of progress given by Alice Gardner, it was not the increase of knowledge or power over nature or even human co-operation that counted with Gladstone and Acton; it was the increase of liberty. In Hicks's first visitation charge and in his addresses to his diocesan conferences in Lincoln he repeatedly urged his hearers to believe in freedom. That was, perhaps, a platitude which all his hearers could interpret, each in his own particular fashion. The cutting edge of his remarks was the association of freedom with democracy and the labour movement.

Here he stood apart from the generation of Acton and Gladstone who had been brought up to think democracy a disease, and of Ruskin, who never trusted it. Even its advocates among church-men could not quite shake off their unease. Hicks himself was aware of its dangers. In the 1906 sermon quoted above, he admitted that already the old faith in democracy, the democracy of Mazzini and de Tocqueville, had lost its spell. Let them consider that demo-cracy had not committed one thousandth part of the crimes of oligarchy or tyranny.

Anxiety about the possible perils of democracy surfaced among church leaders in various ways. The use of words like discipline and character were indicators of that unease. The importance of 'character' had been a prominent theme of F. D. Maurice's *Social Morality* back in 1859. T. C. Fry contributed an article on 'Char-acter' to the *Commonwealth* in January 1900, in which he asked whether the democratic movement was aiming at the enthrone-ment of character or simply more time and more money. Those are simply examples of a recurrent theme. Hicks generally displayed more faith in the workings of democracy, but was not unaware of its need for self-control.[15] His advocacy of women's suffrage was made all the stronger by his belief that democracy needed leavening by women's insights. The concern for character was, in one sense, a continuation of the old liberal belief in the indi-vidual; but that belief had come to mean something different with the increasing emphasis on social determinants of personal beha-viour.[16] It is important, however, to notice the relation of this theme of character to the continuance of capitalism. There were enthu-siasts for socialism who rejected all such moralism as typical of a stage of human society which would be transcended with the end of the capitalist system. Whatever might be thought about such an utopia, they were right in seeing a connection between the work-ing of the system and its need for personal morality to underpin it. It has been argued that this moral base was a legacy of Pur-itanism which was progressively eroded by secularization.[17] The

---

[15] See e.g. *Diary*, 19 Oct. 1913 (at Gainsborough), and address at Labour Party meet-ing in Spalding 19 Feb. 1918.
[16] Harris, *Private Lives, Public Spirit*, 230 ff.: 'Social Theory and the Social Problem'.
[17] See Kenneth Medhurst and George Moyser, *Church and Politics in a Secular Age* (Oxford 1988), 26 ff.

Liberal churchmen did not theorize about its origin in Puritan-
ism, but they were concerned not to lose its controlling influence
in the emergence of a democratic society.

One other feature of Liberalism in the decades before the outbreak of the First World War was a growing acceptance of some
form of collectivism. It cannot be described as an uncriticized
assumption, even if that term could be applied rhetorically to ideas
of progress or liberty. It was indeed constantly criticized, because
it seemed so foreign to the Liberal tradition. Old-style free-traders
saw it as a threat. Gladstone never overcame a deep mistrust of it.
Capitalists in the Liberal Party, encouraged by the political economists, convinced themselves that it was in no one's interest.
Evangelical churchmen, in spite of the Calvinistic legacy which
they had received, with its predestinarian basis, subscribed to a theology which exalted individual responsibility. Even the recovery of
belief in the corporate reality of the church as the Body of Christ,
in the Tractarian tradition, did not necessarily carry with it the
complementary idea of the 'body politic'. But the experience of
the effects of industrialization in poor urban parishes forced some
churchmen to modify their theology and renew their understanding of the corporate dimension of human life. The readers and the
writers of the *Commonwealth*, however much they might differ
in detail, were all groping for some form of collectivism. Hicks
moved cautiously along the road to socialism of a sort, till in 1912
he declared that the collectivist ideal was superseding individualism. In a more brash way T. C. Fry could speak of the subordination of the individual as the only hope of the future; though there
must be some suspicion that he knew who should be doing the
subordinating.

The example of Hicks indicates the need for care and dis-
crimination in characterizing Liberal churchmen. The specificity
of time and place must not be forgotten. Equally when we turn to
the history of the Christian social movement, his example and his
relationship with other reforming churchmen tend to modify some
accepted generalizations. Two of these deserve further examination. They relate to the influences which affected the reformers;
and the significance of the Christian Social Union. To begin with
the question of influences: it is a natural tendency of church historians, in tracing the origination of ideas, to look for precedents
within the tradition of the church. So it is not surprising that the

involvement of leading churchmen in social questions is normally seen as a confluence of the theological and ecclesiastical streams deriving from Maurician and Tractarian sources. There were, however, many churchmen and women in the movement for social reform whose motivation was not primarily theological or ecclesiastical.

The Revd W. Tuckwell has been mentioned as a strong Liberal and an advocate of land nationalization. It is not clear what set him on his chosen path, but we can find hints in his published writings. The choice of characters in his *Pre-Tractarian Oxford*[18] suggests that he looked back to a tradition which owed nothing to the Tractarians or the theology of F. D. Maurice. It is noticeable that when he summarizes the common features of his gallery of portraits, and lists five headings, he puts politics first and theology last, and the theology is of a latitudinarian type, 'between the bibliolater and the rationalist'. In his *Reminiscences* he makes it clear that his ideal of the church is derived from Copleston, Whately, and Arnold. The church's only claim to its property lies in representing the nation, and its call is to be unsectarian. He was admittedly a minor figure in the movement for social reform, but he earned a warm, if critical, appreciation from Hicks in a review article in the *Manchester Guardian* of 6 July 1905 and another from the ever-appreciative Scott Holland. 'No one now goes forward with such flying banners and with all the trumpets blowing.'[19] He evidently passed on to his daughter Gertrude something of his burning concern for social justice. She took up the work of organizing the Women's Trade Union League and campaigned against the sweating prevalent in women's employment. In her case the political, rather than theological, context is evident. She was related by marriage to Sir Charles Dilke, the radical politician, and was appointed his literary executor. It was not necessary to accept, perhaps not even to understand, the theology of F. D. Maurice or Charles Gore in order to take up the cause of social reform.

Some reformers were politically motivated. Others derived their interest from contact with T. H. Green. His influence was not very significant among Liberals generally,[20] but it clearly affected many religiously minded men, and indeed women, at Oxford.

[18] The Revd W. Tuckwell, *Pre-Tractarian Oxford: A Reminiscence of the Oriel 'Noetics'* (1909).
[19] *Commonwealth* (Mar. 1905), 253–5.   [20] See Freeden, *New Liberalism*, 55 ff.

The connection between Green's philosophy and his social and political convictions is not obvious, since those convictions were shared by others who never adopted his idealistic philosophy, and some who did adopt it, such as Edward King, remained politically conservative. But Green had been indirectly influenced by F. D. Maurice's teaching; and there is no doubt that his example, in breaking the barrier between academic and municipal Oxford, counted with some undergraduates, and led to their involvement in schemes of social amelioration. Among those who supported settlement schemes there were those who found in their social commitment what was virtually a substitute for Christianity, rather than an expression of Christian belief. For them it amounted to little more than an easing of conscience; but for others, such as Clement Attlee,[21] it was a gateway into political life.

Political and philosophical ideas, however, need a medium to grow in, and when they are of an altruistic nature that medium is the conscience. The activation of conscience in the middle classes, and even the higher echelons of society, owed much to the evangelical revival. What is distinctive of the latter part of the nineteenth century is the redirection of conscience from the reformation of individuals to the reformation of society. To bring about that change, there was need of prophets. The prophetic voices of Wesley and Whitfield had stirred consciences before, but within the framework of Christian belief. When consciences were agitated afresh, the prophets were not Christian preachers but laymen with at most a loose attachment to mainstream religion. There were special reasons why Ruskin exercised so much influence on Hicks. Not only did Hicks come directly under his influence at Corpus, but his mentor in epigraphical studies, Charles Newton, was a personal friend of Ruskin. Ruskin was one of those remarkable figures in public life whom no educated person could possibly ignore. Perhaps his economic theories might be suspect, though in J. A. Hobson he had an academically respectable follower, but what counted with many of his readers was the prophetic zeal with which he denounced the inhumanity of the commercial system. He was not an Anglo-catholic, though he responded to the aesthetics of ritual, nor even a Maurician, though he knew Maurice well and

---

[21] Attlee was in early life a supporter of the CSU. The November issue of the *Commonwealth* in 1908 carried a letter from him advocating the formation of CSU branches in public schools.

worked for him at the Working Men's College. But Scott Holland, claiming to speak for the CSU, said 'We exist in memory of Ruskin. Surely, his spirit has been our inspiration. He is alive in us.'[22] Ruskin himself acknowledged his debt to Carlyle,[23] whose influence went back to the 1830s when *Sartor Resartus* was published, but who continued to exercise a strong influence till his death, and beyond. The young G. M. Trevelyan, a staunch Liberal, thought *Sartor Resartus* 'the greatest book in the world'.[24] But the difficulty in estimating the influence of these prophetic figures is to know exactly what kind of influence they exerted,[25] particularly when we are considering Liberal churchmen. Educated people are always inclined to be eclectic, and to pick and choose even among the ideas of those they admire. This is exemplified by G. W. E. Russell, who combined Liberalism with ritualism, and declared that Matthew Arnold was his 'loved and honoured master'. Could a ritualist revere the author of *Literature and Dogma*? Evidently the answer was Yes. He was quite capable of discriminating among the opinions of his master, just as Hicks discriminated among the opinions of those he called prophets. But there was a temperamental difference between those who responded with enthusiasm and those, like Mandell Creighton, who disliked prophets and warned young people against the influence of Ruskin.[26]

It is also inadvisable to work with a schematic model of development in Christian social thought. Any such model is likely to be determined by hindsight, and that itself will be dependent on the specific point in history from which the backward look is cast. A clear example of selective hindsight is Hudson and Reckitt's *The Church and the World*. Part IV (vol. III) of that work looks back from September 1939 and implies a lineage from the Oxford Movement and Maurician Christian Socialism via the CSU and Christian socialist groups of the late nineteenth century to the 'Christian sociology' of the Christendom group and the Anglo-catholic summer schools. It was, no doubt, true that those who participated in the activities of that group could see in the teaching of Maurice

[22] *Commonwealth* (Dec. 1902), 371.

[23] Hobson, *John Ruskin*, 25: Ruskin's 'two great masters' were Turner and Carlyle.

[24] David Cannadine, *G. M. Trevelyan: A Life in History* (1992), 29.

[25] For a valuable discussion of the influence of 'prophets' see esp. Kitson Clark, *Churchmen*, ch. 11: 'The Dismal Science and its Enemies', 290–313.

[26] Creighton, *Life and Letters*, i. 325.

and the earlier Anglo-catholics a preparation for their gospel and so claim them as their forerunners in social thought. What is not true, however, is to see a particular later movement as the proper, let alone the single and inevitable, inheritor of the traditions within the Anglican Church which they laid under contribution. In 1939 it seemed clear to Hudson and Reckitt that they were the proper heirs, as if there was some sort of inevitable progress in Christian social thought. 'The outlook of the Christian Social Movement has been moving in recent years to a far more explicitly theo-centric position away from the shallower assumptions of liberal humanism.' Its orientation 'has equally been changing . . . from ethics to sociology'.[27] Nearly half a century later it looks as if that movement led to a dead end. But it was not the terminus of Christian social thought, only the end of a branch line.

There was a strong element of medievalism in the Oxford Movement, a hankering after an integrated Christian society which acknowledged the authority of the church. Although its origins were theological and ecclesiastical, there was a parallel movement of ideas outside the religious sphere to which Ruskin gave a fillip with his biting criticism of commercial society and with imprac-tical schemes such as the Guild of St George. That tradition was carried further by William Morris, and expressed attractively in his utopian *News from Nowhere*. Guild Socialism and J. N. Figgis's 'community of communities' are in the same line of succession. It was a development which had no appeal for Hicks. His love of liturgical worship in the Anglican tradition was sorely tried by the innovations, or retrogressions, of his friend Duncan Jones at St Mary's, Primrose Hill. Tradition, for him, was something always in process of formation. Medieval Christendom was part of that tradition, but could not offer much that was relevant to the mod-ern, democratic, industrialized society which the church was called to serve.

As we take a retrospective view of the Christian social move-ment we cannot see it as the Christendom group saw it in the 1930s. The reason is, put simply, the secularization and growing pluralism of British society. That requires us to ask whether there could be another viewpoint which might equally be called a theo-centric position. It was taken by the Christendom writers as being

---

[27] Hudson and Reckitt, *Church and World*, 201.

nearly synonymous with a church-centred position. It still seemed possible, at the time of T. S. Eliot's *The Idea of a Christian Society* (1939) to imagine that Britain was, or could be made into, the outward and visible sign of a Christian society, with norms derived from theology applied in the form of a 'Christian sociology'. There was always, however, an alternative view. It was possible to see the church as an agency for change within a society which did not consist of Christians, and which was so marred by social injustice that it could only be called Christian in having inherited some Christian values from the past. That, roughly speaking, was how Hicks saw the church. It was meant to be a brotherhood of devoted souls to convert the nation to God. Whether that was a less theocentric view than a traditional 'catholic' image is a matter of definition. Perhaps the world, all human society, was theocentric, and the church called to exercise its role in different ways as human societies changed.

God and his will for the world was central to Hicks's whole ministry. The Church of England had a particular historic calling which was directly related to the condition of English society, and because that society was being transformed through the adoption of a democratic system the established church must work out anew the implications of the gospel. In 1890, at a time when there were many groping attempts to study how society worked and to bring some scientific discipline into the study,[28] Hicks had declared, in preaching at Manchester Grammar School, that Christians were called for the first time to 'study the problem of misery, to deal with the science of human life'. He was perhaps echoing the statement of the purposes of the CSU, with its emphasis on common study; yet he turned its wording round and spoke of beginning with the study of society, not study of the principles of Christianity in order to apply them to social problems. In fact, some of the leaflets issued by the Oxford branch of the CSU have hardly a word of religion in them, and the reading lists include practically no writings by theologians. The intention of the founders was to develop a theologically based critique of society; the practice of the groups tended to focus attention on specific problems to which answers were sought on the simple basis of decent human relations and conditions of living.

[28] Harris, *Private Lives, Public Spirit*, 222.

The Christian Social Union has suffered some sharp criticisms. The burden of these criticisms has been, either that it encouraged a feeble version of socialism, as compared with the clearer, more vigorous, versions offered by such groups as the Guild of St Matthew or the Church Socialist League; or else that it was a mere intellectual exercise of middle-class moralism. There is substance in these criticisms, though each one exposes its critics to scrutiny in return. The first depends on three assumptions, which are not self-evident: that the role of the CSU was to advocate a comprehensive remedy for the ills of society, that there was some hope of overturning the system of capitalism, and that the Christian church had inherited from its past a pattern for the ideal society which ought to take its place. To which it may be replied, that the CSU did not claim the role proposed for it; that very few, if any, of its supporters envisaged the overthrow of the whole capitalist system; and that only incurable romantics could suppose that the existing church, in Britain or elsewhere, offered a model of human relationships. Hicks and those who thought like him pursued limited ends which they considered to be achievable; though he certainly believed that there was a slow movement in society which was replacing individualism with collectivism. He was painfully aware of the evils of the existing system, but advocated Christian engagement with politics to restrain, and perhaps to abolish, those evils. And he saw the church, not as a model for society at large, but as an agent for the reformation of society. Those were rational beliefs to hold, and in holding them he was more representative of the movement for reform among church people than the committed socialists who were the critics of the CSU.

The other criticism, that it was an example of middle-class moralism, has limited validity.[29] If it is suggested that its members ignored the typical culture or ethic of working people, we need much caution before accepting the criticism without reservation. The 'culture of the working class' is a doubtful concept. A recent analysis of urban popular culture[30] proposes the distinction of different elements which coexisted in it: a reformist leisure culture, itself distinguished into a religious and a secular form; an artisan

---

[29] Edward Norman, *Church and Society in England 1770–1970* (Oxford 1976), 165: 'insensitivity to the cultural values of the working classes'.

[30] H. Cunningham, 'Leisure and Culture', in F. M. L. Thompson (ed.), *The Cambridge Social History of Britain*, ii: *People and their Environment* (Cambridge 1990), 299 ff.

leisure culture, exclusive and male-dominated; and a more respectable family-based culture, which gradually replaced the artisan culture towards the mid-nineteenth century. Men like Hicks or Peter Green, though they would not have used this terminology, would have been aware of different life-styles among working-class people and would have known that there were strong elements of self-help and independence to which they could appeal. More than once Hicks expressed his appreciation of the vigorous enjoyment which marked working-class life, even if he could not help wanting to offer to working people the kind of artistic and cultural enrichment he felt privileged to enjoy, and which he believed might wean them away from morally dangerous alternatives. But Hicks also learnt that there were structural faults in industrial society which needed to be attacked from above, by legislation. And he and many members of the CSU tried, and in some instances succeeded in their efforts, to bring about change by legislation, which released the inherent energies of working people. At the historic moment at which the Liberal Party was moving back into the position of government the CSU was one of a large number of pressure-groups advocating new restraints upon the exercise of irresponsible power by commercial and industrial magnates.

But how does the CSU fit into the general picture of the Church of England? It is tempting to place it in a largely Anglo-catholic tradition, because most of its best-known figures were undoubtedly Anglo-catholics. But the details of Hicks's connection with it and a consideration of its general membership raise questions about that assumption. Hicks's own view of it was affected by the fact that he had most to do with it as it operated away from Oxford and London. The two successive Bishops of Manchester, Moorhouse and Knox, who gave their patronage to the local branch, were equally distant from the outlook of the Anglo-catholics. That was also true of Chavasse, the Bishop of Liverpool, who was a staunch evangelical, but approved of the CSU. The general temper of church life in the Diocese of Manchester was decidedly 'Low Church', and yet the Manchester branch was as flourishing as any outside London with the single exception of Oxford. Details of branch programmes, given from time to time in the *Commonwealth*, hardly ever indicate study of the way in which 'the Christian law' was to have 'authority to rule social practice', as declared in the Union's objects; or indeed study of what that law was taken to mean. Without detailed information about what actually went on in the branch meetings, we are tempted to conclude that all kinds of church people were glad to participate in the study and discussion of practical social questions, whatever their theology or their churchmanship. If we look at the contributors to the *Commonwealth* we see a variety of churchmanship, which can include Bishop Percival, Hastings Rashdall and T. C. Fry, who were certainly not Anglo-catholics; and if we notice those who are quoted with approval the spectrum is further extended beyond the limits of the Church of England. We are left with a strong impression that the main function of the CSU was to act as a rallying-point for churchmen who were exercised about the 'condition of England question', without much regard for their churchmanship.

Hicks had come to accept practical co-operation across denominational boundaries, initially through his work for the UKA, and he found no difficulty in accepting a broad base for study and action over social questions within the Manchester CSU. It would be gratuitous to assume that he was the only one to do so. In fact, the CSU was not simply a carrier of socialistic ideas within the Anglo-catholic tradition. The next phase of the Christian social movement was inaugurated, we might say, by the Report of the Archbishop's Committee on 'Christianity and Industrial Problems', set up after the National Mission of Repentance and Hope. Its report had wide circulation. It was published in 1918 and reissued in 1927 when the original run of 29,000 copies had been exhausted. It expressed many of the criticisms of capitalist society which had exercised the CSU in earlier years. But its members were deliberately chosen for their expertise without regard for their churchmanship. They included Christopher Turnor, whose background and sympathies were at the Protestant edge of the church, along with the Anglo-catholic George Lansbury. Most important of all its members was R. H. Tawney, whose churchmanship, though genuine, was never very definite, and certainly not identified with any party in the church.[31] In the wider church we may add Bishop F. T. Woods, who became an advocate of socialistic ideas in the period immediately after the First World War. He came from a firmly evangelical background, although, in Hensley

---

[31] Ross Terrill, *R. H. Tawney and his Times* (1973), 263 ff.

Henson's typical verdict, he displayed 'the familiar phenomenon of an Evangelical in process of being assimilated to the Sacerdotalists' after his consecration.[32] Perhaps no one could have claimed to stand more surely at the centre of the Christian social movement in the inter-war period than William Temple; and he was no Anglo-catholic.

There is a question-mark against the claim that the Christian social movement was in some fashion the nurseling of Anglocatholicism. Certainly evangelicals were severely restrained from taking a leading part in social thought by their overwhelming concern for individual salvation. But some Anglo-catholics were equally individualistic in setting their sights on regular confession and attendance at Mass. Social concern cannot simply be correlated with varieties of churchmanship. Nor can it depend on the existing bases of Christian thought in different church traditions. Because it must attempt to handle the details of changing historical circumstances, it cannot arise simply from study of the scriptures, least of all from the words of Jesus. And the tradition of Christian social teaching, which related to the post-Constantinian church and society, could only be made to appear relevant by a great deal of ingenuity. The practice, rather than the theory, of the CSU was right: to start from a patient study of social problems and the consideration of possible remedies. Its members brought their different theologies with them; but when it came to practical action they found them largely irrelevant. For a few years, with the Liberal Party in power and committed to social reform, they could exert some useful pressure.

Then came the war, which shattered the mirror they held up to society. The picture of a nation being gradually reformed under the guidance of the Liberal Party was irretrievably broken. Reform was shelved while the nation's energies were directed to meet the demands of war. Instead of clearing the slums, men were forced to dig themselves new slums in the mud of Flanders. Instead of creating the conditions which made decent family life possible, the government dragged men from their homes and left children fatherless. But fragments of the Liberal picture remained. Temperance measures were introduced. The movement for women's franchise became irresistible. And fragments of the socialists' picture

---

[32] Henson, *Retrospect*, ii. 290.

began to appear, too. Industry and commerce were made to serve the nation's needs. Food was more equitably distributed and much malnourishment mitigated. Soon great estates began to be broken up by death duties. Even in the established church there were signs of change. The National Mission, nowadays widely described as a disaster, offered (as Hicks thought) a chance for the church to confess its failure and renew its image; not failure to convert individuals and make them church-goers, but failure to side with working people against those who exploited them; not renew an image of authority and control, but change that for the image of a prophetic witness to the fellowship of all within the nation. But the grand design, fostered by the New Liberals, fell apart with the coupon election.

After the First World War there was no longer any significant sense in which it was possible to identify a group of Liberal churchmen. The study of Hicks's life and ministry reveals a well-defined historical moment at which such a group briefly coalesced, along with the emergence of the New Liberalism. The CSU represents, not an unsatisfactory episode in Christian socialism, but a hopeful moment for Liberals. On that basis we can offer some modification of the picture of church parties and their relationship, at least by indicating that at a time of vigorous partisanship within the Church of England there were intelligent churchmen who had other things on their mind, and were happy to adopt without acrimony the best insights of each tradition. To have written the biography of Henry Bazely; to have followed happily in the footsteps of Edward King; to have befriended and defended James Thompson; and to be a respected bishop—all that taken together may only show that Edward Lee Hicks was, as Dean Fry said, 'tolerant beyond the most tolerant I have known'. Or else it may foreshadow a necessary temper in a pluralistic society.

Sources and Bibliography

PRIMARY SOURCES

I. *Manuscript Sources*

1. *Family Papers*

There is a considerable collection of family papers held by the bishop's grandson, Mr Timothy Hicks. The largest single item is a bound volume of letters and papers, put together by Edward Lee Hicks for his family. This consists mainly of letters written by his mother Catherine Hicks between 1871 and her death in 1897. These are prefaced by a manuscript compendium of family history written by Hicks himself. The volume also contains a few miscellaneous letters from other members of the family. The latest item is dated 1907.

The collection also contains many miscellaneous items, including letters from Sir Wilfrid Lawson, Julia Gaskell, Lady Henry Somerset, Lady Cecilia Roberts, W. T. Arnold, Josephine Butler, and a variety of scholars (R. C. Jebb, Prof. Michaelis and others). They are mostly very brief.

Agnes Hicks seems to have begun a collection of autographs while still living in Prof. Palmer's house and to have continued this practice after her marriage. Much of this collection has been preserved, as well as the Visitors' Book from the Old Palace, Lincoln.

2. *Episcopal Diaries*

Two large volumes of a manuscript diary were left to the See Library in Lincoln, and have now been deposited in the Lincolnshire Archive Office. Extensive extracts have been published by the Lincoln Record Society (1993). They cover the entire period from Hicks's consecration to his death. Various news cuttings, programmes, etc. are pasted into them. The unpublished material is mostly records of visits, ordinations, etc. without personal comment.

3. *The Honnold Library Collection*

The Honnold/Mudd Library of the Claremont Colleges, California, holds the Edward Lee Hicks Miscellaneous Letters collection, acquired by William

W. Clary. It consists of twenty-four letters addressed to Hicks from a variety of correspondents including Dean Farrar, J. Rendel Harris, F. G. Kenyon, H. D. Rawnsley, Frederick Temple, John Wordsworth, Dean Kitchin, J. B. Lightfoot, John Morley, and G. W. E. Russell. Some are very brief. It is probable that they, like many items in the Family Papers, were originally kept for the sake of the autographs.

4. Lincolnshire Archives

There is a limited collection of Hicks's official correspondence in the Lincolnshire Archive Office (Cor. B and TSJ 13).

5. Other letters

There are individual letters by Hicks in a number of different collections, viz.: Bodleian Library:
    Ms.Eng.Lett.d.181
    Ms.Top.Oxon.e.554
British Library:
    Campbell Bannerman Papers 41235 fo. 160
    C. P. Scott Papers (7 May 1915)
    Gladstone Correspondence 46,053 fo. 222
Manchester Guardian Archives (Manchester University John Rylands Library):
    C. P. Scott letters, 128/157 & 332/108

6. Other manuscript material

Herbert J. Torr diaries (Aubourn Hall, Lincs.)
Hereford Record Office (Bishop Percival's papers)
Madresfield Court Archives (Worcs.)
Warden's Log Book (1888–92) at Hulme Hall

II. Selected writings of Edward Lee Hicks

Hicks's greatest output of writing on religious topics was occasional, and consisted mainly of letters and articles. The list below contains some of the more interesting articles, sermons, and other writings which have been consulted in preparation for this book. It does not include any of his contributions to the *Manchester Guardian*, which were extensive, and included regular weekly articles under the pseudonym 'Quartus' from November 1904 to April 1910. Individual sermons are accessible in the Bodleian Library and Manchester City Central Library.
1868:   Latin Essay Prize: 'Quaenam sit mythologicae quam vocant scientiae utilitas?' (Bodleian Library).

1880: 'Inscriptions, Greek', in *Encyclopaedia Britannica* (9th edn. 1880).

1882: *A Manual of Greek Historical Inscriptions* (Oxford). (2nd edn with G. F. Hill, 1901.)
'On the Names of the Greeks', *The Nineteenth Century* 11 (Jan.–June), 389–402.

1886: *Henry Bazely, the Oxford Evangelist: A Memoir.*

1887: 'On some Political Terms employed in the New Testament', *Classical Review* 1, 4–8, 42–6.

1888: *How to Supply the Defects of the Parochial System by Means of Evangelising Work*, Church Congress Official Report (1888).

1890: 'The Bread by which Man Lives' (Sermon).

1895: 'The Duty of the Church in relation to the Temperance Movement' (Address to Manchester Temperance Conference).

1896: 'St Paul and Hellenism', in *Studia Biblica et Ecclesiastica: Essays Chiefly in Biblical and Patristic Criticism by Members of the University of Oxford*, iv.

1897: 'To Make Life Sweeter, Purer, More Fruitful of Good' (Jubilee Sermon of the Lancashire and Cheshire Band of Hope and Temperance Union).

1898: Sermon in memory of George Henry Greville Anson, sometime Archdeacon of Manchester.

1899: 'The Duty of England' (Sermon); 'The Present Phase of the Temperance Question', *Contemporary Review* (July).

1903: *Addresses on the Temptation.*

1904: 'The Religious Point of View', in *Is Christianity True? A Series of Lectures Delivered in the Central Hall, Manchester.*

1905: 'Christian Art in Relation to Christian History', in A. S. Peake (ed.), *Inaugural Lectures Delivered by Members of the Faculty of Theology, Manchester (1904–5).*

1912: *Building in Troublous Times* (Episcopal Charge). 'The Church and the Liquor Traffic' (Lees and Raper Lecture). 'Early Days of Hulme Hall', *Hulme Hall Magazine*; 'Hellenism as a Force in History', *Proceedings of the Classical Association*, Presidential Address.

1913: 'Christianity and Riches' (Cambridge University Sermon), *The Christian Commonwealth* (May).

1914: 'The Church and the War', *The Political Quarterly* (December), reprinted as an Oxford Pamphlet (1915).

III. *Journals consulted*

Alliance News
Amateur Historian
Banbury Guardian

Church Quarterly Review
Church League for Women's Suffrage Monthly
Church Times
Commonwealth
Contemporary Review
Ecclesiastical History Society Papers
Guardian
Leamington Spa Courier
Leamington Warwick and County Chronicle
Lincoln Diocesan Magazine
Manchester Evening Chronicle
Manchester Guardian
Modern Churchman
Nineteenth Century
Optimist
Parish Magazine for Kineton, Harbury, etc.
Stratford-upon-Avon Herald
Times Literary Supplement

IV. *Archival Sources*

Brasenose College Oxford Archives
Church Army papers (1898–1917)
Chronicle of Convocation: Reports of Upper House
Church Congress Reports
Corpus Christi College Oxford Archives
Fawcett Library Papers
Imperial War Museum: St George's Gazette
Imperial War Museum: 'Recollections of the Great War' by Olive Mary Taylor
Imperial War Museum: Papers of Major C. H. Emerson
Imperial War Museum: Diary of Revd J. M. S. Walker
Lambeth Palace Library:
  Bishops' Committees
  Davidson papers
    vol. 336: Germany
    vol. 348: Conscientious Objectors
    vol. 375: Temperance
    vol. 409: League of Nations
    vol. 515: Women
Lincoln Diocesan Conference Reports (1910–16)
Oxfordshire County Records
Pusey House Papers

Rylands Library Minutes (1905–10)
Warwickshire Census (1881)
Warwickshire Record Office (Heurtley and P. C. Hine)
Worcester Cathedral Library (Add. MS. 56)

BIBLIOGRAPHY

(The place of publication is London unless otherwise stated.)

ACTON, Lord, *Letters to Mary, Daughter of the Right Hon. W. E. Gladstone*, ed. Herbert Paul (1904).

ALBERTI, JOHANNA, *Beyond Suffrage: Feminists in war and peace 1914–1928* (1990).

ANGELL, NORMAN, *The Great Illusion: A Study of the Relation of Military Power in Nations to their Economic and Social Advantage*, 3rd edn. (1911).

ANGELL, NORMAN, 'Peace Movements', in Edwin R. A. Seligman and Alvin Johnson (eds.), *Encyclopaedia of the Social Sciences*, xii (1934).

ANNAN, NOEL, *Our Age* (1990).

ARCH, JOSEPH, *From Ploughtail to Parliament: An Autobiography* (Cresset Library reprint 1986).

ASHBY, M. K., *Joseph Ashby of Tysoe, 1859–1919* (Cambridge 1961).

AYERST, DAVID, *Guardian: Biography of a Newspaper* (1971).

BACKSTROM, PHILIP N., *Christian Socialism and Co-operation in Victorian England: Edward Vansittart Neale and the Co-operative Movement* (1974).

BALFOUR, ARTHUR JAMES, First Earl, *Chapters of Autobiography* (1930).

BEBBINGTON, D. W., *The Nonconformist Conscience: Chapel and Politics 1870–1914* (1982).

BELL, E. MOBERLEY, *Josephine Butler* (1962).

BELL, G. K. A., *Randall Davidson, Archbishop of Canterbury*, 2 vols. (Oxford 1935).

BENSON, A. C., *The Leaves of the Tree* (1911).

—— *The Life of Edward White Benson* (1899).

BENSON, E. F., *As We Were* (1930).

BENTLEY, JAMES, *Ritualism and Politics in Victorian Britain* (Oxford 1978).

BENTLEY, MICHAEL, *The Liberal Mind 1914–1929* (Cambridge 1977).

BINYON, GILBERT CLIVE, *The Christian Socialist Movement in England* (1931).

BOLTON KING, R., BROWNE, J. D., and IBBOTSON, E. M. H., 'Bolton King, Practical Idealist', in *Warwickshire Historical Society*, Occasional Paper 2 (1978).

BOUTFLOWER, ANDREW, *Personal Reminiscences of Manchester Cathedral* (Manchester n.d.).

BOWEN, DESMOND, *The Idea of the Victorian Church* (1968).

BOWLE, JOHN, *Politics and Opinion in the Nineteenth Century: An Historical Introduction* (1954).

BRENT, RICHARD, *Liberal Anglican Politics* (1987).

BRIGGS, ASA, *Victorian Cities* (1963).

BRIGHOUSE, URSULA W., *A Lincolnshire Childhood* (Stroud 1992).

BROOKE, CHRISTOPHER N. L., *A History of the University of Cambridge*, iv (Cambridge 1993).

BROUGHALL, MARJORIE S., *A Pastel for Eliza* (1961).

BRUTON, F. A. (ed.), *The Roman Fort at Manchester*, 2nd Annual Report of the Classical Association, Manchester and District Branch (Manchester 1909).

BURTON, HUMPHREY P. W., *Weavers of Webs* (1954).

BUTLER, PERRY, *Gladstone: Church, State and Tractarianism* (Oxford 1982).

CANNADINE, DAVID, *G. M. Trevelyan: A Life in History* (1992).

CAREY, WALTER, *Good-bye to my Generation* (1951).

CARPENTER, JAMES, *Gore: A Study in Liberal Catholic Thought* (1960).

CARPENTER, S. C., *Winnington Ingram: The Biography of Arthur Foley Winnington Ingram, Bishop of London 1901–1939* (1949).

CARTER, HENRY, *The Control of the Drink Trade: A Contribution to National Efficiency 1915–1917* (1918).

CHADWICK, OWEN, *Victorian Miniature* (1960).

—— *The Victorian Church*, 2 vols. (1966, 1970).

—— *The Secularization of the European Mind in the Nineteenth Century* (Cambridge 1975).

—— *Hensley Henson: A Study in the Friction between Church and State* (Oxford 1983).

CHARLTON, H. B., *Portrait of a University 1851–1951, to Commemorate the Centenary of Manchester University* (Manchester 1951).

CHITTY, SUSAN, *The Beast and the Monk: A Life of Charles Kingsley* (1947).

CLARK, KENNETH, *Ruskin Today* (1964).

CLARKE, P. F., *Lancashire and the New Liberalism* (Cambridge 1971).

COLLINGWOOD, W. G., *The Life of John Ruskin* (1900).

CONDELL, DIANA, and LIDDIARD, JEAN, *Working for Victory: Images of Women in the First World War 1914–1918* (1987).

CONWAY, R. S. (ed.), *Melandra Castle*, Report of the Manchester and District Branch of the Classical Association, with an Introduction by the Revd E. L. Hicks, President of the Branch (1905).

COREN, MICHAEL, *Gilbert: The Man who was G. K. Chesterton* (1989).

—— *The Invisible Man: The Life and Liberties of H. G. Wells* (1993).

COULSON, JOHN, *Newman and the Common Tradition* (Oxford 1970).

COVERT, JAMES THAYNE, *Memoir of a Victorian Woman: Reflections of Louise Creighton, 1850–1936* (Bloomington and Indianapolis 1994).

COWAN, I. R., 'The Work of the Salford School Board' (University of Durham M.Ed. thesis 1965).

COWLING, MAURICE, *Religion and Public Doctrine in Modern England*, ii: *Assaults* (Cambridge 1985).

CREIGHTON, LOUISE, *Life and Letters of Mandell Creighton 1803–1901 by his Wife* (1904).

CROSS, COLIN, *The Liberals in Power 1905–1914* (London 1963; Westport, Conn. 1976).

CROSS, F. L., *Darwell Stone, Churchman and Counsellor* (1943).

CROUCH, DAVID, and WARD, COLIN, *The Allotment* (1988).

DAKERS, CAROLINE, *The Countryside at War 1914–1918* (1987).

DAVEY, ARTHUR, *The British Pro-Boers 1877–1902* (Cape Town 1978).

DAVIDSON, R. T., and BENHAM, W., *Life of Archibald Campbell Tait, Archbishop of Canterbury*, 2 vols. (1891).

DAVIES, R., GEORGE, A. R., and RUPP, G., *A History of the Methodist Church in Great Britain*, ii (1978).

DEARDEN, JAMES S. (ed.), *The Professor: Arthur Severn's Memoir of John Ruskin*, (1967).

DEARMER, NAN, *The Life of Percy Dearmer* (1941).

Departmental Committee of Inquiry into Allotments (1969) HMSO Cmnd 4166.

Dictionary of National Biography articles: Robert Aitken, W. T. Arnold, T. C. Fry, C. A. Heurtley.

DIGGLE, JOHN W., *The Lancashire Life of Bishop Fraser* (1891).

Doctrine in the Church of England, The Report of the Commission on Christian Doctrine appointed by the Archbishops of Canterbury and York in 1922 (1938).

EDWARDS, D. L., *Leaders of the Church of England 1828–1944* (Oxford 1971).

ELLIOTT-BINNS, L. E., *Religion in the Victorian Era* (1936).

—— *The Development of English Theology in the Later Nineteenth Century* (1952).

ELTON, Lord, *Edward King and Our Times* (1958).

ELVY, JOHN M., *Recollections of the Cathedral and Parish Church of Manchester* (Manchester 1913).

ENGEL, A. J., *From Clergyman to Don: The Rise of the Academic Profession in Nineteenth Century Oxford* (Oxford 1983).

FABER, GEOFFREY, *Jowett: A portrait with a Background* (1957).

FIGGIS, J. N., *The Fellowship of the Mystery* (1914).

FITZGERALD, PENELOPE, *The Knox Brothers* (1977).

FLETCHER, SHEILA, *Maude Royden: A Life* (1989).

FOAKES-JACKSON, F. J. (ed.), *The Faith and the War: A Series of Essays by Members of the Churchmen's Union and Others on the Religious Difficulties Aroused by the Present Condition of the World* (1915).

FOX, ADAM, *Dean Inge* (1960).

FREEDEN, MICHAEL, *The New Liberalism: An Ideology of Social Reform* (Oxford 1978).

FRY, T. C., *A Social Policy for the Church* (1893).

FULLER, PETER, *Images of God, The Consolations of Lost Illusions* (1985).

GARDINER, A. G., *Pillars of Society* (1914).

GAUT, R. C., *History of Worcestershire Agriculture and Rural Evolution* (Worcester 1939).

GIBBINS, H. DE B., *The Industrial History of England* (1892).

GORE, CHARLES (ed.), *Essays in Aid of the Reform of the Church* (1902).

—— *Lux Mundi* (1889).

GORE, JOHN, *Charles Gore: Father and Son* (1932).

GRAVES, RICHARD PERCEVAL, *A. E. Housman, the Scholar Poet* (1979).

GREEN, V. H. H., *Oxford Common Room: A Study of Lincoln College and Mark Pattison* (1957).

GREENE, GRAHAM, *A Sort of Life* (1971).

GRICE, FREDERICK, *Francis Kilvert and his World* (Horsham n.d.).

A GROUP OF CHURCHMEN, *The Return of Christendom* (1922).

GUPPY, HENRY, *The John Rylands Library: A Record of its History 1899– 1924* (Manchester 1924).

HAGGARD, H. RIDER, *Rural England: Being an Account of Agricultural and Social Researches Carried Out in the Years 1901 and 1902* (New York and Bombay 1902).

HAMER, D. A., *The Politics of Electoral Pressure* (Hassocks 1977).

HAMMOND, J. L., *C. P. Scott of the Manchester Guardian* (1934).

HAMMOND, J. L., et al., *C. P. Scott 1846–1932: The Making of the Manchester Guardian* (1946).

HARRIS, JOSÉ, *Private Lives, Public Spirit: A Social History of Britain 1870– 1914* (Oxford 1993).

HARRISON, BRIAN, *Drink and the Victorians: The Temperance Question in England 1815–1872* (1971).

HARRISON, FREDERIC, *John Ruskin* (1903).

HARVIE, CHRISTOPHER, *The Lights of Liberalism: University Liberals and the Challenge of Democracy* (1976).

HASTINGS, ADRIAN, *A History of English Christianity 1920–1985* (1986).

HAW, GEORGE (ed.), *Christianity and the Working Classes* (1906).

HAYLER, MARK H. C., *The Vision of a Century: The United Kingdom Alliance in Retrospect* (1953).

HEENEY, BRIAN, *The Women's Movement in the Church of England 1850– 1930* (Oxford 1988).

HENNELL, MICHAEL, *The Deans and Canons of Manchester Cathedral 1840– 1948* (Manchester n.d.).

HENSON, HERBERT HENSLEY, *Cross-Bench Views of Current Church Questions* (1902).

—— *Letters*, ed. E. F. Braley (1950).

—— *Retrospect of an Unimportant Life*, i (1942).

HEURTLEY, C. A., *Wholesome Words: Sermons on Some Important Points of Christian Doctrine*, with a prefatory memoir by the Revd William Ince (1896).

HIBBS, JOHN, *The Country Chapel* (1988).

HICKS, KATHLEEN NUGENT, *From Rock to Tower* (1947).

HOBSON, J. A., *John Ruskin, Social Reformer* (1898).

HOLLAND, HENRY SCOTT, *Our Neighbours: A Handbook for the C.S.U.* (1911).
—— *Personal Studies* (1905).

HOLLIS, CHRISTOPHER, *The Mind of Chesterton* (1970).

HOOPER, E. B., *Daniel and the Maccabees*, with a foreword by E. L. Hicks (n.d.).

HORN, PAMELA, *Rural Life in England in the First World War* (New York 1984).

HOUGHTON, WALTER E., *The Victorian Frame of Mind 1830–1870* (New Haven and London 1957).

HUDSON, CYRIL E., and RECKITT, MAURICE B., *The Church and the World, Being Materials for the Historical Study of Christian Sociology*, iii: *Church and Society in England from 1800* (1940).

HUGHES, ROBERT, *The Red Dean: The Life and Riddle of Dr Hewlett Johnson* (Worthing 1987).

HUGHES, THOMAS, *James Fraser Second Bishop of Manchester: A Memoir 1818–1885* (1887).

HUTCHINSON, F. W., *Reminiscences of a Lincolnshire Parson* (Ely n.d.).

HYNES, SAMUEL, *The Edwardian Turn of Mind* (Princeton 1968).
—— *A War Imagined* (1990).

INGE, W. R., *Assessments and Anticipations* (1929).
—— *Diary of a Dean: St Paul's 1911–1934* (n.d.).
—— *England* (1926).
—— *Outspoken Essays*, 2nd series (1922).

IREMONGER, F. A., *William Temple, Archbishop of Canterbury: His Life and Letters* (1948).

JONES, PETER D'A., *The Christian Socialist Revival 1877–1914: Religion, Class and Social Conscience in Late-Victorian England* (Princeton NJ 1968).

KENT, JOHN, *The Unacceptable Face: The Modern Church in the Eyes of the Historian* (1987).
—— *William Temple: Church, State and Society in Britain 1880–1950* (Cambridge 1992).

KING, EDWARD, *The Love and Wisdom of God* (1910).
—— *Pastoral Lectures*, ed. E. Graham (1932).

KITCHIN, G. W., *Edward Harold Browne, D.D., Bishop of Winchester: A Memoir* (1895).
—— *Ruskin in Oxford and Other Studies* (1904).

KITSON CLARK, G., *Churchmen and the Condition of England 1832–1885* (1973).

KNOX, E. A., *Reminiscences of an Octogenarian 1847–1934* (1935).

KNOX, R. A., *A Spiritual Aeneid* (new edn. 1950).

KOSS, STEPHEN, *The Rise and Fall of the Political Press in Britain* (1981).

Koss, Stephen (ed.), *The Pro-Boers: The Anatomy of an Anti-war Movement* (Chicago and London 1973).

A Lady, *Five Days and Five Nights as a Tramp among Tramps*, with a preface by the Revd Canon Hicks (Manchester 1904).

Lancelot, J. B., *Francis James Chavasse, Bishop of Liverpool* (Oxford 1929).

Lawrenson, T. E., *Hall of Residence: Saint Anselm Hall in the University of Manchester, 1907–1957* (Manchester n.d.).

Leon, Derrick, *Ruskin: The Great Victorian* (1949).

Lincoln Central Library, (D30), *The Kirkstead Story* (n.d.).

—— *Fancy a Man from Pond Street Knowing His ABC: 75 Years of the Lincoln W. E. A.* (Lincoln n.d.).

—— *The Old Hangar Church Cranwell* (n.d.).

Lloyd, Roger, *The Church of England 1900–1965* (1966).

Lockhart, J. G., *Cosmo Gordon Lang* (1949).

Londonderry, The Marchioness, *Retrospect* (1938).

Longmate, Norman, *The Water Drinkers* (1968).

Lubbock, Percy (ed.), *The Diary of A. C. Benson* (n.d.).

McCrimmon, B., 'W. R. S. Ralston (1828–89): Scholarship and Scandal in the B. M.', *British Library Journal* 14/2 (Autumn 1988).

Machin, G. I. T., *Politics and the Churches in Great Britain 1869–1921* (Oxford 1987).

MacIntyre, Alasdair, *Secularization and Moral Change* (1967).

Mackenzie, Norman and Jean, *The Time Traveller: The Life of H. G. Wells* (1973).

Mackinnon, Donald M., *Borderlands of Theology and Other Essays* (1968).

Manchester Transvaal Leaflets (1899).

Mansbridge, Albert, *Edward Stuart Talbot and Charles Gore* (1935).

—— *Fellow Men: A Gallery of England 1876–1946* (1948).

Marrin, Albert, *The Last Crusade* (Durham, NC 1974).

Marsh, Margaret, *Hastings Rashdall: Bibliography of the Published Writings* (Leysters, Herefordshire 1993).

Masterman, C. F. G., *The Condition of England* (1911).

—— *In Peril of Change: Essays Written in Time of Tranquillity* (London 1905).

Matheson, P. E., *The Life of Hastings Rashdall D.D.* (1928).

Mathew, David, *Lord Acton and his Times* (1968).

Maurice, F. D., *Social Morality* (1859).

Mayor, Stephen, *The Churches and the Labour Movement* (1967).

Medhurst, Kenneth N., and Moyser, George H., *Church and Politics in a Secular Age* (Oxford 1988).

Mews, S. P., 'Religion and English Society in the First World War' (Cambridge University Ph.D thesis 1973).

—— 'Urban Problems and Rural Solutions: Drink and Disestablishment in the First World War', in Derek Baker (ed.), *The Church and the*

Countryside, papers read at the seventeenth summer meeting and the eighteenth winter meeting of the Ecclesiastical History Society (Oxford 1979).

MILL, JOHN STUART, *Autobiography*, ed. Jack Stillinger (Oxford 1971).

MILLS, DENNIS R. (ed.), *Twentieth Century Lincolnshire* (Lincoln 1989).

MORGAN, DAVID, *Suffragists and Liberals: the Politics of Woman Suffrage in England* (1975).

MORGAN, KENNETH O. (ed.), *The Age of Lloyd George* (Historical Problems, Studies and Documents 12 1971).

MOULTON, W. F., *James Hope Moulton* (1919).

MOYSER, G. (ed.), *Church and Politics Today* (1985).

MUNSON, JAMES (ed.), *Echoes of the Great War: The Diary of the Reverend Andrew Clark 1914–1919* (Oxford 1985).

MURRAY, GILBERT, *Five Stages of Greek Religion* (1935).

MURRAY, GRAHAM, *Founders of the National Trust* (1987).

NETTLESHIP, R. L. (ed.), *Works of Thomas Hill Green*, iii (1891).

NEVILLE, GRAHAM, 'Bishop King: Right Heart, Wrong Head', *Modern Churchman* NS 28/3 (1986), 15–19.

—— *Edward Lee Hicks, Bishop of Lincoln 1910–1919* (Lincoln 1994).

—— 'Edward Lee Hicks: A Liberal Rector of Fenny Compton', *Warwickshire History* 9/4 (1994/5).

—— 'Ruskin and Victorian Values', *Modern Believing* NS 38/2 (April 1997), 15–23.

NEWMAN, J. H., *The Idea of the University* (1852).

NOCKLES, PETER B., *The Oxford Movement in its Context: Anglican High Churchmanship 1760–1857* (Cambridge 1994).

NOEL, CONRAD, *An Autobiography*, ed. Sidney Dark (1945).

NORMAN, EDWARD R., *Church and Society in England 1770–1970* (Oxford 1976).

—— *The Victorian Christian Socialists* (Cambridge 1987).

NORTH, J. L., ' "I Sought a Colleague": James Hope Moulton, Papyrologist, and Edward Lee Hicks, Epigraphist, 1903–1906', *Rylands Library Bulletin* (Spring 1997).

NURSER, JOHN, *The Reign of Conscience: Individual, Church and State in Lord Acton's History of Liberty* (New York 1987).

OBELKEVICH, JIM, ROPER, LYNDAL, and SAMUEL, RAPHAEL (eds.), *Disciplines of Faith: Studies in Religion, Politics and Patriarchy* (1987).

OLDFIELD, SYBIL, *Spinsters of this Parish: The Life and Times of F. M. Mayor and Mary Sheepshanks* (1984).

OLNEY, R. J., *Rural Society and County Government in Nineteenth-Century Lincolnshire* (Lincoln 1979).

OMAN, SIR CHARLES, *Memories of Victorian Oxford and Some Early Years* (1941).

PAGET, STEPHEN (ed.), *Henry Scott Holland: Memoir and Letters* (1921).

PALMER, BERNARD, *High and Mitred: A Study of Prime Ministers as Bishop-makers 1837–1977* (1992).

Pan-Anglican Congress Papers (1907–8).

PARMOOR, Lord, *A Retrospect: Looking Back over a Life of More Than Eighty Years* (1936).

PARSONS, GERALD, and MOORE, JAMES R. (eds.), *Religion in Victorian Britain*, 4 vols. (Manchester 1988).

PATTISON, MARK, *Memoirs* (1885).

PEAKE, A. S. (ed.), *Inaugural Lectures Delivered by Members of the Faculty of Theology* (Manchester 1905).

PETERSON, WILLIAM S., *Victorian Heretic: Mrs Humphry Ward's Robert Elsmere* (Leicester 1976).

POOLE, MICHAEL, 'Mr Dean: A Study in Personalities', *Manchester Cathedral News* (1973).

POPE-HENNESSY, JAMES, *Queen Mary* (1959).

PRESTIGE, G. L., *The Life of Charles Gore* (1935).

PRICE, M. G., 'Canon Peter Green: A Study of his Pastoral Work in Salford 1901–1951' (Manchester University M.Ph. thesis 1994).

POWELL, DAVID, 'The New Liberalism and the Rise of Labour 1886–1906', *Historical Journal* 29/2 (1986), 369–93.

RASHDALL, HASTINGS, *Principles and Precepts*, ed. H. D. A. Major and F. L. Cross (1927).

—— *Ideas & Ideals*, ed. H. D. A. Major and F. L. Cross (1928).

RECKITT, MAURICE B., *Faith and Society: A Study of the Structure, Outlook and Opportunity of the Christian Social Movement in Great Britain and the United States of America* (1932).

—— (ed.), *For Christ and the People: Studies of four Socialist Priests and Prophets of the Church of England between 1870 and 1930* (1968).

—— *Maurice to Temple: A Century of the Social Movement in the Church of England* (1947).

—— *P. E. T. Widdrington: A Study in Vocation and Versatility* (1961).

REYNOLDS, J. S., *The Evangelicals at Oxford 1735–1871* (1953).

RICHTER, MELVIN, *The Politics of Conscience* (1964).

ROBERTS, ROBERT, *The Classic Slum: Salford Life in the First Quarter of the Century* (Manchester 1971).

ROBSON, R. (ed.), *Ideas and Institutions of Victorian England* (1967).

ROE, W. G., *Lamennais and England* (Oxford 1966).

ROEDER, CHARLES, 'Roman Manchester Reconsidered', *Transactions of the Lancashire and Cheshire Antiquarian Society* 17 (Manchester 1900).

ROTHBLATT, SHELDON, *The Revolution of the Dons: Cambridge Society in Victorian England* (1968).

ROWLAND, PETER, *Lloyd George* (1975).

RUSKIN, JOHN, *The Political Economy of Art* (1857).

—— *Fors Clavigera: Letters to the Workmen and Labourers of Great Britain*, (1871–84).

—— *The Lord's Prayer and the Church* (1879).

—— *Praeterita* (1885–1889).

—— *Unto This Last* (1862).

RUSSELL, G. W. E., 'The New Liberalism', *Nineteenth Century* 26 (1889), 492–9.

—— *Afterthoughts* (1912).

—— *Fifteen Chapters of Autobiography* (n.d.).

—— *An Onlooker's Notebook* (1902).

—— *Seeing and Hearing* (1907).

—— (ed.), *Sir Wilfrid Lawson: A Memoir* (1909).

—— *Social Silhouettes* (1906).

RUSSELL, REX C., *The Water-Drinkers in Lindsey: 1837–1860* (Barton Branch, WEA, 1987).

RUSSELL-GEBBETT, JEAN, *Henslow of Hitcham: Botanist, Educationalist and Clergyman* (Lavenham 1977).

St Philip's Centenary Brochure (Salford) 1825–1925.

SANDAY, WILLIAM, *Form and Content in the Christian Tradition* (1916).

SANDFORD, E. G. (ed.), *Memoirs of Archbishop Temple by Seven Friends* (1906).

SHEEN, H. E., *Canon Peter Green: A Biography of a Great Parish Priest* (1965).

SHEILS, W. J. (ed.), *The Church and War* (Ecclesiastical History Society 1983).

SIBTHORP, R. E., *The Memoirs of a Minor Canon* (Sussex 1990).

SMYTH, CHARLES, *Church and Parish: Studies in Church Problems, Illustrated from the Parochial History of St Margaret's Westminster* (1955).

SPENDER, J. A., *Life of the Right Hon. Sir Henry Campbell-Bannerman, G.C.B.*, 2 vols. (1923).

SPINKS, G. STEPHENS, ALLEN, E. L., and PARKES, JAMES, *Religion in Britain since 1900* (1952).

STEPHEN, LESLIE, *Some Early Impressions* (1924).

STEPHENSON, A. M. G., *The Rise and Decline of English Modernism* (1984).

STEPHENSON, GWENDOLEN, *Edward Stuart Talbot 1844–1934* (1936).

STORR, VERNON F., *The Development of English Theology in the Nineteenth Century 1800–1860* (1913).

STRACHEY, RAY, *The Cause: A Short History of the Women's Movement in Great Britain* (1928/1978).

STREETER, B. H. (ed.), *Foundations* (1913).

SUTHERLAND, JOHN, *Mrs Humphry Ward: Eminent Victorian, Pre-eminent Edwardian* (Oxford 1990).

SWAYNE, W. S., *Parson's Pleasure* (Edinburgh and London 1934).

TAINE, H., *Notes on England* (1872).

TAPLIN, OLIVER, *Greek Fire* (1989).

TAYLOR, A. J. P., *From the Boer War to the Cold War: Essays on Twentieth-Century Europe*, ed. Chris Wrigley (1995).

TEMPLE, William, *Life of Bishop Percival* (1921).

TERRILL, ROSS, *R. H. Tawney and his Times* (1973).

THOMPSON, DAVID M., 'War, the Nation and the Kingdom of God: The Origins of the National Mission of Repentance and Hope, 1915–16', in W. J. Shiels (ed.), *Ecclesiastical History Society Papers* (1983).

THOMPSON, F. M. L. (ed.), *Cambridge Social History of Britain 1750–1950* (Cambridge 1990).

THOMPSON, J. A. K., and TOYNBEE, A. J. (eds), *Essays in Honour of Gilbert Murray* (1936).

THOMPSON, J. M., 'My Apologia' (printed for private circulation 1940).

THOMPSON, KENNETH A., *Bureaucracy & Church Reform: The Organizational Response of the Church of England to Social Change 1800–1965* (1970).

THWAITE, ANN, *Edmund Gosse: A Literary Landscape 1849–1928* (Oxford 1985).

TOLLEMACHE, LIONEL A., *Recollections of Pattison* (1885).

TREHERNE, JOHN, *Dangerous Precincts* (1987).

TREVELYAN, G. M., *Life of John Bright* (1913).

—— *British History in the Nineteenth Century* (1922).

TREVOR, MERIOL, *The Arnolds: Thomas Arnold and his Family* (1973).

TUCKER, MAURICE G., *John Neville Figgis* (1950).

TUCKWELL, W., *Reminiscences of a Radical Parson* (1905).

—— *Pre-Tractarian Oxford: A Reminiscence of the Oriel 'Noetics'* (1909).

TURNER, FRANK M., *The Greek Heritage in Victorian Britain* (Yale 1981).

University of Manchester Publications, *The Department of Education in the University of Manchester* (Manchester 1911).

TWELVE CHURCHMEN, *Anglican Liberalism* (1908).

URWIN, E. C., *Henry Carter, CBE* (1955).

VIDLER, ALEC R., *Essays in Liberality* (1957).

—— *The Orb and the Cross: A Normative Study in the Relations of Church and State with Reference to Gladstone's Early Writings* (1945).

VON HÜGEL, BARON FRIEDRICH, *Selected Letters 1896–1924*, ed. Bernard Holland (1927, reissued 1933).

WAGNER, DONALD O., *The Church of England and Social Reform since 1854* (New York 1930).

WAKEFORD, JOHN, *Not Peace but a Sword* (Biggin Hill n.d.).

—— *Rock or Sand? Is Christianity True or False?* (1907).

WAKEMAN, H. OFFLEY, *An Introduction to the History of the Church of England*, rev., with an additional chapter by S. L. Ollard (8th edn. 1914).

WALVIN, JAMES, *Victorian Values* (1987).

WARD, MRS HUMPHRY (trs.), *Amiel's Journal: The Journal Intime of Henri-Frédéric Amiel* (1901).

—— *A Writer's Recollections* (1918).

WARD, W. R., *Victorian Oxford* (1965).

WARWICK, PETER (ed.), *The South African War: The Anglo-Boer War 1899–1902* (1980).

WATSON, E. W., *Life of Bishop John Wordsworth* (1915).

WAUGH, EVELYN, *The Life of the Rt. Rev. Ronald Knox* (1959).

WEBB, C. C. J., *Religious Thought in the Oxford Movement* (1928).

WELLDON, J. E. C., *Forty Years On* (1935).

WELLS, H. G., *Experiment in Autobiography* (1934).

—— *Mr Britling sees it through* (1916).

—— *The Soul of a Bishop* (1917).

WESTCOTT, ARTHUR (ed.), *Life and Letters of Brooke Foss Westcott*, 2 vols. (1903).

WESTCOTT, B. F., *Aspects of Positivism* (1874).

—— Address to the Church Congress (1890).

WILKINSON, ALAN, *The Church of England and the First World War* (1978).

—— *The Community of the Resurrection: A Centenary History* (1992).

—— *Dissent or Conform?* (1986).

WILLIAMS, B. H. GARNONS, *A History of Berkhamsted School* (printed for the school 1980).

WILLIAMS, N. P., and HARRIS, CHARLES, *Northern Catholicism* (1933).

WILSON, DUNCAN, *Gilbert Murray O.M. 1866–1957* (Oxford 1987).

WILSON, G. B., *Looking Back* (United Kingdom Association 1946).

—— *Leif Jones, Lord Rhayader* (1948).

WILSON, JAMES M., *An Autobiography* (1932).

WILSON, JOHN, *C.B.: A Life of Sir Henry Campbell-Bannerman* (1973).

WINTERBOTTOM, D. O., *Doctor Fry: A Study of Thomas Charles Fry* (Berkhamsted 1977).

WOODS, EDWARD S., and MACNUTT, FREDERICK B., *Theodore, Bishop of Winchester: Pastor Prophet Pilgrim* (1933).

WOOLLEY, E. F. R., 'Memoirs 1895–1920' (Lincolnshire Archive Office, typescript).

WRIGHT, T. R., *The Religion of Humanity: The Impact of Comtean Positivism on Victorian Britain* (Cambridge 1986).

YOUNG, G. M., *Victorian England: Portrait of an Age* (1953).

Index

COPEC 309
Corben, Miss 167
Cowie, Dean B. M. 117
Cranwell 254
Creighton, Bishop Mandell 40, 42, 50,
    194–5, 215
Creighton, Louise 59, 162
Crete 246
Crimean War 247
Crooks, Will 159
Cross, Colin 185
Crumpsall (Lancs.) 101, 108
Curzon, Lord 164

dancing 9
Darwin 287
Davidson, Archbishop Randall 4, 28, 193,
    226, 240, 245
Dearmer, Mabel 258
Dearmer, Percy 49, 123, 152, 203, 243
democracy 15, 215–7, 221, 242, 280, 323
Denison, Archdeacon 196
Dilke, Sir Charles 325
Dill, Sir Samuel 43, 100
disestablishment 37, 129, 175, 202,
    208–12, 214
    Campbell-Bannerman and 119, 123
    Henson on 303
    Gladstone and 177
Disraeli 195
dogma 294–5, 298–9
Donaldson, F. L. 17, 307
Dulwich College 124
Duncan Jones, A. S. 165, 243

Eaton, John 56
Ecce Homo 155
Ecclesiastical Commission 121–2
Economic Review 296
Ede, Dean W. Moore 249, 258
Education Bill (1906) 197–8
Egerton, Lord 95
elections, general:
    (1886) 200
    (1900) 191–2
    (1906) 155–6
    (1910) 245
    (1918) 222, 266–7, 334
Electoral Reform Bill 166, 264
Eliot, T. S. 329
Ellicott, Bishop C. J. 275
Elliott, Miss 229
Ellis, Thomas 201

emigration 74
Emmet, C. W. 275
Employers' Parliamentary Council 171
English Association 18
English Church Union 232
epigraphy 45–6, 68, 95–6
Essays in Aid of the Reform of the Church
    226
Essays & Reviews 13, 35, 298
eugenics 134, 216, 301, 322
evangelicalism 47, 180
evolution 287

Factory Acts 171
faddism 5–6
fellowships (Oxford) 40
Fenny Compton (Warwicks.) 32, 63, 65
    church 65, 70
    Co-operative shop 80
    highway robbery 73
    murder 69, 73
    North End 74
    reading room 79
    school 79–80
    temperance 81
    Tunnel Houses 71
Figgis, J. N. 214, 298–9, 328
flitting 239–40
Fly-sheets controversy 27
Foakes Jackson, F. J. 321
Foster, C. W. 231
Fowler, J. H. 18, 100
Fowler, W. Warde 231
Fraser, Bishop J. 89, 117, 120
freedom:
    Gladstone and 177
    Hicks's belief in 168, 311
    Inge on 301
    Liberal Party and 313
    of thought 214, 281, 297
freedom, positive 143, 182, 313
freehold of clergy 110, 213
Friends, Society of 131, 237, 266, 290
Frome (Somerset) 66
Fry, Dean T. C. 152, 159, 195, 323
    cathedral chapter 233–4
    character 235, 312
    church reform 168, 226
    militarism 252
    Peace League 249
    political views 156, 197, 201, 220, 324
    theological liberalism 311
Furness Clerical Society 53–4